God's Marshall Plan

God's Marshall Plan

*American Protestants and the Struggle for the
Soul of Europe*

JAMES D. STRASBURG

OXFORD
UNIVERSITY PRESS

OXFORD
UNIVERSITY PRESS

Oxford University Press is a department of the University of Oxford. It furthers
the University's objective of excellence in research, scholarship, and education
by publishing worldwide. Oxford is a registered trade mark of Oxford University
Press in the UK and certain other countries.

Published in the United States of America by Oxford University Press
198 Madison Avenue, New York, NY 10016, United States of America.

CIP data is on file at the Library of Congress

ISBN 978–0–19–751644–7

DOI: 10.1093/oso/9780197516447.001.0001

1 3 5 7 9 8 6 4 2

Printed by Integrated Books International, United States of America

Contents

Acknowledgments

I am deeply grateful to the community of scholars, family, and friends who supported and cheered me on as I researched and wrote this book. In particular, a long line of teachers and scholars have shaped my work as a historian. At Duke Divinity School, both Grant Wacker and Kate Bowler were excellent teachers who invited me to ponder the global engagement of American Protestants in the twentieth century. Their teaching helped inspire the earliest stages of the research that would appear in this book. At the University of Notre Dame, Mark Noll proved to be a tremendously gracious, generous, and kind mentor. His perceptive insights and thoughtful questions about this research project greatly sharpened it. He has been a tireless advocate ever since, and I am deeply grateful for his guidance and support. I can only hope to emulate his example of scholarly rigor, humility, and kindness. John McGreevy, Wilson Miscamble, Gerald McKenny, and Darren Dochuk likewise gave early drafts of this work a close read. Their thoughtful comments and suggestions for revision improved it immensely. Finally, the Colloquium on Religion and History at Notre Dame provided a lively intellectual community and a hospitable environment to test out early drafts of chapters as well.

Beyond these scholars, I would also like to thank Jan Stievermann, the Heidelberg Center for American Studies, and the Ecumenical Institute at the University of Heidelberg. They provided numerous opportunities to present my research in Germany and offered a productive environment to revise drafts of the manuscript. At the University of Leipzig, Peter Zimmerling helped open up to me the depth and richness of Dietrich Bonhoeffer's theology. Matthew Avery Sutton also offered his perceptive critiques on drafts of this manuscript and helped save me from several embarrassing mistakes. I am exceedingly grateful for his help and insight. Mark Ruff likewise gave helpful feedback at a crucial point in the drafting process, while Ansley Quiros provided her insightful wisdom and helpful edits on several chapters. Finally, the peer reviewers at Oxford University Press sharpened this book in myriad ways and opened up new avenues of inquiry that I could not have seen without their input. At Oxford, Theo Calderara and his editorial team went above and beyond in helping get this book to the finish line. They proved incredibly patient through several snafus. It has been a privilege and an honor to work with them, and I would like to thank them for their patience and graciousness, as well as for taking a chance on a first-time author like myself. A special thanks goes to Prabhu Chinnasamy and Dorothy Bauhoff as well for shepherding this book through its final stages. Tucker Adkins also came through with terrific work on the index. All told, I am sincerely grateful to all of these scholars for their support. The strengths of this work are theirs, the weaknesses wholly mine.

Researching and writing this book would also not have been possible without the support and tireless work of archivists in the United States, Germany, and Switzerland. Dirk Ullmann at the Archiv für Diakonie und Entwicklung in Berlin proved a most kind and gracious guide to their extensive resources. Anne-Emmanuelle Tankam-Tene at the World Council of Churches pointed me toward helpful collections, facilitated some exciting archival discoveries, and helped me navigate copyright permissions. Katherine Graber at the Billy Graham Center and Wheaton College Archives generously gave her time in helping me track down collections and figure out image permissions. Omee Thao at Denver Seminary was remarkably kind in granting me access to hard-to-find fundamentalist journals. The librarians at Michigan State University Special Collections and Wichita State University Special Collections also went above and beyond in helping with the final stages of research. Finally, Brenna Wade and Pam Ryan at Hillsdale College tolerated my numerous requests for obscure fundamentalist articles and journals and never failed to acquire them.

In writing this book, I also incurred a great debt to institutions that generously supported my research, including the Fulbright Program, Duke Divinity School, the History Department at the University of Notre Dame, the Institute for Study of the Liberal Arts at the University of Notre Dame, the Nanovic Institute for European Studies at the University of Notre Dame, the Andrew Mellon Foundation, and Hillsdale College. I am grateful to these institutions for giving me a chance and believing in this project.

Finally, I could not have reached the finish line without the loving support of friends and family along the way. Jonathan Riddle, Karie Cross, and Alex Wimberley have been especially dear friends and supporters since we navigated the highs and lows of doctoral work. It has also been a joy to now support one another in our respective vocations. Heath Carter has always been amazingly generous with his time, a tremendous mentor, and an inspiring friend. Nathan has been a faithful friend who always cheered me on as I spent my life's "prime meridians" in dusty archives. Last but not least, I would like to thank my family, to whom I dedicate this book: my parents for their constant presence, encouragement, and steadfast example of love; my grandparents for pouring so much of their time, energy, and love into my life and inspiring my interest in history with their stories; and my brother and sister, for always being there. I love you all very much.

Introduction

On August 7, 1945, American Protestant pastor Stewart Winfield Herman, Jr., arrived in Berlin, Germany, unable to recognize the city he had once known so well. Following countless bombing raids and a final Soviet assault, the Nazi capital lay in ruins. Although months had passed since the guns of the Second World War had fallen silent, little progress in reconstruction had been made. Navigating between piles of rubble and debris, Herman set out to make sense of the city's new landscape.

The young minister first visited the burned-out remains of his old church, the American Church in Berlin, where from 1936 to 1941 he had served as pastor in the throes of Adolf Hitler's dictatorship. The church had succumbed to Allied bombing in the heat of war, leaving behind only the skeleton of its once grand Gothic exterior. Once inside, Herman sifted through the ashes of charred hymnals, burned Bibles, and scorched pews. He left the church having managed to salvage only a few personal belongings that he had stashed in the church's safe before the Nazis had interned him in 1941.

Pressing onward, Herman passed by the badly damaged *Reichstag*—the German parliamentary building—and made his way to the Brandenburg Gate. As he pulled up to that historic monument, he could not help but notice that a large portrait of Soviet premier Joseph Stalin stood at the center of *Unter den Linden*, Berlin's main boulevard. Soviet flags had flown just months before over the parliament, announcing the Soviet triumph over Berlin. In response, Herman's concern grew that secularism and Soviet communism would spread among Germany's spiritual and civic ruins. If Germany fell, he feared, all of "Christian Europe," and even "Christian America," would be at risk. Germany's so-called *stunde null*—the "zero hour"—thus symbolized something much more alarming to Herman: the survival of "Christian civilization" itself was now at stake.[1]

Herman left Berlin with these concerns about Germany's postwar fate burning in his mind. He was not alone. Since the outbreak of the First World War, American Protestants had been discussing what they called "the German problem." They had found Germany to be both a conundrum and a paradox.

God's Marshall Plan. James D. Strasburg, Oxford University Press (2021). © Oxford University Press.
DOI: 10.1093/oso/9780197516447.003.0001

While they lauded Germany as the historic birthplace of their Protestant faith, they also puzzled over its path to authoritarian government, its hyper-nationalism and militarism, and its theological liberalism. With the rise of Nazi fascism, American Protestants had come to believe that the same nation that had ignited the Protestant Reformation had also paradoxically threat-ened to destroy the "Christian West" altogether. Although Allied powers had triumphed over Axis armies and had prevented such a fate, the difficult tasks of reforming Germany, reconstructing Europe, and forging a new Christian world order remained. As the burned-out sanctuary and destroyed parlia-ment lingered in his mind, Herman thus pondered how Americans could restore Germany and the European continent to full spiritual and political health. With fascism defeated and communism on the move, the American pastor summoned his nation into action. He called on the American govern-ment and American Protestant churches to make good on the war they had just won. In particular, he and other leading American Protestants identified Germany as the prime territory for creating a new Christian and democratic world order in the heart of Europe, one that could dispel any new totalitarian threat, whether spiritual or political.[2]

Herman's mission activated in particular the energies of a group of American Protestants that described themselves as "ecumenists." From the turn of the twentieth century onward, these "ecumenical" Protestants had worked to overcome doctrinal differences through commitments to a modern and progressive faith. They also had pursued interdenominational unity through creating a powerful national church organization they called the Federal Council of Churches (FCC). They believed their ecumenical co-operation enhanced their efforts to "Christianize" their nation, and to spread the Protestant faith and democracy across the globe. They accordingly envisioned themselves at the center of what they called "World Christianity," an imagined global community that was ecumenically Protestant in its spir-ituality and democratically oriented in its politics. Through the trials of war, they worked to unify the world's Protestant churches in the World Council of Churches (WCC), a global church body which they thought of as a spir-itual complement to the League of Nations and then the United Nations. In sum, they tended to be proponents of progressive governance, ecumenical religion, and spiritual values such as responsible citizenship, democratic equality, and multilateral organization.[3]

When Herman and other American ecumenists joined army platoons in occupying Germany, they did so reflecting these particular beliefs about their faith and their nation's purpose in the world. Their sense of global mission naturally led them now to intervene in Europe and to seek to spiritually rebuild the continent in the American image. This course of action flowed out of their steadfast conviction that their faith and their nation possessed the spiritual and civic acumen needed to advance the cause of world peace and to create a new Christian world order rooted in democracy and Protestant ecumenism. They marshalled their spiritual and political energies to oppose any perceived "totalitarian" threat to such an order—including communism and secularism, as well as Catholicism and Protestant fundamentalism—both at home and across the European continent.

These Protestant ecumenists indeed sensed they were not the only ones interested in spiritually reconstructing Europe. They were especially eager to not cede spiritual ground to the Vatican in the heartland of their faith. Believing that Protestant Christianity alone provided the proper spiritual foundation for political democracy, they rushed to match and outdo the Vatican's relief and reconstruction efforts. American Protestant "evangelicals" also raised their alarm by sending squadrons of preachers and revivalists to Germany and the continent. Shortly after Herman arrived in Berlin, rising evangelical preacher Billy Graham embarked on his first preaching tour through Europe, where he would perfect his pitch before taking the United States by storm. Graham and his evangelical partners wanted to spread a different set of American spiritual and political values abroad. In contrast to Herman, they promoted biblical fundamentals and conversionary mission as the proper theological expression of Protestant Christianity. They also identified individual liberty, limited government, free market capitalism, and an America-first foreign policy as their nation's proper political values. Led by Graham, these evangelical Protestants worked to resurrect Europe and establish their own countervailing evangelical order abroad. Together, these ecumenists and evangelicals began a struggle for the soul of Europe that would remake politics and theology on both sides of the Atlantic.[4]

This book narrates the origins and history of these competing American Protestant missions to Germany and Europe. In particular, it examines how ecumenical and evangelical American Protestants used the onset of two world wars and an era of reconstruction as rationale to spiritually and politically intervene in Europe. As they did so, Germany and Europe became proving grounds for the respective world orders these American ecumenists and evangelicals desired to create in the early to mid-twentieth century. This volume also documents how this spiritual struggle for Europe activated and advanced American Protestantism's long-standing Christian nationalism—the belief that the United States was a Christian nation with an exceptional role to play in the world. In pursuit of Europe's spiritual reconstruction, both groups lived out tenets of what Francis B. Sayre, a prominent 1930s American diplomat, called his nation's "conquering faith"—its spiritual impulse to shape, lead, and transform the globe through the spread of Protestant Christianity and American democracy. In pursuit of such a cause, ecumenical and evangelical Protestants alike mobilized for world war and pursued strategic partnerships with federal officials, foreign policymakers, and the American military. Through these efforts, they hoped to spread democratic values and Protestant Christianity to Europe, and as such, to remake the continent in the American image.[5]

As they pressed abroad, however, America's ecumenical and evangelical Protestants also came to see that they had developed dramatically different plans for rebuilding their world out of the ruins of war. Germany and the European continent therefore became an early battleground between them for the spiritual leadership of their nation and the so-called "Christian West." While their respective missions to Germany provided a spiritual rationale for a new cold war against communism, they also refined competing spiritual agendas that would begin to fracture American politics, diplomacy, and religion in the decades that followed.

Their spiritual advance would also not go uncontested abroad: European Protestants firmly challenged aspects of these American Protestant missions to their continent as well. As the Cold War intensified, leading European theologians forged a "third way" theology of their own that mediated between Moscow and Washington and called for peace and reconciliation across the world. Faced by this counter-response, a growing number of American Protestants were challenged to rethink the contours of their global mission and their relationship to the American nation-state in the Cold War. They examined anew how their loyalties to their nation aligned with their commitments to the global church. They questioned more fully whether God's global kingdom could be advanced through America's global primacy. They reconsidered where their true citizenship lay.

While American Protestants had thus pressed abroad to remake Europe, Europe had instead begun to remake them. Forsaking their wartime Christian nationalism, a growing number of American Protestants embraced an emerging Christian globalism that placed commitments to Christ over the nation and challenged the imperial contours of their global activism. A fresh wave of Protestant spiritual warriors ensured, however, that the Christian nationalist cause and struggle for Europe's soul would continue deeper into the Cold War. The spiritual struggle for Europe thus left American Protestants deeply divided and at odds over their global mission. It ultimately forged competing theologies of global engagement—Christian nationalism and Christian globalism—that transformed the United States, diplomacy, and religion in an era of world war and beyond.[6]

At heart, *God's Marshall Plan* explores how American Protestants have come to see their place and role in the world in such differing and competing ways. Although most American Protestants today accept that their nation is a global superpower, they often disagree sharply on the promise and perils of that particular identity. While some celebrate the United States as God's chosen nation, others ponder how to live faithfully in the world's new Babylon. The American Protestant mission to spiritually reconstruct Europe reveals that these contemporary tensions are not new. In fact, American Protestants have long wrestled with how their faith relates to the particulars of their nation's identity and its international engagement.

To examine the roots of these tensions, this book begins its storyline at the turn of the twentieth century, when American Protestants were just beginning to make sense of their nation's rise as a world power. The three global wars that ensued—the Great War, the Second World War, and the Cold War—offered American Protestants an extraordinary opportunity to redefine their nation's role in the world. Many American Protestants began to broadly agree that their nation had a divine commission to solve the trials of their age. Their isolationist and pacifist tendencies began to fade as they supported new global interventions and launched missions to remake the world in their image. By 1945, their nation's ascent seemed near complete. Following the Second World War, America's military spanned the globe and its economy dwarfed all others. In the view of many American Protestants, the United States also possessed the clearest claim to moral and spiritual leadership of the world. Yet despite that preponderance of power, American Protestants had come to sharply disagree over how exactly the United States should use its newfound standing in the world and to what ends. The spiritual fight for Europe exposed this growing divergence between American Protestants over the proper political and diplomatic expressions of their faith.

This book explores the origins of these sharp disagreements through considering how American and European Protestants responded to the outbreak of world war and the rise of totalitarian regimes in the early to mid-twentieth century. To do so, it recovers a lost transatlantic world that reshaped Protestant political thought and international engagement on both sides of the Atlantic. Zooming in further, it focuses its narrative especially on the German-American Protestant relationship from the turn of the twentieth century into the early Cold War. It explores how the German-American exchange in this era was arguably much richer, more complex, and more transformative to international religion and politics than previously recognized.[7]

At the turn of the twentieth century, Protestants across the North Atlantic world were beginning to make sense of the rise of the United States and Germany as new global powers. Following respective wars of national unification in the 1860s and 1870s, both the United States and the German Reich endeavored to become powerful nation-states and internationally respected empires. The American government emerged from the American Civil War (1861–1865) eager to consolidate its control over the North American interior, as well as to unify its northern and southern sections under the banner of a shared Protestant culture. In the Spanish-American War, the United States proceeded to stretch its "frontier" thousands of miles from home into the Pacific and the Caribbean, in the process becoming a new empire. Meanwhile, following the Franco-Prussian War in Europe (1870–1871), Otto von Bismarck, the militant "blood-and-iron" minister of Prussia who had unified the German states through war, worked to strengthen Prussian and Protestant hegemony through a domestic culture war on Catholicism and socialism. He also sought to win the new German empire continental respect and to establish German colonies through "carving up" the African continent. By the turn of the century, both nation-states had become imperial powers and had developed commanding positions in their era's industrializing international economy. Both had also sought to forge Protestant national cultures at home and were pursuing Protestant foreign missions abroad that aimed to "civilize" and "Christianize" the world.[8]

Against this backdrop, religion proved to both connect and divide American and German Protestants. As the twentieth century approached, transatlantic revivals, social reformers, and liberal Protestant theology had built religious bridges between Protestants on both sides of the Atlantic. Yet despite these points of connection, the rapid rise of both nations heightened how American and German Protestants came to believe they advanced rather different spiritual and political traditions in the world. Moreover, both American and German Protestants equally claimed divine sanction for their respective world-historical missions. While American Protestants affirmed that they stood behind the sacred cause of a democratic faith and politics, they argued that German Protestants had grown to promote an authoritarian spiritual and political culture. As a range of American Protestants saw it, their counterparts' proclivity for autocratic governance and theological modernism had led them to support the Kaiser's march to war, to reject the liberal democracy of the Weimar Republic, and to welcome Nazi fascism and its militaristic nationalism. In contrast, German Protestants often criticized their American peers for pursuing the "Americanization" of the world, for practicing an unbridled spiritual activism, and for advancing the cause of American empire. American Protestants in response viewed defeating and reforming this German tradition as one of the central tasks of two world wars and a military occupation. Moreover, integrating Germany into a newfound international Protestant order stood out to them as one of the most decisive undertakings in the early Cold War. In these ways, the "German problem" loomed large as one of the most central spiritual and political issues for American Protestants of this era, just as German Protestants equally harbored fears of America's "spiritual imperialism."[9]

This book accordingly surveys how American Protestants became so focused on reforming Germany and documents their prolific efforts to change Germany's political and spiritual culture. It follows a host of Protestant pastors, revivalists, diplomats, and spies who responded to the outbreak of trench warfare, observed the rise of fascist dictatorships, mobilized against the Axis powers, and began to identify Germany and Europe as in need of saving. After two tumultuous wars, they then launched far-reaching missions to spread their faith and democracy across the Atlantic. Their spiritual interventions solidified their sense of moral and spiritual exceptionalism and presaged a new American activism in the world as a defender and promoter of democracy.[10]

While Americans drew energy from their mission to save Europe, that mission also fractured American Protestantism through further pitting "ecumenical" and "evangelical" Protestants against one another as spiritual foes. Historians have long debated how exactly to define these respective movements within American Protestantism. The boundaries between these two groups were at times fluid and permeable, and a wide middle ground often existed between them. Nonetheless, scholars have pointed to the "Fundamentalist-Modernist Controversy" of the 1920s as one significant point of theological departure between these two Protestant wings. While historians most often recount this moment as an early twentieth-century struggle over theology and the teaching of evolution, the controversy was never just about doctrine and science alone. It also had to do with vastly differing notions of mission, eschatology, politics, and foreign policy. It is these differences that ultimately inspired the competing ecumenical and evangelical missions to Europe.[11]

In the lead in crossing the Atlantic were the "ecumenical" Protestants, or "ecumenists," who stemmed from the broad tradition of liberal mainline American Protestantism. Theologically, these ecumenists tended to be "modernist" and "liberal" in their theological orientation, which meant they were more open to synthesizing their faith with new intellectual currents flowing from Europe, such as biblical higher criticism and modern evolutionary science. Drawing upon such insights, they revised traditional Protestant doctrines that they felt no longer held up to scientific scrutiny, such as a six-day creation and Christ's virgin birth. Their openness to the discoveries of modern scientific methods also overlapped with a growing tolerance for doctrinal difference. They sought to overcome once-sharp confessional disputes and to unify America's powerful mainline denominations in the Federal Council of Churches, a national Protestant church organization designed to coordinate Protestant mission efforts and public engagement. The idea of Protestant "ecumenism," drawn from the Greek word *oikumene*, meaning the "inhabited world," developed from this effort to unify Protestants across denominations. Until the early twentieth century, national ecclesial unity had proven elusive for these Americans, who lacked the national church structures of Europe and experienced firsthand the enduring denominational fragmentation of the Reformation. Yet American ecumenists believed they could reverse such effects, not only at home but also abroad. Through their collaboration, they strove to complete the "Christianization" of their country and to unify the world under the banner of their modern faith and democratic politics.[12]

Beyond their ecumenical leanings, ecumenists also gravitated to postmillennialism, an eschatological school of thought which foretold that a thousand-year era of peace and justice would precede Christ's triumphant return to the earth. They believed they had a role to play in ushering in this millennial era through progressively improving human affairs. They therefore practiced a social activism that sought to transform human society, reform industrial capitalism, and uplift international relations to a higher moral plane. They affirmed that their mission of Christianizing and even Americanizing the world helped establish this anticipated kingdom of God on earth. In pursuit of a more harmonious world, they also began to downplay conversionary proselytization in favor of new mission methods focused on institution building, social service, and humanitarian aid.[13]

Their postmillennialism also tended to align them with the aims of progressive politics and diplomacy. They especially supported Woodrow Wilson's foreign policy of world democratization and multilateral global governance, which they hoped would quicken the creation of a harmonious world. Along with Wilson, they set their sights on remaking the world through the global spread of America's liberal democratic and Protestant Christian values. While the brutality of the Great War challenged their postmillennial optimism, their commitments to pursuing peace and progress nonetheless endured. They strove to spiritually complement Wilson's League of Nations through global ecumenical partnerships that they hoped would infuse international diplomacy with an underlying Christian character. They likewise worked to establish a new global institution for Protestant Christians, which culminated in the creation of the World Council of Churches. Through this spiritual fellowship, ecumenists hoped they could promote ecumenical values abroad, overcome the nationalism, secularism, and totalitarianism that threatened their globe, and create a lasting foundation for a peaceful and just world.[14]

In contrast, twentieth-century Protestant "evangelicals" found their roots in the "fundamentalist" response to these currents of Protestant modernism. In a series of booklets titled *The Fundamentals: A Testimony to Truth* (published in the 1910s), these theologically conservative Protestants opposed evolutionary theory, affirmed that the Bible was infallible and absolute in authority, and insisted that doctrinal differences and the confessional autonomy of local congregations continued to matter. Through defending these "fundamentals" of the faith, they laid the foundation for a national, interdenominational movement that aimed to challenge Protestant modernism and ecumenism on a global scale. Their movement seemed to be dealt a decisive blow in the mid-1920s when the Scopes-Monkey Trial, argued over the teaching of evolution in Tennessee public schools, gave these "fundamentalists" the pejorative reputation of being anti-intellectual, backward plain folk. While conventional wisdom suggests fundamentalists then retreated out of sight, they in fact began to build their own national networks that rivaled the Protestant mainline's powerful hold on American society. Moreover, they sought to shape their nation's politics and culture through campaigns against evolution and alcohol.[15]

The signs of the times led Protestant fundamentalists to develop their own competing sense of global mission that rooted itself in their premillennial eschatology. Having defended traditional doctrines such as the atoning work of Christ, they accordingly stressed the enduring importance of conversionary mission in saving as many souls as possible from sin and the eternal fires of hell. Their interpretations of ancient biblical texts and daily news headlines also led a more radical wing within their ranks to believe the world was not getting progressively better, but rather, in its sinful corruption, was coming to a violent, tragic, and imminent end. Such convictions reflected an eschatology—dispensational premillennialism—that drew on biblical prophecies to outline the six dispensations of human history that purportedly preceded Christ's return and the foretold millennium. Believing that they lived in the sixth dispensation, these "radical evangelicals" anticipated that Christ's faithful followers would be raptured from the Earth, while a powerful dictator known as the Antichrist would take over the world and spark an apocalyptic battle before the final judgment and onset of the millennium.[16]

Far from leading these fundamentalists to withdraw from the world, however, such apocalypticism actually emboldened their activism even more. As historian Matthew Sutton has illustrated, premillennial evangelicals drew inspiration from the apocalypse to "occupy" their country for Christ and to prepare their world for Christ's imminent return. They felt a tremendous urgency to save souls and to oppose the forces of evil in the world until the very end. In particular, they opposed the "collectivism" of ecumenical councils, big government programs, and Wilsonian internationalism—any development that they feared would centralize power and could aid the coming Antichrist. To counteract such trends, they championed their own Christian politics of limited government, spiritual liberty, and free-market capitalism. When it came to international affairs, their apocalypticism led them to call for independence from international influence and multilateral organizations such as the League of Nations. Along with their muscular faith, their apocalypticism also led them to support a strong military in times of conflict, unilateral interventions abroad, and the pursuit of holy war against evil.[17]

The Second World War electrified American fundamentalists even further. In 1942, a core group within their ranks sought to give their movement a fresh public image through rebranding themselves as "neo-evangelicals." They likewise hoped to challenge the Federal Council and to restore their nation to its proper theological heritage through institutionally forming the National Association of Evangelicals (NAE). While these evangelicals sought to foster a "new" identity, in many ways, they were still very much fundamentalists at heart. Following the war, they sought to gain a new hold over American public life through promoting a public theology of "faith, freedom, and free enterprise." Paradoxically, they advanced these commitments even as they developed a closer relationship to an increasingly expansive federal government in the Cold War. As that conflict developed, they emerged as their nation's fiercest spiritual warriors in the struggle against Soviet communism.[18]

These ecumenical and evangelical traditions stood behind the competing spiritual missions to Europe. In short, Protestant ecumenists aimed to usher in a new era of democracy and ecumenical religion across the Atlantic and to build multilateral spiritual and political institutions that they hoped would undergird a new American-led Christian world order. In contrast, American evangelicals desired to preach a gospel of liberty in its spiritual, political, and economic forms, to spread biblical fundamentals, and to defeat the evils emanating from Europe, including theological modernism, "pagan Nazism," and atheistic communism. These varying theological commitments ultimately compelled a broad range of American Protestants to fight for the soul of Europe and to seek to establish competing transatlantic spiritual orders.

God's Marshall Plan also considers how both Protestant traditions played a role in facilitating the rise of Christian nationalism and Christian globalism as competing twentieth-century theologies of global engagement. It does so through investigating the historical roots of these theologies, in particular through examining the ways Protestant figures on both sides of the Atlantic made sense of the relationship between the church and the nation-state in this era. In one sense, how to draw the line between God and Caesar had always troubled Christians. A host of political theologies had been developed to solve this dilemma, from the bishop Eusebius baptizing Constantine's

Roman Empire as a vessel of God's providence, to Augustine differentiating the heavenly and the earthly cities, to the Reformation-era Anabaptists rejecting the sword and withdrawing from the magisterial state. Such tensions no less concerned twentieth-century Protestants. As historian Brian Stanley has put it, the history of twentieth-century Protestant Christianity can be read in part as the story of the faith's engagement and "compromise" with the creeds of nation, race, and empire. In particular, Protestant Christians on both sides of the Atlantic had generally come to espouse the central tenets of Christian nationalism—the belief that a divine partnership existed between the Christian God and their respective nation-states. The nation and its corresponding empire appeared to many North Atlantic Protestants as an agent of God's will and work in the world.[19]

Making matters more complex, twentieth-century Protestants likewise grappled with powerful political ideologies—such as democratic liberalism, fascism, and communism—that swept over the North Atlantic world and vied for their political loyalties. More often than not, their national and political allegiances overpowered their religious commitments. In particular, such loyalties often challenged their faith's summons to love of neighbor, regardless of that neighbor's nationality, race, or politics. Christian nationalism likewise clashed with the biblical admonition to prioritize peacemaking and to seek the welfare of the wider world. Finally, it undercut the biblical mandate to hold a higher citizenship in heaven and to declare a greater devotion to a kingdom that knew no borders.[20]

This book in part examines the elaborate and complex process through which Protestants on both sides of the Atlantic came to terms in the twentieth century with the unholy alliances that had formed between their faith, nationalism, and political ideology. It proved difficult for American and European Protestants alike to untangle the thicket of connections between their churches and such creeds. In particular, it took time for many to see the nation-state itself as the human construction it was, an "imagined community" that drew upon history, culture, race, and religion in order to police the national boundaries of belonging, to oppose the perceived enemies of the state, and to undergird world-historical missions. Yet a host of twentieth-century developments—in particular, the onset of tumultuous wars, the emergence of new spiritual networks, the rise of totalitarian regimes, and the global growth of the Christian faith—led Protestants on both sides of the Atlantic to begin to question Christian nationalism and its corresponding projects. These fundamental upheavals prompted American and European

Protestants to develop a new global identity that challenged nationalism, racism, and imperialism. Yet as this book shows, Christian nationalism continued to find faithful adherents across the North Atlantic world and still finds expression in today's global political and religious debates.[21]

In the American context in particular, Christian nationalism powerfully shaped how many twentieth-century American Protestants viewed the globe. As a theological mode of thought, American Christian nationalism asserted that the United States was a Christian nation—by which Christian nationalists meant Protestant—that possessed an exceptional purpose and messianic mission to spread Christianity and democracy across the world. This theological conviction had already fostered a bold array of foreign initiatives in the nineteenth century, including efforts to conquer the North American continent in the name of Christ and liberty, as well as the Spanish-American War—a conflict many American Protestants viewed as an opportunity to dispel the backward "Catholic" empire of Spain and to liberate tens of millions living in Cuba, Puerto Rico, the Philippines, and Guam. In the early twentieth century, Christian nationalism also found expression in American Protestant campaigns to "Christianize" the world and to spread America's democratic civilization abroad. While some American Protestant nationalists rejected the "old-style" imperialism of Europe as exploitative, they still believed Americans needed to practice a "spiritual imperialism" in the world—what they described as a more benevolent and enlightened form of empire that undercut the power-hungry ways of European nations.[22]

Christian nationalism was not just about America's role abroad, however. It compelled American Protestants to narrowly define and police the national identity of the United States as well. On the home front, Christian nationalists often argued that "Christian America" needed to be defended from enemies both foreign and domestic. They sought to protect the privileged domestic standing of white American Protestants and warned that numerous threats—including European immigrants, communists, Catholics, and Jews—imperiled "Christian America" and the Protestant character of the American nation. In response, they often practiced a nativist politics of racial and religious exclusion. In this regard, Christian nationalism was an illiberal form of nationalism. It aimed to define American identity not on a set of inclusive liberal principles and civic ideals, such as the revolutionary proposition that all human beings were created equal and entitled to "certain unalienable rights," as well as foundational freedoms such as religious liberty, but rather on a narrow and exclusive understanding of "Americanness" that limited itself to Anglo-Saxon Protestants. American Christian nationalists countered the revolutionary vision of the United States as a safe haven for the world's oppressed, and advanced the idea that America was a vulnerable fortress that needed to be defended from a multitude of threats.[23]

To be clear, Christian nationalism was not civic patriotism. For some American Protestants of this era, patriotism rightly understood constituted a "cautious" and tough love of country. It entailed a dedication to America's liberal ideals and did not hesitate to criticize and admonish when Americans failed to live into these principles. This kind of civic patriotism likewise nurtured the aspirational longing toward what Martin Luther King, Jr., described as the "beloved community." It promoted the kind of solidarity, mutuality, and equity that could bind a diverse society together and form the foundation of a just common life. It understood Nazi fascism just as much as a summons to vigilance abroad as a call to reform of injustice at home. In an increasingly interconnected world, it also overlapped with commitments to wider global fellowships that helped temper and mediate it. In contrast, Christian nationalism corrupted and distorted this kind of civic good. It endorsed exclusionary and insular politics at home and abroad, asserted notions of national greatness, fostered myths of national exceptionalism, and claimed divine sanction for the nation's pursuits. Christian nationalists at times sought to cloak their commitments in the garb of patriotism, but there was always a crucial distinction between a measured devotion to country and their deification of the flag.[24]

In accounts both academic and popular, historians and journalists have tended to credit Protestant evangelicals as the harbingers of Christian nationalism in the twentieth century, and with good cause. Evangelicals were indeed often at the forefront of arguing that the United States was a Christian nation, heir to a divinely ordained heritage of evangelical theology and political and economic liberty. In response to German imperialism, Nazi fascism, and Soviet communism, they fostered Christian nationalist revivals at home and called for the kind of robust militarism that they hoped could eradicate such evils in the world. They likewise tended to promote an "America First" mentality that rejected international institutions and alliances and instead called on the United States to unilaterally and muscularly use its military might to defeat foreign enemies. Yet far from retreating from the world as isolationists, Protestant evangelicals also proved eager to remake the globe in America's evangelical, democratic, and capitalist image.[25]

In contrast, several historical accounts have portrayed Protestant ecumenists as transcending and eschewing Christian nationalism. In particular, the foreign mission field and the ruins of war provided soil for an alternative theology of global engagement to grow. Through the trials of the twentieth century, some American Protestants began to espouse this counter-theology, which this book describes as "Christian globalism." In the aftermath of the Great War, a small yet committed group of ecumenical Protestant missionaries began to seriously question and critique the notion of Christian nationhood itself. As historian Michael Thompson puts it, these ecumenical Protestant missionaries began to place their "commitment to the ethics of Jesus above the nation." As such, they challenged the common American Protestant belief that their nation's cause and God's cause were inherently one and the same. They likewise opposed the exceptionalism and imperialism that flowed from such convictions. Forsaking the nation, they instead pursued "wider solidarities" within a global fellowship of Protestant Christians and developed an ethic of pacifism and justice in an increasingly interconnected world.[26]

In the words of historian David Hollinger, these ecumenical missionaries also began to espouse a "cosmopolitanism" that sought to reverse "the provinciality of American life." They especially devoted themselves to promoting a global mentality at home that was more tolerant to difference and diversity. They desired to build new global institutions that would promote peace and understanding and proved willing to partner with other confessions of faith in pursuit of peace, justice, and equality across the globe. In this regard, they were in the spiritual business of reforming a provincial Protestant nation into a pluralist and egalitarian member of a broader global community. When the Cold War set in, these Protestant globalists favored an ethic of peace and mediation between the United States and Soviet Union. They refused to position themselves as proponents of the American way, but rather chose to be ministers of reconciliation in a broken world. They likewise supported pacifism in the face of nuclear proliferation and defended human rights in an era of Jim Crow segregation and decolonization.[27]

While Christian globalism without question grew in prominence during the interwar years, this book considers how Protestant ecumenists also continued to advance a Christian nationalism of their own well into the mid-twentieth century. While their patriotism and sense of national exceptionalism were indeed at times "cautious" and tempered, their engagement with Europe also activated their enduring belief that "Christian America" had a Wilsonian duty to Christianize and democratize the world. Through the trials of war and reconstruction, they affirmed that their churches and their nation possessed the spiritual resources and political skill needed to undertake such a world-historical mission. They accordingly viewed international relations as a venue through which they could use state and ecclesial power to spread Christianity and democracy abroad. As historian Emily Conroy-Krutz has documented, this kind of international engagement—what she terms as "Christian imperialism"—had deep roots in the nineteenth-century American Protestant missionary experience. Twentieth-century American ecumenists—the self-proclaimed successors of the missionary project—practiced a "conquering faith" of their own through seeking to remake the Europe along ecumenical and democratic lines. Their growing global awareness and ethic of international responsibility yielded a mission to create a new Christian world order premised on the American way and American global leadership. Their faith drew upon Wilsonian convictions and a confidence in the American system as they worked to establish American-led spiritual, economic, and political networks across the Atlantic and to inaugurate what they called a new "American Century." In these pursuits, some Protestant ecumenists also espoused religious and racial prejudice and proved resistant to movements for interfaith and racial equality. Overall, many remained protective of their establishment status both at home and abroad.[28]

Building on these insights, this book suggests that the boundaries between Christian nationalism and Christian globalism often proved blurry in the American mission to Europe. It examines how Christian globalism only more fully emerged within American Protestantism through an arduous, contested, and complex process, one that especially involved pushback from European and global partners. To explore these themes, this book especially tracks how a core group of American ecumenists tied to the Federal Council of Churches and America's foreign service—including Protestant giants such as John Foster Dulles and Reinhold Niebuhr, alongside lesser known figures such as Stewart Herman, Henry Smith Leiper, and Samuel McCrea Cavert—made sense of their duties to their faith and their duties to the state in their mission to Europe.

These leading Protestant figures often stood at the nexus of American religion and foreign policy. In an era of totalitarian ideology and growing global interconnectedness, the American government viewed them as prized assets for several reasons, including their extensive international experience, their intimate knowledge of foreign languages and cultures, and their central standing in the mainline Protestant establishment that dominated Washington. While a pacifist ethic had long defined their movement, the specter of Nazi totalitarianism in part led these ecumenists to embrace Niebuhr's Christian realist ethic, which had outlined the tragic need for the use of restrained force in order to limit evil, create order, and achieve a semblance of justice. Drawing on this ethic, they called for American intervention against the Axis powers while also seeking to place ethical limits and restraints on the use of American power abroad.[29]

This book examines how these leading ecumenists ultimately blended elements of Christian nationalism and Christian globalism in their mobilization for war and their mission to Europe. Even as these leading ecumenists embraced aspects of Christian globalism—such as the need for multilateral and global institutions—some also affirmed the belief that it was their nation's particular responsibility to rebuild and remake the world through the spread of its Christian and democratic ideals. They accordingly came to see an era of world war and spiritual reconstruction as their nation's ascendant moment. They therefore worked to establish for "Christian America" an advantageous, even hegemonic, position in the international arena, as well as to rally their nation into a defense of the Western world's "Christian civilization." Their wartime service for Christ and country sent them out as diplomats, advisors, and spies across the Atlantic, where they advanced national and ecumenical interests in tandem in a shared defense of democracy and faith against the Axis and Soviet threat. They viewed such service as the surest way to give their nation and their movement a fighting chance to create a new global order. In pursuit of such ends, they readily used their nation's military and diplomatic power, at times sanctifying it with spiritual purpose, at other times seeking to purify and restrain its excesses.[30]

Through the turmoil of two world wars, these mid-century ecumenists also came to identify Germany as the prime location to build a new Christian world order in the heart of Europe. Following the Second World War, they embedded in occupying army platoons and orchestrated a wide-reaching campaign to reconstruct Germany's churches along ecumenical and American lines. To carry out their spiritual and political intervention, they used the World Council of Churches as a tool of America's global project and forged alliances with German partners inclined to their flavor of ecumenism and democratic politics. Through ecumenical aid and reconstruction campaigns, they moreover sought to change what Germans believed, how they worshipped, and how they voted. They then held up Germany's spiritual reconstruction as a blueprint for the promotion of ecumenism and democracy across Europe, which they viewed as their era's major scene of confrontation with spiritual threats such as communism, secularism, and Catholicism. In this sense, the American ecumenical movement itself became a vehicle for securing Europe as an American and Protestant sphere of influence.[31]

Historians have indeed argued that the postwar hour marked the triumph of the United States' "empire by invitation" in Europe and the rise of its "hidden empire" across the globe. This book considers how these Protestant ecumenists were spiritual architects of this new kind of American presence in the world, one that relied less on colonies and control by bayonet and more on subtle measures such as economic networks and cultural appeal in order to establish America's global standing. Unlike the empires of old, these ecumenists desired their new world order to be predicated upon a kinder, gentler, and more benevolent American presence in the world. They provided vital energy and institutional resources for the creation of a host of multilateral institutions and Cold War initiatives, such as the United Nations, a new multilateral hub of global governance, and the Marshall Plan, an economic infusion of American funds and aid that the US government implemented in order to revive Europe's postwar economies. The Marshall Plan, ecumenists and policymakers alike agreed, was a sign of America's benevolent global activism. While the Plan indeed reflected humanitarian commitments, it also was about establishing and solidifying the American system in Europe and securing for the United States a new hegemonic position in the world.[32]

In this regard, the Marshall Plan serves as an apt metaphor for the ambitions of American Protestants in Europe. As the American government worked to remake the continent's markets and politics, American Protestants complemented these efforts through tent revivals, theological exchanges, and reconstruction programs designed to revive the continent's soul. In effect, they worked to establish an American empire of the spirit. They hoped that exporting their faith's values abroad and creating new ocean-spanning religious networks would provide spiritual support for America's new transatlantic democratic order. Through these efforts, they strove to make good on the promise of the "American Century" and to create a new world order rooted in American values, ideals, and institutions. Here again, globalist and nationalist sentiment blurred together, at once tying American ecumenists to a transnational community while also asserting American leadership over this new global order.[33]

As the occupation of Germany matured and the Cold War began, these same ecumenists continued to work alongside their government in designing foreign initiatives to circumvent communists and secularists in postwar Europe. They worked to activate the latent energies of Europe's lay Protestants as Christ's foot soldiers in the "re-Christianization" of the continent. As they rehabilitated German Protestants as new allies in this spiritual struggle, they articulated many of the political and spiritual concerns that led to a Cold War revival of Christian nationalism at home. All the while, many of these ecumenical leaders sought to protect the privileged place of ecumenical Protestantism in both the United States and Europe. They mobilized against what they described as the spiritual totalitarianisms of Roman Catholicism, Protestant fundamentalism, and secularism and thereby turned Europe into a spiritual battleground.

Yet as these American Protestants pressed abroad to change Europe, some began to find that Europe in fact remade them. Such a pattern was not necessarily new. As historian David Hollinger has shown, American Protestants often went out with confidence to change the world, only to discover that their foreign engagement could equally change them in return. Time spent abroad could also foster a self-critical spirit that transformed their global imagination. In pressing abroad to promote the American system in Europe, a growing number of American Protestants began to leave such a project behind in search of a more global fellowship and a more prophetic witness.[34]

While numerous global encounters facilitated this shift, this book probes how the Protestant turn to Christian globalism resulted in part from this European pushback to America's spiritual crusade. It shows that German and European Protestants were far from passive recipients of America's global project. German Protestants in particular had long held deep concerns about American Protestant "activism" in the world and the shallow nature of American theology. They championed their own German form of Christian nationalism that made equal claims about Germany's chosen status in the world. German Protestants used their conservative nationalist theology to support the cause of empire, excoriate the liberal Weimar Republic, laud national renewal under Hitler, and condone German warfare. German Protestant bishop Otto Dibelius perhaps best illustrated this thinking when he greeted Hitler's rise to power with professions that the state was to be "hard and ruthless" and to oppose the nation's enemies "without mercy." Such conservative nationalism lingered into the postwar era. Protestant nationalists in particular protested the Allied occupation of their "fatherland" and sought to

set their defeated nation on equal spiritual and moral terms with the victorious Allied powers.[35]

Yet for some German Protestants, the devastation of the war and a realization of their complicity in Hitler's regime began to challenge such
premonitions. In the ruins of Hitler's Reich, radical German reformers called
for pathbreaking changes within German Protestant churches. They began
to forsake their own Christian nationalism and to foster the slow postwar
transformation of their congregations. They developed a new public voice
that contested their faith's long-standing apathy to socialism, their country's
Cold War division, and the remilitarization of their lands. They spoke back
to Americans in powerful ways, challenging American Protestants in particular to reconsider their conflations of church and nation and their
contributions to Cold War tensions. These German Protestants, now joined
by other European Protestant pastors and theologians, instead articulated a
"third way" position for the world's Protestants that would mediate between
Moscow and Washington and engage Protestants across borders in pursuit
of global peace, reconciliation, and justice. Faced by the European challenge
to their conquering faith, some of the same American Protestants who had
served their nation in war and reconstruction now more fully embraced the
theology of Christian globalism. They returned to theologies of prophetic
protest, peace, and racial justice. They more readily challenged American
militarism in the Cold War, attacked economic inequality at home and
abroad, and pushed for civil and human rights in an era of Jim Crow segregation and decolonization. Not to be left behind, some evangelical Protestants
also began to experience their own global turn as they listened to evangelical
partners from across the world and developed a growing social concern for
the poor.[36]

Yet Christian nationalism continued to hold Protestants spellbound on
both sides of the Atlantic. All along, America's Protestant evangelicals had
also mobilized for holy war against the German Kaiser, Hitler, and Soviet
communists. They used these three wars to assert themselves as their country's
most faithful Christian nationalists. With each wave of conflict, they increasingly strove to occupy the center of American public life and to restore their
nation, as well as Europe, back to what they viewed as its proper theological and political heritage. As they pressed abroad to share their gospel of
liberty along the Iron Curtain, they called for rugged militarism at home

and practiced a politics of "containment" and "rollback"—to borrow phrases from the Cold War lexicon—that sought to suppress and repel Soviet communism, New Deal liberalism, and Protestant ecumenism, as well as to slow down progressive reform movements for civil rights. As the Cold War heated up, they provided the backbone for a powerful postwar consensus of Christian nationalism and anti-communism and forecasted a different kind of aggressive American presence in the world. They would eventually find themselves ascendant in domestic and international politics while Protestant ecumenists began to experience a slow decline. Indeed, these Protestant Cold Warriors viewed postwar Europe as a major staging ground in their broader spiritual mission to retake their nation and the globe. As they looked abroad, they forged new evangelical and anti-communist alliances with German and European fundamentalists and sought strategic partnerships with politicians like Konrad Adenauer and anti-communist German bishops like Otto Dibelius. Ironically, conservative German nationalists like Dibelius, who had been most opposed to the Allied occupation, became America's strongest Cold War allies due to their fervent anti-communism and notions of Western exceptionalism.[37]

Against the backdrop of this evangelical resurgence and renewed Cold War hostilities, Protestants on both sides of the Atlantic found themselves increasingly divided. The struggle for Europe's soul simultaneously challenged, changed, and reinforced the political and religious convictions of American and European Protestants alike. With a particular focus on the American context, this book documents how this spiritual struggle ultimately fostered competing visions for America's role in the world and left American Protestants divided and at odds over their global mission. Certainly, other international developments—such as the status of postwar China, the wars in Korea and Vietnam, decolonization, and the pursuit of global human rights—played a formative role in shaping American Protestant international attitudes and merit careful consideration. This book adds an important chapter to the story by showing how the American effort to spiritually reconstruct Europe emboldened, fractured, and converted American Protestants in myriad ways.

The ramifications endure. As American Protestants continue to make sense of their world, a muscular Christian nationalism still challenges a cosmopolitan Christian globalism as their faith's definitive mode of global engagement. Ideally, careful study of these twentieth-century episodes can help make plain the pitfalls and possibilities of these theologies, from the hazards of imperial interventions and exclusionary nationalisms to the promise of charitable engagement at home and abroad within mutual and hospitable global partnerships.

1

Spiritual Conquest

In November 1918, just as troops began to depart from the trenches of the First World War, American Protestant ecumenist Henry Smith Leiper reflected on the state of disorder that had swept over the globe. Over the prior four years, the young missionary had watched with grave concern as a cataclysmic world war had broken out and disrupted American Protestant efforts to win over the world for Christ and democracy. In response, Leiper and his ecumenical colleagues had pinned such troubles on German imperialism. They also had interpreted Germany's wayward course as a mandate to claim the leadership of transatlantic affairs and to guide the world to a peaceful future. Backing Woodrow Wilson's internationalist aims, they argued that Americans needed to spread abroad their "spiritual democracy" through the sacred cause of world mission and world democratization. Through such efforts, Leiper believed Americans could foster a newfound global spiritual order that was ecumenical, democratic, and a true rival to the German empire.[1]

Leiper, however, was not the only American Protestant eager to advance America's cause. Protestant fundamentalist William Bell Riley also called his nation to war against the Germans. Yet in contrast to Leiper's ecumenical aims, Riley desired to stamp out Germany's theological modernism that he believed had corrupted the Protestant faith and had fostered German militarism itself. Through mobilizing for war, Riley and his partners pledged to battle evil both abroad and at home. They worked to establish their own "fundamentalist empire" as they contested ecumenical understandings of the Bible, Christian mission, and world diplomacy.[2]

Despite their diverging spiritual commitments, one thing stood clear to both Leiper and Riley: Germany was the major problem. Whether it was Germany's autocratic ambitions or its liberal theology, a growing number of American Protestants saw the German threat to "Christendom" as requiring an American response. An era of world mission and world war ultimately activated the Christian nationalism and spiritual imperialism of these disparate American Protestants. Yet the challenges of the war, along with the ruins of

God's Marshall Plan. James D. Strasburg, Oxford University Press (2021). © Oxford University Press.
DOI: 10.1093/oso/9780197516447.003.0002

the postwar landscape, also led some Americans to adopt a new self-critical spirit that questioned these notions of Christian nationhood and empire altogether. These competing theologies of global engagement—Christian nationalism and Christian globalism—would decisively shape American Protestant activism to Europe, and more broadly to the world, in the decades that followed.

Henry Smith Leiper came of age in the heyday of American Protestant foreign missions. Throughout the nineteenth century, American Protestants had primarily focused their missionary efforts on "home missions," or as some American Protestants put it, the effort to "Christianize" the continental United States. Yet following several decades of rapid industrial growth and the "closing of the continental frontier," as one prominent thinker of the era phrased it, Americans were increasingly looking abroad for new markets to capitalize, societies to civilize, and souls to redeem. Congregationalist minister Josiah Strong captured such sentiment in 1885 when he called on his fellow American Protestants to not only complete the "spiritual conquest" of the American West but to also press onward in pursuit of "the evangelization of the world." "The world is to be Christianized and civilized," Strong wrote. He added that God had chosen American Protestants to "stamp the peoples of the earth" with the imprint of America's political and spiritual culture.[3]

Strong's rhetoric reflected the powerful Christian nationalism, as well as the notion of a benevolent Christian imperialism, that motivated many American Protestants to spread American civilization across the globe. Freed from the political authoritarianism, rigid ecclesial hierarchy, and the backward economics of the European "Old World," American Protestants believed their nation's religious, democratic, and market-based culture destined them to remake the world. In the nineteenth century, some American missionaries had called for simply preaching the gospel alone, limiting the spread of American culture abroad, and instead creating "self-supporting, self-propagating, and self-governing" indigenous churches. Yet by the early twentieth century, many others had embraced the imperial spirit of their age and had come to see conversionary mission as a spiritual complement to military intervention, capitalist expansion, and the spread of American civilization. As one missionary organizer put it, American Protestants offered a "spirit of Christian imperialism" that enhanced their nation's imperial advance in the world. Reflecting the racial outlook of their era, many white American Protestants also believed their efforts would enlighten the "less civilized" and "heathen" peoples of the world. Moreover, some affirmed their nation's global expansion was helping usher in the millennium—a thousand-year era of peace and justice that would precede Christ's triumphant return.[4]

This triumphal and imperial pursuit of Protestant mission united American Protestants in an endeavor that cut across denominational lines. Unlike many of their European counterparts, American Protestants had no single, unified national church. Many longed to see their disparate denominations work more closely together both at home and abroad. They strove to see past doctrinal differences as they focused on the common goal of evangelizing and civilizing the world. Reflecting this trend, leading "mainline" Protestant denominations officially came together in 1908 as a federation of national churches they called the Federal Council of Churches (FCC). While the Federal Council's creation reflected the desire of American Protestants to unify all Protestant churches under one national banner, it also upset some Protestants who saw ecumenism as overlooking important differences in fundamental doctrines. These Protestants also argued that ecumenism undermined the independence of local congregations. Ironically, ecumenism bred unity and division in equal measure.[5]

From its outset, the ecumenical mission of the Federal Council rallied American Protestants to a cause that served both Christ and country. These intertwined commitments had already appeared in the remarks of ecumenical speakers at the 1905 Inter-Church Conference on Federation. Woodrow Wilson—then president of Princeton University, a close friend of Protestant missionary organizers, and a committed southern Presbyterian—blended religion and democracy together in a sacred cause when he charged attendees to rise up to "the mighty task before us," which "welds us together. It is to make the United States a mighty Christian Nation, and to Christianize the world." As another attendee added, American Protestant mission could "bring about an ideal Church and an ideal State" through promoting the sacred partnership of Christianity and democracy. Reflecting the imperial ambitions of ecumenical cooperation, one observer noted that the ecumenical conference represented "nearly all the Protestant faiths of the country whose aim is a world conquest for Christianity." The gathering illustrated how American ecumenists readily blended together commitments to Christ, democracy, and global expansion. They saw their churches and the state as complementing one another in the cause of spreading America's democratic and Protestant spirit across the globe. The American state, with its relatively limited foreign service, had also looked to Protestant missionaries as non-state actors of foreign policy. American ecumenists hoped this collaborative partnership would continue on in the global promotion of democracy and Christianity. The blending of these spiritual and political interests foreshadowed how ecumenical and governmental activism would often overlap seamlessly in the decades to come.[6]

Civic supporters like Wilson certainly helped advance the cause, but it was really missionary organizers like John R. Mott that inspired young Americans like Leiper. Perhaps no other American Protestant captured the spirit of Leiper's age better than the charismatic evangelist. In calling for "the evangelization of the world in this generation," Mott reflected American Protestantism's urgency, optimism, and global ambition. While a student at Amherst College, Leiper came under Mott's spell and immersed himself in the Student Volunteer Movement, a missionary recruiting organization that inspired thousands of young Americans to go abroad in mission. At one summer meeting, Leiper made exactly such a commitment. Upon graduation, he went on to pursue missionary training and theological study at Union Theological Seminary, which was quickly becoming a flagship institution in training young Americans like Leiper, as Union put it, to "peacefully conquer the world." Above all, the Seminary was developing a missiology that highlighted American commitments to practical service in medicine, government, and agriculture. Such endeavors were part and parcel of spreading American civilization abroad and ushering in the foretold kingdom of God.[7]

In bolstering their missionary departments, mainline seminaries like Union especially wanted to retain America's best students. From the 1840s onward, many of America's brightest young Protestant students had embarked to German theological faculties for advanced training. Steeped in centuries of tradition, these German faculties seemingly towered over American mainline seminaries. While young evangelical theologians from the United States flocked to the Pietist centers of Berlin and Halle, others headed to the theology faculties of universities such as Göttingen to study German rationalism. Once abroad, they absorbed ideas that would inspire new theological developments within American Protestantism itself, including a growing interest in biblical higher criticism and scientific rationalism. With time, this infusion of "liberal theology" into American Protestantism would drive a wedge between the "modernist" Protestants who welcomed its arrival and the "fundamentalist" Protestants who rejected its insights.[8]

In his theological studies, Leiper embraced the modernist, ecumenical perspective. Having studied the methods of biblical higher criticism, he could no longer accept biblical literalism. Having embraced ecumenism, he could no longer see mission as a purely confessional and conversionary endeavor. Instead, Leiper soaked up a commitment to practical Christian service at Union. He especially embraced the "social gospel" theology of Walter Rauschenbusch, who called on American Protestants to establish the "kingdom of God" on earth through their missionary outreach. Leiper began to believe that American Protestants had a special responsibility to transform and uplift societies in the world. American Protestants, he concluded, needed to be at the front lines of fostering harmonious international relations, promoting democracy abroad, and creating a global "brotherhood" of believers. In these pursuits, many ecumenical Protestants identified progressive reformers and the American government as crucial allies. They especially hoped that the church and the state could collaborate to foster a Protestant culture at home and a more harmonious world abroad.[9]

Despite the inspiration ecumenical Protestants drew from German liberal theology, they also began to discern worrisome developments across the Atlantic. Leiper's life path especially contrasted with that of a young German Protestant naval officer named Martin Niemöller. Born in 1892, just one year after Leiper, Niemöller grew up in an era in which Germany was quickly rising in the world as a powerful international empire. Fueled by a successful war of national unification from 1870 to 1871, Germany began to strive for international glory. Germany's Protestants readily supported their emperor, Wilhelm II, in his imperial ambitions. As a young man, Niemöller regularly heard proclaimed that God had providentially chosen the German nation to be a vessel of divine salvation in the world. Readily adopting such ideas, Niemöller affirmed that the German cause of "throne and altar" were one and the same. In other words, Germany's conservative nationalist faith naturally led Niemöller to support the Kaiser, political authoritarianism, and imperial expansion. Seeking to advance these causes, Niemöller became a cadet in the quickly expanding German imperial navy at the age of eighteen.[10]

Leiper and Niemöller's respective storylines pointed to competing visions of godly global order at work on both sides of the Atlantic. Despite crucial differences, American and German Protestants aligned in the Christian nationalism that shaped their churches. In other words, both groups believed that God had chosen their nation for a sacred cause in the world. While

American Protestants endeavored to spread America's "benevolent" civilization abroad, German Protestants advanced a national religious culture that celebrated the Kaiser, authoritarian politics, and ecclesial hierarchy.[11]

For American ecumenists, this distinction between democracy and autocracy was crucial. In their view, the United States promoted godly order, while Germany fostered devilish disorder. In response, American Protestants authored blistering assessments of Germany's spiritual culture and church-state relations. Congregationalist minister Josiah Strong had already provided a working framework for many American Protestants when he argued that a providential connection existed between Protestantism, democracy, and the United States. Strong affirmed that the Protestant Reformation had birthed a "pure spiritual Christianity" free from Catholic hierarchy, coercion, and control. This free religion of conscience in turn had provided a spiritual foundation for democracy and "civil liberty" through its affirmation of spiritual equality and the "priesthood of all believers." Americans like Strong therefore assumed that Protestantism, when rightly practiced, ought to naturally yield political democracy. Although such ideals had originated in the lands of the Protestant Reformation, Strong argued Germans had neglected their spiritual and civic birthright. "Protestantism on the continent has degenerated into mere formalism," he penned. In his view, Germany's state Protestant churches had become as spiritually dead as "Romanism"— the faulty faith of Catholicism. Their faith was cultural and nominal, not living and voluntary. Moreover, from the Reformation onward, he suggested, German Protestants had looked to the king and magistrate for spiritual leadership, not to lay believers and individual congregations. In his reading, the German state churches stifled lay activism, promoted hierarchy, and opposed democracy. While some American Protestants recognized the German Pietists as an exception to this perceived norm, they began to believe Germany had become mired in an authoritarian spiritual and political culture.[12]

In response, Strong had high praise for the American Protestant tradition. The Congregationalist minister lauded Americans as heirs to the highest ideals of the "Anglo-Saxon" heritage. In his view, "Anglo-Saxon Americans" possessed a genuinely free "spiritual life and power" and "a genius for self-government." He suggested that God had worked providentially through human history to make the United States the heir of such a political and spiritual legacy, which had spread from Germany to Great Britain and then had found its fullest expression on the other side of the Atlantic. Through great spiritual awakenings and a democratic revolution, American Protestants had developed an unprecedented tradition of democratic spirituality and politics. America's adoption of lay-based congregationalism and activism had made American churches into the spiritual schoolhouses of American democracy. In Strong's view, Protestant congregations nurtured the art of voluntary association and prepared Americans for moral action in a democratic civil body politic. Meanwhile, the constitutional provisions of religious freedom and disestablished religion allowed American Protestants to pursue an "informal" partnership with their government and to freely foster a national Protestant culture that strengthened their republic's moral and civic fiber. Such a model was not only exemplary, Americans like Strong thought. It was desperately needed across the world.[13]

For all these reasons, Strong called on American Protestants to respond with decisive action. First and foremost, Americans needed to "Americanize" the immigrants and "Romanists" from the Old World who threatened their nation's Protestant culture. For him, "Americanizing" these European migrants marked the first step "in promoting Christian civilization" both at home and abroad. Yet "Anglo-Saxon Americans" could not stop there. They also had to accept their special responsibility to promote such values abroad, even in the heartland of the Protestant faith itself. Through their foreign mission, they believed they could ignite spiritual and democratic transformation across the world, and in the process, establish God's kingdom on earth. Such confidence in their faith, their politics, and their nation showcased the strong Christian nationalism that informed their thought and provided the foundation for visions of spiritual intervention in Europe. It also pointed to the "racial providentialism" and Christian imperialism that shaped American Protestant thought. Simply put, Strong felt God had chosen white American Protestants to lead the globe to Christ and democracy. His theology translated into diplomatic support for an expansive and ambitious global role for the United States.[14]

As Strong's writings suggested, American Protestants had often looked to Great Britain as a special partner due to their shared Protestant culture, Britain's constitutional tradition, and its powerful global empire. Yet by the turn of the twentieth century, American missionaries were also seeking to establish themselves as the new leaders of international Protestantism. Their efforts especially appeared at the 1910 World Missionary Conference in Edinburgh, a gathering which Leiper followed with careful attention. With mission recruiting and training shifting into high gear, American

Protestant missionaries had come to outnumber continental European missionaries two to one and had outpaced their British counterparts in both financing and in total missionary numbers. Out of the 1,215 delegates at the conference, over half came from the United States. An additional third hailed from Britain, making the conference a decisively Anglo-American affair. With a lion's share of the seats, Americans gave the proceedings an imperial tone. As co-chair of the Conference, Mott noted the need for a "vast enlargement" in missionary numbers in order to seize the "opportune time" and take the gospel into all the world. Meanwhile, former US president and Spanish-American War Rough Rider Theodore Roosevelt sent a letter to the Conference lauding the coordinated efforts to "Christianize humanity." An American commentator also praised the "leading place" Americans took at Edinburgh. While continental Europeans were keen on deep intellectual discussion, Americans outlined an aggressive and practical mission of "world conquest." They depicted Protestant missionaries as the soldiers of a Christian army with "marching orders" to advance on a spiritual crusade in the world.[15]

Lay American Protestants back home readily adopted the rhetoric of conquest and Christian nationalism to make sense of their own role in such an endeavor. From the pews to the pulpit, many everyday Protestants affirmed that the cause of the cross and the flag were one and the same. In particular, "Rally Day" ceremonies—kickoff events for Sunday Schools after the summer holiday—sacralized the nation and taught young Protestants the language of spiritual conquest. These liturgical celebrations featured the first use of the Christian and Conquest flags, the latter emblazoned with Constantine's famous phrase "By this sign conquer." Turn-of-the-century American Protestants designed these flags "to rally, unite, lead, and inspire God's people for the conquest of the world." Lay Protestants used them in elaborate "pageants" and liturgies that called on young Americans to "renew the memory" of "Patriots" long dead who had secured their "birthright of freedom." Meanwhile, the students marched as "Sunday-School Armies" that would defend "the institutions of liberty" and save the American nation "from foes without and within." They also carried the "Conquest Flag" to affirm their belief "that only through the Cross of Christ can the world be conquered for righteousness." To hammer the point home, one Rally Day organizer instructed Sunday School pupils to dress up "as Crusaders armed with spear and shield." As they processed behind the Conquest Flag, they bellowed out "Onward, Christian Soldiers." The organizer of the ceremony

"Rally Day" festivities encouraged everyday American Protestants to "spiritually conquer" the world. This Rally Day button paired the American flag with the Christian "Conquest Flag," which was emblazoned with the Constantinian phrase, "By this sign conquer." Such rhetoric captured the imperial impulse at work in American Protestant mission in the early twentieth century.
Courtesy of American Baptist Historical Society, Mercer University, Atlanta, Georgia.

noted the Crusaders' contemporary relevance to the American people: "there is just as urgent a call for crusaders now as there was during the Middle Ages."[16]

The abundant use of imperial terminology at Edinburgh suggested to some German Protestants that Americans indeed desired to conquer the world. German critiques of American mission focused on how America's promotion of "spiritual democracy" was actually a form of "spiritual imperialism," an effort to spiritually conquer the world and remake it in America's image. Already in 1900, German missiologist Gustav Warneck had blasted the Americans for equating the "Christianization" of a country with its

"Americanization." Heinrich Frick, another German mission theorist, also attacked the "Americanism in modern evangelical missions." In his view, Protestant mission aimed at establishing an Anglo-American democratic order in the world. Americans erred, he believed, when they identified themselves as God's "chosen people" and connected "God's preferential order with democracy" and the "spread of typical American ideals . . . with evangelical mission." In contrast, Frick saw American mission as shallow and hollow. It lacked a "transnational feeling of solidarity" and possessed "no consciousness of ecumenical Christianity." The German missiologist leveled the charge that American mission fed off the "conviction that America was the source and center of a worldwide Christianization." For all these reasons, he criticized the "Americanism" of Protestant mission as a dangerous form of spiritual imperialism.[17]

In response, Frick charged that Americans failed to account for the cultural and ethnic particulars of foreign peoples in the ways that German missionaries did. Frick and other Germans called for the creation of *Volkskirchen*, or "people's churches," rooted in the indigenous soil of national cultures. While these Germans believed they were more sensitive to cultural difference, their use of the idea of *Volk*—which they defined as a people group with its own divinely given cultural, historical, and ethnic traits—depended heavily upon theories of racial and civilizational hierarchy. In calling on German missionaries to guide "less civilized" peoples to higher levels of spiritual development, the German missionary establishment sanctified the idea of race as God-given and opened itself to "nationalistic and even racist distortions of the faith."[18]

While American activism inspired a chorus of dissent from Germany, American Protestants left Edinburgh enthralled about the prospects of increased international cooperation, especially with their British counterparts. Conference delegates organized new international Protestant committees dedicated to discussing further collaboration and to increasing unity on questions of faith and doctrine, as well as mission and service. American ecumenists secured donations from American banker J. P. Morgan to fund the cause. In the decades that followed, they would seek to take commanding leadership roles within these committees and their international meetings, which would culminate in the formation of the World Council of Churches. While Edinburgh thus laid a foundation for transnational cooperation, it also emboldened American ecumenists to assert themselves as the movers and shakers within an emerging transatlantic spiritual movement.[19]

The theological tension that defined Edinburgh in 1910—Anglo-Americans versus continental Germans—in part prefigured the military conflict that submerged Europe into trench warfare in 1914. While Niemöller prepared that summer for combat with the German imperial navy, Leiper found himself pursuing further studies at Columbia University. He and other American Protestants were alarmed when leading German Protestant theologians defended the Kaiser and the German war effort in the "Manifesto of the Ninety-Three." Adolf von Harnack, one of Germany's leading liberal theologians, called on Germans to protect Western Europe with "their bodies and their blood" against "Asiatic Russia." Through rejecting "false ideologies" like communism and internationalism, these ranking German Protestants viewed the war as an opportunity to further revive and purify the German "fatherland." As the Great War dragged on, Niemöller concurred. He worked his way up to the command of a U-Boat submarine that would terrorize the open seas.[20]

Not all German Protestants endorsed the rush to war, however. Friedrich Siegmund-Schultze proved to be one German Protestant critical of the German nationalist and imperial project. Siegmund-Schultze's alternative track in part stemmed from his transatlantic engagement with the Protestant social gospel. In 1910, the young German pastor had accepted a posh pastoral post from Kaiser Wilhelm II at the *Friedenskirche* in Potsdam, the site of the imperial palace of Sans Souci. Yet following visits to "settlement" homes that cared for the downtrodden and poor, including Toynbee Hall in England and Jane Addams's Hull House in Chicago, he drew inspiration from the lived theology of social reformers and left the imperial courts in favor of the "Christian social work" he had found so inspiring. Resisting the pull of nation and empire, the up-and-coming German pastor began to pursue ministry in the working-class neighborhood of Berlin-Friedrichshain, far from the halls of power. Veering from his conservative nationalist colleagues, he also committed himself wholeheartedly to the transatlantic peace movement. In particular, the German pastor played a leading role in the World Alliance for Promoting International Friendship through the Churches. The alliance gathered in August 1914 in Cologne, Germany, only to have their conference interrupted by the outbreak of battle. As the delegates departed, Siegmund-Schultze and English Quaker delegate Henry Hodgkin pledged to one another, "We are one in Christ and can never be at war." That summer in Europe, however, such professions of peace through Christian fellowship ultimately proved few and far between.[21]

On the other side of the Atlantic, many American Protestants initially called for neutrality in response to the outbreak of hostilities. Yet Germany's invasion of Belgium, tales of German war crimes against civilians, and unrestricted submarine warfare shocked a growing number of American Protestants, who viewed these steps as barbaric actions taken by a wayward empire. When Woodrow Wilson appeared before the Federal Council in December of 1915, just months after German submarines had sunk the British passenger ship *Lusitania* on the open seas, he stressed the tie between Christianity and democracy and hinted at America's special mission to fully democratize European civilization. He argued that Americans could "spread their spirit" and values far and wide through their "peaceful conquest" of the continent.[22]

Wilson would soon lead the American nation into the war and depict the conflict as a righteous progressive crusade. In January 1917, his cause was bolstered when the infamous "Zimmermann Telegram" revealed that the Germans were conspiring with Mexico to attack the United States. Germany's simultaneous resumption of unrestricted submarine warfare further strengthened Wilson's rationale for formally entering the war. The statesman played to his progressive audience through branding the war effort as an opportunity for Americans to reform Germany and incorporate the country into a new international order of liberal democratic nations. Only the United States could rise above the fray of European imperialism and militarism, Wilson asserted, and as a selfless, benevolent Christian nation, create a new world order based on progressive principles. "The Old World had deviated from God's plan," Wilson concluded, yet God had ultimately "willed the universal embrace of American principles." With bold rhetoric and a certainty about the direction of history, Wilson now depicted the military fight as a "war to end all wars" and called on Americans "to make the world safe for democracy." The United States would fight to spread democratic reform to Europe and to lay the foundation for a world order "remade in America's image and therefore permanently at peace."[23]

In making the case for intervention, Wilson and his allies also shared his vision for an imagined network of North Atlantic democracies that some American Protestants would eventually call the "Christian West." In Wilson's formulation, this international order would be tied together by a shared commitment to the democratic values outlined in his "Fourteen Points," including open diplomacy, consent of the governed, self-determination, right over might, liberal freedoms, and an association of nations. The American president likewise championed the underlying Christian character of this transatlantic community, which appealed to the ecumenical hope of Christianizing the world and creating a peaceful and enlightened world order. Such an order, Wilson hoped, would further "enhance and perpetuate the primacy of the United States." Meanwhile, Wilson's War Department partnered with Columbia University, where Leiper had studied, in order to examine American connections to Europe. The collaborative effort generated the first university classes on "Western civilization." Notably, the effort urged Americans to see the war as a struggle for this civilization itself, of which Americans were the purported heirs.[24]

While pacifist Protestants like the Quakers and Mennonites refused to support the war effort and pro-German lobbies proved hesitant to support the cause, Wilson's gospel found devoted acolytes among a wide array of ecumenical Protestants. For his part, Leiper especially admired Wilson's leadership and vision. "What a statesman and world leader he is," he acclaimed. A modernist-ecumenist like Leiper indeed welcomed America's opportunity "to make the world safe for democracy." He saw Wilson as leading the charge for "a spiritual democracy ... born in Christian hearts and guided by the mind of Christ thinking." Other Protestant ecumenists echoed such sentiments and spoke about Wilson's goal of world democratization as if it were the Great Commission itself. Congregationalist theologian Henry Churchill King, for example, called on Americans to "extend the sway of democratic principles over the whole earth." America's progressive Protestants likewise backed Wilson's vision for the League of Nations. In fact, they viewed their own ecumenical Protestant organizing as promoting such a world government rooted in Christian morality and dedicated to international peace and justice.[25]

Overall, Protestant ecumenists aggressively supported the Wilsonian mission of conquering and reforming Germany's militaristic imperialism, its autocracy, and its nationalistic religion. Presbyterian divine William Pierson Merrill worked to rally American Protestants through arguing that the wayward German empire had ultimately "turned to tread the old, discredited, disgraceful, pagan path to greatness through force and dominion." Merrill thus called on American Protestants to oppose "cold-blooded, hard-hearted, efficient Prussia" and its "pagan and anti-Christian" ways. With their benevolent and selfless demeanor, Americans could "radically change" the "Prussian system," rid the world of Germany's "international anarchy," and make the world "a safe place for democracy."[26]

The Christian Century, ecumenical Protestantism's ranking periodical, publicized similar sentiment when it depicted the war as "the final battle of supremacy" between the "forces of good and evil." Writing for the periodical, Frank Lowden, the progressive Republican governor of Illinois, condemned the German Protestant clergy for their "subordination to the state" and their support of "this monstrous doctrine that might makes right." The Germans ultimately worshipped the "German God" of power, he claimed—that "old savage god called Woden," the pagan god of war. The war thus stood as a chance to preach to Germany the authentic gospel of "pure Christianity" and "democratic liberty." America's Methodist-Episcopalians fully endorsed such sentiment. They urged their country to give "the Central Powers and the heathen nations a soul, the spiritual idealism of the great democracy of the West." In their reading, Americans rightfully were intervening in order to civilize Germany.[27]

Federal Council leaders concurred when they argued that German Protestants had discredited themselves through their support of German empire. The Germans, in their view, were the epitome of anti-Christian behavior as they espoused "pagan nationalism" and "distorted patriotism." They had carried out "secret diplomacy," were brutally selfish, and had sought to "destroy weak neighbors." In contrast, Federal Council ecumenists held up America's "Christian nationalism" and "Christian patriotism" as exemplary models for Germany. In their view, a genuine Christian spirit—one that was selfless, benevolent, and democratic—had shaped the United States into a lodestar of righteous nationhood for all. Ecumenical Protestant leader Lyman Abbott likewise justified the war as an opportunity for America—the messianic Christian nation—to sacrificially redeem Germany. In his view, Christian America rightly opposed "pagan" Germany, where "the poor serve the rich, the weak serve the strong, and the ignorant serve the wise." In response to such a backward society, Americans proved a moral beacon of "organized Christianity" where "the rich serve the poor, the strong serve the weak, and the wise serve the ignorant."[28]

Writing on the "failure of German-Americanism," up-and-coming theologian Reinhold Niebuhr also pointed out that German-American immigrants had failed to adopt the civic and moral responsibilities which were needed in a democratic republic. Niebuhr criticized members of his church who lobbied for a policy of non-confrontation with the German empire. The son of a German immigrant, Niebuhr himself had wrestled with throwing off the political and spiritual culture of the Old World. After studying at Yale

Divinity School, the young pastor scoffed when he received his first assignment at Detroit's Bethel Evangelical Church, a congregation that was "three-fourths German." In this post, Niebuhr overcame the congregation's fatal flaw—being "too German"—by making "Americanization" his guiding ideal for his new ministerial role. In other words, Niebuhr set out to make Bethel more civically active and politically engaged. He would draw upon this model of Americanization repeatedly in his thinking on the "German problem." Across the American nation, it had broad appeal. Anti-German propaganda even pressured German-American religious groups, above all Lutherans and Mennonites, to abandon German liturgies and halt instruction in German at parochial schools in order to prove their Americanness. It was a compelling sign of how Protestants from across the ecumenical mainline seamlessly wove together commitments to their faith, democracy, and their nation. The war activated their Christian nationalism, as well as their Christian imperialism, as they organized to spiritually conquer Germany in the name of Christ and democracy.[29]

The Great War did not just mobilize America's ecumenical Protestants. It also activated the energies of Protestant fundamentalists who opposed the modernist assault on biblical inerrancy, conversionary mission, and congregational autonomy. By the 1910s, fundamentalists were by no means a nationally organized movement, but rather were widely spread out across the nation's major Protestant denominations. While they worked and prayed alongside theologically liberal Protestants in America's mainline congregations, the Great War and the perceived modernist threat of Germany galvanized them into becoming an independent and unified outfit. Their wartime mobilization would also transform them into some of their nation's most fervent proponents of Christian nationalism.

As the war broke out, some Protestant fundamentalists developed diverse theological critiques of the conflict and the Christian nationalist currents overtaking their country. Because of their dispensational premillennialism, some found little credence in Wilson's war cause at first. Drawing upon Scriptural passages from Daniel, Ezekiel, and Revelation, these premillennialists had come to believe the world's violent, tragic end was imminent. They therefore refused to support the war because they considered world democratization to be a pointless pursuit. Social reform, they argued, would not solve the underlying and fundamental problem of human sin. Preach the atoning gospel, they suggested, and social conditions might improve. Pacifist fundamentalists also argued that violence remained fundamentally irreconcilable with Christ's refusal of the sword. They point-edly questioned the redemptive potential some American ecumenists had assigned to armed conflict.[30]

Other fundamentalists also argued that the ideas of Christian nation-alism and imperialism were unbiblical. Nations could not be Christian, they pointed out, only individuals could. As fundamentalist Leonard Newby wrote, "There is not, and never has been, such a company of peoples as a Christian nation, and never will be until the Lord comes." Adding a fine point, he concluded, "It is impossible for us to find in this dispensation a Christian nation." A leading fundamentalist periodical, *The King's Business*, agreed, stating, "such a nation does not exist on earth, and never has existed." Blind patriotism thus stood out to these fundamentalists as a concerning sin. Faithful Christians were ultimately loyal to God's kingdom, not to the nation-state. So too was the sanctification and forceful promotion of democ-racy ill advised. As *The King's Business* added, it seemed inherently wrong to "force Democracy upon Germany by bomb and bayonet." How would Americans would feel if Germany forced "[a]utocracy upon us in the same way," the editors asked.[31]

As Wilson led the nation into war and initiated a draft, however, fundamentalists were forced to consider their duties to their government and nation. Their readings of Christian Scripture, namely Romans 13, led some to see obedience to the governing authorities as a biblical require-ment. Moreover, their initial lack of enthusiasm for the war raised the ire of some ecumenical Protestants, who accused them of being "suspiciously Teutonic" in their anti-war demeanor. Revivalist preacher Billy Sunday, one of the most famous Protestants of the day, responded in turn through popularizing a muscular and militant Christian nationalism among his followers. In revivalist sermons, he affirmed to his listeners that "no man can be true to his God without being true to his Country." If God had used nations before in the time of the Israelites, he reasoned, so too could God use the American nation now. To Sunday, being a good Christian therefore meant honoring the state and serving the nation. For faithful Americans, the evangelist argued, it ought to be a clear-cut choice. "In these days," he stated, "all are patriots or traitors, to your country and the cause of Jesus Christ."[32]

In his sermons, Sunday also inspired support for the war through depicting the German empire as wholly evil. The evangelist railed in one address, "If you turn hell upside down, you will find 'Made in Germany' stamped on the bottom." The revivalist called on all Americans to oppose the "God-forsaken bunch of hot-dog degenerates" and summoned the Protestant faithful to march with him "under a flag of patriotism to Berlin or Hades to defeat the Kaiser." Before Congress, he prayed that God would "strike that great pack of hungry, wolfish Huns, whose fingers drip with blood and gore." Through his wartime revivals and colorful rhetoric, Sunday popularized Christian nationalism among fundamentalists and sanctioned military interventions against Germanic evil.[33]

"Germanic trends" likewise compelled fundamentalists to support the war effort. In particular, they identified Germany as the central source of theological modernism, including biblical higher criticism and the rationalist, scientific perspective that they believed corrupted authentic Scriptural interpretation. As the war began, Baptist minister William Bell Riley reflected at length about the danger of "German Kultur." In his reading, Germany was diabolically anti-Christian and a threat to authentic faith due to its promotion of evolutionary science. As Riley put it, evolution was "German in cultivation and world-wide in devastation." The Baptist fundamentalist believed the philosophy of German intellectual Friedrich Nietzsche best illustrated the dangers that resulted from such evils. As he wrote, Nietzsche, "the greatest exponent of evolution known to the age," had declared the death of God and reduced human existence to a perpetual struggle for power and survival. Having made Nietzsche's atheistic thought "the basis of all German education," the Germans had naturally embraced such "superman philosophies," along with militarism and the cross of iron. Modernism thus had led the Germans to "baptize the world in blood."[34]

Many fundamentalist evangelicals agreed in this basic calculation. Fundamentalist luminary French Oliver added, "The beer-soaked theologians of Germany have done more to preach infidelity in the form of Higher Criticism into the world during the past forty years than all other educators combined." Another fundamentalist preacher quipped that German chemical weapons paled in comparison to the "poison gas . . . German university professors" had "been belching" into American seminaries. These evangelicals saw at stake in the Great War the very modernist evils that corrupted their pure faith. They therefore supported the war effort in order to defeat modernism and "German destructive criticism" at its very source.[35]

Beyond condemning German modernism, fundamentalists also depicted the "German way"—Germany's spiritual and political order—as a threat to America's evangelical and constitutional roots. As A. C. Dixon, editor of *The*

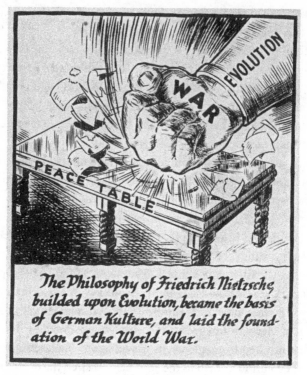

The Philosophy of Friedrich Nietzsche builded upon Evolution, became the basis of German Kulture, and laid the foundation of the World War.

American fundamentalists saw much to condemn in "German Kultur." In their view, German culture had not only promoted theological modernism and evolution, it also had yielded the atheistic, power-hungry philosophies of Friedrich Nietzsche. In response, American fundamentalists supported their nation's entry into the First World War in order to defeat these intellectual currents.

Fundamentalist, put it, German philosophers and scientists had attacked the evangelical foundation of the American republican experiment through their intellectual modernism. In contrast to Germany's political and spiritual corruption, America stood firmly on "the Bible, Plymouth Rock . . . democracy and freedom, and the principles of Abraham Lincoln." Another theologically conservative Protestant, David Kennedy, contrasted America from Germany by stating his native land "was born of moral progenitors and founded on an eternally moral foundation. Her ancestors were Christian of a high order . . . her foundation is the Bible." These fundamentalists argued their evangelical faith was in fact the very bedrock of their Christian nation. In their reading, Jesus Christ himself had brought the American nation into existence and divinely authored its tradition of limited government and free markets. Any departures from this sacred order, which for some fundamentalists also included a clear social, racial, and patriarchal gender order, were sacrilegious. In their view, Protestant modernists—both at home and abroad—gravely imperiled the Christian American experiment and were foes to be opposed.[36]

In confronting German "Kultur" and defending American civilization, Protestant fundamentalists also advanced visions of apocalyptic holy war against evil. Although initially hesitant to support the war effort, by 1918 the editors of *The King's Business* called for holy warfare against Germanic malfeasance: "the Kaiser threw down the gage of battle—infidel Germany against the believing world—Kultur against Christianity—the Gospel of Hate against the Gospel of Love. Thus is Satan personified. . . . Never did Crusader lift battle-ax in holier war against the Saracen than is waged by our soldiers of the cross against the Germans." As another fundamentalist put it, through making war against the Kaiser, Americans were holding back the "world-tidal wave of barbarism, savagery, and immorality." Casting Germany as Satan on earth, fundamentalist evangelicals found cause to sacralize America's warfare against the Kaiser. They strove to prove their mettle as defenders of the Christian nation and promoters of America's sacred cause in the war.[37]

In these ways, the Great War actually brought together progressive ecumenists and fundamentalist evangelicals in identifying Germany as the central problem threatening "Christian civilization," even as they differed greatly on why Germany was a threat. While ecumenical Protestants targeted Germany's autocratic traditions and evangelicals focused on its modernist beliefs, leading Protestants on both sides of the theological aisle ultimately backed America's entry into the war as a sacred cause. For ecumenists, that cause entailed conquering Germany with progressive values, reforming German imperialism, and creating a new democratic world order. For fundamentalists, it involved defeating the source of theological modernism, curbing the forces of evil, and protecting America's Christian heritage. These disparate causes all found a place under the Christian nationalist banner that led the United States into war.

These differing rationales for wartime mobilization foreshadowed competing ecumenical and evangelical missions to Europe after the war. Protestant ecumenists seized upon the postwar hour to create a new "Christian world order" led by the United States and shaped by ecumenical values and multilateral institutions. In contrast, the war galvanized American fundamentalists into becoming a new national, interdenominational movement with global ambitions to defend biblical fundamentals, pursue conversionary mission, and oppose the forces of the Antichrist. They also called for an America-first foreign policy that championed independent neutrality in the face of new entangling alliances.

In the war's aftermath, American ecumenists outlined a mission to create a new international system rooted in Wilsonian principles. For these ecumenists, the brutality of the war had exposed the faulty spiritual foundations of what they described as "European Christendom." In the Federal Council's reading, it now fell upon "Christian America" to make the continent more authentically Christian and to promote a democratic spirit abroad. As these ecumenists had argued during the war, America's "Christian nationalism" and "Christian patriotism" were exemplary. Their nation's self-less, benevolent, and Christian spirit could yield a new kind of "Christian internationalism" that would "Christianize international relations" through open diplomacy, multilateral institutions, and benevolent humanitarianism. The Federal Council called on American Protestants to promote this Christian spirit within their congregations, the halls of power in Washington, and America's fledgling foreign service. So too would they need to advance this Christian spirit abroad and make every nation a genuinely Christian nation, purging European countries in particular of selfish nationalism and militarism, and in the process, creating the possibility for a "warless world." Through such efforts, they could yield a new international system, a "familyhood" of Christian nations, as they put it, dedicated to Wilsonian and ecumenical principles. In this way, ecumenists could make good on the German defeat and establish, as Federal Council leaders wrote, a new "Christian world order." For these ecumenists, promoting "Christian internationalism" both at home and abroad was an important step toward creating a more just and tolerant international system that constrained nationalism. Their postwar activism also carried forward, however, their Wilsonian quest to spiritually conquer the continent for Christ and democracy.[38]

The Federal Council's vision found widespread acceptance among ecumenical Protestants who affirmed their nation's spiritual and democratic values needed to be ascendant both at home and abroad. After the war, for instance, American Methodists drew inspiration from both Wesley and Wilson when they called on their congregants to treat "the world as their parish" and to peacefully conquer the globe. Drawing from Wilson's wartime rhetoric, they affirmed that "the only safe basis for a permanent peace is a Christianized world, and the only safe way to Christianize the world is to send the Gospel to all people." They added that they stood ready to accept "the responsibility of uniting a world Christianity with a world Democracy." Protestant divine George Henry Hubbard also urged American Protestants to assume "world leadership" and to carry out the "spiritual conquest of the nations." The "American horizon," he affirmed, had "extended itself a hundredfold." The stakes were too high to retreat into isolation. Methodist-Episcopal pastor John Chadwick likewise called to mind that "a far more titanic and fateful struggle" was now unfolding—"a contest for the spiritual supremacy of Christ in the life of the world." After the war, mainline ecumenists thus continued to provide vital energy to their nation's pursuit of the world's democratization and Christianization. For them, "Christian internationalism" itself was impetus for an ascendant "Christian America" to spiritually conquer the globe and to create a new Christian world order.[39]

Presbyterian preacher William Pierson Merrill likewise endorsed Wilson's internationalism in his landmark postwar book *Christian Internationalism*. Despite its title, the book in fact portrayed "Christian America" as an exceptional nation destined to usher in a new Christian and democratic international order. Merrill indeed called on American Protestants to "Christianize international relations" and to "lift the world to a better and higher life." In his view, the Vatican was ill-equipped for such a task due to its "imperial internationalism" that brought the world under Roman tyranny. He condemned as well the "extreme pre-millenarians" for their "pitiful" posture toward international affairs. Instead, he argued, enlightened ecumenists needed to lead the world to its "democratic destiny." Channeling Strong's rhetoric, Merrill wrote that selfless American missionaries had spread out across the globe, "standardizing" the world and preparing it for democratic governance and America's "pure Christianity." Americans could build upon this spiritual foundation through supporting the League of Nations and fostering a new Christian world order. In Merrill's telling, "Christian internationalism" was but the natural extension of America's world-historical mission.[40]

The ecumenical pursuit of internationalism, however, faced fierce resistance from Protestant fundamentalists. The Great War had clarified for fundamentalists the modernist evils threatening their nation and had heightened their apocalypticism. These twin conduits of modernism and apocalypticism further electrified their movement. Building on their wartime mobilization, leading fundamentalists soon formed an interdenominational movement with global ambitions to defend biblical fundamentals and convert lost souls. On May 25, 1919, nearly 6,000 ministers, theologians, and evangelists descended upon Philadelphia to found the World's Christian Fundamentals Association. Led by William Bell Riley, the Association denounced the doctrinal shallowness and modernist teachings of the Federal Council and German Protestantism. The conference organizers urged those gathered to combat the "thousands of false teachers" at work "throughout Christendom." Riley felt a new era had dawned in Christian history. "The hour has struck for the rise of a new Protestantism," he heralded following the conference. He compared the gathering as surpassing in historical magnitude "the nailing of Martin Luther's ninety-five theses." Attendees left inspired to establish a new spiritual empire of Christian fundamentals across their nation and the globe. A unified, national fundamentalist movement with global ambitions had been born.[41]

When it came to foreign affairs, fundamentalists above all applied their apocalyptic perspective to the emerging debate over the League of Nations. Wilson's dramatic expansion of federal power during the war itself had already alarmed premillennialists. Their concerns over the Antichrist accordingly weakened their enthusiasm for Wilson's international reforms. They reasoned that such dictatorial trends surely would accompany the end times. So too would the potential establishment of diplomatic organizations with supranational authority. Some feared that the Antichrist might use an international organization like the League of Nations to terrorize the world. Fundamentalists therefore displayed a consistent "anti-internationalism" in their politics. They tended to believe that if the United States had to act in the international arena, it ought to do so unilaterally.[42]

They also rallied behind a Senate faction that opposed Wilson's internationalism after the war. Wilson's vision for postwar order failed in part at home when this Republican contingent torpedoed the ratification of the Treaty of Versailles, sinking ecumenical and Wilsonian hopes for a multilateral world order in the process. Led by "America First" Republican Henry Cabot Lodge, this senatorial squad feared American involvement in the

League of Nations would ultimately threaten America's national interests and perhaps even draw the nation into another costly European war. Lodge warned that the League also cut against the long-standing American principle of independent neutrality. As he put it, such "internationalism" was "Bolshevik" in nature and anti-American. As such, he could never declare loyalty to the League's "mongrel banner."[43]

Lodge's rhetoric paralleled the first "Red Scare" and "Red Summer" that swept over the United States in 1919. That summer, as massive strikes crippled the American economy, anarchists detonated bombs in major cities, and African American veterans and workers organized in pursuit of their constitutional rights, many white Protestants feared their country was succumbing to a sinister plot from enemies both foreign and domestic. As fundamentalist John McDowell warned, a "radicalism" was "abroad in America." New "enemies"—in particular "European imports" such as foreign-born anarchists and socialists—threatened the American way and wanted to "paganize" the United States. Billy Sunday quipped in sensational fashion, "I would stand every one of these ornery, wild eyed I.W.W's, anarchists, crazy socialists, and other types of Reds up before a firing squad." Following the successful 1917 Bolshevik Revolution in Russia, fundamentalists surmised that the growing tide of ecumenical modernism and workers' movements for social justice went hand in hand with the Bolshevist materialism that sought to remove religion from society. Fundamentalist Arno Gaebelein warned that unless Americans took preemptive action against such threats, America's "civilization and religion" would "*be totally destroyed*!!!" Many American Protestants thus supported the "America First" foreign policies of independent neutrality and anti-internationalism and opposed movements for workplace and racial justice. They also resisted European, Catholic, and Jewish influence upon their nation and worked to protect its Anglo-Saxon Protestant identity. In the aftermath of the war, a large swath of ecumenical and evangelical Protestants contributed to this revival of Protestant nativism, as well as to a "second coming" of the Ku Klux Klan, which advanced the banner of "true Americanism" in response to Catholics, socialists, black Americans, and the nearly twenty million Europeans who had migrated to the United States between 1890 and 1920. Reflecting this nativist and illiberal spirit, the US Congress passed restrictive immigration legislation in the 1920s that cut off the flow of immigrants from Southern and Eastern Europe and almost entirely from East Asia.[44]

The turbulence of the postwar hour and the uptick in nativism also led some Protestant ecumenists, however, to call for a more tolerant approach to racial and religious difference both at home and abroad. A budding interfaith movement emerged in response to Protestant nativism that sought to recognize Catholics and Jews as genuine partners in the American democratic experiment. So too did the failures of the war lead some American ecumenists into deep self-reflection about their faith's nationalistic commitments. In the war's aftermath, a small yet committed group, led by ecumenists such as Sherwood Eddy, John Mott, and Robert Speer, started to significantly question the notion of Christian nationhood altogether. Drawing from indigenous mission theory, they instead articulated a vision for a global church that entirely transcended national boundaries. They especially listened to Protestants from the non-Western world. Ecumenical missionary conferences became venues for these non-Western Protestants to voice their deep concerns about Western imperialism and racism. These ecumenists accordingly began to recover Christian opposition to racism as a foundational theological practice. So too did they call on American Protestants to declare their highest loyalty not to Christian America but to the body of Christ—a global fellowship of believers. These missionary-ecumenists thus began to articulate a new theology of global engagement—Christian globalism—that drained the American nation-state of its salvific, messianic potential, rejected racial hierarchy, and promoted the pursuit of genuinely mutual partnerships with Protestant Christians across the globe. In the ruins of the war, a more tolerant and cosmopolitan perspective was therefore also emerging.[45]

Some liberal ecumenists took such sentiment a step further in calling for a more tolerant, less imperialistic approach to non-Western religions. The roots of that reform lay deeper in the Protestant missionary experience itself, as American Protestants who had gone abroad developed a deeper respect for non-Western cultures and foreign religions. In response, ecumenists began to rethink their commitment to conversionary mission and instead focused on fostering a "Christian spirit" both at home and abroad. Direct conversionary mission only caused friction and misunderstanding, they reasoned, thereby hampering the realization of the peaceful and harmonious kingdom of God. This sentiment appeared in *Marks of a World Christian*, a 1919 devotional authored by Daniel Fleming, one of Leiper's professors in missions at Union Theological Seminary. Downplaying conversionary mission, Fleming instead encouraged American Protestants to exhibit "respect

for other peoples" and "responsiveness to human need." He also called everyday believers to the "Christianization of the social order" and "the enterprise of world friendship." Fleming's work elevated humanitarian service and
the building of democratic and Christian institutions as the surest path to
international peace.[46]

The particulars of Protestant mission proved to be another fault line, however, between ecumenists and fundamentalists. Seeing individual human sin
as the culprit of human disorder, the most responsible thing fundamentalists
believed they could do was to convert the lost through conversionary mission. Their apocalyptic politics also led them to seek to transform the
American republic into a godly nation worthy of Christ's call at the last day.
Without doctrinal purity, they reasoned, Christian civilization itself would
crumble. Fundamentalists accordingly launched national campaigns that
opposed the teaching of evolution in schools, the consumption of alcohol,
and the spread of theological modernism. They likewise sought to purge
modernists from leading seminaries and denominations. Meanwhile, they
began to make use of business partnerships, radios, and journals to create
a new and powerful national network of fundamentalist Protestants. Their
standing grew so prominent that Harry Emerson Fosdick, the dean of
Protestant modernism, asked pointedly in 1922, "Shall the fundamentalists
win?" The growing divide also appeared in a 1924 article from *The Christian
Century* which stated plainly: "The God of the Fundamentalists is one God.
The God of the Modernists is another."[47]

The spiritual conflict also went abroad. As the Great War ended, Henry
Smith Leiper began to grapple with fundamentalist Protestant missionaries
in the foreign mission field as well. A student of Fleming's, Leiper dedicated
himself to making "the spirit of America known and understood" from his
missionary outpost in North China. Downplaying direct conversionary mission, he instead aimed to share America's "spiritual democracy" through education, medicine, and humanitarian service. He refused to equate Chinese
culture with heathenism. Instead, he desired to forge mutual partnership in
"clasping hands with noble Chinese brothers and sisters in their hard up-
hill fight for light, liberty, and righteousness." Leiper also hoped his mission would foster greater understanding between the peoples of the "East
and West." In his view, Protestant ecumenists could practice "Christian
statesmanship" as they promoted America's ecumenical and democratic
values abroad and fostered a new kind of Christian order across the globe.
Fundamentalists in the field notably opposed Leiper's methods.[48]

As Leiper returned to the United States from China in 1922, his ecumenical sensibilities increasingly focused him on promoting this "Christian spirit" in Europe. German missiologist Julian Richter especially heightened American ecumenical concerns through the postwar reports he dispatched to the Federal Council. Richter warned that the "unchristian" and "materialistic" movements of socialism and secularism were now at work across Germany and the European continent. The German churches in particular had suffered a "terrible collapse" underneath the Weimar Republic. "Nominal Christianity" now pervaded the country. In the ruins of war, Richter feared "the breakdown of Europe and of European culture." The German missiologist professed his hope, however, that "Christian America" might come to Europe's aid in such a growing crisis. Reports of Catholic activism also alarmed American Protestants. Risking financial insolvency, the Vatican had expended more than 82 million lira to care for beleaguered civilians and prisoners of war. Under the new Pope Pius XI, an era of Catholic "militancy" began in opposition to communism, which would soon lead to partnerships with fascist states in Europe.[49]

Such premonitions led American Protestants to perceive Europe as a continent in need and a new mission field in itself. In response, American ecumenists began to launch material relief programs across the continent that they hoped would demonstrate "the moral strength of America" and "its spirit of freedom fostered by Protestant principles." The Federal Council likewise supported American Relief Administration efforts to feed starving European children. Postwar relief, the Council suggested, could promote Christian and democratic principles across a continent they believed sorely needed them. In contrast, fundamentalists forged transatlantic partnerships with the so-called free churches in Europe—the Baptist, Methodist, and evangelical churches that existed independently of the modernist "state churches"—in order to promote conversionary mission and to distribute postwar relief.[50]

Following his own 1923 tour of Europe, Reinhold Niebuhr became further convinced of the continued role the United States and American Protestants needed to play across the continent. Niebuhr believed that while Americans were not necessarily more virtuous than Europeans, they were nonetheless ideally positioned to help Europe recover. He wrote, "We have no virtue above Europe but we have good fortune, and if we were to exploit it morally, we could save Europe." As Niebuhr backed postwar relief to Europe, the formation of his own realist ethic was well underway. While Niebuhr tempered any claims of American exceptionalism, he still called on the United States to act "responsibly"—to use its power to stabilize a disordered continent. In the ruins of the postwar landscape, American ecumenists thus continued to find rationale for American engagement abroad. Although he opposed Wilsonian activism, even Republican president and practicing Congregationalist Calvin Coolidge believed the United States could maintain its independence while being the "magnanimous republic" and "Good Samaritan" to Europe.[51]

As European nations experienced growing instability in the interwar years, American ecumenists also sought to strengthen ecumenical partnerships across the Atlantic that would promote a spirit of peace and international understanding. At a League of Nations assembly in 1925, leading American ecumenist Harry Emerson Fosdick preached that Christians across the North Atlantic and the entire world needed to "concentrate on the creation of an international spirit, based on cooperation amongst nations as an offset to the danger of nationalism, and thus rid the world of war forever." Fosdick continued to voice the ecumenical hope that Americans could "Christianize" international relations and foster international peace. Multilateral arrangements—such as the 1921 Washington Naval Conference which promoted demilitarization, the 1924 Dawes Plan which restructured Germany's war debts, and the 1928 Kellogg-Briand Pact which outlawed war altogether—renewed the ecumenical confidence that a warless world and Christian international order remained within reach.[52]

Yet even as ecumenists like Fosdick called for transnational fellowship, others still espoused an ethic of American exceptionalism and Christian nationalism. The paternalistic language of "older" and "younger" churches that American Protestants adopted to describe their relationship to non-Western congregations could not hide the sense of spiritual superiority that still shaped their view of the globe. Nor did leading ecumenists refrain from calling on Americans to continue to practice "the fine spiritual imperialism" of the Christian faith. Even as more American ecumenists began to envision themselves as part of a global body of Protestants, some would still strive to be that body's mind, heart, and soul. They would work to make their aid, conferences, and organizations into the sinews that held that body together. Their democratic and ecumenical theology, they hoped, would animate that body's purpose. Eventually, they would look to that ecumenical body itself to be the agent of an American-led world order.[53]

The ruins of world war had therefore left American Protestants increasingly at odds over their sense of global mission. In a period when

Americans were still working out their nation's relationship to the world, the contours of Christian nationalism and Christian globalism began to appear. Sharp differences continued to exist between ecumenists like Leiper and fundamentalists like Riley on a host of issues, including the viability of conversionary mission, the ethical quandary of violent force, the importance of multilateral institutions, and the need for new attitudes toward race relations and non-Protestant religions. Yet despite these divisions, American Protestants still generally agreed that the United States was a Christian nation with an exceptional role to play in the world. Across the North Atlantic world, that identity entailed either building a new Christian order or defeating evil and defending the true faith. In such endeavors, American Protestants worked to reshape the world through American values and outlined a vision for global spiritual conquest. As they faced a severe global depression and new totalitarian regimes rose to power, however, they also began to grow uncertain whether they would conquer the world or the world would conquer them.

2

World Chaos

Henry Smith Leiper had never witnessed such an international crisis. The missionary-ecumenist had lived through the Great War and the divisive American debate over the League of Nations. He had also observed the rise of Mussolini and Stalin and had begun to weather a severe depression that had tanked the transatlantic economy. Yet nothing troubled him quite as much as the rise of Hitler and the Nazis in the early 1930s. In Leiper's reading of the times, the Nazis' totalitarian politics, fervent nationalism, and heretical theology threatened to submerge the North Atlantic world into unprecedented chaos. In response, Leiper saw the emerging crisis as a mandate for spiritual activism. As he put it, either "world chaos" or "World Christianity" would prevail. He worked to ensure that the ecumenical Protestant church would triumph over Nazi disorder.[1]

From 1933 to 1936, Leiper therefore traveled to Nazi Germany on behalf of the Federal Council of Churches in order to diagnose the crisis and formulate a response. Serving as the Council's secretary for ecumenical relations, he relayed to American Protestants chilling tales of antisemitism and alarming examples of Nazi nationalism. As he documented such concerns, he drew upon the emerging Christian globalism of his era and called on Protestants on both sides of the Atlantic to declare a higher loyalty to Christ than to the nation. Such a commitment, he hoped, would foster a global ecumenical order that could keep Nazi fascism, hyper-nationalism, and racism at bay. Yet American ecumenists, he argued, would also need to pursue broad-reaching reforms of the transatlantic world and of their own society. In particular, he urged American Protestants to promote spiritual democracy, morally sound economics, and interfaith cooperation both at home and abroad.[2]

As Leiper reported back to the Federal Council, fundamentalist Protestants were likewise heeding the signs of the times—only their reading of "world chaos" focused on the "collectivist" trend rapidly sweeping over the world. Not only did fundamentalists see the rise of fascist dictators as signs of the coming Antichrist, they also found cause for concern in the advance of Soviet communism, planned economies, and the New Deal.

God's Marshall Plan. James D. Strasburg, Oxford University Press (2021). © Oxford University Press.
DOI: 10.1093/oso/9780197516447.003.0003

Whereas ecumenists called for the creation of a new Christian world order, fundamentalists pushed for individual conversion, crusades against evil, and consistent opposition to these collectivist trends. While both ecumenical and fundamentalist Protestants identified Nazi fascism as a dangerous threat, they formulated dramatically different plans to save their faith and their world from the impending chaos.

As Protestant ecumenists worked to create a new Christian world order, Nazi fascists rose to power in the ruins of the failed postwar peace. When the Great War came to an end, German liberals had called the democratic Weimar Republic into existence and began Germany's tumultuous fourteen-year experiment with democracy. German Protestants especially found much to dislike in the new arrangement. The abdication of the German Kaiser and the 1919 Weimar Constitution had dissolved the historic tie between "throne and altar," leaving Protestant pastors to feel they had lost their revered national and monarchical standing. In response, they condemned Weimar Germany as a "godless republic" and expressed their support for conservative nationalist political movements. Lacking political consensus, the new Weimar parliament lurched through successive failed political coalitions, while runaway inflation and crushing reparation payments mandated by the victorious Entente crippled the economy. German Protestant fears grew that Bolshevist revolutionaries, who had just struck in Russia, might seize upon the political and economic instability and take over their desperate country.[3]

With the weight of Versailles and Weimar on their shoulders, German Protestants sought to strengthen their humiliated nation through the church. Leading German Protestant theologians pursued a Christian nationalist revival at home in order to strengthen ecclesial defenses against Bolshevist communism and democratic liberalism. Theologians such as Paul Althaus, Emanuel Hirsch, and Friedrich Gogarten in particular advanced a theology of "divine orders" that emboldened Protestant nationalists to see the German *Volk*, the authoritarian state, and the German family as vessels of God's salvific work in the world. Many German Protestants seized the Weimar era as an opportunity to revive and strengthen these pillars of the German nation. In the aftermath of the First World War, these theological developments tied German Protestantism all the more thoroughly to a fervent nationalism which grew in response to Germany's international humiliation. Overall, the

Volk and the nation informed the German Protestant vision of godly order in the era of "godless" Weimar.[4]

In these turbulent times, Germany's leading conservative theologians and clergy also challenged the Anglo-American-led ecumenical movement. German missiologist Heinrich Frick in particular argued that the postwar peace merely advanced "the Spiritual Expansion of the Anglo-American Empire." Frick claimed that the same Anglo-American spirit present at the 1910 Edinburgh Conference could be seen at work in the postwar hour. Both Edinburgh and Versailles, he wrote, were the product of "the Americanism in modern evangelical missions." In Frick's view, both Edinburgh and Versailles advanced America's spiritual empire in the world. The seizure of German Protestant mission property, mandated in Section 438 of the Treaty of Versailles, only aggravated Frick and his colleagues further. In response, the prominent German missiologist called on German Protestants to oppose the missiological and ecumenical currents crossing the Atlantic. The German animosity toward internationalism also appeared in the work of German theologian Paul Althaus, who declared, "there can be no understanding between us Germans and the victorious nations in the world war." Whoever thought otherwise, Althaus added, disowned "the German destiny."[5]

German Protestant Martin Niemöller personified all these developments in personal detail. In the chaotic postwar landscape, Niemöller counted himself among the many disillusioned conservative nationalists who openly opposed the Weimar Republic, as well as the socialists and Bolshevists active in German politics. To further advance the conservative cause of the German nation and the church, he made his way from the command of a U-Boat to that of a preacher's pulpit. For Niemöller, the two roles went hand in hand in service of his church and his people. As the new pastor watched Weimar Germany suffer from economic and political instability, he longed for a strong political leader who would promote national unity and restore German honor. In the 1924 parliamentary election, Niemöller cast his vote for the National Socialist Party, believing that Adolph Hitler might fulfill exactly those aims. As Hitler campaigned for office, he emphasized the importance of Christianity in Germany's renewal, a commitment which greatly appealed to Niemöller.[6]

One voice cried out from the wilderness, however. Swiss theologian Karl Barth puzzled over how his German colleagues had become so drunk on the wine of nationalism. In his now-famous commentary *The Epistle to the*

Romans, Barth sought to correct the errors he identified in Germany's nationalistic theology. The Swiss pastor argued that God was not immanently present in the German people or nation, or in any people or nation, for that matter. Rather, God entirely transcended the created world. God's salvific work in the world, he reasoned, could therefore never begin with human designs. As Barth put it, God delivered a thunderous "Nein!" to any such anthropocentric schemes. In his reading, Jesus Christ was the sole source of otherworldly revelation and this world's only means of salvation. In these ways, Barth drained the nation—as well as all human striving—of salvific significance. The German *Volk* and nation could therefore never be seen as exceptional; only Christ could. In response, faithful Christians had one task: like John the Baptist in the famous Isenheim altarpiece of Matthias Grünewald, all they could do was point to the crucified and resurrected Christ. Barth's treatise soon sent shockwaves throughout the German theological world. Aspects of his theology would eventually find a receptive audience among some American Protestants as well, such as Reinhold Niebuhr, who had grown disillusioned with the shortcomings of liberal Protestant theology in their own American context.[7]

Despite his best efforts, however, Barth's "Nein" to the German Protestant nationalist project could not temper the enthusiasm many of his peers felt for a rising militaristic, nationalist, and authoritarian German political party. In response to the instability of the Weimar era, the National Socialists pledged to restore law and order, revive German greatness, spark economic growth, and defeat Germany's supposed Bolshevist and Jewish enemies. After a failed putsch in 1923 and an abbreviated jail sentence, Adolf Hitler helped the Nazis vie for national prominence in the late 1920s and early 1930s. When the Nazis won a bare plurality of parliamentary seats in the 1932 federal elections, German president Paul von Hindenburg eventually agreed to appoint Hitler as chancellor of the Weimar Republic, hoping that seasoned coalition members could keep the wily politician in check. Yet just two months later, the German *Reichstag* went up in flames. Seizing upon this national emergency, the Nazis accused a Dutch communist of the crime and moved quickly to suspend civil liberties. Shortly thereafter, they began to silence political opposition through incarceration in concentration camps. In the chaos that ensued, the German parliament granted Hitler emergency powers as chancellor. His twelve-year dictatorship had begun.[8]

In light of these events, Federal Council of Churches leader Samuel McCrea Cavert tasked Leiper with gathering intelligence on the political and ecclesial situation in Hitler's Germany. Both Cavert and Leiper were eager to maintain contact with German Protestants and to make sense of the dramatic political and religious changes sweeping over Europe. During his trips, Leiper encountered a German church that was just as much in transition as the American. As modernist and fundamentalist Protestants in the United States sparred over biblical inerrancy and mission theory, German Protestants likewise found themselves at odds. One extreme Protestant nationalist movement, the *Deutsche Christen* ("German Christians"), had begun synthesizing Christianity with German nationalism and the Aryan racial ideology of the Nazis. While only numbering 600,000 parishioners in a church of 41 million, the German Christian movement still commanded the loyalty of about one-third of the German Protestant church's roughly 18,000 clergy. Under their direction, German Protestant theology underwent alarming alterations, starting with Aryan revisions of Jesus's racial identity. For these Germans, worshipping a crucified Jew did not square with an Aryan ideology in which Jews were less than human. German Christian biblical scholars and anthropologists therefore conducted research into the Aryan origins of Jesus and denied he was a Jew. They also set out to reinterpret Christian doctrine and sacraments in light of the German racial concept of *Volk*. Baptism now became a ritual that facilitated a German's sacred entry into the German people, and holy communion meant receiving the *Blut und Boden* ("blood and soil") of the German *Volk* itself. Meanwhile, they lauded Germany and the German *Volk* as God's chosen nation and people.[9]

In calling for "positive Christianity," the Nazi party aligned itself with the aggressive, muscular, and heretical theology of the German Christian movement. More broadly, Nazi relations with the churches fit into Hitler's strategy (*Gleichschaltung*) of bringing all national institutions into line with the new Nazi state. In addition to pursuing a Concordat with the Vatican in 1933, the Nazis pledged they would restore the privileged place of the Protestant churches in German society. They likewise urged on the Protestant desire for a single, unified national church, a new *Reichskirche* ("Reich Church") which would join together the various regional churches spread across German lands.[10]

From the perspective of the average German Protestant in 1933, the promises of Adolf Hitler and the National Socialists had their allure. Hitler and the Nazis satisfied the German Protestant preference for conservative leadership and a national Christian culture. The Nazis were also outspoken foes of Bolshevism, a stance which greatly pleased German Protestants and

Catholics alike. After the Nazis' seizure of power, signs of national revival also began to appear in mass baptisms, fewer church withdrawals, and a ban on atheist associations. Due to German Protestant political theology, which based itself on the German reformer Martin Luther's "Two Kingdoms" doctrine, a majority of German Protestants also relegated the church's duties to a spiritual realm and conceded the public realm to the state. The church existed to proclaim the gospel, they reasoned, whereas the state served to create order. The two entities complemented one another in separate spheres of earthly life but were not to interfere in the other's affairs. Citing Romans 13 and its teaching on governmental authority, many believed God worked through the government to order the world and would continue to do so through Hitler. German bishop Otto Dibelius preached exactly such a message on March 21, 1933, just two days before the *Reichstag* passed the Enabling Act that granted Hitler dictatorial power. Dibelius declared, "We have learned from Martin Luther that the church cannot get in the way of state power when it does what it is called to do. Not even when [the state] becomes hard and ruthless." The state "ruled in God's name," Dibelius added, when it opposed the nation's enemies and all those who "vilify death for the Fatherland." Such sentiment led most German Protestants to welcome and normalize Hitler's ascent to power.[11]

In the fall of 1933, Leiper was on hand to observe the aftermath of the Nazi takeover. He studied in particular the outcome of that summer's Protestant church elections for the new German-wide "Reich Church," which was coming into existence under Nazi direction. The defeat of the German Christian candidate, Ludwig Müller, in the original election frustrated the German Christians and the Nazis alike. In response, Nazi agents began intimidating, firing, and suspending church leaders who opposed the German Christian movement. The growing political pressure led to a new church election in July. Before that second election, the German Christians received the official endorsement of Hitler himself. Müller won in a landslide. Through the church elections and strong-arm tactics, the German Christians soon claimed control of multiple regional churches and worked to secure the Reich Church as part of Hitler's program of national renewal.[12]

In response, Leiper voiced his opposition and skepticism to the German Christian movement. The American ecumenist clearly questioned Müller's character, noting that the former naval chaplain and "his most vociferous supporters" were "not impressive as close followers of Jesus." He also took a hard line against Nazi religious, political, and racial policies. He especially condemned a German Christian rally that November when it publicized the German Christian vision for a de-Judaized Christianity, which included removing the "Jewish" Old Testament from the Bible. German Christian leaders had also announced their support of the "Aryan Paragraph," a Nazi measure designed to remove all Jews from public offices. They argued it should also apply to the Protestant pastorate. When the event publicized the heretical extremism of the German Christians, Leiper lamented that the German church had been reduced to "an instrument for a dictator" to advance his sinful order upon the world.[13]

Leiper saw, however, hopeful signs of resistance. A vocal group of German Protestant pastors protested the church elections as a Nazi intrusion into the church's independent spiritual realm. Drawing from his critique of the German Protestant liberal tradition, Barth especially voiced his opposition to both Müller and Hitler in 1933. Niemöller's warm welcome of Hitler also cooled once the Nazi leader began to interfere in the affairs of the Protestant church. A stalwart believer in Luther's "Two Kingdoms," Niemöller claimed that the Nazi state was improperly interfering in the church's realm. The German captain-turned-pastor likewise watched with concern as German Christians claimed leadership roles within his Prussian regional church and destroyed its doctrinal integrity through their heretical teachings. In order to oppose Nazi interference in the church's life, Niemöller organized a Pastor's Emergency League, which rallied together roughly 6,000 pastors in opposition to the German Christians and the Reich Church. Increasingly, Niemöller and the League called for an abrupt break from the German Christian–controlled church. Their movement formed the foundation for the so-called Confessing Church, a break-away church body that argued the witness of Christ and the integrity of the Protestant confessions necessitated separation.[14]

In addition to the Pastor's Emergency League, a group of German Protestants led by conservative bishop Theophil Wurm likewise protested Nazi interference in the churches but proved more hesitant to take such a schismatic course. The German Christians had not come to dominate their regional churches quite to the extent as they had elsewhere in Germany, such as in Niemöller's Prussian church, where the Emergency League proved most popular. As a result, conservative Protestants like Wurm felt their regional churches remained intact and that schism was premature. While they protested the German Christian takeover of the church and supported the Confessing Church, they hoped they could reason with Hitler and dislodge

German Christians from leadership, thereby preserving the integrity and unity of the German Protestant church itself.[15]

While Leiper admired their opposition, he also observed a pattern, even among these protesting Protestants, that elicited his concern. Niemöller and Wurm certainly opposed the German Christians and Nazi interference in the churches, he noted, yet they also desired to remain faithful servants of Germany's church-state order. Although German Protestant leaders protested state interference in the church, their conservatism, nationalism, and militarism led them to rarely challenge the Nazi state outside of this spiritual realm. As Nazi attacks targeted German Jews and political leftists, German Protestant leaders largely remained silent. They wanted to be both good churchmen and good statesmen. In contrast, Federal Council leaders pressed these protesting German Protestants to respond more robustly to Nazi ecclesial and racial initiatives. In 1933, for instance, American Presbyterian E. G. Homrighausen penned a series of essays in the liberal Protestant periodical *The Christian Century* praising Barth's opposition in the German church crisis. Drawing from his personal meetings with Barth in Bonn and his ecumenical work in the World Presbyterian Alliance, Homrighausen called on more Germans to follow Barth's lead.

Beyond Barth, American ecumenists likewise lauded peace activist Friedrich Siegmund-Schultze for aiding German Jews, an effort which led the Nazis to deport him from Germany. Siegmund-Schultze's advocacy was a rare exception, however, to the antisemitism that dominated German Protestant churches. After the first public boycott of Jewish stores in Germany, Federal Council leaders were flummoxed when their German colleagues said nothing. In May 1933, Cavert wrote in *The Christian Century* that "the German churches have not, it has to be said regretfully, made any public protest against the injustice done to the Jews." Reinhold Niebuhr concurred, stating that German Protestants were failing to address "the total tragic problem" of antisemitism.[16]

By 1933, Niebuhr had arisen as a leading figure in American Protestant circles. He would also emerge as one of America's most outspoken critics of Nazi fascism. In 1928, with the support of Sherwood Eddy, Niebuhr accepted a professorship at Union Theological Seminary, one of the flagship seminaries of Protestant modernism. At Union, however, Niebuhr would increasingly leave behind his liberal convictions and social gospel optimism. Instead, he began to outline a new school of American Protestant thought known as Christian realism. The so-called Christian realists dramatically departed from Protestant modernists in their assessment of the human condition. In part influenced by Karl Barth's theological breakthrough, they now emphasized the fallen sinfulness of humankind. Due to their seriousness about sin, they increasingly doubted that humankind could realize the kingdom of God in this world. While sinful as individuals, Niebuhr reasoned that the human tendency toward evil only increased when individuals worked together in societal groups. In his view, the Nazis were the prime example of this reality. In response, Niebuhr argued that Christians had to accept concrete ethical responsibilities in order to curtail such forces. Although they might never realize the kingdom of God in this life, they could still reform sinful social structures and achieve a semblance of justice through imperfect means. They were therefore called to active engagement in public life and morally responsible action in the world, even to the use of violent force to check evil and tyrannical regimes. To Niebuhr, such was the hard reality of power, politics, and ethics in a fallen world.[17]

On this point, Niebuhr especially critiqued Barth and other continental theologians for having what he described as an inadequate social ethic. The American professor charged that Barth's "otherworldly" theology led to quietism, "pessimism," and "sanctified futilitarianism" when it came to earthly life. In his view, the Swiss theologian neglected the concrete ethical responsibilities Christians needed to assume in pursuit of justice. The Swiss preacher from Safenwil countered that his theological ethic was not wholly apolitical or quietist. The church, Barth maintained, had a prophetic responsibility to pray for the state and even to suffer persecution when the state became "demonic." The church also needed, he added, to challenge the state to carry out just policies, as well as to remind the state that it had to conform to the rule of God. Yet in Niebuhr's reading, Barth's theology still lacked the more robust and urgent ethic of worldly responsibility that could keep fascist regimes in check. It would not be the last time the two theological giants clashed. In the years and decades ahead, American and continental Protestants would continue to disagree sharply over their faith's political and societal responsibilities. Such differences would show up in opposing plans for postwar reconstruction and diverging attitudes toward Cold War hostilities. Yet for the time being, they most immediately led American Protestants like Niebuhr to believe the German and continental Protestant response to Nazi fascism lacked the vigor, vigilance, and urgency required to counteract Nazi fascism.[18]

These observations of realists like Niebuhr led them to call on Americans to spread their spiritual and ethical values abroad as a counter-response to Nazism and Germany's perceived theological inadequacies. Dietrich Bonhoeffer, one of the younger German Protestants protesting Hitler's interference in the churches, especially raised their hopes that their concrete ethic of responsible action could counteract Nazi fascism. Leiper and Niebuhr had already met Bonhoeffer when the young German churchman had studied at Union from 1930 to 1931. In their reading, America's Protestant milieu had infused into Bonhoeffer what his European environment lacked: a sense of civic activism and ethical responsibility for public life. Such attributes, they surmised, enabled the young German to approach the growing crisis in Germany from a different angle. In particular, they saw in Bonhoeffer a unique and bold German visionary who had the courage to protest Nazi totalitarianism and antisemitism. Such observations only strengthened their confidence in the importance of their American civic theology. Increasingly, Niebuhr and Leiper would hold up Bonhoeffer as an example of how American spiritual values could transform German Protestants into responsible actors in the public sphere.[19]

Like many German Protestants of his era, however, Bonhoeffer initially scoffed at American Protestant theology. In his application for the exchange, Bonhoeffer had expressed his interest in "studying the development of systematic theology in a completely different setting." With a doctorate in hand and a second theological tome published at the age of twenty-four, he was already a theological mastermind. Yet when Bonhoeffer arrived at Union in the fall of 1930, he dismissed the theology he encountered. In one report back home, he reflected the Americans were "completely clueless with respect to . . . dogmatics." They were "intoxicated with liberal and humanistic phrases" and "talk a blue streak." He concluded bluntly, "There is no theology here." More broadly, he criticized the Seminary's curriculum and philosophy of education. He noted, "academic preparation for the ministry is extraordinarily poor . . . theological training is practically zero." Reflecting the pragmatist spirit of the Progressive Era, the Seminary pursued "truth largely in light of the practical community." In contrast to Germany's doctrinal transcendence and confessional precision, Union's theology planted its feet firmly on the ground. In the world of Niebuhr, theology was an attempt to speak a critical and instructive word to concrete social realities.[20]

Bonhoeffer was still not impressed. He felt that the Americans were too focused on "after-the-fact" activity. They exhibited strong ethics but lacked a solid theological and confessional grounding for that activism. Bonhoeffer's experiences with numerous white, mainline Protestant churches only confirmed that conclusion. "In New York," he wrote, "they preach about virtually everything; only one thing is not addressed . . . namely the gospel of Jesus Christ." The preachers dabbled in "ethical and social idealism" as they merely commented on "newspaper events." Beyond the hollow preaching, the young German criticized these churches for being nothing more than "social corporations." Bonhoeffer had hoped he might find a "cloud of witnesses" in the "New World" living as faithful disciples, but his encounter with white mainline Protestantism left him disappointed.[21]

Despite Bonhoeffer's stingy critiques, Union's practical orientation still shaped him. The young theologian absorbed what was lacking in his German environment—"the grounding of theology in reality." In his later reflections, Bonhoeffer stated that his sojourn in America had helped him turn from "the phraseological to the real." Above all, Bonhoeffer left Union with a stronger commitment to practical ministry, social engagement, and civic action. His time in New York helped him start to become a public theologian committed to living out theological ideas through responsible action in the public sphere. The transformation came in part through interactions with Union's activist scholars and engaged students. Methodist professor Charles Webber, for instance, offered coursework in social ministry and faith-based organizing, such as the seminar "Church and Community" that immersed Bonhoeffer in New York City's social ministries. As part of the course, Bonhoeffer paid weekly visits to "settlements, YMCA, home missions, cooperative houses, playgrounds, children's courts, night schools, socialist schools, asylums, youth organizations, Association for advance of coloured people [sic]." Bonhoeffer wrote that the agencies' work was "immensely impressive" and stated that the course was "the most valuable experience I had at the seminary." Immersing him in New York's progressive activism amid the poverty of the Great Depression, Bonhoeffer's field work began to open a path from the academic theology of the university to the lived theology of the streets.[22]

Niebuhr's yearlong seminar on ethics also nudged Bonhoeffer along in this direction. In his response to one of Bonhoeffer's term papers, Niebuhr critiqued the German's conception of grace as "too transcendent." He charged the young scholar with robbing the "ethical significance" from grace. Instead, he advised "obedience to God" required concrete actions that could be "socially valued." Niebuhr's comments worked in Bonhoeffer like yeast in dough. Upon his return to Berlin, he reflected that "it is the problem of concreteness that at present so occupies me." He set out to "speak of God at the center of life" and to ponder how Christians ought to lead life "as responsible human beings." Once back in Berlin, Bonhoeffer threw himself into social ministry, working on behalf of the unemployed, raising funds for charities, and starting a youth club. His theological insights bore fruit four years later, when he penned *Nachfolge* (The Cost of Discipleship). In this classic text, Bonhoeffer criticized the "cheap grace" that he felt characterized German Protestantism. He instead called for "costly grace" that required concrete obedience to the commands of God.[23]

Beyond shaping in him a new social concern, Bonhoeffer's year in the United States also helped mature his commitments to the ecumenical movement. Before Bonhoeffer came to the United States, the young prodigy had spent a year serving as a vicar in a German Protestant congregation in Barcelona, Spain. During his final months, he delivered a series of lectures to the congregation that showed his stripes as a German nationalist. Mirroring the theological currents of his era, he suggested that God could work through the nation and the German people as vehicles of salvation. He likewise stated that to die in defense of one's *Volk* stood as a noble honor. Such views were held widely across Germany in an era of national resurgence. Bonhoeffer entered into his year in New York City still entertaining such notions. Friendships forged at Union, however, in particular with French exchange student Jean Lasserre, began to shift such views. While the Germans and the French harbored deep historical and nationalist grievances against one another, Bonhoeffer came to see Lasserre as a Christian brother. Beyond forming such friendships, Bonhoeffer also engaged with the Federal Council of Churches and attended its annual meeting in 1930. He was moved when the assembly passed a resolution rejecting the sole war guilt clause of the Treaty of Versailles. For him, this gesture illustrated that Christians could work together across national boundaries to right past wrongs. By the time he departed New York City, Bonhoeffer had begun to leave his nationalistic theology behind. As he sailed back to Germany, he declared, "my sojourn in America made one thing clear to me: the absolute necessity of co-operation." Once back home, Bonhoeffer threw himself fully into the ecumenical movement.[24]

While Union reshaped his theology, the most powerful influence on Bonhoeffer came from outside America's ecumenical establishment. American ecumenists felt confident that their theology could help reform German Protestantism, but it was really the black church's prophetic witness and theology of suffering that most profoundly changed Bonhoeffer. Through Frank Fisher, a black classmate at Union, Bonhoeffer was introduced to Abyssinian Baptist Church, one of New York City's historically black congregations. Bonhoeffer dove head first into Abyssinian's life. He soon began to teach Sunday School at the church, to lead the Wednesday evening women's Bible study, and to organize youth clubs and musical events. While Bonhoeffer had found white mainline congregations to be lacking in theology and substance, the fellowship of Abyssinian overpowered him. He wrote home, "I heard the Gospel preached in the Negro churches." He added, "Here one can truly speak about sin and grace and the love of God . . . the Black Christ is preached with rapturous passion and vision." Bonhoeffer had finally found his cloud of witnesses.[25]

At Abyssinian, Bonhoeffer was immersed in a community living under the conditions of systemic injustice and racial violence. The young German wrote that he discovered "the other America"—the America "hidden behind the veil of the words in the American constitution that 'all men are created free and equal.'" Building on this direct encounter, he became a focused student of the plight of black Americans in the United States. While he had read newspaper stories of lynching in the American South, his extensive travels throughout the region shocked him all the more. He described the Jim Crow system "as really rather unbelievable." Meanwhile, he studied Harlem Renaissance literature and black Christology that portrayed Jesus as one who abided with the oppressed of the world, such as the victims of lynching, and not with the oppressors. As he walked alongside this community, he learned to see life from the position of the sufferer, as well as to look for Christ in and with the downtrodden. Christ was a "vicarious sufferer," he would later write, who came into the world hidden in weakness and suffering and assumed "responsibility" for others. Such insights in part explain why Bonhoeffer would stand out as one of the few German Protestants to defend persecuted Jews. Harlem had granted him a different perspective, one that allowed him to see Nazi Germany in ways that his counterparts could not. He now identified himself with the outsiders on the margins. He saw the Christian's purpose as one of solidarity with and responsibility for "the least of these."[26]

As an outsider himself to the United States, Bonhoeffer was especially primed to see how racism and nativism tarnished the American Protestant witness and exposed the imperfections of American democracy. Years later, the German theologian wrote that racial justice stood as "the most decisive future task for the white churches" in the United States. Upon his return to

Germany, he likewise came to realize that such currents transcended the Atlantic. American nativists protected "pure Americanism" just as much as the Nazis defended "Aryan purity." Protestant nativism and racial prejudice thus found full expression on both sides of the Atlantic. In Germany, the Nazis had even looked to American eugenics laws as models for their own racial purity laws. Hitler had likewise praised America's restrictive immigration laws as exemplary. Bonhoeffer proved one of the rare Protestants who had eyes to see these connections clearly. Some Protestant ecumenists in the United States also recognized the racial injustice and inequality festering within their society, but many within their ranks often situated these shortcomings within a gradualist framework, claiming that in a democratic system, such problems would be gradually overcome. Bonhoeffer's observations, however, raised in him deeper questions about the vitality of American democracy. Far from being a perfect state form, he concluded, it could harbor significant inequality and injustice. Having urged white American Protestants to stand up for justice, the German theologian knew he too would have to counteract Nazi racism once he returned home.[27]

Once back in Germany, Bonhoeffer indeed applied the lessons he had learned at Union and in Harlem. Arguably, his sojourn in America enabled him to respond to the German crisis in a vastly different way than his German colleagues. In particular, Bonhoeffer emerged as one of the most resolute German Protestants in his spiritual and political opposition to Hitler and the German Christian crusade. Two days after Hitler's ascent to chancellor, Bonhoeffer was already warning Germans in a radio address of the dangerous idolatry surrounding the Nazi politician's leadership cult. Bonhoeffer cautioned that such a charismatic leader (*Führer*) could very well turn out to be a "seducer" (*Verführer*) who led the people astray.[28]

In authoring "The Bethel Confession," Bonhoeffer also attacked Protestant complacency toward the "Aryan Paragraph." When German theologians watered down his pro-Jewish protest in their edits of the "Confession," Bonhoeffer refused to sign the final version of the document. He felt a growing frustration in his church's lack of boldness. Increasingly, Bonhoeffer discerned he was heading in an altogether different direction than his peers. Having seen racial injustice firsthand in America, he now called on the church to defend the persecuted Jews in three crucial ways. In a 1933 essay titled "The Church and the Jewish Question," he began by arguing that the church needed to remind the state of its responsibilities to protect the rights of all of its citizens. Next, he added that the church must also be ready to aid the victims of state action. Finally, if all else failed, the church needed to "jam a spoke in the wheel itself." As Bonhoeffer put it, "such action would be direct political action." Bonhoeffer's principled plan of protest fell on deaf ears, however. Other German Protestant theologians found his ethic to be far too radical. In particular, he had called on the church to interfere in the state's affairs, a glaring violation of the Two Kingdoms doctrine. Moreover, they believed they held a limited responsibility to aid the Jews, who, in their prejudiced estimation, had created their own difficulties.[29]

While Protestant dissenters rejected Bonhoeffer's calls for radical intervention and solidarity with German Jews, by 1934 they had nevertheless resolved to more decisively protest Nazi interference in the churches. Karl Barth and Martin Niemöller brought together the core group of opposition Protestants in the town of Barmen and organized a dissenting church body called the Confessing Church. Together, they hammered out "The Barmen Declaration," a theological treatise that asserted the Christian church could answer to no other power than Christ. The document offered a strong rebuttal of Nazi interference in the churches and claimed the state fell under the lordship of Christ. Yet beyond that, it did not venture to reject the Nazis as a political or national movement, nor did it question Nazi racial policies. For Bonhoeffer, it was still a step too tepid.[30]

Although Leiper found the development promising, he too worried that German Protestantism lacked the capacity to counteract Nazism as a whole. He wanted a total rejection of Nazi fascism, but on that point, even the Confessing Church remained silent. A deeper question thus continued to linger: did German Protestantism contain within it the theology and spiritual practices that could halt totalitarianism in its tracks? Leiper certainly found the Confessing Church's spiritual dissent promising, yet he also pondered why they were not politically challenging the Nazi regime. As he noted, "the protesting pastors are still for the greater part pathetically trustful of Hitler's motives." Moreover, the Germans seemed to readily "sign away every vestige of their political rights" to an authoritarian power. In his view, German Protestantism had not developed the spiritual and theological culture needed for a robust democratic politics. Consequently, he noted, "steadily and relentlessly the Nazi Juggernaut has advanced."[31]

Samuel McCrea Cavert confirmed Leiper's findings. Following his own tours of Germany, Cavert argued, "the traditional readiness of German

Lutheranism to regard the State as absolute in the temporal sphere is part of the explanation of the rise of the totalitarian State in Germany." In response, Cavert called on Americans to help German Protestants counteract this "state absolutism." As they made this case, ecumenists like Cavert and Leiper in the United States were mindful of honoring "Germany's contributions to World Christianity." They noted the "debt of all churches to the reformers, scholars, preachers, missionaries, and prophets Germany has given to the world." Yet they also saw in the German Church Struggle a troubling set of patterns. In particular, the church-state conflict led them to believe German Protestants lacked the theological convictions needed to fully counteract totalitarian politics, nationalism, and racial persecution.[32]

Leiper and Cavert thus decided it was time to mobilize a more robust American ecumenical response. Leiper in particular more fully supported the Confessing Church as Germany's true Protestant church and protested the "Aryanism and extreme nationalism in the New Church of Germany." Meanwhile, he urged the Federal Council to postpone receiving an ecumenical delegation from the Reich Church. At a 1934 ecumenical gathering in Fanø, Denmark, Leiper likewise went on the offensive against Nazi meddling in the church's affairs. While there, he counseled a distraught Bonhoeffer on how to best proceed when a growing number of Protestants saw the young German's dissent as increasingly antithetical to the "new Germany." Bonhoeffer was moreover frustrated that the ecumenical movement proved slow in fully supporting the Confessing Church as Germany's one true church. He felt the ecumenical witness proved weak when it needed to be at its strongest. Instead, British and American ecumenists wanted to preserve ties to all church factions in Germany, including the German Christian–led Reich Church and the Confessing Church.[33]

While Leiper agreed with Bonhoeffer, he maintained his confidence in the ecumenical movement's capacity to handle the crisis. When the world's Baptists gathered in Berlin for the 1934 Fifth Baptist World Congress, for instance, Leiper took courage in the Congress's condemnation of the Nazis' racism and antisemitism. While the Congress praised Hitler for restoring "morality" back to German society, it also identified Nazi "racialism" as a "violation of the law of God." The Congress condemned "all racial animosity and every form of unfair discrimination towards Jews, towards colored people, or towards subject races in any part of the world." For an ecumenist like Leiper, it was exactly this kind of theological ethic that the worldwide fellowship of Protestant Christians could offer in such a crucial hour.[34]

Leiper indeed saw in the ecumenical movement a transnational global spiritual order that could undermine totalitarian states like Nazi Germany. His two major publications in the 1930s, *The Ghost of Caesar Walks: The Conflict of Nationalism and World Christianity* and *World Chaos or World Christianity*, disseminated these views. In these works, Leiper argued that Nazi fascism laid total claim to the political and spiritual loyalties of the German people. He and other mainline ecumenists depicted "World Christianity" as a countervailing spiritual order that laid similar totalitarian claims upon the commitments and devotion of its members. As "world chaos" proliferated, Leiper's confidence in the "spiritual force of a united Christendom" endured. In his view, Protestant ecumenism offered a truly universal set of values that counteracted racial injustice, promoted democratic equality, and undermined the "revivified State worship of Nazi Germany." Leiper thus believed ecumenical loyalties to Christ could resolve the crisis.[35]

As Hitler's dictatorship matured, Leiper continued to see the Nazi threat with noteworthy clarity. As he wrote from Germany in 1935, "I am more than ever disgusted and alarmed at the character of Hitlerism and its menace to the best things in human culture and religious heritage." The Nazis were a gang of "lawless thugs" who used brutal tactics to terrorize minorities. They also "trampled" the churches "under the heel of a modern Caesar" and were well on the way to establishing a "pagan state religion" that glorified the Teutonic gods. He also rejected the common German Protestant claim "that Nazidom conquered Bolshevism and saved Christianity" as wholly "shallow." Meanwhile, he lamented the "frightful state of the Jews." The Nazis had made Aryanism into "a sacred doctrine . . . and a holy crusade," Leiper warned, and even worse, they had pledged "to eradicate a whole race." Although Leiper saw the situation clearly, not all Protestant ecumenists and American policymakers shared the urgency of his protest. His calls for the United States to boycott the 1936 Berlin Olympic Games, for instance, in protest of Nazi antisemitic policies, went largely unheeded.[36]

Leiper remained steadfast in his protest, however, and soon began to forge new coalitions to counter the Nazi threat. His observations of Nazism had strengthened within him a commitment to religious pluralism and an inclusive understanding of American identity. The American ecumenist had come to conclude that the Nazis threatened nothing less than the central tenets of Western civilization itself, which in his view was founded upon the shared truths of monotheistic religions, including "faith in a moral order, a moral imperative, and the sacredness of personality." The Nazis also endangered the West's moral code, including "Mosaic law, prophetic ideals, the Sermon on the Mount, the Cross, and the universal Father God." Leiper's assessment reflected the new Judeo-Christian ethic that was emerging in some Protestant circles in response to Nazi fascism. In response to Jewish persecution, he had taken a step beyond the traditional Protestant hostility to Judaism and Catholicism, identifying the three monotheistic religions as the wellsprings of Western political and spiritual culture. He accordingly called on all "men who believe in God" to form a "common front" against the Nazis and to preserve the liberal tenets of the Western world. Leiper soon joined Rabbi Stephen Wise in issuing Jewish-Christian statements against antisemitism. Wise spoke with national authority for American Jews and gave voice to their staunch opposition to Hitler and Nazism. The American rabbi had likewise traveled throughout Europe in 1933, meeting with Jewish refugees in major European capitals. Similar to Leiper, Wise and many Jews in the United States identified National Socialism as a major threat to liberal democratic values, including the freedom of religion and international goodwill.[37]

Leiper's collaboration with Wise stood out in a decade when antisemitic views were prolific not only in Germany but also in the United States. For taking such a stand, Leiper received hate mail from German and American antisemites, with one letter threatening to "get rid of such trash" like the "Jew Pastor Leiper." Leiper worked to change the status quo, however, through contributing to the National Conference of Christians and Jews, a national organization founded in 1927 that promoted religious pluralism and the Judeo-Christian heritage of American democracy. This development paralleled the "tri-faith idealism" that Franklin Delano Roosevelt popularized in response to the threat of Nazi fascism. Roosevelt pointed to the three monotheistic faiths of Protestantism, Catholicism, and Judaism as the spiritual wellsprings of democracy. While Roosevelt sought to forge a more inclusive religious pluralism in response to the Nazis, many American Protestants still resisted such interfaith activism.[38]

Some within mainline Protestant missionary elite, however, came to see interfaith cooperation as a useful antidote not just to Nazism but to secularism as well, which they viewed as a new pressing threat across the globe. In particular, the 1933 Laymen's Report, a study into American Protestant mission in East Asia funded by Protestant philanthropist and Standard Oil heir John D. Rockefeller, Jr., called on the world's faiths to band together in a common offensive against the globe's "secularizing" forces, including "the philosophies of Marx, Lenin, and Russel." To achieve this goal, the report urged Protestant missionaries to forgo direct conversionary mission and to instead forge new interreligious partnerships in pursuit of peace, "social improvement," and "righteousness." Protestant mission societies in Chicago and New York responded in kind, focusing their efforts all the more on the "world service" of "mankind's basic needs." In calling for interreligious cooperation and social service, the Laymen's Report signaled the rise of a new cosmopolitan missionary ethic and the search for a united spiritual front against atheism.[39]

Beyond leading them to promote a more tolerant approach to other religions, the threats of Nazi fascism and secularism also compelled ecumenists to search internally for additional traces of disorder within their own society. Leiper's self-critical spirit in particular recognized that the United States had its own set of problems with racism, prejudice, and economic inequality to overcome. In response to the Nazi threat, Leiper urged his fellow Americans to "strengthen the safeguards of democracy and to make it more vital and effective a thing in our own national life." As such, consistent opposition to secularism and Nazi fascism abroad aligned with calls for democratic reform at home.[40]

In addition to opposing racial and religious prejudice, some ecumenical Protestants also argued that their national economy needed reform. In the midst of the Great Depression, growing poverty and wealth inequality especially alarmed the ecumenical Protestants at the helm of the Federal Council of Churches. They reflected critically on America's untamed capitalist marketplace, which they believed had contributed to the Depression and the political instability of their era in the first place. They therefore welcomed Roosevelt's initiatives to provide relief, promote recovery, and manage the economy through federal action. In this regard, the Federal Council claimed that the New Deal represented Christian economic principles such as the "religious significance of daily bread, shelter, and security." The New Deal's defense of the common good, fair distribution of wealth, provision of social security, and promotion of economic equality appealed to these liberal Protestants. In their estimation, the political program advanced the central tenets of the social gospel. Many black Protestants rightly pointed out, however, that the New Deal racially discriminated against black workers and heightened racial inequity across the nation. In this sense, the ecumenical quest for full democratic equality at home and abroad was far from complete.[41]

For some ecumenists, economic recovery and ecumenical organizing could also keep in check Soviet communism, another emerging international movement they followed alongside Nazi fascism. Reinhold Niebuhr especially warned that communism advanced "historical materialism" in the place of God and functioned like a "new religion" in the world. He cautioned that it could sweep like a deluge over colonized regions frustrated with Western imperialism. Following a fact-finding trip to the Soviet Union, Methodist bishop G. Bromley Oxnam agreed. He likewise found the Soviets to be far more effective than Protestant ecumenists in their appeal to peoples living under colonial regimes. After his trip, he called for opening relations with the Soviets, a move which found a wide backing among diplomatically inclined, multilateral ecumenists. Moreover, he urged ecumenists to further engage non-Western partners and to foster their own ecumenical world order that could compete across a decolonizing and religiously plural globe. Together, these Federal Council leaders hoped that the transnational church would indeed quell the chaos and create a more just, tolerant, peaceful, and faith-filled world.[42]

As these ecumenical leaders responded to Nazi fascism, global recession, and Soviet communism, American fundamentalists likewise followed the emerging "world chaos" with concern. Yet in contrast to the ecumenical response, the fundamentalist reading of international and domestic events heightened their apocalypticism, emboldened their opposition to "collectivism," and further strengthened their Christian nationalism. For many within their ranks, Nazi fascism, the New Deal, and Soviet communism all seemingly resulted from the same collectivist trend. These developments also bore traces of theological modernism and doctrinal impurity. In their estimation, the entire Western world seemed to be turning to centralized political power in response to the Great Depression. Such developments abroad compelled them all the more to oppose the evils that threatened their Christian nation.[43]

Many fundamentalists considered the rise of European dictators and the New Deal as certain signs of the coming end times. These transatlantic developments confirmed their apocalyptic reading of Scripture. Drawing from the books of Daniel, Ezekiel, and Revelations, premillennial fundamentalists believed that Mussolini, Hitler, and Stalin were certain portents of the coming Antichrist. They warned that this diabolical world leader would revive the Roman Empire, while a great "northern kingdom" would persecute and attack the Jews in Palestine. For them, the expansion of government at home was intimately tied to their worries about dictators abroad. They closely followed Mussolini's invasion of Ethiopia, Hitler's persecution of Jews and Christians, and Roosevelt's New Deal. They then wove these events together into an apocalyptic interpretation of world events.[44]

Kansas fundamentalist Gerald Winrod especially voiced such concerns and views. Winrod had earned his fundamentalist stripes in the 1920s as he worked alongside William Bell Riley as a "Flying Defender of Fundamentalism" and lobbied for anti-evolution legislation in Minnesota, California, and Kansas. In 1925, Winrod had also founded the notorious "Defenders of the Christian Faith" to promote his fundamentalist convictions. By the 1930s, he saw tremendous cause for concern in the events sweeping across Europe and the United States. While Mussolini seemed to be setting the stage for a revival of the Roman Empire, Winrod likewise believed that Hitler was a skilled demagogue who would certainly play a role in leading the world to its apocalyptic doom. In his 1933 tract *Hitler in Prophecy*, the Kansan fundamentalist condemned Hitler as a "wild beast that will not be controlled." The Führer was an "egotistical fanatic," he wrote, who thought of himself as a "superman anointed of divine providence in the same way that the Kaiser seemed to think of himself as being ordained of God to slay the world." In his view, Hitler's iron dictatorship was even more sinister and evil than Mussolini's, which made the Führer a far greater danger than Il Duce. Following Hitler's seizure of power, Winrod also predicted that another world war was inevitable. His reading of Ezekiel 38 led him to believe that Hitler, despite his professed hatred of Bolshevists, would soon ally with Russia and aid the powerful northern confederacy foretold in Scripture. The prophesied "Gomer" would serve the "Gog" of the north in its quest for power, Winrod warned. Moreover, Hitler's antisemitic policies were already driving Jews back to Palestine, yet another important precursor to Armageddon in Winrod's premillennialist timeline.[45]

Like many premillennial fundamentalists, Winrod tied his concerns about Hitler to his opposition to the New Deal. His prophetic reading of the "Blue Eagle" that adorned the seal of the National Recovery Administration, one of Roosevelt's landmark programs, highlighted his apocalyptic opposition to the president. In particular, Winrod worried the emblem was preparation for "the trademark of the Beast." "Study the Blue Eagle," he opined. "One wing has seven feathers. The other ten," just like the "beast" in Revelation with

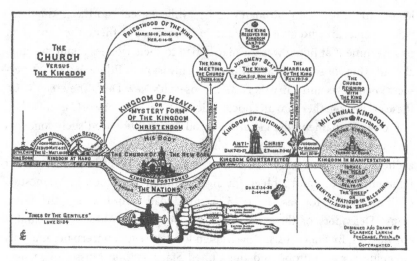

Clarence Larkin excited the evangelical imagination with his elaborate premillennial charts. This particular chart depicts several key events in the apocalyptic timeline of premillennial fundamentalists, including the rapture of the faithful, the kingdom of the Antichrist, the seven years of tribulation, and the triumphant second coming of Christ. Such theology inspired fierce opposition to international organizations such as the League of Nations, which fundamentalists feared could become a tool of the Antichrist, as well as vigilance in response to the rise of fascist dictators and "collectivist" governments.

Source: Clarence Larkin, "The Church Versus the Kingdom," *Rightly Dividing the Word* (Philadelphia: Fox Chase, 1921), 54.

"seven heads and ten thorns." The major nations of the world had become "mark-conscious," he warned. The Italian fascists had their axe; the Soviets a hammer and sickle; the Nazis the swastika; the Americans the Blue Eagle. All pointed to the coming Antichrist. Winrod knew with confidence what such developments portended: "the inevitable tendency is to cement all things together into one big system . . . international barriers will be abolished. The Antichrist's dictatorship will reach to the most remote parts of the earth." He continued, "a monstrous monopoly is on the way. It will embrace, regulate, and direct all human affairs, both religious and secular. It will be ecclesiastical as well as political and industrial." For Winrod and other fundamentalists, powerful dictators, economic regulation, international organizations, and ecumenical councils all presaged the coming apocalypse.[46]

Fundamentalists refused to twiddle their thumbs in response, however. They rose up in defense of the "Christian American" way of life. Southern Baptist fundamentalist J. Frank Norris especially warned that the American people had forsaken their nation's Christian foundations in accepting the New Deal. The Baptist preacher had attended the founding conference of the World's Christian Fundamentals Association in 1919, and in the 1920s, had developed a national reputation as a fervent opponent of "that hell-born, Bible-destroying, deity-of-Christ-denying German rationalism known as evolution." A larger than life figure, the Texas preacher had also been indicted twice, once for the arson of his Baptist church and once for shooting and killing a Texas lumber executive in his church office. Acquitted both times, Norris now sounded off against an invasion of "European imports" in the 1930s. To Norris, New Deal Democrats like Henry Wallace represented the "European Way" of doing things. Norris instead defended the "American Way" of limited government and free market capitalism. In his view, "social justice" and the New Deal were the obvious "Trojan horse of European dictatorship." He therefore railed against "the menace of the dictatorship at Washington" and warned his fellow Americans they were "headed with the rest of the world toward a dictatorship of communism or fascism." The New Deal was a "Hitler revolution," he stated, only it was perhaps even more sinister because it had taken place "with American ballots instead of Hitler bayonets." For fundamentalists like Norris, then, the New Deal at home was just as alarming as "Hitlerism" abroad. Norris urged fundamentalists to fervently oppose both developments.[47]

Winrod concurred. He too advanced a robust Christian nationalism in response to such "European trends." Like Norris, Winrod affirmed the American experiment had developed out of a firm rejection of the European way of politics and religion. In a grand historical interpretation, he argued that the Puritans, the true bedrock of the American republic, "had discarded the religious, moral, and governmental practices of Europe." Even more, the Bible had birthed the Constitution and the American republic. As one of Winrod's associates wrote, "the founders of the American republic . . . looked in their open Bibles and brought forth the American constitution." For Winrod, both the Bible and the Constitution were sacred and infallible documents containing "eternal principles" never to be altered. New Dealers were doing just that, however, in their efforts to "scrap the Constitution" and desecrate the Scriptures. Winrod cautioned his fellow Americans that they had already "gone to Europe for false scientific theories, Evolution and

Higher Criticism." They had also "permitted the hierarchy of Rome to invade our national life." Now they were taking the sure road to communism in embracing the New Deal.[48]

Winrod thus warned the American people that they stood at a crossroads. They could go the way of the Democratic liberals and communists and forsake their heritage, or they could mobilize for political battle. He and his colleagues called on all good "Anglo-Saxon" Americans to defend the "most priceless heritage of Christian Americans." They counseled faithful "Christian Americans" that "internal enemies"—evolutionists, modernists, New Dealers, Jews, and communists—were surely "boring from within" to undermine "the American constitutional system, our heritage of freedom . . . and the foundational principles of Christian ideals." These invading forces did not share "the spirit, or the doctrines, of the founders of our Country," Winrod asserted. They advanced "alien ideas, brought over from Europe," which if left unchecked, would "destroy all that is near and dear to the heart of every true American." These radicals were carrying out a grand conspiracy as they worked "night and day, to tear down our ideals, to destroy our patriotic sentiments, to wreck our moral standards, to overcome our spirituality, and to abolish our very system of representative government." Winrod thus urged his followers to gird their loins for battle and oppose "every man" who could "not subscribe one hundred percent" to his Christian nationalist creed.[49]

In fact, some fundamentalists perceived this conspiratorial threat led by Bolshevists to be so severe, they were willing to revise their initial views of Hitler. Like many American Protestants, fundamentalists especially feared that the Soviets were aggressive atheists who ardently opposed Christianity. In 1933, they were taken aback when Roosevelt opened diplomatic relations with the Soviet Union. In response, they condemned Protestant ecumenists for underestimating the Soviet threat. Even more, their growing concerns over communism now led some to see the Nazis as potential allies in a Christian crusade against this new source of world chaos. As they developed sympathy for Hitler's Germany, they gave voice to the extremism, nativism, and antisemitism that defined notable swaths of American Protestantism in this era.

In 1935, Gerald Winrod led the charge after he took a pilgrimage to Germany to study the Protestant Reformation. Along with a tour of the Castle Church in Wittenberg and a hike to the Wartburg castle in Eisenach, his firsthand experiences with Nazi Germany led him to drastically revise his estimation of Hitler. So too did *The Protocols of the Elders of Zion*, a 1903 chronicle of a secret meeting of powerful Jews planning to take over the world. While ultimately discredited as a forgery, the *Protocols* still inspired conspiracy theorists and antisemites like Winrod, who began to theorize that "international Jews" stood behind Soviet communism and the New Deal. In response, Winrod now praised Hitler and the Nazis. They had "dared to try and completely extricate" themselves, he wrote, "from the control of international Jewry." They were "fighting atheistic Communism," he added, and "smashing Bolshevism into oblivion." Winrod found an ally in Riley, who blamed the Jews for warranting their "own rejection" on "the day" they "crucified Jesus Christ." As a result, Riley admired Hitler for making the Germans the "enemies of the Jews." Moreover, he also praised Hitler for saving "Germany from the very jaws of atheistic communism." Like Winrod, he erroneously believed the Jews were behind an international cabal to control the world and were the originators of Bolshevism.[50]

Following his brief journey abroad, Winrod became one of Hitler's most fervent American supporters. When he returned home to Kansas, he burned the remaining copies of his pamphlet *Hitler in Prophecy*, which had condemned Hitler. He also welcomed pro-Nazi German Protestants to the United States to bolster his cause, such as Methodist bishop Otto Melle, who visited Winrod in the mid-1930s. Melle affirmed Winrod's view that God "in providence" had "sent a Leader who was able to banish the danger of Bolshevism in Germany and rescue the nation from the abyss of despair." An outspoken defender of Hitler's regime, Melle and his tours of the United States were a crucial tool of Nazi foreign propaganda.[51]

Winrod was also inspired to wage political battle of his own. In 1938, he ran for a US Senate seat in the state of Kansas in order to defend "Christian America" from the New Deal. The publicity of the race did him in, however. After investigating his record of antisemitism, the American press billed him as "the Jayhawk Nazi," a Nazi "fifth columnist," and a leader of America's "racist-nationalist fringe." Yet his fame was still growing. Winrod's *The Defender Magazine* now boasted a purported readership of over 100,000, far outpacing many mainline journals such as *The Christian Century*.[52]

In 1939, the cause of homegrown Nazis like Winrod gained national prominence when 22,000 Americans gathered at a "Mass Demonstration for True Americanism" in New York's Madison Square Garden. The "German-American Bund" had organized the event in order to carry out "George Washington Birthday Exercises." Swastikas, Nazi regalia, and American flags adorned the "monster rally" as hundreds of American "stormtroopers" marched into the arena. The organizers proceeded to condemn the "Jewish controlled press" and called for "Gentile-controlled" government and labor unions free from "Moscow-controlled domination." Winrod also found common cause with the event's organizers who urged "Aryan, Nordic, and Christians" to "wake up!" and "demand that our government return to the people who founded it." Winrod's fellow travelers had taken Manhattan for the evening and hoped to achieve much more. In the weeks ahead, American fascists continued to follow the Nazi playbook through attacking the free press, promoting conspiracy theories, and championing exclusionary understandings of American identity.[53]

Winrod's associate, the popular Canadian preacher Oswald J. Smith, proved to be another Nazi admirer who lauded the New Germany following his trip there. Smith claimed he encountered an ideal Christian society that perfectly replicated his commitments. Indeed, he believed the German people were experiencing a "spiritual awakening" under the Nazis. The Nazis promoted "positive Christianity," opposed Bolshevism, esteemed the family, and enforced eugenics laws. As Smith put it in eugenicist terms, "No longer can weak-minded, imbecile parents bring such children into the world. Hence, Germany is destined to become a strong and healthy nation." Winrod and his peers illustrated how the most extreme Christian nationalists found much to praise in Nazi Germany. Hitler may have been a dictator, but he was creating their ideal kind of "Christian" society. While they often criticized centralized power, fundamentalists like Winrod readily lauded the state when it served their interests. It would not be the last time they looked to strong-arm politicians to advance their agenda.[54]

While nowhere near a fascist like Winrod, Baptist fundamentalist J. Frank Norris also succumbed to the temptation to see Nazi Germany as an anti-communist defender of the faith. Making his own trip to visit fundamentalist Europeans in the summer of 1937, Norris shared his transatlantic voyage on the Queen Mary with a group of modernist ecumenists bound for the 1937 Oxford ecumenical conference. He readily debated them on the social gospel and the responsibility of the church in economic and political matters. Norris felt that these modernists, with their focus on "reformation, social service, international peace, and economic justice," were far from "the Acts of the Apostles" and "the New Birth." After visiting Baptists in Germany, he reported that these ecumenists had also overblown the German Church Struggle. "I worshipped just like we do in America," he stated. Far from being persecuted, Germany's Baptists "were singing, praying, preaching, and teaching the fundamentals of the Christian religion." In contrast, the Soviets stifled religious freedom and had even denied Norris entry into their country. Although Norris clearly admitted Hitler was a dictator, he concluded the German people were "happy" and "not in fear." They took "new hope" as Hitler had "scrapped the impossible treaty of Versailles." In his journal *The Fundamentalist*, Norris also widely disseminated the views of German Protestant Coyus Fabricius, who condemned Leiper's narrative of Nazi Germany. The Nazi state had not been "deified" or "worshipped," as Leiper claimed. Rather, the Nazis were rightly honored for opposing "neo-paganism" and promoting spiritual awakening.[55]

In contrast to Winrod and Riley, however, some fundamentalists followed the growing Nazi persecution of the Jews with significant concern. From the outset of Hitler's regime, they perceptively identified the Nazis' murderous intent. Their readings of the end times affirmed that Jews would face mounting persecution and eventually be driven to Palestine. In response, a considerable number of fundamentalists defended the Jews and affirmed they were still God's chosen people. Numerous fundamentalists were therefore outspoken on Jewish persecution when many ecumenical Protestants remained silent. Baptist fundamentalist John R. Rice especially denounced the "barbarous persecution of Jews." He claimed it should "shock . . . true Christians throughout the entire world."[56]

The growing persecutions also led J. Frank Norris to shift course. A few months after his return from Germany, Norris began to condemn Hitler again, claiming that he could actually be the Antichrist. "Hitler is rapidly becoming a Messiah to his people," Norris warned. Moreover, the Germans were intoxicated with "the worship of might." In a "gospel mass meeting and Americanism rally," Norris made his revised views public through burning both the Nazi and the Soviet flags. He also rejected the *Protocols*, claiming that "those who believe in the Premillennial coming of Jesus Christ should certainly do everything in their power to help the Jew." Later, Norris also publicly denounced Riley and Winrod as "pro-Hitlerites and anti-Semites." While he did not share Leiper's interfaith ethic or commitment to social democracy, he did see Nazi antisemitism as a malicious manifestation of evil. Shaped by his apocalypticism, he and other leading fundamentalists would urge on decisive action against Nazism both at home and abroad.[57]

While Norris and Winrod now viewed Hitler and Jewish persecution differently, their interwar rhetoric still had fired up the Christian nationalist cause. In response to the "world chaos" of their era, Protestant fundamentalists affirmed the Christian founding of the American republic, outlined an exceptional role for "Christian America" in the world, and drew boundaries between insiders and outsiders, those who were pure Americans and those who were European threats. For them, promoting this flavor of Christian nationalism was the surest way to defend their understanding of the American way of life. Not only was it a surefire defense against foreign dictators, it also was the best means to counteract dangerous political and spiritual developments at home.

Henry Smith Leiper took in all these developments with growing worry. "World chaos" had inspired tremendous divisions between German and American Protestants, as well as between American ecumenists and fundamentalists. American Protestants could not agree whether to see Hitler as a heretical tyrant or a savior of their faith. Many found themselves somewhere in the middle, cautiously sympathetic to the new Germany. Try as he might, Leiper struggled to forge a united Protestant opposition to Nazism. As Hitler's dictatorship marched on, he would look to a young ecumenical pastor who had found his way to the Nazi capital. There in Hitler's Berlin, Leiper hoped that the American Lutheran pastor Stewart Winfield Herman, Jr., would be able to help quell the chaos of Nazi fascism.

3
The Lonely Flame

In 1935, Federal Council of Churches leader Henry Smith Leiper left Berlin discouraged. The American Church in Berlin, an American Protestant congregation in the Nazi capital, was about to close its doors. Leiper hoped to find a suitable new pastor to lead the congregation. In his view, the church could serve as a valuable outpost of American Protestantism and a beacon of ecumenical values in a troubled Germany. The longer the pastoral post remained vacant, he feared, the weaker the witness of Protestant ecumenism would grow in the heart of the Nazi Reich.

Leiper did not anticipate, however, that a young American ecumenist, Stewart Winfield Herman, Jr., had not only been studying in France and Germany for some time but was also looking for a temporary pastoral post. Born in 1909 the first son of a Pennsylvania preacher, Herman had come of age in the heyday of Protestant ecumenism. As he made his way through his studies at Gettysburg Lutheran Theological Seminary, he sensed that his life path lay beyond his father's Pennsylvania pulpit. He desired to pursue an ecumenical and international career, one that would take him abroad in order to build the kingdom of God on earth and strengthen the global Protestant faith. Upon assuming the Berlin pastorate in 1936, Herman endeavored to spiritually nourish and uplift this solitary outpost of American Protestantism in Hitler's Germany. As he put it, he sought to keep "the lonely flame" of ecumenical Protestantism ablaze in Berlin.[1]

When he arrived in the Nazi capital, Herman was a relatively unknown Lutheran pastor, dedicated to ecumenical Protestantism and American democracy. In his view, Protestant ecumenists were rightly seeking to create a Christian world order. In this regard, Leiper and other leading ecumenists could not have found a better protégé than Herman. Yet Herman's sojourn in the Nazi capital from 1936 to 1941 illustrated how Protestant ecumenists struggled to speak with one voice when it came to Hitler's dictatorship, the German Church Struggle, and Jewish-Christian relations. Even more, the young American's conflicted response to Nazism and Berlin's Jews revealed how aspects of Christian nationalism—in particular, religious and racial

God's Marshall Plan. James D. Strasburg, Oxford University Press (2021). © Oxford University Press.
DOI: 10.1093/oso/9780197516447.003.0004

prejudice—continued to shape the interwar work of some of the most committed Protestant ecumenists. Under Herman's watch, ecumenism's lonely flame ultimately grew dim in Hitler's Berlin.[2]

As a budding ecumenist, Herman naturally found himself pulled abroad. After his graduation from Gettysburg and ordination into the United Lutheran Church, the young American won a fellowship to study theology at the University of Strasbourg in Strasbourg, France. Herman arrived in the French border town in 1934, just over a year after Hitler had assumed dictatorial powers in Germany. As a student, he spent his days perfecting his French, studying theology in a new intellectual environment, debating faith and politics with his European classmates, and admiring the narrow lanes and timber-frame homes of his host city. He also became a keen observer of European events, especially in neighboring Germany.

Herman's observations and extended stay in Europe revealed the conflicted mind of some Protestant ecumenists on the dramatic political changes sweeping over Germany. While an ecumenist like Leiper had quickly and resolutely condemned Hitler, Herman initially expressed a cautious optimism about German national renewal under the Nazi leader. Following a first trip into southern Germany in the fall of 1934, for instance, he noted that despite Hitler's seemingly absolute control over German society, the Nazi dictator's "unified program" still struck him as "pacific." Like many Americans of German ancestry, Herman felt that Hitler was restoring Germany to a semblance of respect and confidence following what he perceived to be the unfair postwar peace of Versailles.[3]

Studying in the French-German borderlands, the young American also found himself in a region that was a prized possession in Hitler's expansionist quest to restore the "Greater Germany" that Versailles had dismantled. In January 1935, the residents of the neighboring Saarland, one such contested territory, overwhelmingly voted to be reunited with the German Reich. Having traveled there to witness the vote, Herman noted the "spirit" of revelry and celebration "was so contagious" that he and his classmates "could not desist from flagging up our arms in the Roman salute and yelling 'Heil' (although we did not add 'Hitler!')." When Hitler renounced the Treaty of Versailles that spring, Herman stated, "it's a relief to see someone cut a clean line for once, even though he may be half-crazy." Under Hitler's watch, he added, Germany was at least "getting back her self-respect" in the international community. He opened his next letter back home with a playful "Heil Hitler!" While he was far from a convert, Herman still expressed his "confidence" in "Hitler's honesty" as a diplomat and political tactician. His respect for some of Hitler's aims showed that not all Protestants saw the Nazi leader as an immediate threat or clearly understood the Nazis' intentions.[4]

Herman soon had a chance, however, to develop fuller observations of the "New Germany," and in particular, the intensifying German church situation. After his exchange year in France ended, he won a fellowship to study across the border at the revered theology faculties of Göttingen and Tübingen. Before he enrolled at the German institutions, he traveled to Berlin to brush up on his German. While there, he studiously visited an array of German Protestant churches. He also connected with German clergy who expressed their support of Hitler. Herman was taken in by their example. "I am beginning to see how a preacher can be in favor of this government," he wrote, "and be absolutely sincere in his homiletic and pastoral work." Hearing Confessing Church pastor Martin Niemöller preach, however, also tempered Herman's openness to pro-Nazi clergy. Niemöller's critique of Nazi interference in the church's affairs, he reported, was "really strong stuff." Equally impressed by these different groups of clergy, Herman hoped to maintain his neutrality in the emerging church struggle and to develop a deeper understanding of German Protantism in the months ahead.[5]

As was his custom in most German cities he visited, Herman also made a point of visiting Berlin's Jewish sector. He had arrived in Germany just after the passage of the 1935 Nuremberg Laws, which had stripped German Jews of their citizenship and forbade Jews from marrying Aryan Germans. Herman noted that "the ghetto" was eerily silent. He wrote home that he "saw few Jewish noses on the streets and none of the uproarious hilarity that usually characterizes the ghetto because of the many children." Far from expressing solidarity with Berlin's Jews, however, Herman's tone instead remained that of a distanced observer. Moreover, his casual use of racial stereotypes—the same ones Nazis and antisemites at the time were using to dehumanize the Jews—revealed an underlying prejudice that would soon be on fuller display.[6]

As he settled into a new semester at Göttingen, Herman's prolonged exposure to Hitler's Reich confirmed his earlier conclusions about German renewal. In his estimation, the Germans were "trying to work out not only their economic but their spiritual salvation with much more honesty and effect than any other nation in Europe today." In an age of economic and spiritual depression, he noted that Germany was "the only nation . . . taking clear-cut and decisive steps in an attempt to stem and defeat this Decline of the West." On this point, the threat of "Bolshevism" across Europe especially loomed large to Herman. Like many American and German Protestant clergy of his era, Herman felt Protestants ought to "be frightened by the inroads of Bolshevism and every effort ought to be made to stamp it out once and for all." Perhaps Nazi propaganda had overly shaped his thinking, he confessed, but he still felt the Nazis were at least trying to counteract the Soviet threat. Other ecumenists such as Leiper, however, had long dismissed such claims as ill-founded. In espousing these anti-Judaic, anti-communist views, as well as cautious sympathy for the nationalist aims of Hitler's "New Germany," Herman veered closer to the convictions of fundamentalist nationalists than to those of ecumenical globalists.[7]

At the same time, Nazism also startled Herman. He wrote home, "I like these Germans from all angles except the political angle." In particular, he noted, the Nazis were "absolutely ruthless in running individuals thru the Nazi mill." With a sense of horror, he feared they desired to seize "not only the loyalty and support of the people but their very hearts and souls." The hyper-nationalism of his German peers also alarmed him. The Germans had become "intoxicated" with their "fatherland," Herman warned. He grew weary of countless university lectures on "Blut and Boden" and the "necessity of dying for the country." Even worse, Herman stated, was the Nazi belief that "the Christian doctrine of love consists in loving your own Volk." The American pastor sensed such *völkish* doctrines were an omen of storm clouds on the horizon. It was a "fresh bottle of the same stuff that gave" the Germans "the last headache," he wrote.[8]

Herman certainly sensed the gravity of such developments. He noted "the next couple of decades are going to be very important for religion (and theology)." "I feel like a small boy behind his fort in a snowball battle," he said, admitting, "I haven't even now nearly enough 'ammunition.'" The budding theologian hoped he could "put in a 'few good licks' for the spiritual side" and be of service "if the battle becomes another 'World War.'" For Herman, that "spiritual side" was both ecumenically Protestant and American-led. His observations of Nazi Germany strengthened his own confidence in the spiritual mission of the United States. In particular, he hoped Americans could forsake the ways of exploitative imperialists and build a new kind of global order rooted in American-led Christian institutions.[9]

Taking stock of these thoughts, the young American recognized that he had always thought of himself as "more or less 'cosmopolitan.'" He had often thought his commitments deserved "some such magnificent label as 'universal' or 'international.'" "I was wrong," he confessed. Having lived for a short while abroad, he now recognized that "the subtle nationalism of U.S.A." had "permeated" his "very marrow." He wrote he considered America "as being superior to the rest of the world," just as the Germans expressed confidence in their own nation. His ecumenical commitments thus did not preclude a high certainty in his nation's spiritual and civic exceptionalism. He believed Americans were naturally the kind of spiritual leaders who would lead the way to a new democratic and ecumenical world order.[10]

As Herman's desire to be of service in such a spiritual struggle grew, his interest in remaining in Göttingen also weakened. His advisor at the university—German Protestant theologian Friedrich Gogarten—had proven more challenging than he had anticipated. He also felt a growing uncertainty about pursuing an academic vocation altogether. Instead, he desired to more fully prepare himself for ecumenical work that would build up the church. He therefore began to seek out short-term pastoral work to complement his studies. At that point, the council of the American Church in Berlin unexpectedly offered him a temporary post after the church's pastor had grown ill. Herman had some hesitation due to the extensive summer travel plans he had lined up, but he ultimately realized "the chance of preaching and doing some real work in that run-down church" proved "exceedingly attractive." His path was thus set: he transferred his studies to Berlin and embarked for the Reich capital.[11]

Upon his arrival, Herman's first forays into pastoral life revealed to him the significant and even overwhelming role he had accepted. He was now no longer a casual observer of German Protestantism and the Nazi state. Instead, he was dealing directly with Nazi officials and ministering to a congregation in a tense church-state context. He wrote home, "I have not stepped gingerly, toe by toe, into the whirl of Berlin's public life. I have been tossed headlong in the deep waters and left to swim for myself, grasping and choking . . . I am even impressed myself . . . by the incredible chance I've had."[12]

Herman was soon keeping company with Nazi officials, Hohenzollern royalty, and leading American diplomats at "stiffly formal dinners" and "opera parties." In his first days as a Berlin pastor, Nazi officials called upon him to deliver a prayer to open a luncheon celebrating George Washington, whom they eagerly compared to Hitler. Herman agreed, without considering how this "Christian invocation at an official Nazi function" would come across to the public. With Leiper distancing the Federal Council from the Nazis and the German Christians, an American ecumenist "blessing" a Nazi event did not go over well back home. Yet Herman also infused ecumenical values into his prayer for "brotherly love" among all nations. He recounted, "I think it was a blow to some of them to have Grace said. The one I said was even more of a blow."[13]

Yet the Nazis would soon strike back themselves. Just a month after arriving in Berlin, Herman casually exited the *Nollendorfplatz* subway station on his way to the American Church. He proceeded into a silent throng of German citizens making the Nazi salute following a speech given by Hitler. As he navigated his way through the crowd, a Nazi sympathizer pushed Herman onto the square's cobblestones due to his lack of respect for the Führer. Quickly surrounded by several other accosters, Herman pled his ignorance as an American, but his original assailant had already slipped into the crowd.

Back in the United States, American newspapers ran headlines announcing a "fanatical" and "overzealous" Nazi had "attacked" Herman. While Herman felt the press was overblowing the incident, the international media attention did grant Herman and the American Church a more visible profile. Gestapo agents soon visited Herman to apologize for the assault. Herman at first wrote the incident off as the action of a deranged zealot. A friend warned him, however, that the Gestapo had tapped his phone. Agents were also purportedly reading his mail. The discovery startled him. Perhaps Hitler's regime was not as peaceful and serene as he initially thought. He now began to exercise a newfound caution so as not to raise the ire of his Nazi hosts.[14]

Brushing the incident off, Herman soon found his stride in building up what he described as the "American colony" in Berlin. For the young ecumenist, serving the Anglo-American expat community and advancing its spiritual interests stood paramount to him. In his own words, he believed the American Church represented the "spirit of American Christianity" in Germany. As he informed his congregation, they had the lofty mission of fostering "an unbreakable faith in the super-national power of Christian love and brotherhood." Herman desired to rally his church "as a community of Christian Americans" to expand "the kingdom of God." "It is especially necessary," he wrote, "to keep this lonely flame of American Christianity burning in a Europe so upset as it is." Confident in America's global Christian mission, Herman thought he had a unique "chance to set up a bit of typical American Christianity in the midst of the German national church." He envisioned himself faithfully occupying a lonely outpost of American Protestantism. He hoped he might play his own small part in promoting ecumenical values in a country that he felt sorely needed them.[15]

In his initial four-month stint as pastor, Herman also aimed to strengthen the American Church's ties to the American diplomatic community in Berlin. He surmised that American diplomats and ambassadors had a tangible opportunity to infuse American foreign policy with moral vitality and Wilsonian activism. He therefore sought to capitalize on his first Fourth of July service, which he had learned always drew the largest congregation of the year. The service would prove one of the most crucial moments in his quest to grow the church and establish his pastorate. The service accordingly dazzled in its display of American civil religion. While he delivered what he saw as a compelling sermon on the "right to life, liberty, and happiness," his song selections of "America the Beautiful" and "God Bless Our Native Land" played to the nationalist feeling of the holiday. A presentation of a new American flag from Douglas Jenkins, consul general in Berlin, bolstered the spiritual-diplomatic connection Herman wanted to see developed in the Nazi capital.[16]

All seemed to go smoothly until an unexpected American fundamentalist in attendance challenged him after the service. The Moody Bible Institute graduate approached Herman, stating, "I am here for bread this morning and I got a stone! Preach Jesus, young man, nothing but Jesus." The man then offered to "pray for him" and inquired whether or not he was "saved." Clearly, the Moody graduate had other concerns than celebrating the United States. He was about the business of saving souls. Herman recounted that it was a "blow to the belt" that left him feeling "pretty blue." While he realized that "his sort of Christianity wouldn't suit me more than mine suited his," he admitted he felt "rattled around like a dry pea in a pod." Such episodes led Herman to harbor growing doubts about his spiritual mission. He continually wrestled with whether he was inspiring his congregants to build the kingdom of God in their midst.[17]

Despite his best efforts, Herman also grew frustrated at the lack of interest American diplomats showed in the church's affairs. They neglected a golden opportunity, he wrote, to "represent . . . the spirit of Christ and the spirit of a Christian nation." While he desired to recruit them to "Christianize" their diplomacy, he grew frustrated as he faced an "indifference" to such a task "thru out our whole foreign service." He concluded, "the pretenses of being a Christian country is very hollow." Like other ecumenists, Herman believed both deacons and diplomats had a responsibility to advance "Christian America's" mission in the world. Together, the church and the state could work in tandem to create a new order of peace and harmony.[18]

Over the months that followed, Herman accordingly launched an aggressive campaign to expand the social and spiritual life of "the colony." Beyond organizing a choir, a sewing club, and Sunday School classes, he hosted church dinners and recruited leading diplomats, such as ambassador William Dodd, to join the church council and attend key events. To finance these pursuits, Herman consistently pursued the patronage of wealthy American businessmen, bankers, and media moguls living in Berlin, some of whom were American Jews. Through his efforts, the social fellowship of the American Church grew. Noting the church's buzzing social life, the church council renewed Herman's contract.[19]

Along with his first Fourth of July service, the 1936 Summer Olympics also provided an opportunity for Herman to further establish the social and spiritual presence of the "American colony" in Berlin. While Leiper had demanded an American boycott of the Games, Herman saw the festivities as a crucial chance to strengthen his pastorate and his church. He launched a special sermon series and networked with North American delegates in town for the Games, including the track star Jesse Owens, and the founder of basketball, James Naismith. The Olympics that summer also coincided with Sherwood Eddy's "Steamship Seminar" series. Privately, Herman expressed a special distaste for these "internationalist" seminars. He found Eddy, a leading figure in the transnational ecumenical movement, to be a "not very impressive sort of person." Later, he complained about the delegates Eddy would send to Berlin, including a group of Jewish rabbis who "spewed venom" and "pure poison" toward the "new Germany." That particular summer, Reinhold Niebuhr also was in tow. Herman considered Niebuhr to be "more likeable and far more capable" than Eddy. He offered Niebuhr the pulpit while the Union theologian was in Berlin, but Niebuhr declined, noting that "he wouldn't feel free to say what he thought." He sensed that his harsh rebuke of the Nazis and his word against antisemitism would not have found a receptive audience in the church.[20]

Beyond leading ecumenists, the Summer Games also brought into town the eccentric American evangelist Frank Buchman, a practitioner of Keswick holiness Christianity, whose pursuit of conversionary mission contrasted with Herman's ecumenical ministry. Buchman had once been a committed modernist and ecumenist himself, until a 1908 tour of Britain had turned him into a devotee of Keswick Higher Life spirituality, a movement within British Protestantism dedicated to disciplined moral lifestyles, the "entire sanctification" of the individual, and the "second work" of the Holy Spirit. Having experienced "a great spiritual shaking up" at a Keswick conference, Buchman launched a transatlantic crusade of promoting holiness Christianity and encounters with the Holy Ghost. He eventually took his movement to Oxford University, where his successful efforts at recruiting Oxford students earned his movement the name the "Oxford Group."[21]

When Hitler came to power across the Channel, Buchman made the Nazi leader his new evangelistic target. In 1932 and 1933, he made routine trips to Berlin to host house parties similar to the ones he held in Oxford. Through strategic networking, he hoped he might meet Hitler and convert him to an authentic Christian faith. With a "twice-born Führer" in charge of one of the world's most powerful nations, Buchman believed "every last, bewildering problem" could be solved.

While he never gained an audience with Hitler, Buchman still lavished praise on the Führer that reflected the anti-communist commitments of many American Protestants. As he put it, he thanked God "for a man like Adolf Hitler, who built a front line of defense against the anti-Christ of Communism." He continued to dream of meeting the German leader, imagining what a "God-Controlled Dictatorship" could do for the world.[22]

While Buchman's inroads to Hitler failed, he did develop a friendship with Heinrich Himmler, the leader of the *Schutzstaffel*. Although Buchman failed to persuade Himmler to accept Christ into his heart, the friendship did provide him with insider access to the 1935 Nazi rally at the Nuremberg parade grounds. The production value of the large gathering left Buchman inspired to organize similar mass events, only for the cause of Christ. In 1935, 5,000 Americans traveled to Stockbridge, Massachusetts, for the Oxford Group's first national assembly and soon made the movement a "household term," as the *New York Times* put it. When quickly converting Hitler and Himmler proved more difficult than anticipated, the Oxford Group launched evangelistic ventures into Norway, Denmark, and Germany in order to inspire conversions and gain a stronger continental following; 60,000 even gathered at Olerup, Denmark, for an Easter assembly. Buchman's efforts foreshadowed the emergence of a mid-century evangelization style that targeted the rich and powerful and used high production value to draw in large crowds.[23]

In response, ecumenical Protestants sharply criticized Buchman's approach. "It is difficult to restrain the contempt which one feels for this dangerous childishness," Niebuhr wrote. The realist theologian considered it foolish to think one could "save the world by bringing the people who control the world under God-control." The international crisis would not be resolved through a single conversion, he reasoned. Rather, it bubbled up from "the decadent forces of a very sick society." Convert Hitler, yet the social forces that placed Hitler in power would remain untouched. What religion could offer to Hitler and Nazi Germany was the prophetic judgment that reformed society. Beyond this, Niebuhr criticized Buchman for his "first-class travel" and attempts to win over "big men in the luxurious first-class quarters of ocean liners." German Protestant theologian Dietrich Bonhoeffer also found the plan ludicrous: "The Oxford Group has been naïve enough to try to convert Hitler—a ridiculous failure to understand what is going on—it is we who are to be converted, not Hitler." For Niebuhr and Bonhoeffer, the path to a godly global order lay not in converting evil tyrants. Rather, it required fundamental transformation of sinful society itself.[24]

Upon meeting Buchman in Berlin, Herman wrote, "he may be a prophet to some people but to me he is just a celebrity-sniper." He critiqued Buchman for being too focused on "medals, money, and titles" and expressed concern over his efforts to "add Hitler's scalp to his belt." All the while, however, Herman also sought to recruit the top American diplomats and businessmen to attend and fund his church. Moreover, his favorable views of Hitler's anticommunism matched Buchman's quite well. When Herman saw Hitler at the 1936 Winter Olympic Games, he wrote, "I must say that I was impressed by his appearance—not as a true-leader-of-men sort but as a sincere and simple man full of honest effort and good intentions." Despite their "crazy messianic tendency," Herman recollected that the Nazis had been on their "best behavior" at the Summer Games, leaving most American visitors "duly impressed" by the "New Germany." Even then, Herman continued to be duped like many other Americans who encountered the Nazis at the Games.[25]

That summer, Herman also still believed that the German churches and Hitler's regime could cooperate with each other. Like some of his Protestant peers, he felt that Hitler had a prime opportunity to marshal the German churches in his pursuit of national renewal. Such an observation showed Herman's conflicted view of the German Church Struggle. Upon his arrival in Berlin, he often went to hear Confessing Church leader Martin Niemöller preach. He admitted he found the "Confessional men" like Niemöller to be "courageous." They were the "real *Protestants*" who preached with fiery passion and conviction, he felt. He loved attending their services, which reminded him of "early Christians gathering in the catacombs." At the same time, Herman thought the more radical members of the Confessing Church disrupted ecumenical unity. He therefore proved reluctant to initially endorse the movement. Before the Summer Games, he even refused to help its pastors promote "a short statement in English of their position." At that time, he voiced his "disappointment" to them due to their schismatic views. In order to protect the American Church from Nazi reprisals, he even refused the Federal Council's request "to bring greetings from America" to a series of Confessing Church prayer meetings during the Olympics. While he attended and found the services liturgically moving, he noted a meeting of Confessing Church clergy recounted "tales of confiscations, arrests, and searches" that "seemed scarcely credible." Although Herman had recognized by then that the most ardent Nazis cared little for religion and were undertaking "a deliberate movement" to "erase Christianity from the minds of the people," he still struggled to believe the stories he heard of brazen interference in Confessing Church parishes. Instead, he argued that "the Confessionals" were too "adamant in their refusal of all compromise, even to talking it over." In his view, their posture amounted to "bullheadedness."[26]

That first summer in Berlin, Herman thus proved reluctant to take a clear stand. He even initially expressed a willingness to learn more about the *Deutsche Christen* before coming to any hard and fast conclusions. As Herman pursued further conversations, however, he did find the German Christians to be just as heretical as Leiper had indicated. He found their "Blut und Boden" theology shocking and routinely refuted their view that Jesus was not a Jew. Yet beyond disavowing their theology, Herman did not know where exactly to stand. He found himself caught in the thick of the church crisis. Earlier that year, the Confessing Church had actually divided into competing wings, the more radical side, led by Martin Niemöller, and the other more moderate, led by regional bishops such as Theophil Wurm. At that point, Herman found himself most sympathetic to the many church members who opposed "Niemöller's uncompromising stand" and instead wanted "harmony" with Hitler but "without government control." Having surveyed the ecclesial landscape more thoroughly, he decided that he felt a stronger affinity in the church struggle with the "old, conservative stalwarts" like Wurm, as opposed to the "violent radicals among the confessional churchmen."[27]

In 1937, however, Herman's professed neutrality began to turn when the Nazis arrested Niemöller and clamped down further on Confessing Church parishes. It became clear to him he should not have doubted their earlier stories. Charged with treason for protesting Nazi interference in the churches, Niemöller was eventually imprisoned in the Sachsenhausen and Dachau concentration camps, where he remained from 1938 to 1945 as Hitler's personal prisoner, alongside other enemies of the Nazi state. Herman's earlier hesitations about the Confessing Church were beginning to fade underneath more overt signs of Nazi oppression.[28]

For many American Protestants back home, Niemöller's "martyrdom" at the hands of Hitler helped foster a narrative of Protestant resistance to the Nazis. In particular, American Protestant Ewart Edmund Turner, one of Herman's pastoral predecessors at the American Church in Berlin, heralded Niemöller's "colossal action" to protect the church against the "brown invasion" of the Nazis. Just a year later, *TIME Magazine* followed this line of thought in depicting Niemöller as a "German martyr" on their front cover. Meanwhile, American churches held vigils for the imprisoned pastor. They lauded Niemöller and the Confessing Church for practicing the "totalitarian nature of the Christian faith" and acting as a spiritual counterweight to Nazism. Niemöller's example, they believed, demonstrated how Christ made more powerful claims on the lives of Christians than any fascist dictator. Yet they were also sorely mistaken. Even as Niemöller languished away in concentration camps, in 1939 he still offered to captain a U-Boat when the Second World War broke out. Moreover, he never opposed Hitler as the leader of the German state. In contrast, Hitler's imperial and racial policies found a wide backing, not only with Niemöller, but also among many German Protestant clergymen, who believed that if Germany fell, the "West" itself would fall. They therefore willingly supported the march to war and prayed for Nazi victory. Nonetheless, a myth of total resistance had been born.[29]

As the Nazis clamped down on the Confessing Church, Herman's role representing the American ecumenical movement abroad grew all the more important. Having already attended ecumenical meetings as a student in 1935, Herman earned an invitation to the 1937 ecumenical conference in Oxford, where he connected with leading Protestant ecumenists from the United States and Europe. American ecumenists Samuel McCrea Cavert and John Foster Dulles delivered speeches that moved Herman in their affirmation that the ecumenical movement could instill in the world community the universal spiritual values it lacked. For many of these American ecumenists, their study of Nazi nationalism had led them to more fully question whether the nation-state could be a vessel of God's work in the world. They likewise condemned Nazism as a dangerous manifestation of a kind of "secularism" that sought to eliminate all traces of religious belief from the world. In response, the delegates called for the formation of a World Council of Churches, a "counter-totalitarian" spiritual order that would make equally "totalizing" claims upon the world's Protestants and thereby rival the totalitarianism of regimes like Hitler's, as well as the nationalism, militarism, and racism such regimes espoused.[30]

Herman would play a small yet important role at Oxford. When the Nazi government prohibited most German Protestants from traveling to the conference, he offered what firsthand news he could from German colleagues, such as Hanns Lilje, who claimed Herman "was of great service to the German church . . . cut off from Oxford." Leiper likewise praised Herman for his ambassadorial work. Herman in turn soaked up the ecumenical atmosphere. Following the Conference, he preached to his Berlin congregation that Oxford's "true ecumenicity" would stand as a "guiding light" for Protestant Christians in the decades to follow." For his part, Dietrich Bonhoeffer continued to question why the ecumenical movement still sought to maintain ties to all church factions in Germany. The time had long passed, he felt, to recognize the Confessing Church as the true church in Germany.[31]

After the conference, American hopes grew that the proposed World Council would be a Protestant vehicle for a new global order. Yet despite their optimism, their statements and speeches could not halt Hitler's expansive endeavors. After the Nazis successfully annexed Austria in March 1938, Herman admitted that he "reluctantly admired" how Hitler secured "what Germany wants" through "clean cut action." Months later, the Nazi leader would add the Sudetenland to this growing list of spoils. Ecumenists like Herman praised the 1938 Munich Agreement's "appeasement" for preventing armed conflict, but it was becoming clear to more perceptive observers such as Reinhold Niebuhr that Hitler's intentions were far more severe and the ecumenical response far too tepid.[32]

As Hitler accelerated Germany's march to war, Herman's ministry revolved all the more around the "Jewish question" in Germany. Over the spring and summer of 1938, German persecutions of Jews provided overt evidence of the Nazis' brutal intentions. While Herman recorded these scenes of persecution with noting alarm, he often proved reluctant to aid the Jews who came to him seeking relief. Entrusted with tremendous responsibility as an ecumenical pastor in the heart of Nazi Germany, he would exhibit in word and deed a clear anti-Judaism—a theological hatred of the Jewish faith—and at times a streak of antisemitism—a sociopolitical and racial hatred of the Jews. Herman's conflicted record on Jewish-Christian relations revealed how the currents of religious and racial prejudice continued to appear even within committed ecumenical Protestant circles.

Herman realized that the "Jewish question" would occupy much of his pastorate just weeks after he had arrived in the Nazi capital. At that point, two German Jews sought Herman's help in securing lodging and American visas. Privately, he expressed his bemusement that they had come to an "American 'Protestant' minister in Berlin" for help. Placing emphasis on his identity as a "Protestant," Herman revealed that he initially saw little need to care for those who did not share his faith. His lukewarm response also pointed to his conviction that genuine friendship between Jews and Christians remained impossible outside of Jewish conversion. The American ecumenist confessed that he thought the Jews practiced "an inferior religion" and needed to be redeemed from their erring ways. "We must go after the Jew and bring him into our Christian faith," he proclaimed. If the Jews refused to convert, Herman even entertained a more sinister option. In that case, he wrote, "we must throw him and his inferior religion out of our society (because Judaism at its highest is not equivalent to Christianity at its highest)." At that point, Herman's plain words left open the possibility of forcibly removing Jews from cities and towns, an occurrence he would eventually witness before his own eyes. Until the Jews converted, he implied, he would not consider them his spiritual or civic neighbors. On this matter, Herman was not alone. In both the United States and Germany, anti-Judaism found broad expression among Protestants of the interwar era. Drawing from a long-standing theology of supersessionism, many Protestants believed that Christians had supplanted, or "superseded," the Jews as the people of God. Protestant leaders struggled to see in this era how their supersessionist theology and religious hostility could actually undergird racial antisemitism itself. Numerous others openly expressed such racially rooted hatred of the Jews. In particular, very few German Protestants openly condemned Nazi antisemitism. They proved far more concerned with preserving the church's autonomy.[33]

Herman's posture on Jewish-Christian relations, however, did incline him to help what he described as "non-Aryan" Christians in need. He often treated Jewish Christians with respect and welcomed them in the American Church, even in the face of congregational opposition. When a Jewish Christian medical doctor contacted Herman about fleeing the Nazi Reich, for instance, the American pastor contacted foreign missionaries to see if they could provide him a post. Herman also often urged fellow German Protestant clergy to more proactively care for Jewish Christians. The American ecumenist thus proved most willing to help fellow Christians in need. Throughout his time in Berlin, he kept his focus on protecting and serving the interests of his co-religionists and the American Church.[34]

Although Herman called for Jewish conversion, when Jews came to him seeking to convert and be baptized, he often doubted their motives and proved resistant to administer the sacrament. When two Jewish Americans married to German Protestants sought baptism in 1936, for instance, Herman admitted "these questions" of whether or not to comply gave him "a real headache." He took significant time to discern whether the two women were "politically" motivated, as he put it. He suspected they might simply be seeking a degree of Christian protection from Nazi persecution following the passage of the Nuremberg Laws. Herman also faced pressure from some of his congregants who were stalwart antisemites. They had called for a complete ban on baptizing the growing number of Jews who visited their church. Beyond the resistance of his reluctant congregation, Herman also worried about potential ecclesial and diplomatic ramifications. He was cautious to interfere in what he felt was a German Protestant responsibility, as well as to potentially endanger the standing of the American Church and diplomatic corps in the Nazi capital. In this instance, however, Herman felt he had a right to get involved due to the two women's tangible connection to the United States and what he deemed to be their genuine desire to convert. Despite some congregational opposition and a non-committal response from the US Embassy, Herman baptized the two women in a quiet and private ceremony that moved them to tears.[35]

In practice, however, Herman often hesitated to help the Jews who came to him. In 1938, even more sought the sacrament following an alarming "uptick in antisemitic outbursts" across Berlin and the rest of Germany. Many only had a single Jewish parent and had been educated as Christians. While they were well-versed in the Christian faith, Herman ultimately turned them away, informing them that they had "waited too long." He reckoned that their worsening political situation solely motivated them. When one German Jew sought out of such "political reasons" to be baptized, he retorted back that such dishonest motives caused the "Jewish-Christian trouble" unfolding across Germany in the first place. In making such a claim, however, Herman overlooked that for centuries, Christians had actually been the root cause of the issue. They had often demonized the Jews, forced their conversion, and pushed them to the margins of society. Moreover, he showed a double standard. While "political" conversions were inappropriate for Jews, they were not for American diplomats who would advance his ecumenical cause.[36]

Beyond doubting their motives, Herman came to other rationalizations for his inaction. As an American minister, he often felt the Germans were ultimately responsible to care for those suffering in Berlin. Moreover, he was a foreigner, he reasoned, living under the threat and intimidation of the Gestapo. He claimed he did not want to harm "a good diplomatic relationship" between the American and German governments, nor to endanger the standing of the American Church. As he put it, "The last thing I desire is to have anybody think that the pulpit of the American Church is trying to undermine the German government." If the Nazis caught the American Church somehow aiding Jews, Herman feared, perhaps they would shut it down, effectively putting out the flame of American Christianity in the heart of Germany. In the end, Herman felt he was "very helpless" as an American pastor in the face of such "evident distress." His reflections illustrated how even a young and promising Protestant ecumenist, full of idealism and eagerness to improve the world, justified his decision to not get involved.[37]

Deep down, however, Herman also remained indifferent due to the racial prejudice he harbored against Jews. In particular, when wealthier Jews came to him for help navigating visa applications, he stated he had no time or patience for these "international" Jews. He thought that they acted in an entitled manner and believed America "owed them a way out." He added that it was these "anxious non-Aryans" who were "the refugees" he was "least anxious to help." In private correspondence, the American ecumenist also used antisemitic tropes to describe what he described as "entitled" Jews. In one letter home, Herman wrote that "these panic-stricken people" reminded him of "a rat I once caught and threw in the ashcan before he was quite dead." He added, the rat's "terror-struck, beady eyes and his babyish squeal almost made me forget for a moment that he was a rat to whom I must give the coup de grace." Such diatribes continued when Billy Rose, a prominent Jewish-American orchestra leader, threatened to blackball the career of the young American singer Miriam Verne after she performed before Hitler. Herman wrote, "Of the two gentlemen, I prefer Mr. H[itler]. . . . Rose is typical of the sort of rotten Jewry that we could well dispense with in America." In making such remarks, Herman clearly dehumanized the Jews and perpetuated a ghastly tradition of comparing them to vermin and refuse. His hostile views toward wealthy Jews also mirrored the sentiment of *The Protocols of the Elders of Zion*, which erroneously maintained that an affluent cabal of "international" Jews stood behind the world's troubles. In expressing such views, Herman was certainly not alone. Many of his Protestant peers back home and in Berlin either overtly or subtly expressed such religious and racial prejudice. As an ecumenical leader, however, Herman neglected the theological resources available to him, namely Protestant ecumenism's budding interfaith, anti-racist ethic. Such an ethic enabled other ecumenists to see Hitler's brutality as a dictator and to oppose the virulent antisemitism that surrounded them.[38]

Witnessing violent persecutions of the Jews firsthand, however, Herman also experienced an internal conflict about his faith's troubled record on antisemitism and race relations. As a student, he had opposed European classmates who suggested Americans should "send all Negros back to Africa at once" or sequester them in "less populated states." He recoiled when they claimed "racial persecutions" could align with an ethic of Christian charity. He clearly opposed such state-sponsored violence. As a pastor in Berlin, he also privately wondered how "pogroms" were "possible" after meeting a friendly Jewish businessman. Based on such encounters, Herman shared with a Harrisburg rabbi that "reports of rising antisemitism" back home "greatly perturbed him." He desired to learn more from the rabbi "about the next step necessary in the Christian attitude" toward the Jews. At times, Herman did not seem far from beginning to embrace Leiper's interfaith ethic.[39]

Yet even then, Herman often proved lukewarm about supporting movements for racial equality. At times, he defended Nazi racial policies, stating that the reality of "racial inequality at this stage" made it clear that racial "intermarriage" could not be tolerated in the United States or Europe until greater racial equality across society had first been achieved. Herman had thus welcomed Jesse Owens to advance his church's cause, but he ultimately found limited reason to swiftly alter Owens's second-class citizenship back home. Instead, Herman called Nazi policies banning interracial marriage "clear-cut and decisive steps to stem and defeat this Decline of the West." Even more, he claimed the eugenic quest to purify a race "was perhaps a fine idea." Herman's own conflicted reflections showed that even committed ecumenists were not immune from the nativist, racist sentiment that defined much of American Protestantism in the 1930s. In his first years in Berlin, his record proved conflicted and his thinking torn. His uncertainty at this point translated into inaction and an acceptance of the status quo.[40]

Herman's posture began to somewhat change when he woke up on November 10, 1938 to streets of broken glass. In vicious rampages across Germany, the Nazis had openly attacked and destroyed Jewish shops and synagogues. They then blamed the Jews for the destruction and forced them to pay for the cleanup. The severity of *Kristallnacht*—"the night of broken glass"—began to jolt Herman into a more serious grappling with Christian antisemitism. He wrote that he felt "sick in the stomach from the sights of murderous vandalism" all around him. With a note of empathy, he added, "These are days of tears and despair for thousands of Jews, and days full of bitterness and disgust and shame for many thousands of Germans." The burning of synagogues especially revolted him and challenged him to reconsider his own quietism in response to such blatant persecution. The following Sunday, he delivered an especially sharp sermon to his congregation that sought to "put steel in their Christian convictions." He called out his congregants for their opposition even to Jewish Christians and reduced them to tears for their seeming indifference to the Jews.[41]

Beyond his congregation, the Germans' apathy to the events frustrated Herman as well. Throughout his Berlin years, Herman had sought to develop a sympathetic reading of the changes sweeping across Germany. In particular, he consistently disassociated everyday Germans from Nazi extremists. Like many other Americans in the 1930s, he was inclined to see "average" Germans, even Hitler himself, as virtuous, hard-working, and fair. In the United States, Germans had readily assimilated themselves into America's body politic, especially after World War I. They constituted that "old stock" of European immigration that easily fit the Anglo-Saxon ideal. The idea of the "good German" lived just as strongly in Herman's mind as it did in those of most white American citizens. Yet *Kristallnacht* challenged his notions of the "new Germany." Herman wrote home, "I feel as though all my effort to paint a fair picture of Germany" had "been cold-bloodedly sabotaged." Witnessing such violence firsthand proved a turning point that began to align him more firmly with the Federal Council, whose interfaith ethic led it to resolutely condemn the attacks.[42]

Yet even as his sympathy for the Jews grew, in the weeks that followed, Herman still proved hesitant to help the growing number of "non-Aryan Christians" and German Jews that showed up at the American Church. Some felt they had no other place to worship in the worsening environment. Others sought the support of the American pastor amidst their deteriorating political situation. Herman stated it was a "delicate" problem whether to leave the Church's doors open to them. He ultimately decided he would neither encourage nor discourage their attendance. Keeping the doors open, he reasoned, could at least provide them with an opportunity to convert to the Christian faith.[43]

As Nazi persecution mounted, Herman indeed continued to identify conversion as the faithful Christian response. As he wrote, "It's a great time for Jewish mission work!" He now confessed his belief in the "necessity of a more far-sighted plan which takes into consideration the very regeneration of the Jewish race itself. Sorry as I must feel for those who come sniveling to me in their extremity, nonetheless I cannot look upon them as desirable spiritual neighbors . . . *unless* (here is the point!) some effort is made to give their own prophetic religion back to them." In a moment when many Jews needed partners and allies, an ecumenist like Herman rejected antisemitic persecutions but proved slow to aid the Jews or to stand in solidarity with them. As the violence mounted before him, he continued to see limited possibility for genuine partnership between Protestants and Jews outside of their conversion.[44]

After *Kristallnacht*, more German Jews also pressed Herman for help in applying for an American visa. The American pastor continued to do relatively little for them. In letters home, he complained of wealthy Jews coming to him for help "with their fatty flabby hands which haven't done a day of manual labor . . . repeating over and over the catalogue of all the great Hebrews." He again returned to antisemitic tropes, stating, "They look at me in a way which I can compare only to the terrified, glistening glance of a mouse which I once had to kill." Even as the evidence began to amount before him, Herman gravely misestimated that the Nazis' real intentions were indeed to kill. At that point, he dismissed the possibility of a "final solution," claiming that such an outcome "seems impossible when one only thinks of the sheer number—500,000—eligible for this honor."[45]

Yet just weeks later, the displays of violence eventually led Herman to ponder whether a more sinister plot was now unfolding. He now acknowledged "the inevitable solution of the Jewish problem is to drive them all out of Germany . . . there is no doubt that the eventual fate of those who remain is . . . death." His premonition seemed confirmed when a German Jew, "from the chosen race," as he quipped, came to him "with his shaved head" and gave him firsthand testimony of his imprisonment in a Nazi work camp. The Jewish man had been forced to live in "very primitive quarters without adequate water supply . . . beds were four deep and more like shelves." He continued, "my witness told me that processions of caskets went out of the place every week." With the evidence mounting before him, Herman was finally recognizing that Germany's Jews were in an extremely vulnerable position. Whether he would choose to aid them, however, still remained in question.[46]

Such tensions lingered through the next summer as the Nazis prepared for war. At that point, Herman welcomed the opportunity to leave Berlin's troubles behind for a long trip across the Baltics and Scandinavia. He especially relished the time away after the theology faculty in Berlin had rejected his dissertation. Herman admitted the dissertation lacked quality, but he felt it was "good enough for Berlin." He ultimately concluded that the Nazified faculty did not appreciate his "sensational" and "picturesque" style as an American and had conspired against him.[47]

As Herman departed for vacation, Leiper and Niebuhr received distressing letters from Dietrich Bonhoeffer. Since 1935, Bonhoeffer had devoted himself to the ecumenical movement and the Confessing Church, even illegally training seminarians for the Church in secret. Bonhoeffer's frustration with the ecumenical community meanwhile grew. It had still done nothing more to concretely counteract Nazism other than issue what he felt were toothless statements. The movement was clearly failing, Bonhoeffer thought. As Germany prepared for war, he found himself conflicted on what to do if he were drafted. Fearing that Bonhoeffer "might end up in a concentration camp," Leiper and Niebuhr extended an invitation for him to teach at Union Theological Seminary and minister to German refugees. He accepted.[48]

Once in New York City, however, Bonhoeffer sensed he had made a grave mistake. Just weeks after arriving, he reversed course and sailed back to Germany on the last steamer to leave before the war broke out. Niebuhr was flummoxed. "I do not understand it at all," he wrote to Leiper. In a letter to Niebuhr, Bonhoeffer explained his motivations: "I made a mistake in coming to America. I have to live through the difficult period of our national history with the Christians in Germany. I will have no right to assist with the restoration of Christian life after the war in Germany if I do not share the tests of this period with my people." Bonhoeffer also explained that the Nazis threatened "Christian civilization." He needed to be on the front lines in defending "our civilization" that he shared with Niebuhr, a civilization that recognized "Christ as formative for its life and values." Back home, Bonhoeffer put into motion the radical ethic he had outlined in 1933. He joined his brother-in-law in a military assassination plot against Hitler. He was one of the few German Protestants to take such a bold, radical step, one that had grown out of his critical engagement with Niebuhr's realism and his immersion in Harlem. As Bonhoeffer wrote to his fellow co-conspirators in 1942, they had learned to see the "great events of world history from below, from the perspective of the outcasts, the suspects, the maltreated, the powerless, the oppressed and reviled, in short from the perspective of the suffering." It was that ethic of suffering, solidarity, and responsibility that ultimately shaped Bonhoeffer's path. While Buchman had sought to convert the tyrant and Herman reluctantly admired him, Bonhoeffer would seek to kill him. While he believed that murdering Hitler would be a sinful action, he could wager no other course of action in light of the evil Hitler represented. For him, it was the only responsible thing to do.[49]

As Herman and Bonhoeffer settled back into Berlin in early September from their respective travels, they sensed the changed mood of the city. "The air is heavily charged with serious preparation," Herman wrote home. Days later, on September 1, 1939, Nazi Germany invaded Poland. The war had begun. Following the outbreak of hostilities, Herman secured a position at the American Embassy in Berlin in its "Department of Non-US Interests." While the position offered him a needed degree of diplomatic immunity in a worsening political environment, he also hoped to strengthen the American spiritual-diplomatic connections he wanted to see develop in the foreign service. He began to oversee Embassy affairs for non-Americans in Germany, a role which had him translating documents, visiting prisoner-of-war and internment camps across Germany, and aiding visa applicants. For Herman, the new diplomatic position came as a relief. It especially allowed him to share his thoughts more candidly in letters back home that he could now send via the secure diplomatic pouch of the Embassy. With church numbers dwindling as Americans left Berlin, he also offered to volunteer as the American Church's pastor and headed up the American Emergency Relief Committee, which provided relief services to Allied prisoners of war.[50]

As the war intensified, Herman wrote home about midnight air raids and dealing with diminished rations. He also relayed how the war further clarified his view of the "New Germany." He had learned that *Shutzstaffel* and Gestapo officials viewed him as a threat. They were secretly attending his services and monitoring his activities, even interrogating his housekeeper. If the United States entered the war, a contact had shared, they had decided Herman would be the first American they would arrest. He even suffered a short stint in Gestapo detention after American officials seized German commercial ships docked in American harbors. Seeing Hitler invade neutral countries and being on the Gestapo's hit list helped Herman realize more clearly the true nature of the Nazi regime.[51]

So too did the continued struggles of the Confessing Church. Herman now gravitated much more strongly to the protesting movement. While he had once turned down their entreaties, he now began to aid them, at times storing their literature—an illegal activity in wartime—and smuggling it to other pastors. He also led a secret prayer service for Confessing Church youth in an air-raid shelter. The young men exhibited "such evidences of splendid faith," Herman wrote. Yet even then, he kept up his guard, lest he slip up and run afoul of the authorities. While he stated that he "longed to open up my heart to them," he was "non-committal on every subject" that "could be considered political or dangerous." The worsening situation of the young "lads" clarified for him, however, that the Nazis indeed aimed to "do away with the churches altogether."[52]

Herman also found himself mired in internal conflict as the situation of Berlin's Jews deteriorated under wartime conditions. By September 1941, all "non-Aryans" were required, as Herman put it, to wear the "yellow badge" in public. Soon thereafter, "non-Aryans" were altogether banned from attending public events. Herman recorded that he had "the unpleasant task of being oily and diplomatic" when "non-Aryan Christians called up or wrote . . . about permission to continue attending" his church. In order to protect the congregation, he felt he had no other choice but to ask them to not attend.[53]

Then the Nazis announced their intention to forcibly deport all Jews from Berlin to a ghetto in Poland. In the following days, Herman found himself overwhelmed by what he described as a sea of "mental cases and nervous wrecks." While he recognized he was "unnecessarily gruff and ungracious" with these Jews seeking refuge, he wrote he could not stand "their whining, moaning, hand-wringing despair." Yet again, Herman expressed his sense of helplessness in what he felt was an impossible situation. He reminded himself that he followed the policies set by the American government that refused to lift the nativist immigration restrictions against European Jews. Despite his Judeo-Christian ethic and close political alliance with American Jews,

American president Franklin D. Roosevelt felt hamstrung by an American public that overwhelmingly favored neutrality and feared refugee assistance might draw their nation into war. In the end, Americans did relatively little to aid Europe's Jews in the years before the Holocaust.[54]

Following the deportation order, however, Herman found the courage to take some action to help the Jews. He first condemned the "anti-semitic plague" from the pulpit in a sermon that he claimed "hit the bell." He also agreed to help a Confessing Church pastor hide an elderly Jewish couple on the run and supported a German Protestant mission to rescue Jewish Christian children from the deportation order. But even then, he ultimately wrote that he believed such endeavors were futile, and he finally concluded that such efforts "need not concern me." Beyond their conversion, he decided, the fate of the Jews lay outside of his purview as a Christian ecumenist.[55]

In early December 1941, a "non-Aryan Christian" approached Herman in the American Church. The man rather directly asked Herman if he hated Jews. Herman "gave him a pointblank 'No.'" Yet the man's question haunted him. He recognized "there are probably a lot of Berlin Jews who think I am unsympathetic simply because I brace myself to refuse their impossible pleas for help." Days later, Herman continued to find himself overwhelmed by visa applicants. He wrote home that his "abnormal existence" in Berlin had given him "the willies." He was experiencing a "funk," he stated, "which makes strong men weep or get drunk or smash everything in sight." He wished he could "hire a sparring partner" he could "sock" every time he got an "itch to let fly at some harmless old lady" who "asked an abysmally stupid question . . . a whole series of them" at the Embassy. Herman would ultimately not need such a defenseless partner. The very next day, the Japanese attacked the American naval base of Pearl Harbor. When Germany declared war on the United States days later, Herman would soon find himself interned as a member of the American Embassy staff.[56]

As he sat in internment, Herman reflected on his conflicted response to the challenges of his sojourn in Berlin. He wrote in his diary, "These past years have been very depressing, largely because I had to observe without being able to help." Herman felt he had offered what opposition he could. He had tried to help Jewish Christians, had called for Jewish conversion, and had gradually begun to support the Confessing Church. Yet his time in Berlin ultimately revealed the tensions that hamstrung Protestant ecumenism in the 1930s. He was a gifted young ecumenist that Leiper and other Oxford delegates wholeheartedly trusted as their ambassador in Berlin. He fully understood the theology behind their interwar Christian globalism. Yet in his public and private dealings, he often struggled to act on such convictions. His record of inaction stands out not just due to the prominent position he held in Berlin, but also for how it showcased views widely held by interwar Protestants. While he was in many ways a product of his times—and indeed, few of his American or German peers had acted any differently—his ministry among Berlin's Jews revealed the religious and racial prejudice that continued to shape Protestant ecumenism during the interwar years. In this regard, it proved difficult to differentiate the Christian ecumenist from the Christian nationalist in Hitler's Berlin.[57]

Moreover, while ecumenists ultimately condemned Nazism in principle, they often proved reluctant to concretely counteract the regime and its policies. In the end, stories of tangible Protestant resistance to the Nazis proved few and far between. Such a reality stands as a painful reminder that the religious, racial, and national allegiances of American Protestants often trumped their Christian responsibility to care for the most vulnerable. Many remained inactive and on the sidelines in the face of an impending holocaust. Nonetheless, individuals like Friedrich Siegmund-Schultze, Henry Smith Leiper, and Dietrich Bonhoeffer did choose to act. They marshalled their experiences and their beliefs to raise their voices in protest. They put their lives on the line. The solitary nature of their resistance has challenged many since to ponder how they might have acted had they lived in such a trying time: would they have spoken up? The historical reality suggests not, which makes such questions, as well as critical reflection on the failures of the past, all the more important today.

Considered together, the interwar worlds of Herman, Leiper, and Bonhoeffer show how Protestant ecumenism was far from monolithic or fixed in its views on the era's challenges. Should Hitler be converted, tolerated, or assassinated? Were the Jews friends in faith, wayward souls to be converted, or enemies to be rejected? Was racial equality an urgent necessity, a gradual goal, or an unnecessary illusion? Was the Confessing Church a faithful remnant or a schismatic threat? These questions burdened the ecumenical movement and fractured its witness. Ultimately, Protestant ecumenists struggled to meaningfully counteract Nazi fascism. As Herman awaited his deportation to the United States, he felt that reality weigh on his soul. News from the front only increased the burden. The Nazis continued to wage *blitzkrieg* with devastating effect. In the depth of that winter, he and other ecumenists sensed that their lonely flame had grown dim. Its light obscured, darkness now seemed to surround them.

4

For Christ and Country

When the Japanese attacked the American territory of Hawaii in December 1941, ecumenical and evangelical Protestants in the United States had already been urgently preparing their country for a spiritual defense of the "Christian West." Across the board, they sensed that Nazi fascism and Japanese imperialism imperiled what they felt was the world's only Christian civilization. Led by Christian realist Reinhold Niebuhr, a core group of ecumenists, including Stewart Winfield Herman and John Foster Dulles, called on their nation to responsibly exercise its power abroad in order to defeat "pagan" and "irreligious" Nazism and create a new multilateral order based on American leadership, Christian ethics, and Western democratic norms. Their efforts proved far ranging, from covert missions to infiltrate the World Council of Churches to nationwide crusades for a new United Nations. They ultimately looked to an Allied victory in Germany as a foundation for making the defeated nation the European cornerstone of their new American-led Christian world order.

While their spiritual rationale for intervention differed, American evangelicals seized on the war as an opportunity to breathe new life into their beleaguered movement, to prove themselves as faithful Americans, and to reclaim a central role in American public life. Yet their competing understanding of Christianity and democracy led them to articulate an alternative vision of America's role in the world, one that defended and advanced their commitments to conversionary mission, liberty, and unilateralism. They would emerge from the war emboldened to reclaim their country for evangelical Christianity and to press abroad in pursuit of the evangelization of Europe and the globe.[1]

The consequences of these ecumenical and evangelical wartime mobilizations were dramatic. Perhaps no other conflict more decisively shaped how American Protestants thought about their role in the world than the Second World War. Once the United States had been drawn into the conflict, Protestant ecumenists and evangelicals alike affirmed that their nation had a special role to play. The ensuing struggle emboldened their respective styles of Christian nationalism and refined their sense of moral and

God's Marshall Plan. James D. Strasburg, Oxford University Press (2021). © Oxford University Press.
DOI: 10.1093/oso/9780197516447.003.0005

spiritual exceptionalism. Meeting the trials of the hour, they activated their long-standing "conquering faith"—the American impulse to spread abroad Protestant Christianity and democracy—and seized the conflict as an opportunity to remake the world in America's image. The war revealed, however, that ecumenists and evangelicals had come to dramatically different understandings of what that image entailed. While both groups felt called to save the "Christian West," they would outline competing missions that would transform the postwar landscape into a spiritual battleground.[2]

Up until the Japanese surprise attack, Stewart Herman counted among the numerous Protestant ecumenists who wanted to avoid America's armed entry into the war at all costs. At the American Embassy in Berlin, the American pastor found himself surrounded by diplomats who thought otherwise. They consistently urged US president Franklin Delano Roosevelt to intervene on behalf of Great Britain against the Nazis. Herman's initial opposition to such a course of action rooted itself in the peace ethic that had dominated Protestant ecumenism in the interwar era. Having drawn lessons from the Great War, Herman initially disavowed armed intervention as a path to world peace. While Nazi fascism and Japanese imperialism deeply concerned him, he feared that entering the war would activate all the worst aspects of "American Empire," including a tendency for exploitative colonialism and brazen militarism. Instead, he hoped that "by proper inspiration and leadership," Americans "could blaze the way into a new world where empires will no longer be necessary." As he stated, "in the midst of the ferocity of totalitarian war, we all sense the futility of armed conflict." Instead, Herman envisioned an activist "peace force" as being the best solution for the time being. As an advocate of neutrality, he outlined the need for a "selective training in the arts of peace . . . a peace which is not merely the absence of war, but so virulent that it can wipe out militarism more effectively and painlessly than Germany mopped up Denmark." In contrast to the war-mongering Nazis, Herman believed the United States had the exceptional opportunity, as well as the needed spiritual skill, to remake the world through an activist pacifism.[3]

Due to his pacifist ideals, Herman opposed the war even after he learned of the Nazi T4 euthanasia program, a secretive campaign that murdered hundreds of thousands of disabled Germans whom the Nazis had classified as "lives unworthy of life." While Herman admitted "all of this stuff is horrible," he still claimed it was no cause for entering the war. Additionally, he opposed Roosevelt's decision to lend the British fifty naval destroyers in September 1940. While the deal granted new life to a democratic partner on the brink of defeat, Herman believed it placed a "noose" around America's neck. It was a "bargain" that marked "the beginning of an imperialistic policy which, if logically pursued," would "lead either to American world supremacy or to national disaster." Herman did not want to see a militaristic "Christian America" arise in the world. Rather, he desired to see America's ecumenical faith peacefully restore world order through enlightened diplomacy and Christian fellowship.[4]

To a Christian realist like Reinhold Niebuhr, ecumenical neutrality and isolationist pacifism amounted to moral irresponsibility. While Niebuhr had also been a pacifist in the 1920s, his clear-eyed understanding of fascist regimes had led him to believe that there were "historic situations" that required the use of violent force, such as "defending the inheritance of a civilization" against "tyranny and aggression." "War is one of the most vivid revelations of sin in human history," Niebuhr admitted, yet simply "disavowing" war was also morally irresponsible in the face of Nazi fascism. As Niebuhr watched the British succumb to defeat at Dunkirk in May 1940, he believed an unprecedented "crisis" of Christian civilization was unfolding. As he put it, "the most powerful state in Europe has sworn to destroy our North Atlantic civilization." As the Nazis pushed the British out of the continent and neutralized the French, Niebuhr warned, "on the eastern shores of the Atlantic, freedom has disappeared from an entire continent."[5]

Niebuhr clearly thought such a crisis demanded an American response. He accordingly founded a journal, *Christianity and Crisis*, in February 1941 to counteract the pacifist isolationism of his ecumenical colleagues and *The Christian Century*. In the journal's opening editorial, the dean of Christian realism reflected on his nation's special responsibility to defend the West. His argument rested on his view of the "North Atlantic world," or what he deemed the cradle of Christian civilization. The "North Atlantic Basin" constituted a spiritual-democratic zone that had nurtured the defining ideals of the "Christian West," including the dignity of the human person and ordered liberty. These "qualities of the human spirit," he wrote, flowed from the "priceless legacy" of "both the Reformation and Renaissance." In particular, these Western virtues had given life to American democracy and its voluntary religious culture. Now these principles needed a defender. As Niebuhr put it, Americans were "the trustees of this North Atlantic society . . . the heirs of this freedom." While he resisted the claim that the United States was somehow more virtuous or exceptional as a result, he did believe the time for responsible international action had arrived. In the near term, that meant passing the "Lend-Lease Bill," which would provide the British with additional military aid in their fight against Nazi Germany. In January 1941, Niebuhr testified before the Senate Foreign Relations Committee in support of the bill. In the long term, however, it meant mobilizing for war.[6]

Niebuhr's vision found allies in the presidential administration of Franklin Delano Roosevelt. In 1938, Francis B. Sayre, Roosevelt's assistant secretary of state, had already outlined the growing transatlantic crisis in Niebuhrian terms. As Sayre put it, the "titanic forces" of fascism, Nazism, and communism were in "irreconcilable conflict with the fundamental teachings of Christ and many of the precious values of Western civilization." In response, Sayre called on American Protestants to revive their "conquering faith" and make their "Christianity more virile and dominant in the world today." A professed Wilsonian internationalist, Roosevelt also believed the United States needed to defend Western democratic freedoms and religious faith in the world. While hamstrung by a domestic mood favoring neutrality, he nonetheless affirmed that the United States stood with Britain in the democratic freedoms outlined in the Atlantic Charter. In October 1941, he then warned the American public that the Nazis planned to eliminate all religion in the world and replace the "God of love and mercy" with "a god of blood and iron." Roosevelt increasingly made the war about protecting these precious American values—religious freedom, democracy, and international goodwill—and extending them to the rest of the world.[7]

With time, even a cautious ecumenist like Herman found the realist reasoning of Niebuhr, Sayre, and Roosevelt convincing. The Japanese surprise attack on Pearl Harbor especially sobered Herman's pacifist idealism. His months-long internment with the US Embassy staff in Berlin also granted him time to reassess what he saw as an ethical response to war. On December 14, 1941, Herman and the Embassy staff, including leading diplomat George Kennan, were relocated to a hotel in Bad Nauheim, Germany, where they remained interned until their repatriation to the United States in May 1942. Sitting in Bad Nauheim, Herman began to sketch out a book about National Socialism that brought together his various encounters with Hitler's regime and observations of German Protestantism. His reluctant admiration of

Hitler's tact as a diplomat had ceased. Instead, he now sounded like a converted realist in condemning "the secular church-state" of Nazi Germany for creating "the crisis of our civilization."[8]

Upon his repatriation to the United States, Herman got to work sounding the alarm. Tales of his internment and arrest by the Gestapo had turned him into a minor celebrity. The "ex-captive of Nazis" took advantage of the moment. He embarked on an international speaking tour in order to educate American and British Protestants about the Confessing Church's struggle against the Nazis. Beyond addressing multiple American colleges and Protestant assemblies, he toured the British Isles for six weeks at the behest of the British Council of Churches, delivering stirring addresses about the Nazi threat to Protestantism and calling for transatlantic spiritual solidarity against Hitlerism. Herman's own transformation—from neutral pacifist to sober yet principled advocate of American intervention—reflected the transition many American ecumenists made that same winter and spring in the face of Japanese militarism and Nazi *blitzkrieg*.[9]

As Herman returned home from his speaking tour, he knew he wanted to somehow play a role in offering a lasting spiritual solution to the emerging civilizational crisis. He found one such outlet in a visiting professorship in ecumenism at Hamma Divinity School in Ohio, where he taught on "Christian world order, the world church, and post-war reconstruction." He relished the opportunity to form a new generation of Protestant ecumenist-diplomats who could help make good on ecumenism's global mission and complement their nation's diplomatic mission.[10]

Yet Herman also sensed he wanted more: he also desired be in the field taking the fight to the Nazis. He had already come to view the American state as a valuable ally in the ecumenical quest to build a new Christian world order. He now hoped to supply the American war cause with an underlying spiritual dimension. Together, the ecumenical movement and the American state could defeat fascism and create a new international system premised on peace, multilateralism, and democratic values. To advance this dual ecumenical and national cause, Herman inquired with contacts in the War Department whether the government had "all the information that it needed from the Christian underground in Europe." Perhaps the churches could be mobilized as an anti-Nazi force in the conflict, Herman suggested. The fledgling Office of Secret Services—a wartime spy agency organized under Roosevelt's watch—found Herman's vision alluring. The young American's religious and diplomatic connections in Germany, along with his terrific language skills, made him an ideal recruit.[11]

In November 1943, Herman thus found himself reporting for OSS duty in Washington, DC. In Maryland's Catoctin Mountains, he underwent an intensive training regimen in the art of espionage and war. In several respects, the transition was jolting. The one-time pacifist pastor was leaving behind sermons for spy craft, catechisms for covert operations, and the pulpit for pipe bombs. Yet Herman also found that his pastoral skills—including the art of persuasive communication, a knack for languages, and a deep knowledge of German history—lent themselves well to the work of espionage in the European theater of the war. The budding spook shortly thereafter received his first assignments to the OSS Western and Central European Special Operations units. Stationed in London, Herman began to recruit and assess agents for covert missions against Nazism across Europe. In particular, he drew up plans for small guerrilla units that would harass Nazi platoons and trained "lone-wolf" operatives to wreak havoc behind Nazi lines. As he planned warfare against Hitler, he also provided intelligence on German religious and political life, networked with the German exile community in London, and met regularly with British clergy to plan postwar reconstruction work. "Wild" Bill Donovan, the director of the OSS, praised Herman for his "intimate knowledge of the enemy" and noted that the pastor-turned-spy greatly assisted the government in its quest to defeat Nazi fascism. In working for the intelligence agency, Herman was just one of the many American Protestant pastors and missionaries who sought to bring the Axis powers to an end and create a new Christian world order out of the ruins of war.[12]

Herman's story illustrated the calculated journey many American ecumenists made as the war unfolded. They had initially seen war as morally evil and in conflict with Christ's nonviolent example. Yet the Axis threat to Christian civilization had led a growing number of ecumenists to embrace Niebuhr's realism and accept the war as a sobering necessity. The war itself could be a refining fire, they hoped. The United States could defeat the Axis, subdue the world's chaos, and create a new kind of world order. As Henry Luce, the son of Protestant missionaries put it, the American war effort could mark the dawn of the "American Century"—a moment of ascendancy for "Christian America" and an unprecedented opportunity for the United States to expand the American system across the globe. Luce's bold vision reflected the enduring confidence of some American ecumenists in the moral exceptionalism of their country and their churches. They believed that the church and the state together could lead the way to a more just, tolerant, and peaceful world order premised on American leadership, the American system of democracy and free markets, and multilateral spiritual and diplomatic networks. In this regard, American ecumenists revived a sense of spiritual and national exceptionalism of their own, one that wed the cause of Christ and country together and invigorated their long-standing commitment to Wilsonian internationalism. Granted, many American ecumenists still clothed their wartime nationalism in caution. They remained resistant to what they described as an exploitative, power hungry, and unilateral style of American imperialism. They also were not hesitant to critique their government for indiscriminate bombing campaigns and the tactics of total war. Yet even with this note of caution, their wartime mobilization also revived older notions of Christian nationalism and fostered visions of "Christian America" redeeming and remaking the world.[13]

As they mobilized for war, American ecumenists indeed began to draft bold plans for the creation of a new Christian world order out of the ruins of war. In surveying the crisis of their civilization, they began to target Germany as the prime territory for constructing a new kind of international system along democratic and ecumenical lines. They accordingly planned a reconstruction campaign to spread America's ecumenical values to Germany, promote spiritual and civic reforms within German churches, and integrate the defeated country into a multilateral federation of nations. Through fostering a spiritual and political reformation in the heartland of Protestantism itself, they believed they could resurrect Germany as a Christian and democratic partner and a bulwark against the "global giants" of fascism, communism, and secularism.

Given his firsthand experiences and rising stature as an ecumenical pastor and spy, Herman played a leading role in identifying Germany's perceived shortcomings and casting a vision for its postwar reconstruction. In 1943, he gathered his reflections on Nazism and German Protestantism in his first major publication, *It's Your Souls We Want*. Dedicated to the Confessing Church, the book narrated National Socialism's quest to destroy Christianity and the German church's courageous response. It likewise outlined a religious rationale for taking the fight to the Nazis. In contrast to his blurred interpretations as a young student, hindsight helped Herman develop a clear-cut take. Instead of an honest diplomat, Hitler was now depicted as a pagan demagogue. Herman likewise portrayed Nazism as a totalitarian and pagan movement that enchained the "souls" of the German people. So too had the Nazis attacked the democratic freedoms of the West, namely religious liberty, and used the German Christian movement as an instrument to implement their political will. For all these reasons, Herman argued, Americans needed to oppose Hitler and support the global ecumenical movement. His analysis received mostly glowing reviews. While *The New Republic* lauded the book as "persuasive and brilliant," Henry Smith Leiper named the "colorful" treatise the "best" he had found on the Nazi "threat to Christianity." Union Theological Seminary professor Henry van Dusen likewise acclaimed the work as "splendid and comprehensive" and stated "Herman has done us all a service."[14]

Besides firing up Christian realists, Herman's analysis also contributed to the emergence of a wartime myth of heroic Protestant resistance to Hitler. In Herman's view, the Confessing Church's opposition in church affairs amounted to wholescale defiance of Nazi totalitarianism. His firsthand perspective overlooked, however, the ways in which German Protestants, Confessing Church leaders included, had actively supported Hitler's rise to power. The American pastor also neglected to robustly reflect upon Protestant ecumenism's struggle to grapple with Nazi antisemitism. Instead, Herman lauded the Confessing Church for its limited operations to help Christian Jews escape Germany. In these efforts, Herman claimed the "Confessional" churchmen had "acquitted themselves heroically." Herman ultimately absolved Germany's Protestants for being generally "helpless to mitigate" the Nazi "growth of terror" against the Jews. That interpretation fit his observations about his own experience: it was "impossible" to help the Jews or to counteract Hitler. A mostly praiseworthy review in the *New York Times* subtly identified some of these oversights. The reviewer wrote that Herman "leans over backward to be fair and sympathetic to the great silent body of Germans who distrust Hitler but go along with him for various reasons of their own. Perhaps he is too sympathetic and too quick to condone the cowardice and apathy of the majority."[15]

Like many ecumenists of his era, Herman struggled to see clearly the uncomfortable truths about the 1930s. The myth of the church's righteous resistance hid its real record of accommodation and admiration. While German Protestants had certainly protested Hitler's interference in the churches, they had largely remained silent on matters of the state and racial discrimination. Herman's account illustrated how in the war and the ruins it left behind, Protestant ecumenists would increasingly come to see themselves as the most fervent opponents of Nazism. In their view, that identity also made them the most heroic hope in the present crisis. Yet it absolved them as well of their inaction and prevented a deeper level of critical reflection about their complicity with antisemitism, the Holocaust, and Hitler's regime.[16]

In contrast, Herman and other ecumenists had their eyes fixed on the spiritual reconstruction of Germany they desired to pursue after the war. Herman's book developed a grand spiritual diagnosis of German spiritual sickness that drew a direct line from Luther to Hitler and prescribed an American cure. "From the Reformation to the National Socialist Revolution," Herman wrote, the German church had "been sheltered under the arm of the German state." Consequently, the Germans never knew "the religious independence" so emblematic of their American peers. Nor had the German church undergone the same "religious phenomena" as American Protestantism, such as the Great Awakenings which "blew with such destructive and cleansing force" through the United States. As a result, Herman surmised, American Protestantism had developed a robust congregationalism, a spirit of lay activism, and a critical public role. The ecumenist-turned-spy believed these Protestant values in turn had nurtured an ideal democratic and civic society. In contrast, he reasoned, German churches had grown to rely on compulsory taxation and hierarchical bureaucracies. In his view, their lack of activism resulted in civic and spiritual quietism that only aided the rise of totalitarian regimes. The Confessing Church marked a promising development to Herman, however. It had begun Germany's spiritual renewal and democratic transformation and stood out as a promising partner in the mission to renew Protestant Christianity and promote democracy in the heartland of the Reformation.[17]

Herman accordingly concluded the book by making the case for an ascendant "Christian America" in the postwar world. The Nazis had gone for the souls of the people, he claimed. Americans would need to likewise win over the hearts and minds of the Germans in order to promote a vibrant Christian democracy in the center of Europe. He called for a "new era" in German spirituality, assuring his American audience that the Germans knew "to a very great extent the imminent need for a complete reorientation of Christian faith and life." He noted that only international communism could rival the Christian churches in their ability to awaken the hearts and minds of the people. The church in Germany and throughout Europe proved weak, however. It needed American aid and guidance. Only "Christian America" had the know-how and selfless spirit to promote an "ecumenical brother-hood among Christians" and "establish an international order." In response to Germany's wayward course, Americans would need to activate their polit-ical and spiritual energies in a far-reaching reconstruction effort. As Herman put it, the resurrection of Europe would not be solely a matter of "economic rehabilitation, nor even of re-education in an academic sense." It would also be a moment of "spiritual reformation and revival."[18]

Herman's vision resonated with his fellow ecumenists, who were quickly embracing a wartime ethic of "global responsibility." In the midst of the con-flict, American Lutherans especially called for transatlantic activism. As American Lutheran Church pastor Arnold Jahr wrote, German Protestants had once aided fledgling American congregations in the nineteenth century. Yet a century later, the situation had decisively reversed itself. Two world wars had led to Germany's decline and America's ascent. Jahr now declared, "Today Germany and the Scandinavian countries with the rest of the world look to America as the center from which Lutheran world action must ema-nate." In the ruins of the war, Jahr reported, Europe's cry resounded: "Come over and help us! Make haste!" It was now time, as Jahr put it, to "repay our debt" through preparing a broad program of aid, relief, and reform. Reinhold Niebuhr likewise believed Americans had a special responsibility to promote Western norms and a democratic order in the world, starting in Germany. He rejected the "irresponsibility" of "isolationist imperialism" and instead wanted to wield America's great power in the exercise of "world responsi-bility." He especially believed the United States stood primed to create "a tol-erable system of mutual security" and a new kind of international system, one that was multilateral and based upon mutuality and consensus.[19]

Niebuhr indeed identified Germany as ground zero in America's transat-lantic mission to create this kind of order. In 1944, the American realist had lamented, "Of the many tragic aspects of our age, none is greater than the failure of Germany. It is the failure of a great people, fallen to as low a state of moral and political corruption as we are likely to see for centuries." He likewise reflected that the Germans had never achieved "the foundation for democracy" due to their "old aristocratic military tradition." He thus called on Americans to guide Germany's postwar democratization, first building the spiritual foundation needed for democracy, then establishing "civil liber-ties," "free elections," an "open society," and a critical public spirit. The Allies would also need to remove high-ranking Nazis and outlaw Nazi institutions. Finally, Niebuhr called for substantial American investment in Germany and the issuance of interest-free loans to bankroll recovery. He outlined a postwar program of reconstruction that found broad acceptance among Federal Council leaders.[20]

For many of these ecumenists, remaking Germany was but the starting point for establishing an entirely new world order of democracy, human rights, and multilateral security. To advance such a cause, the Federal Council organized the Commission on a Just and Durable Peace and campaigned for multilateralism at home. Chaired by Presbyterian lawyer John Foster Dulles, the Commission channeled Wilsonian internationalism and ecumenical values into its "Six Pillars of Peace," which included international collaboration, peaceful change, armament control, economic cooperation, self-determination, and religious liberty. At heart, the Commission drew up a moral framework for the new United Nations. Protestant ecumenists recognized such a multilateral vision had already experienced defeat in the United States after the Great War. They were determined not to let that happen again. To rally support among everyday Protestants, FCC member churches organized national crusades under the banner of "Christian Mission on World Order." One such crusade sent a "flying squadron" of preachers, politicians, and diplomats to over a hundred cities across the nation. An impressed politician heralded it as "the greatest crusade since Jesus sent his twelve disciples out to preach the brotherhood of man." As Niebuhr put it, American Protestants could no longer "disavow" their "responsibilities for the preservation of our civilization against the perils of totalitarian aggression." Niebuhr thus summoned American Protestants to "the tragic duty of saving the present world from tyranny" and "the task of rebuilding a new world." Not only was Protestantism a source of democracy itself, he believed, it also could pare back the excesses of American nationalism and foster ecumenical cooperation in the world. Ecumenists thus envisioned the war as America's moment to create a new world order that in their view had been a long time coming.[21]

As they reflected on postwar reconstruction, some American ecumenists also engaged in critical self-reflection about America's own shortcomings. Plans to remake Germany abroad prompted calls for reforms at home. In particular, as the war ended, Federal Council leader G. Bromley Oxnam reflected on the "seedlings" of Nazism in the United States. "The Nazis aren't licked yet," Oxnam warned. Too many Americans rejected the human dignity of their fellow citizens, just like the Nazis did. Oxnam especially compared Nazi racism to Jim Crow segregation in the South. He also called on Americans to achieve full "economic democracy" for their workers. Similar to Leiper in the 1930s, Oxnam found in Nazi Germany a reminder for American Protestants to "take an active and personal interest" in achieving a just democracy at home.[22]

Even before Oxnam called for reform, however, black service members in the US military had already begun such campaigns. In joining the war effort, nearly one million black soldiers worked to defend and spread democratic freedoms abroad that they scarcely enjoyed at home. In this regard, the black Protestant tradition spoke a powerful prophetic rebuke to the exceptionalism of Christian nationalists. For some, the United States was less so the chosen Israel and more so the oppressor Egypt. Nonetheless, black Americans put their lives on the line for change. One black cafeteria worker, James Thompson, hoped the war could purify the American nation itself, making it a "true and pure democracy." He defied those at home who perpetrated "ugly prejudices" and were "seeking to destroy our democratic government just as surely as the Axis forces." In 1942, black Americans built on Thompson's call for a "double victory" and announced the Double V campaign that called on Americans to defeat Nazism abroad and Jim Crow at home. As black sociologist Horace R. Cayton, Jr., put it, Americans needed to exorcise the "Hitler that lives in us" as well, not just in Germany. The campaign further galvanized the black freedom struggle for full democratic equality in America. Some ecumenists such as Oxnam rallied to the cause. They embraced racial equality at home as a central component of an Allied victory. Yet not all mainline Protestants followed Oxnam's example, with some preferring a more gradualist approach to civil rights. Others proved reluctant to engage at all, in part due to underlying racist attitudes, as well as a fear that such "radical" change would undermine "order" in American society. Some white Protestants would even cast civil rights as a communist plot to inspire insurrection and instability at home.[23]

Indeed, even in the midst of the war, the American alliance with the Soviets concerned a growing number of mainline Protestants. Working out of the OSS branch in London, Herman especially grew worried that the Protestant church would be in a weak position in comparison to Marxists and secularists across the European continent. He increasingly sought to elevate the prominence and highlight the importance of the churches in his government's postwar planning. He would soon find himself at the heart of an American mission to use the World Council of Churches as a vehicle of democratization and anti-communism in Germany. That partnership emerged out of a friendship with a like-minded spook named Allen Welsh

Dulles, the younger brother of John Foster Dulles. Allen led an OSS intelligence operation out of Bern, Switzerland, that identified and supported anti-Nazi movements active in Germany.

In that role, Dulles was already hard at work seeking to use the European churches to counteract Nazism. In particular, Dulles had recruited Dutch theologian Willem Visser 't Hooft as an informant. In addition to serving as provisional secretary of the World Council of Churches, Visser 't Hooft also was known as agent "474" in Dulles's spy ring. The Dutchman proved all the ready to collaborate with Dulles on the "German problem," which he saw as "the decisive one for the whole future of Europe, and possibly the whole world." Beyond providing Dulles with direct knowledge of the Nazi plan to "exterminate the Jews," Visser 't Hooft also briefed the American spy on his contacts with three ecumenical conspirators—Dietrich Bonhoeffer, Hans Schönfeld, and Adam von Trot—who were involved in assassination attempts on Hitler.[24]

In his conservations with Dulles, Visser 't Hooft portrayed the churches as an anti-totalitarian bulwark in Germany as well. They stood "against the total victory of totalitarianism," he wrote in intelligence briefings, and were "anti-Communistic forces." He also warned that "pan-Slavism" was on the move. As he put it, Bolshevism was becoming "a tremendous menace to all countries." Yet in response to this threat, he maintained, the churches opposed communism and could become an ally in postwar democratization efforts. Visser 't Hooft nonetheless recognized that the Nazis had destroyed Germany's spiritual and political culture. He likewise estimated that Germany lacked the "long spiritual tradition" that would allow democracy to grow. In particular, the churches "learned from Luther to distinguish sharply between the spiritual and temporal realms" and accepted "complete control by the State." The German churches thus failed to "call the state and nation to order." With the right guidance, however, he thought the German churches could foster the type of "spiritual power" which could promote democratic growth. Visser 't Hooft thus called on the "spiritual forces of Germany and of the whole Western world" to promote the "Christian convictions which are the basis of Western political ideology." Finally, he hoped the OSS and the World Council could aid one another during the ensuing occupation. He warned that a vindictive peace would only allow German nationalism to linger and thwart internal renewal.[25]

The Dutch theologian's advocacy for "federalist European unity" also caught Dulles's attention. Drawing from American and Swiss political thought, ecumenists like Visser 't Hooft believed a confederation of European states could counteract nationalism and totalitarianism in postwar Europe. In particular, he called for a democratic and federal Germany to be integrated into this European union of states. For ecumenists, that federation could extend internationally into a world government. The plan had strong ecumenical and diplomatic backing. FCC president Samuel McCrea Cavert likewise called for a "federated Europe within a federated world," and even Winston Churchill would call for a "United States of Europe" after the war. Not only did such thought align with emerging American plans for a new United Nations, it also signaled the ecumenical origins of a European economic and political community.[26]

Dulles was impressed. He relayed back to Washington that he had identified a crucial foundation for a new German "state based on Democratic and Christian ideals." Moreover, he agreed that the churches could be a crucial ally in defeating communism in Europe after the war. A European continent unified in faith and politics and oriented toward the West would be a great asset to America's postwar ambitions. Following the lead of Herman and Dulles, America's intelligence community increasingly looked to the German churches and the World Council of Churches as vital partners in America's quest to democratize postwar Europe and keep communism at bay. While the Soviets were a wartime ally, Dulles believed a cold war for Europe would continue even after Nazi defeat. Both the OSS and the State Department were therefore outlining plans to swiftly integrate a defeated Germany into a Western postwar order. They called for the prosecution of high-level Nazis, robust reconstruction, and the integration of Germany into the Western capitalist economy. As the OSS drew up occupation manuals for the War Department, it advised that US military officers ought to rely upon German religious leaders and should extend a broad freedom to the purportedly anti-Nazi churches.[27]

Such a vision encountered resistance in Washington, however. In August 1944, Secretary of Treasury Hans Morgenthau opposed the OSS plan and advised reducing Germany to a partitioned agricultural state—demilitarized, deindustrialized, and denazified. In response, ecumenists went on the offensive. Herman and Niebuhr believed their churches needed to "prepare the minds" of the American people "for right relations with the German people after the war." Channeling this ethic of responsibility, Niebuhr wrote that Americans were "in the driver's seat" and controlled "the lines of historical destiny." They needed to pursue a "victory of virtue" and reject "the vengeance of victors." For him and other ecumenists, a vindictive punishment would only weaken potential democratic allies within the "Christian West." As he put it, an "impoverished Germany" would be a "menace to world peace." Americans would have won the war only to squander the peace.[28]

In pushing back against Morgenthau's plan, American ecumenists also warned against alienating "pro-democratic" and "anti-Nazi" partners within Germany. Through his leading work with the American Friends of German Freedom and the American Association for a Democratic Germany, Niebuhr especially trumpeted the Christian Democratic Union (CDU), an interconfessional party that brought together German Catholics and Protestants in pursuit of a democratic future. In Niebuhr's view, the party's goal was "to preserve the Christian West." Niebuhr and other ecumenical Protestants targeted these partners as "the kind of Germans" who could make sure ecumenical reconstruction did not just "impose democracy by force from without." The editors of the liberal mouthpiece *The Christian Century* especially affirmed this approach. Reflecting Herman's ecumenical view of the Confessing Church, they called for "releasing the indigenous spiritual forces in German life" in order to democratize Germany. There were "millions of Germans who may be looked to with confidence as the builders of a future democratic order in Germany," the editors asserted. In particular, with the right amount of American aid and support, Germany's confessional Protestants could help ensure that democracy's "Christian presuppositions" would be cultivated "in the German soul." Ecumenists thus emphasized working with these indigenous spiritual partners who shared their ecumenical and democratic vision.[29]

To enhance the profile of the churches as an anti-Nazi force, Herman delivered further intelligence on German Protestantism that excited Dulles. While Herman recognized the danger of "canonizing" the "martyred church," he still praised the institution for its "energetic" opposition to Nazism. Looking forward, the American pastor noted, "the German Church" provided "the strongest organized basis for stabilizing post-war Germany." In particular, Herman named Hanns Lilje, Eugen Gerstenmaier, and Otto Dibelius as churchmen who had proven "exceptional" in their stand against Nazism. Herman reported they could especially be counted upon "to provide Germany with a new government." In offering such intelligence, Herman overlooked the nationalist conservatism of these ranking church leaders and the internal divisions that riddled the German churches—tensions that would indeed run hot and boil over during the Allied occupation. Yet portraying the churches as an anti-Nazi and anti-communist bulwark fit the ecumenical reading of the situation, as well as the emerging consensus within the American intelligence community. In particular, Dulles had decided to find a way to covertly support the German churches during the postwar occupation, potentially through the World Council of Churches.[30]

Herman had meanwhile grown restless in his OSS post. His schemes for guerrilla war and anti-Nazi agents had not yet been implemented due to logistical challenges, an outcome which disgruntled him. He also lamented that he could not take direct part in "Operation Overlord" and "the grand invasion" of D-Day. He ultimately felt stuck on the sidelines like "a water-boy," he wrote. At the same time, Herman also sensed that such operations were really a means to an end. He found himself most enthralled by the prospect of Protestants leading the charge in building a new Christian world order. One group of Protestant activists meeting in London especially excited him. Of the group, he wrote, "Whenever I see such a gathering at work on postwar plans and become conscious of their innate generosity of spirit, my confidence in the united nations gets a big boost." In the late summer of 1944, a door opened up to pursue such work when Henry Smith Leiper cabled to Herman. Leiper had been keeping tabs on Herman's career since Berlin and now asked the London-based spy to lead the World Council of Church's postwar reconstruction efforts. Herman responded by indicating his great desire to contribute to "the rehabilitation of churches in the postwar period." "Nothing is closer to my heart," he wrote. With his ties to the OSS and diplomatic community, he recognized he could "work closely with the Army and the State Department" during the occupation of Germany. His spiritual connections in London would also enable him to keep close ties to the British Council of Churches, the Anglican Church, and the German "exile community." While Leiper offered Herman an executive leadership role in New York City, he ultimately declined the offer, stating that "sitting in New York appeals to me very little." Instead, Herman wanted to be a "leg man," using his "contacts among the churches and nations" to "re-tie the ruptured bonds" between Germans and the Americans. Herman sensed he possessed the background needed to work directly with the German churches and to steer them in an ecumenical and democratic direction.[31]

When Allen Dulles heard such sentiment from Herman, the spymaster recognized the need for exactly this kind of covert agent in the field. Dulles wanted to see "healthy church connections reestablished as rapidly as possible." Moreover, he considered the "World Council" a "powerful instrument in the pacification of Europe." As such, he suggested that Herman become a covert OSS operative embedded within the World Council. For Dulles, Herman provided a means to tap into the ecumenical organization and further the American state's postwar agenda through it. As the war ended, Herman thus formally resigned his OSS position and became a "deputy director" for reconstruction in the World Council. He was now pursuing "an 'unofficial' mission to the German church," as he put it, on behalf of the American ecumenical movement and the American state. He continued to draw paychecks from Dulles's office, even as he formally resigned from the spy agency. Through this dual role, Herman affirmed he could "serve our churches in America, the German Church, the World Church, world peace, the United Nations and the U.S.A." In his view, the causes of these disparate groups were one and the same.[32]

Herman's covert mission fit his ecumenical sensibilities well. Sensing the hazards of the postwar peace, he wanted to ensure that the occupation would unfold in a way that prioritized German spiritual reconstruction. "I'm absolutely sure that no nation likes to be occupied or dictated to—not even by the U.S.," he wrote. But he still felt his nation had a special role to play in rebuilding Europe, one that reflected his counterparts' deep sense of spiritual exceptionalism. He had therefore accepted an ecumenical role that advanced American state interests as well. Undertaking this informal commission, he hoped, would allow ecumenists to sidestep "going in on the coattails of victorious forces." Avoiding the pretense of empire, he could help restore spiritual partnerships across Europe that would undergird peace and federation while also serving the democratic and anti-communist cause. With the right amount of "our sympathetic interest and support," he wrote, American ecumenists could help lead European churches in an ecumenical and democratic direction. Moreover, Herman envisioned strengthening the standing of the Protestant churches against his faith's spiritual opponents. He sensed that both the Vatican and America's "crackbrained missionaries"—those Protestant fundamentalists—were eager to claim the continent for themselves. Through his postwar work, however, he believed he could transform Europe into a bastion of Protestant ecumenism and hold off these religious foes.[33]

In the summer of 1945, as the postwar occupation of Germany began, Herman made his way to Geneva, Switzerland, where the World Council had set up its headquarters. Willem Visser 't Hooft joined him there after a fundraising and recruiting trip in New York City. The trip strengthened Visser 't Hooft's view that the United States was blazing the way as a global spiritual leader. As he had put it, "the whole future of the Ecumenical Movement" depended on "whether America will discover it alone has the key to the situation." American ecumenists did not disappoint him. Protestant philanthropist John Rockefeller, Jr., donated a million dollars to the World Council for ecumenical reconstruction work. Herman and Visser 't Hooft would use those funds to reconstruct Germany and promote ecumenism and democracy across war-torn Europe. As the war came to an end, they endeavored to build a new Christian world order and to remake the continent through Protestant ecumenism and democracy.[34]

As ecumenists prepared these plans, American fundamentalists outlined their own rationale for supporting the war effort and pursuing postwar reconstruction. With flourishes of Christian nationalism, they called on their nation to rise up and defeat the forces of evil threatening the world. They also positioned themselves to ignite revivalist fires through conversionary missions across the North Atlantic world. Their wartime mobilization emboldened them to pursue a more powerful hold on American public life through public advocacy for evangelical Christianity, limited government, and free market capitalism.

As the clouds of war gathered in the summer of 1939, many American fundamentalists affirmed they had seen such a cataclysmic event coming. A premillennialist like Gerald Winrod, for instance, believed that global wars would naturally precede the end times. Fundamentalists also read major international events, such as the 1939 Non-Aggression Pact between Nazi Germany and the Soviet Union, as definitive fulfillments of foretold prophecies. The unexpected alliance between the two Eurasian powers led some premillennialists to see a surefire premonition of the Gomer-Gog alliance foretold in Ezekiel 38. All signs were pointing to the impending end times and cataclysmic last battles of the sixth dispensation.[35]

For some premillennialists, such forebodings fostered isolationism. Winrod and his colleagues, for instance, initially wondered why Americans should "fight on the soil of Europe" for a once proud "Christian civilization" that had now "reverted to type—back to Paganism" and been "wrecked" to ruin. Instead, Winrod promoted an "America First" and isolationist foreign policy. "We must mind our own business!" the Kansan exclaimed. The Jayhawk Nazi represented the far-right fringe of the nearly 800,000 strong

"America First" movement, which, despite its left-leaning pacifism, also attracted German sympathizers, Nazi admirers, and Aryan supremacists who all sought to keep the United States out of the war. Winrod added an eschatological rationale to the movement. In his view, the United States had been blessed with providential geographic separation from the world's conflicts. Allow the world to eat itself up in the final wars, he reckoned. Meanwhile, the United States could pursue a Christian nationalist revival. As he put it, "The time has come for a speedy return to the old-fashioned, rock-ribbed fundamentals of Christian Americanism. Our supreme need, in this hour of peril, is a spiritual rebirth." The Kansan tied his prophetic reading to pragmatic arguments too. Winrod feared entering the war would greatly enhance the powers of the state, strengthening the trend toward dictatorship in the "land of the free." Moreover, the war effort would submerge the nation in debt, creating conditions that international communists could use to their advantage. To prevent these outcomes, Winrod believed "Christians and patriots simply must demand neutrality in this solemn hour."[36]

Not all fundamentalists called for isolation, however. In fact, many were making the case for military preparedness and intervention even before Pearl Harbor. Resurrecting arguments first forged in the Great War, Baptist preacher John R. Rice saw the war as an opportunity to defeat Axis evil in the world and hold ground until Christ returned. Rice condemned Nazism in no small terms, claiming that Germany, once "the seat of culture for the world," had now "set out to rule the world by murder, by lying, by broken treaties, by Jew-hate, by the slaughter of innocents, by the murder of millions." The Germany of "Luther, Goethe, Schiller, and Wagner" had given itself over "to hate and rapine and murder and beastliness." Texan Baptist Frank Norris fully concurred. "Hitler is Satan Incarnate," he warned, a "beast" who would not stop in his aggressive plans to take over the world. "Shall we submit to the Beast?" Norris asked. "No, not for one second's time." For both fundamentalists, the choice in 1940 was thus simple: support England and France against such "beastly aggression" and prepare for the inevitable war. Rice advised his readers that they needed to be ready "to go and be good soldiers for America and for God." He added, "we should be determined to free the world from Hitler and beast rule." The Baptist fundamentalist affirmed that God had ordained governments to wield the sword in the world against such evil. Christians therefore had a "duty to God to put down blood-shed and wickedness, like that of Hitler." They were "to be against sin and help bring sin to judgement." They likewise needed to resist forces that would "rapidly clear the way for the Antichrist."[37]

Here again, Norris agreed wholeheartedly. He called for the "complete replanning and reconstruction" of America's air forces to counter the Nazi threat. While he had condemned the New Deal, he now urged Roosevelt "to follow your characteristic method, cut all red tape, smash the bottle neck to smithereens, and send Great Britain all resources at your command." The small government preacher became rather pragmatic about federal power with the fate of "Christian America" on the line. He likewise praised the president's expansionist decision to establish "advanced air bases" in Greenland and Iceland. When war came, the United States could "turn out fifty thousand huge bombers a year" that would spell "Hitler's doom." The Nazi flag burner clearly called for war against Hitler's satanic forces.[38]

Once the United States actually entered the war, fundamentalist Protestants continued to stand out as America's most outspoken Christian nationalists. Rice reminded his readership that "real Christianity involves Christian patriotism" and celebrated America's troops as "the agents of government and the agents of God." He also cautioned his fellow Americans that they could not "maintain" their "free government" if they allowed "Hitlerism to spread over the world." Fundamentalist preacher Hyman Appelman likewise reflected on how "God" was "using Hitler to remind America of the religion of the Pilgrim Fathers, the founders of this marvelous land of ours." Even a fundamentalist isolationist like Winrod fell in line. After Pearl Harbor, Winrod's *The Defender Magazine* changed its tagline to read an "evangelical, patriotic publication." It called for a "revival of Christian patriotism" and asked subscribers to bear the American and Christian flags as signs of their Christian Americanism. For these fundamentalists, the war offered a chance for a Christian nationalist revival at home.[39]

Alongside such pleas, fundamentalist evangelicals also sacralized the American nation, claiming it had a purifying role to play in the world. As Winrod now put it, "America" had been "singled out for special duty and holy service" in the last days. Prominent evangelical minister Harold John Ockenga concurred: "We have a providential position in history. Our continent was preserved to incarnate the development of the best civilization. Humanly speaking, it is almost as though God has pinned His last hope on America." For evangelicals, the United States had been founded as a Christian nation on Christian principles; now God had summoned that nation to defend those values in the world.[40]

For many American evangelicals, the American and Christian flags demonstrated their commitments to God and country as their nation waged war. This particular wartime advertisement helped popularize the pairing of the two flags in everyday American sanctuaries.
Courtesy of Wichita State University Libraries, Special Collections and University Archives.

Such a providential role sanctified the use of violent force to defeat evil. While some liberal ecumenists criticized the indiscriminate tactics of total war, such as the Dresden fire-bombing campaign which "obliterated" the city, Ockenga defended such measures. He urged on "the use of force to free the world of the menace of German militarism and Japanese barbarism." To Ockenga, limiting American power was "un-American pacifism" pure and simple. Liberal Protestants, another fundamentalist preacher added, undermined "the national defense" and "the adequate preservation of our liberty by defensive or offensive measures." To strengthen fundamentalist-military ties, Winrod ran profiles of the nation's leading generals, including George Marshall and Douglas MacArthur, heralding them as "Christian gentlemen" and "fighters for freedom." In these ways, fundamentalists became some of the most committed supporters of a new American militarism that would become a mainstay of postwar American life. They also doubled down on efforts to promote morality and revival among the armed services. In doing so, they forged an enduring connection to an institution that would become a permanent national fixture in Cold War America. While the military provided fundamentalist Protestants with a stronger public presence, it also gave them an unprecedented global reach in the postwar hour.[41]

The war also inspired fundamentalists to weaponize prayer and revival as spiritual complements to military offensives. Speaking at the Tremont Temple Baptist Church, Paul W. Rood, president of the World's Christian Fundamentals Associations, declared that faithful Christians gathered together in "prayer bands could win the war." Pondering why Americans were suffering defeat abroad at "the hands of a heathen emperor-worshipping nation," Rood found a clear answer: "we have forgotten God, rejected Christ, and spurned the Bible." America's army, navy, and air fleet, "certainly the greatest in history," would not cut it without "a nation-revival," which could swiftly "win this war" for the American people "in 30 days," Rood predicted. The fundamentalist leader called on "one million prayer warriors" to "change the history" of the United States and prepare America to "fulfill her God-given destiny which is speedily to evangelize the world." In these ways, fundamentalist evangelicals portrayed conversion and revival as meaningful supplements to invading armies.[42]

Rood's urgency for wartime revival pulsated across American fundamentalism. In Chicago, Torrey Johnson answered the call through organizing mass evangelism rallies for American youth under the auspices a new youth ministry, Youth for Christ. While he had once aspired to become a dentist, Johnson now invited America's youth to devote themselves to their nation's highest national and Christian ideals. Youth for Christ's 1944 "Victory Rally" packed 28,000 young adults and service members into the prominent Chicago Stadium. The rally revived Christian nationalism as attendees sang gospel hymns, heard the old-time gospel, honored the service members present, and prayed for spiritual and military victory abroad. The success of the

CHICAGOLAND YOUTH FOR CHRIST
CHICAGO STADIUM
OCTOBER 20, 1944

Youth for Christ's 1944 "Victory Rally" gathered together 28,000 Chicago area youth and service members to pray for revival and a swift victory for American forces fighting abroad. Such events showcased how the Second World War revived Christian nationalism across the United States.
Courtesy of Billy Graham Center Archives, Wheaton College.

rally launched Johnson onto the national scene. He soon recruited an up-and-coming evangelist and former brush salesman, Billy Graham, to join him on circuit tours across the United States, where they would hone their evangelistic style and seek to win their nation back to Christ.[43]

As fundamentalists backed the war effort, they found common cause to take the offensive against spiritual foes at home as well. Wartime operations abroad provided a fitting metaphor for spiritual maneuvers in the US. As American troops stormed the beaches of Normandy, Wheaton-based Baptist John R. Rice asked his flock for the "deepest, heartfelt, and long-continued prayer" for the Allies' "invasion armies." He tied his request for "disaster among the enemies" and "vengeance upon the German armies, for all their crimes against society," to spiritual warfare at home against dictatorship, immorality, and modernism. He especially opposed the "Bible-denying" and "un-American doctrines" of the Federal Council. Echoing evangelical

To advance the cause of Christ and country, YFC's "Victory Rally" prominently featured a color guard and other symbols of American nationalism alongside proclamations of the Christian gospel.
Courtesy of Billy Graham Center Archives, Wheaton College.

arguments about the German Kaiser, Rice claimed the FCC's modernism made "men like Hitler" and warned that "modernism" had been Germany's original sin, leading that nation to "turn her back on the Bible and on God." The Baptist revivalist counseled his people to "confess this horrible sin of modernism" if they desired "God to bless America." They could also counter the decline of America through "revival meetings" that emphasized "the virgin birth of Christ, the blood of atonement, and the resurrection and the second coming of Christ." In this way, fundamentalists tied their fight against Hitler abroad to a domestic battle against Federal Council ecumenists. The Federal Council, in their view, was promoting this source of "theological Hitlerism" in their own country. Revival, prayer, and conversion, however, could transform America into a genuinely Christian nation.[44]

To further oppose the Federal Council and protect the "American Way," fundamentalist Presbyterian Carl McIntire founded the American Council of Christian Churches in 1941 as a militant and separatist ecclesial organization.

McIntire hoped the new institution would displace ecumenists as the "voice of Protestantism." He quickly set its sights on all those "internal enemies" who threatened "American freedoms," above all the ecumenists who supported the New Deal and "economic democracy." The Presbyterian preacher sharply condemned ecumenists as "socialists" and "communists" out to destroy America's "free economy, free enterprise, free system of education, free medicine, and freedom of religion." In response, he defended "capitalism, private enterprise, and the profit motive" as "created by the living God." He encouraged his followers to read Friedrich Hayek's *The Road to Serfdom*, noting that the Austrian's defense of free markets would inspire all good Christians to "oppose" with all their "might a controlled and planned economy." The war thus mobilized McIntire to defend what he saw as America's only proper spiritual and political heritage from threats both foreign and domestic.[45]

Beyond Federal Council modernists and New Dealers, John R. Rice opined that other specters demanded vigilance, including communism, "class and race warfare," lawlessness, and antisemitism. On the final matter, both Rice and Norris targeted William Bell Riley and Gerald Winrod, whose vicious hatred of the Jews and earlier praise of Hitler had placed them under increasing scrutiny. While Riley recanted of his views, Winrod refused to budge. The American government accordingly tried Winrod for sedition due to his pro-Nazi sympathies. Winrod's fortunes turned for the worse as his wife filed for divorce and fundamentalists disowned him. While he had once been at fundamentalism's center in the 1920s, he was now being relegated to its fringes. In a passionate self-defense, he claimed he was America's "Martin Niemöller," a living martyr for the faith. Yet seeing himself as a persecuted victim thwarted critical self-reflection. It freed Winrod from facing the facts: racism had corrupted his faith.[46]

Winrod pressed onward undeterred. He nurtured an alliance with Gerald L. K. Smith, a fellow American fundamentalist and fascist. In 1942, Smith convened a group of fundamentalist and separatist "Christian nationalists" in St. Louis to start the "Christian Nationalist Crusade" and retake the country. In his journal *The Cross and the Flag*, Smith defended the "Christian American tradition" of limited government and capitalism as an eternally fixed order. He also praised German Christian theology that declared Jesus was not a Jew. Later, he would even deny the Holocaust took place and call for the deportation of Jews and racial minorities from the United States. As the war ended, the "minister of hate" rallied his followers to a host of far right-wing causes, from "outlawing communism" to "opposing a world government" to practicing the "George Washington Foreign Policy." All the while, he called on Congress to halt the "indiscriminate admission of aliens" and "prevent the mongrelization and . . . the intermixture of the white and black races." The two Geralds carried the fundamentalist, ultraright crusade into the postwar hour, drawing new recruits for years to come.[47]

As they distanced themselves from Winrod, a core group of fundamentalists wanted to shed the pejorative understanding mainstream Americans had developed of fundamentalism during the interwar years. To foster a new forward-looking movement, over one hundred fundamentalists also gathered in St. Louis in 1942 to found the National Association of Evangelicals (NAE). In the midst of war, they began to strategize ways to reclaim a commanding place in American public life. They all agreed on the fundamentals of Protestant Christianity affirmed thirty years prior: conversionary mission, revival, inerrancy of Scripture, and holy living. Moreover, they shared a common conservative political vision—limited government, free enterprise, America-first diplomacy—that opposed the progressive agenda of Protestant ecumenism. They desired to leave behind, however, the pejorative reputation and in-fighting that had defined their movement in the 1920s and 1930s.[48]

As a way to rebrand their movement, these media-savvy delegates began to refer to themselves as "neo-evangelicals." Their new approach aimed to capture, as the first NAE president Harold Ockenga put it, "the united, corporate testimony . . . of evangelical Christianity in America." Ockenga especially believed that their evangelical understanding of Christianity and democracy, freed from theological liberalism, would save their nation and Western civilization. He made the stakes quite clear: Americans could head down the road to "heathendom," or they could "rescue Western civilization by a re-emphasis of evangelical renewal." Ockenga called on these "new" evangelicals to tap into their powerful network of fundamentalist journals, radio stations, and Bible institutes to get their message back to the heart of American society. Notably, a fundamentalist separatist like McIntire refused to endorse the NAE. He felt the association was too open to Protestant modernists.[49]

Behind the NAE's forward-looking mission still stood, however, many of the Christian nationalist convictions that had long defined fundamentalism. While they condemned Winrod and Smith, even these "new" evangelicals were slow to support movements for civil rights. They ultimately claimed that only the gospel could solve the problem of racial prejudice, arguing that sin and the human heart—not prejudiced laws or social systems—were the root problem. They likewise opposed the emerging wartime movement for women's rights and argued that America's existing social order was God-given. While they welcomed European immigrants in order to convert them, they still contested international influences upon their nation, especially through the United Nations, which some within their ranks panned as "godless, a child of illegitimate alliances, born lame, and due to die." The UN, these evangelicals feared, had succumbed to Protestant modernism. It was shorn of an authentic Christian witness and instead promoted an all-inclusive pluralism. Moreover, they argued its conception of human rights denied God and rested on a secular foundation. For these apocalyptic Protestants, the "anti-Christ world order" of the United Nations also stood as a surefire way for a world dictator to take over, just as it gave other nations undue influence in American affairs. These end-times concerns regarding multilateral organizations fostered a penchant for unilateralism within evangelical ranks when it came to international relations.[50]

As the war ended, J. Frank Norris indicated how his faith's wartime mobilization would continue into the postwar hour. He began with praise for his nation's capitalist economy. "If it had not been for American industry, American tanks and planes and railroads and munitions," Norris stated, "Hitler would have won the war." He then called for continued military preparedness, noting that "we will not disband our armies if we have any sense—this time we will not junk our navy." A strong defense was necessary, Norris warned, because of "the coming war between Russia on the one side and England and America on the other." Norris and his counterparts had already felt called to defeat evil and defend liberty in the world. Their Christian nationalism had guided them through a prolonged war with the Axis powers. Now they would press onward. While their wartime mobilizations had exposed growing fractures within Protestant fundamentalism, many within their ranks could still find common ground in the dual threats of modernism and communism. They would not back down in counteracting such dangers.[51]

On the other side of the Atlantic, European Protestants pondered what these American missions would mean for their continent. Swiss Protestant Adolf Keller noted that "the heart of Europe" was "burnt out, swept empty, and filled with a nostalgia for a new content." Anticipating an American response, he contemplated whether Europeans should expect the fire of American revivals that advanced "a new vigorous and inspiring gospel," or whether Americans might lead "a cultural and educational campaign bringing the 'American Century' to the European centuries, educating them for the new democracy." Following the war, both American ecumenists and evangelicals would launch their own respective campaigns to spiritually re-make Europe. While evangelicals would bring the "pure gospel," ecumenists would advance their "universal spiritual values." In seeking to revive Europe, both would continue to fight for Christ and country. Even more, they would transform the continent into a new spiritual battleground for the soul of Europe and the North Atlantic world.[52]

5

Reviving the Heartland

On July 30, 1945, Stewart Herman departed for Germany from the Geneva headquarters of the World Council of Churches. Having identified Germany's "spiritual reconstruction" to be of "highest priority," the World Council had commissioned Herman to undertake a postwar mission of reconciliation and spiritual aid to the German churches. With the support of the ecumenical agency, the Office of Strategic Services, and the American Military Government (AMG), Herman traveled "by jeep, command car, army sedan, train, and plane all over the prostrate country" as "the first foreign civilian to reach" the German Protestant churches. Throughout his travels, the American pastor hoped to activate the German churches as a "promising instrument for national regeneration on both Christian and democratic lines." With the specters of nihilism and communism stalking Germany's cities and countryside, he hoped German Protestantism could emerge as "a bulwark of Christian principles and democratic procedures in the ex-Nazi state." In joining forces, ecumenists like Herman and state officials like Allen and John Foster Dulles worked to spiritually reconstruct Germany through an ecumenical program of "democratization and re-Christianization."[1]

For decades, American Protestants had anticipated this moment. The Allied triumph over the Nazis and the ensuing occupation made tangible the long-standing mission of bringing the American gospel to Germany. Decades of critical reflection came to fruition and culminated in efforts to promote American values among a war-torn people. This ecumenical quest to revive the Protestant heartland drew upon and refined elements of America's Christian and democratic world mission. In occupied Germany, American ecumenists wed their "conquering faith" to America's newfound project of building the "American Century." They advanced religious and state interests in tandem and used their nation's postwar primacy to build the foundations of an American-led new Christian world order.

To get the job done, Herman and other ecumenists pushed the American government to pursue a program of reconstruction and reconciliation in Germany and to avoid a vindictive peace. They also sought to mediate and

God's Marshall Plan. James D. Strasburg, Oxford University Press (2021). © Oxford University Press.
DOI: 10.1093/oso/9780197516447.003.0006

lessen the power dynamics of the occupation through establishing ties with German Protestants as mutual partners, as well as through activating the German Protestant churches as an indigenous force of spiritual renewal that could remake Germany along democratic and ecumenical lines. They finally strove to establish new international and multilateral networks that could dampen nationalism and provide a foundation for postwar peace.

As the occupation matured, it became clearer to these American Protestants that a new spiritual cold war against secularism and communism was developing. In this intensifying environment, ecumenical and occupation leaders alike worked to recruit German Protestants as Christian partners in their quest to establish a new democratic and Christian alliance against these perceived threats. Yet they also discovered firsthand that the military occupation faced tremendous challenges and could inspire fierce German Protestant resistance. In the midst of postwar ruins, German Protestants were not afraid to rise up as defenders of their defeated nation, to battle with one another for control of their church, or to oppose ecumenical reforms. As a spiritual quagmire emerged, Herman grew nervous that Americans were squandering their opportunity to create a new Christian edifice against spiritual and political totalitarianism.[2]

Herman's postwar mission represented the American ecumenists, diplomats, and policymakers who wanted to swiftly reconstruct Germany as a Christian and democratic partner in the heart of Europe. From the outset, his ecumenical mission depended on close collaboration with the branches of American state power. OSS agent Allen Dulles kept Herman flush with funds and secured the standing orders that allowed him to slip into Germany alongside occupying platoons. The military government's resources, including its modes of transport, its mess halls, and its armed protection, stood fully available to Herman, who made liberal use of them in carrying out his ecumenical mission. The military government in turn looked to a voluntary citizen like Herman to carry out diplomacy as a non-state actor. Commanding general Dwight Eisenhower authorized Herman to serve as an "unofficial liaison" between the military government and the German Protestant churches and expressed his sincere interest in Herman's work. Beyond Eisenhower, Herman reported to leading State Department officials, including Secretary of State James F. Byrnes, and briefed them on religious developments. Finally, when Truman disbanded the OSS in October 1945, Dulles proved all the more eager to work informally through Herman. While ecumenists in principle prided themselves on transcending narrow loyalties to nation-states, they made full use of state and military power in carrying out a mission that was equally ecumenical and national in its purpose. Protestant ecumenists like Herman would accordingly emerge in postwar Germany as crucial non-state agents of American foreign policy.[3]

Yet despite such collaboration, Herman's relationship to the American state was also at times fraught and tenuous. As an ecumenical and non-state ambassador, Herman sought to carry out American foreign policy on what he and other ecumenists argued was a Christian basis. In particular, he maintained that a Christian nation would carry out an occupation of reconciliation and reconstruction, not of retribution. As a result, Herman rejected aspects of the policies adopted at the Potsdam Conference, which split Germany into four zones of military occupation and called for Germany's denazifaction, demilitarization, deindustrialization, and democratization. Additionally, the Conference authorized the "orderly and humane" expulsion of thirteen million Germans living in the Soviet-occupied regions of Eastern Europe, creating in the process an unprecedented refugee crisis. American ecumenists and diplomats alike strongly criticized Truman for implementing what they condemned as Morgenthau's vindictive peace. The editors of *The Christian Century* wrote, "The Potsdam policy of vengeance is far worse than anything that came out of Versailles. In its short-range effects, it is in a fair way to destroy Germany. But in its long-term effects, it is likely to destroy Europe." Herman also stated that the Potsdam policy was "no less detrimental to the Christian cause than Hitler's Nuremberg decrees." In the chaos that was unfolding, ecumenists feared Germany would make a leftward or nihilistic turn and both Europe's spiritual future and America's postwar opportunity would be lost. In contrast, ecumenists, OSS agents, and key diplomats desired to pursue a reconstructionist peace that quickly rehabilitated the Germans as democratic and anti-communist partners. In his unofficial role, Herman therefore sought to give the occupation a different public face and to recruit German pastors as partners in Germany's postwar democratization.[4]

Herman also worked to secure the broader cooperation of the AMG in these reconstructionist pursuits. The intelligence work of Allen Dulles and the OSS had already sought to win the German churches a degree of freedom in the occupation. Recognizing the churches as an anti-Nazi force, and in part due to the sheer logistical challenge of occupying a destroyed nation, the AMG had indeed adopted a hands-off approach to religious affairs. Beyond monitoring the German churches for a rebirth of Nazism and militarism, the AMG granted the churches a broad degree of latitude to regulate their own affairs. Marshall Knappen, who helped lead the AMG's Education and Religious Affairs Branch, proved a key ally to Herman. A former Congregational minister, Knappen also shared Herman's vision of reconstructing the churches on a democratic and ecumenical basis. At the outset of his duties, he noted that Germany's Protestant clergy were leaders "of fine bearing, dignity, and prestige" who had "considerable standing in their respective communities." He recognized that the occupation would fail without their cooperation.[5]

Knappen thus worked with Herman to educate military officers on the ecumenical mission and to establish positive relations with leading clergy. From the outset, their pursuits were filled with tension and difficulty. The problems that plagued the AMG—high turnover in staff, bureaucratic conflicts in policy, and competing Washington pressures—also applied to Knappen's understaffed and underfunded unit, which oversaw Germany's educational institutions and interfaith relations as well. To complicate matters, not all American military officers were sure what to make of the churches as the occupation began. One military chaplain reflected critically on the Germans' "lack of guilt" for the war and the "hopelessly inadequate" nature of German Protestantism's "concept of the state and social ethics." He had serious doubts whether the churches could overcome their "depressing" situation. Still others suspected the Nazis might use the churches as a religious cover to sabotage the occupation. Even more were shocked at the scenes of Nazi death camps and wondered how Germany's Christians had allowed such horror to unfold.[6]

The liberation of Martin Niemöller from Nazi imprisonment strengthened such misgivings. An exhausted and irate Niemöller, now detained under the Americans, delivered a rambling interview with the American press. He declared that he had naturally placed his political trust in the Nazis and affirmed his enduring loyalty to the German nation. As he put it bluntly, "My soul belongs to God but my body to the State." In addition to espousing this kind of dualism, he added that the German people would not accept democracy. As TIME put it, the American public was "shocked." In 1940, the magazine had honored Niemöller as a Nazi martyr. Now he had seemingly condemned America's wartime cause. In response, American ecumenists went into damage control. Federal Council leader Samuel McCrea Cavert petitioned Truman to get Niemöller released from American custody immediately. Herman worked to ensure that Niemöller's views would not discredit the German churches among the military government. He defended the churches among military officers and coached Niemöller on how to deal with the American press moving forward.[7]

Niemöller's remarks should not have shocked American ecumenists, however. European Protestants had long expressed their skepticism of America's Wilsonian project. In 1942, Karl Barth had already penned a "Letter to American Christians" that poked holes in American postwar planning. Barth claimed Americans were caught up in a "mighty dangerous business" of "futurism." They were more focused on conquering the world tomorrow than preaching the gospel today, he argued. Moreover, Christian theology did not align in Barth's opinion with "this or that form of government." "Democracy," Barth pointed out, could not be "an essential, permanent, and universal Christian postulate, to be maintained under all circumstances." This prominent European theologian clearly questioned the inherent link that American Protestants drew between their faith and democracy.[8]

Dietrich Bonhoeffer likewise had expressed his concern about the prospect of America's "world domination." In the war's early years, Bonhoeffer had written to American Protestant Paul Lehmann, a former classmate of his at Union Theological Seminary, to gain a sense of American thinking on the postwar situation. Lehmann sought to assuage Bonhoeffer that Americans increasingly recognized their "interdependence with the destinies of all men round the world." They had forsaken "isolationist democracy" and were ready to create a "world of political and economic democracy." So too were they wary of a "bolshevist triumph over Europe" and the "terror of yet another tyranny." Yet despite Lehmann's reply, Bonhoeffer's fears were not wholly mitigated. In his letter back, Bonhoeffer wrote, "The development that we believe is bound to come in the near future is world domination by America . . . the power of USA will be so overwhelming that hardly any country could represent a counterbalance." Bonhoeffer also doubted that Germans would accept democracy. He instead thought a restoration of monarchy would provide postwar Germany with the most political stability.[9]

As illustrated by Barth and Bonhoeffer, European Protestants harbored their own ideas and concerns about Germany's postwar fate. As the occupation began, German Protestants in particular started to compete over who would lead a defeated Germany in the postwar hour. The same divisions that had hampered the churches during the German Church Struggle itself resurfaced in the aftermath of the war. Led by Martin Niemöller, Confessing Church leaders favored a more radical break with the past, a posture of repentance, and the implementation of democratic practices in the church. The chaos and destruction of the war, however, led many German Protestants to prefer a conservative approach that preserved church tradition and set the Germans on equal terms with the Allies. Germany's Protestant conservative nationalists began to mobilize as defenders of the German nation before the occupying armies, especially the Soviets' Red Army. Their strong nationalism would be on full display during the occupation.[10]

Many American military officials struggled to make sense of the deep historical and theological divisions that riddled German Protestantism. These competing groups of German Protestants accordingly sought to capitalize on the American officers' uncertainty in order to advance their respective causes. In initial meetings with Knappen, Niemöller made the case for radical reformation. He pointed out that the Church Struggle had allowed the "radical reformers" of the Confessing Church to develop a more critical posture toward the state. The one-time prisoner of Hitler now wanted to implement a congregational-based order that would allow grassroots spirituality and civic responsibility to flourish. To bolster Niemöller's cause, the AMG permitted him and other reform-minded clergy to gather in Frankfurt that July in order to plan the reorganization of the Protestant churches. Yet the AMG also proved initially taken with the conservative bishop of Württemberg, Theophil Wurm. In contrast to Niemöller, Wurm wanted to preserve the regional and hierarchical structure of the German churches and maintain much of German Protestantism's traditional theology. He proved open to ecumenical influence, however, and desired to establish a positive relationship with the occupying authorities. Wurm shared his hope to hold a national conference that would reconstitute the German Protestant church, and in actuality, undercut Niemöller's push for more radical reform. The military government backed Wurm as well, giving him an automobile and scarce gasoline to aid him in his organizing.[11]

In these first meetings with the AMG, German church leaders were also quick to establish themselves as opponents of totalitarianism. Wurm portrayed the Protestant church as the "one institution devoted to the establishment of a Christian order opposing equally Nazism and communism." When Wurm shared his vision of the church as a "bulwark against leftist interests," Knappen reminded the German bishop that the Soviets were still America's allies in the occupation. Along with Knappen, some Protestant ecumenists initially hoped the Americans and Soviets could work together in implementing the postwar peace. Their optimism overlooked the difficulty, however, of coordinating policies across occupation zones, not to mention the significant ideological differences between the two world powers. The Americans, British, and French would find it increasingly difficult to work with the Soviets in the Allied Control Council that was supposed to jointly coordinate the occupations. After an initial period of conciliation, the Soviets placed the churches in their zone under increasing strain. In particular, they interfered in the political organizing of the Christian Democratic Union and restricted religious education in schools. With time, Knappen's cooperative perspective would give way to more hostile relations and a divided Germany.[12]

Following these initial meetings, Knappen began to grow frustrated with the limits he encountered within the military bureaucracy. The churches often seemed a low priority to the AMG, which had been tasked with the overwhelming task of stabilizing a country that now lacked a government. Knappen noted with concern, however, the lingering prevalence of "nationalist" and "conservative-monarchical" convictions among many of the German Protestant clergy. The limits placed upon his unit also prevented Knappen and his few officers from more aggressively promoting "an international point of view among German Evangelical churchmen." To this end, Knappen sought out a civilian expert who could more directly engage with the Protestant clergy and shape German church life. He looked to Herman's "voluntary leadership" to maneuver past the limitations he faced. As Knappen put it, "not being uniformed" freed Herman to discuss "all the problems" facing the churches in an open and critical manner.[13]

For his part, Herman was more than ready to play the role that the military government could not. He believed the Potsdam directives dangerously squandered America's postwar opportunity. He also noted that the military government generally lacked an "appreciation" of the role the churches—the "only national institution" that had "resisted complete Nazification"—could play in remaking Germany as a Christian and democratic nation. Beyond Knappen, he felt the military officers tasked to religious affairs had "little vision, initiative, or courage." He wanted the entire military government, from ranking officials to chaplains, to pursue a robust program of spiritual reform and reconstruction. With the backing of ecumenists, Allen Dulles, and the State Department, Herman avoided "the red-tape" of the occupation and began to pursue his ecumenical mission of spiritual reconstruction.[14]

Starting in late July 1945, Herman traveled extensively across Germany. During his first trip from July 30 to August 19, he met with leading Protestant pastors in Freiburg, Stuttgart, Frankfurt am Main, and Berlin. He would return for three additional multi-week tours of Germany that fall and winter. His reports to the World Council and American policymakers over those months provided both parties with firsthand intelligence and observations of the postwar religious situation. They also indicated the type of reforms that he and other American ecumenists hoped would lead Germany to a new democratic and Christian future, as well as the limits they faced in seeking to fundamentally change the spirituality and theology of German Protestantism.

Altogether, Herman's postwar mission drew upon key features of American Protestantism as a guiding paradigm for Germany's spiritual reconstruction. The American ecumenical ambassador believed that German Protestants had an "opportunity for reformation" that they had not seen since the days of Luther. In such a context, he brought to mind the many arguments American Protestants had made about the German state churches and their lack of spiritual vitality. He now encouraged German Protestants to overturn the "the hollow foundation" of rote German tradition. For Herman, public activism, lay voluntarism, and congregationalism would transform the German church into a democratic force and overturn the traditional Two Kingdoms doctrine which separated the church's spiritual affairs from the political arena. Indeed, he encouraged German Protestants to develop a voluntary and active faith that he and others felt would support a "democratic and independent form of government." He also hoped German Protestants would activate the energies of lay believers, much like American churches had in centuries prior. Local congregations could thereby become the seedbeds of a new democratic spirituality. Ecumenical connections could moreover inspire new interest in German and European public life and foster support for a new "global government" and "order among nations." Through promoting these definitive tenets of the American religious experience in Germany, Herman hoped to reform Germany's spiritual culture and facilitate the democratization and re-Christianization of the country.[15]

Once on occupied soil, Herman began to pursue this hoped-for reformation by first restoring ecumenical ties with leading German pastors. He wrote in his first circular letter to German clergy that "the Church of Jesus Christ" needed "to become the cornerstone of a new world community." He added that although "National Socialism and war tried to break spiritual bonds," he was coming "to bring the German pastors back into the fellowship of ecumenical Christianity." As he visited German Protestant pastors and bishops, he urged them in particular to join the World Council of Churches. If they entered this ecumenical network, he and his fellow ecumenist Sylvester Michelfelder assured them that American Protestants possessed a "generous" spirit that would send "millions of dollars of aid" to support German church reconstruction. Before the generosity of American Protestantism would flow, however, they stated that Americans first needed to see "signs of repentance" from their German counterparts. Ecumenists thus in part used the promise of humanitarian aid as leverage to promote their ecumenical reforms.[16]

To further bolster an ecumenical spirit in German Protestantism, Herman also encouraged the purging of Nazi influence from the church. He agreed with leading American clergy that National Socialism had been a "pagan regime" and "Satanic power" that had jeopardized the Christian foundations of the German people. As such, he urged German Protestants to do their "own housekeeping" through removing the heretical "German Christians" from their ranks. He reported back to Washington and Geneva on the swift and robust removal of German Christian influence from the church. As he saw it, this decisive purge qualified the Protestant churches to be rehabilitated quickly as pro-Christian and pro-democratic partners. In taking this stance, however, Herman also did not push the German church to more deeply examine and repent of its complicity with the Nazis. It was not just the German Christians who had voted Hitler into office and had supported the Nazi war machine. Instead, Herman accepted and promoted the narrative of ecclesial resistance to Hitler.[17]

Coupled with the removal of Nazi sympathizers came Herman's call for German Protestants to repent and confess their nation's guilt. In his meetings with German clergy, he repeatedly pushed for "some sort of declaration of responsibility for the events of the last decade." In part, Herman noted that such a confession was what "the churches outside of German expected." He believed such a confession would clear the air, quickly resolve a thorny issue that had hindered interwar ecumenism after the Great War, and provide a strong foundation for the work of reconstruction. The matter proved a point of tremendous controversy, however. Herman noted that some pastors refused "to accept any responsibility for the sufferings" of the war. They instead pointed to the collective guilt of all humanity in the conflict. Others withheld their support because it seemed too similar to the "sole war guilt clause to the Versailles Treaty" that had burdened Germany with full responsibility for World War I. They refused to allow Germany to be humiliated yet again. Martin Niemöller encouraged Herman, though, by calling for "general repentance" among church leaders. Herman found the rest of the Confessing Church to be in line with Niemöller on the issue. He wrote, "The strongest sense of responsibility for what happened in 1933 and after ... is to be found among the men of the Confessional Movement."[18]

In the place of German Christians, Herman accordingly sought to secure the leadership of Confessing Church pastors. He robustly promoted this radical movement, which he described as a "fighting fellowship" and "courageous minority" that had "fought stoutly against all Nazi attempts to swallow or smash the Church of Christ." In his view, these German martyrs had never "ceased fighting the satanic Nazi system." Herman stood convinced that their resistance and the martyrdom of figures such as Dietrich Bonhoeffer "provided the basis for a new beginning" for the German Protestant church. In particular, he believed that pastors such as Niemöller, Hans Iwand, and Hermann Diem were "committed to the reconstruction of Christian communities" and promoted "the democratic principle" of the congregation." Herman especially praised Niemöller for opposing the "enthronement of new bishops" and "episcopal absolutism." Moreover, he noted that these ecclesial radicals looked to the Barmen Declaration as a revolutionary confession of faith that outlined an ethic of responsibility in public affairs. Herman indeed saw such an ethic as the spiritual foundation of a democratic political system that would prevent the re-emergence of totalitarian politics. As the American ecumenist noted, Confessing Church leaders had "become amazingly sensitive to dictation without representation" during the Nazi years. Their newfound civic responsibility, he added, was "incidentally one of the most hopeful evidences of budding democracy to be found in the whole wintry ex-Nazi landscape." For these reasons, Herman urged Confessing Church pastors to fill their provisional church councils. He professed "the spirit of the Confessing Church should prevail throughout German Protestantism."[19]

The Confessing Church also proved so important to Herman and ecumenists because they knew their ecumenical campaign would fail without genuine spiritual partners in occupied Germany. Ecumenists like Herman proved sensitive to the power dynamics of the occupation. British Protestant Cyril Garbett, archbishop of York, especially spoke to the challenge of forcefully changing the spiritual culture of a people. He wrote, "It is easy to say we must reconvert Germany, but in practice it will be very difficult. It is ludicrous to think that the victors can send to Germany missionaries to undertake the task. It must be done by the Germans themselves." When considering continental reconstruction, American ecumenical leader A. L. Warnshuis concurred by adding, "The European churches must determine the program. Americans will not ask Europeans to do for us what we want to do . . . a truly humble mind must characterize our attitude toward Europe." Instead of imposing their will, these American and British ecumenists desired to build mutual partnerships "with the faithful Christians of Germany." Yet in seeking indigenous allies, they also looked to support Germans who most aligned with their ecumenical and democratic convictions. Moreover, these same ecumenists did not hesitate to indicate the reforms they thought were needed in Germany. Nor did they prove reluctant to shape the spiritual agenda at major ecclesial gatherings. Overall, they were eager to recruit German Protestants to their cause of creating a new Protestant world order. In pursuit of that end, they would soon propose a docket of ecumenical reforms and initiatives designed to thwart the spiritual and political totalitarianisms of communism, secularism, Catholicism, and evangelicalism in Germany and across the continent.[20]

In response to these perceived threats, Herman also did not object to working with the "old conservatives" in the church, the German Protestants led by bishops such as Theophil Wurm and Otto Dibelius. During the Nazi years, Wurm had worked with the Confessing Church to oppose German Christian and Nazi interference in the churches and had even been placed under Nazi house arrest. Herman noted Wurm's "neutral" stance in the church struggle had still offered up meaningful "passive" resistance to Hitler. In Herman's estimation, Wurm had especially emerged "the speaker of the resistance" during the war years. Meanwhile, Dibelius had worked "silently, swiftly, and surely" against the Nazis. Yet in reality, the "old conservatives" also were committed nationalists. They had supported the war effort and would emerge as opponents of the occupation. Both Wurm and Dibelius also opposed reforms in the church. They opted for a top-down, conservative approach that maintained the traditional hierarchy of Germany's regional churches. In the place of lay congregations, they envisioned bishops and pastors leading a loosely unified national church of various Lutheran and Reformed regional churches.[21]

Despite these notable differences, Wurm and Dibelius still impressed Herman when they called for the "re-Christianization" of their country.

Dibelius shared his hope with Herman to foster a religious revival and to fill the "German people with a new Christian spirit" in the place of Nazism. The German bishop especially expressed concerns about the nihilist, secular, and socialist spirits that now stalked the defeated nation. He feared that these unseen forces could ultimately steer the nation toward Bolshevism. Fearing the Protestant "loss" of Germany, Herman called on Dibelius and others to seize the postwar situation as an opportunity to "rehabilitate desolate souls." He urged them to pursue postwar evangelization with urgency and to make "regeneration . . . the great war cry of the new church." In the aftermath of the war, Herman's hope for a massive spiritual awakening grew as he encountered increased attendance at German churches and noted great spiritual "energies" were "latent or bubbling within the population." He hoped those "destructive and cleansing" forces of religious awakening would finally blow through Germany, filling the nation with a new Christian spirit and preparing the spiritual soil for Protestant and democratic growth.[22]

In Herman's mind, a surefire way to promote this ecumenical and civic synthesis was for the German churches to "emulate the example of American churches" and become "self-supporting and completely independent of the state." Even as ecumenists called for patient and humble partnership, they also concluded that German Protestantism was built on "a faulty structure" that welded the church to the state and thwarted "responsibility and independence" in the local congregation. Herman therefore impressed upon German pastors the need to "accumulate sizable endowments" and develop independence from the state. Looking around him, Herman had reason to believe such a model would be sustainable in postwar Germany. He noted that attendance at many churches was "three or four times as large as it has ever been" and that freewill offerings to the churches were exceedingly high as well. He found German pastors initially in agreement. In Herman's meeting with Otto Dibelius, the bishop told him, "people are now learning to contribute over and beyond the customary taxes." Herman took the remark as a sign that the Protestant church would be able to cut financial ties from the state. He wrote that the German "church desires to finance itself solely from offerings and collections without the aid from the State." His confidence grew that German Protestants would adopt this model and take an important step toward spiritual independence.[23]

All told, Herman's reports and postwar writings revealed how ecumenists drew upon some of the defining features of the American ecumenical experience as a model for German spiritual reconstruction. In his view, America's

Protestant spiritual culture had fostered a thriving civic and religious sphere in the United States. He and other ecumenists believed these spiritual values could have a similar effect on Germany. They affirmed that their ecumenical and civic theology could enable the German Protestant churches to become a wellspring of democracy. As such, their ecumenical mission revealed a high confidence in the American way and the universality of American beliefs. That confidence led them to identify Germany as prime territory for building a postwar ecumenical order. To advance their cause, they worked alongside the military government and the OSS to ensure that the American occupation fulfilled its spiritual potential. They pursued German partners in the Confessing Church and articulated a vision for reform and reconstruction that promised to transform Germany's spiritual and civic culture. With the promise of aid, they hoped to lay the groundwork for a new democratic and ecumenical German church. These initial efforts provided the foundation for a much wider spiritual intervention in Europe, one that ecumenists felt was needed to oppose potential threats to their postwar ecumenical order, above all secularism and communism. In the ruins of Germany, American ecumenists thus activated their "conquering faith" as they worked to transform German spirituality and to promote the defeated nation's democratization. In their hands, the ecumenical movement's postwar mission to Germany became a vehicle of America's democratic project.

Herman's first trip across occupied Germany preceded a crucial German Protestant gathering at Treysa, a small town in the heart of the defeated nation. From August 27 to 31, 1945, German Protestant leaders gathered together to deliberate over the shape and direction of the postwar church. Aside from Otto Dibelius, very few representatives from the Soviet zone were present. Herman's second extensive tour of Germany coincided with the conference. Flying in from Geneva on a military plane allowed him to make it just in time. With the assistance of the OSS, Herman also arranged for the Swiss theologian and Barmen author Karl Barth to be in attendance. Although Americans hoped the German churches could be marshalled as an ecumenical and democratic force in postwar Germany, the conference revealed that German Protestants had their own competing plans for their church and their nation's renewal that reflected deep internal divisions, personal rivalries, and confessional animosities. While Herman hoped for reform and unity, the conference began to create a spiritual quagmire that solidified resistance to the occupation.

At Treysa, Germany's leading Protestants debated above all the shape of their church's organizational structure. Niemöller's reform-minded contingent faced off with Wurm's conservative wing, while a group of conservative Lutheran nationalists led by bishop Hans Meiser called for the formation of a united church true to the Lutheran confessions. All told, tremendous theological division, historical animosity, and opposing visions came into view at Treysa. Niemöller pushed hard for radical reform. As he put it at the conference, "the day of the State Churches is over; the churches should not be controlled by hierarchies but by the congregations themselves." Yet his vision faced stiff resistance. Many desired to restore the German church structure to its pre-Nazi status and to preserve the strength of the regional churches. The differences in opinion created tremendous gridlock. Wurm's vision of a loose federation of the regional and confessional churches ultimately garnered enough support to prevail. The conference called into formation the Evangelical Church in Germany (EKD). To guide the church and contain the tensions, the attendees organized an ecclesial council composed of twelve leaders. Wurm headed the Council, while Niemöller served as vice chairman and the head of the church's new foreign relations office. Although Herman clearly preferred the congregational model championed by Niemöller, he saw Wurm as more than fit for postwar leadership. He believed ecumenists could work with the EKD and continue to promote internal reforms, even though the EKD seemed far from the vessel of democracy he had desired it to be.[24]

Herman's quest to cultivate German interest in democratic politics indeed received a cold reception at Treysa. Herman's strongest ally seemed to be Niemöller, who he recalled stood out as "one of the boldest champions of democracy in Germany" at the conference. In particular, the radical reformer stated the church held a "responsibility to foster democracy because democracy lives from Christianity." Herman also saw these views expressed in an internal memo authored by reform-minded Protestants titled "A Word on the Responsibility of the Church for Public Life." This document outlined a new responsibility for the churches to "influence much stronger than before the shape of public life and in particular the political community." The radical reformers who authored the document saw the statement as aligning with the trajectory of the Barmen Declaration. Although the Treysa delegates never formally discussed the document due to its controversial nature, it ignited a wider debate. Notably, many conservative Protestants opposed the document and insisted on preserving their traditional political stance of non-interference. Herman noted that these conservative Protestants associated democracy "with the impotence and indecision of the Weimar Republic." They felt democracy had failed them before, and they continued to doubt it would provide the "redeeming formula" to a "German nation in deepest distress." Herman fired back. He criticized their "vague forebodings" about "Anglo-Saxon democracy" and claimed the Germans relied on "second-hand analyses" that "depreciated" America's political and spiritual tradition. Herman's response began to cast occupied Germany as a spiritual and civic battleground between traditionalists and reformers, nationalists and ecumenists. It also exposed the ways in which American Protestant mission itself was tied to a polarizing ideology of democracy and American civilization.[25]

In response, Herman used the conference to network with democratic-minded clergy. He believed that working with these Germans could set "a democratic example" of "civic courage" and "a sense of political responsibility in the reluctant people." These reform-minded pastors in particular called for the creation of an "Evangelical Academy" that would train lay Protestants to apply their Christian faith to the social and economic problems of the postwar era. Some also endorsed the Christian Democratic Union, a new political party that united together Protestants and Catholics in political confession. Herman lauded this political development as "most wholesome" in its affirmation of "democratic" politics "founded on Christian principles." He likewise backed the formation of *Hilfswerk*—the EKD's new relief agency. The organization's leader, Eugen Gerstenmaier, had already been profiled in one of Herman's OSS reports on the German resistance. A former member of the Kreisau Circle that sought to assassinate Hitler, Gerstenmaier now organized internal relief to a nation in desperate need. He pioneered a new practical theology of "self-help" (*Selbsthilfe*). Seeking to nurture a spirit of lay activism and responsibility, "self-help" placed the burden on German Protestants to carry out church reconstruction themselves and to rely on foreign churches only as a second option. As one German supporter noted, "Self-help comes first. If we do not help out one another, we have no right to ask for foreign help." *Hilfswerk*'s organizers thus called for indigenous renewal and aimed to activate the latent energies of the German Protestant laity. Herman and other ecumenists praised *Hilfswerk* and looked to collaborate further with the agency to advance his ecumenical and democratic spiritual cause.[26]

As spiritual divisions strained the postwar church, Protestants could find a semblance of unity in discussing the Soviet occupation zone. Regardless of their differences, many could agree that "Bolshevism" was a threat to the German people. Initially, the Soviets surprised both Herman and German Protestants alike. They anticipated that the Soviets would "liquidate" German clergy and undertake an "antireligious crusade" against the churches. Yet the Soviets, who had refined their own politics of accommodation with the Russian Orthodox churches in order to cement their rule, initially honored religious freedom and had not yet imperiled the German clergy. Herman noted the Soviet occupying authorities had been "unexpectedly tolerant and even friendly" to German pastors. Such occurrences left Herman feeling slightly optimistic about the fate of the churches in the Russian zone. Perhaps the German churches would retain their freedoms there, he hoped, and be able to prevent the total secularization of their nation underneath Soviet influence.[27]

At the same time, Herman and the Treysa delegates expressed deep concerns. The Red Army had carried out a murderous campaign as it had closed in on Berlin. As the occupation began, the Soviets also began to pursue the "deliberate spoliation" of their zone, a strategy that in Herman's assessment promoted "private misery" and the material conditions for "public revolution." The path to a Stalinist dictatorship was already beginning to appear before his eyes. The expulsion of nearly 13 million Germans from Eastern Europe only made the matter worse. The spiritual communities of these refugees had been decimated, Herman lamented. The American ecumenist wrote soberly how the refugees left behind "charred and broken fragments of thousands of churches." It was a "loss sustained . . . by all of Christendom" that left Herman and his German partners pondering how long "Christendom" could "continue to lose its member churches and escape the final reckoning." He feared that many would lose faith "that the world . . . was essentially Christian" and that "the church" was "an agent of a decent world order." It seemed that the devastation of the war and its aftereffects were leading to an abrupt and rapid secularization of the world.[28]

In light of these deteriorating spiritual conditions, the issue of resuming Protestant religious education became all the more important in the occupation zones. While German Protestants felt confident they could reconstitute their church-run schools and religious education in the Western zones, they feared the Soviets would shut down their religious schools and indoctrinate "Nazified youth" into ardent Bolshevists. They worried that a red dictatorship would replace a brown one as communism grew in the ruins of Nazism. Herman sought to rally the churches in response. Where the Soviets limited religious education, he claimed the churches had an opportunity to carry out catechesis outside of the schools. Yet as postwar revivals failed to materialize and the Soviets further limited religious freedom, Herman's opposition to the Soviets only strengthened. He accordingly called on Americans to equip Germany with Christian defenses against Bolshevism and supported the German call for a "Christian counterattack" against the Soviets. As the Cold War began, Americans like Herman would move quickly to recruit Germans as new anti-communist partners.[29]

This shared sense of mission against secularism and communism led Herman to see Treysa largely as a success despite the deep theological and political divisions it had exposed. In contrast, the restoration of pre-Nazi church norms and the failure to enact radical reform led Niemöller to consider the conference a failure. Herman certainly sensed Niemöller's frustration. He admitted there was still much work to be done. In particular, he felt German Protestants still needed time to develop a more robust theology of public responsibility and congregational activism. But Herman hoped the roots of that transformation had been planted. In his view, Treysa had helped create a united church out of the ruins of war. He now hoped ecumenism would work like "leaven in the lump of the whole German Church." Herman thus reported back home with glowing, even exaggerated, descriptions of the conference. He stated that church leaders had acknowledged their "crushing burden of responsibility" for the war. So too were Germany's Protestants pursuing denazification efforts in a "thorough and just way." Moreover, he added that a "new ecumenical spirit" was "brooding over the country." Regarding the internal divisions within German Protestantism, Herman proved optimistic, stating that "a fundamental spiritual unity underlay the Treysa Conference." In Herman, the new German church found a passionate defender, even if these particular descriptions did not wholly match the messy realities on the ground. In his view, the German church indeed appeared to be well on its way to becoming a valuable and reliable partner in postwar work.[30]

Herman's mission certainly renewed a line of contact between American and German churches, yet it also did not stimulate much critical reflection on the past. Seeing the churches as a source of stalwart resistance led him to overlook Protestantism's complicity with Hitler's rise to power and march to war. His postwar reports also remained silent on one crucial issue: the church's failure to counteract Nazi antisemitism. Indeed, Protestant pastors more broadly remained slow to recognize the need to seriously examine their anti-Judaism, their antisemitism, and their complicity with the Holocaust. On this matter, Herman was mute as well. Instead, he continued to maintain that the blemished record of Protestants was "heroic," or as he had frequently stated during his years in Berlin, that Protestants were "helpless" in the face of Hitler's power.[31]

Beyond Herman's reports, American policymakers and military government officials came to dramatically different conclusions about the postwar status of German Protestantism. They struggled to make sense of what they witnessed at Treysa and to grasp the historical and theological divisions that exploded out into the open at the conference and in the postwar hour. Their assessments of Treysa were therefore remarkably mixed. One military officer echoed Herman in noting the "general tenor" of the conference "was excellent." Protestant leaders had found "common ground," he wrote, and were prepared to "establish a moral basis for the new Germany." Others saw through such praise. One State Department official noted, "there is little evidence that the German Protestant Church repented Germany's war of aggression or the cruelties visited upon other peoples and countries." Another added that he too did not find "evidence that the church repented the war of aggression." Both reports pointed to Germany's conservative nationalists who were eager to avoid the question of guilt and repentance. The German people were also forlorn and were beginning to harbor grievances against the occupiers. Increasingly, everyday Germans looked to their Protestant and Catholic leaders as defenders against these foreign invaders and the "hard peace" they were implementing. Their conservative religious leaders were more than ready to defend the German nation against the foreign powers that occupied their lands.[32]

As these military reports indicated, the question of war guilt proved highly controversial for both German and American Protestants alike. In October 1945, Herman led and accompanied a multinational ecumenical delegation to convene with German Protestant leaders and discuss that very question, which had plagued ecumenical relations following World War I. Included in the party were leading American ecumenist Samuel McCrea Cavert and Lutheran delegate S. C. Michelfelder, along with World Council secretary Willem Visser 't Hooft and the Anglican bishop George Bell. Meeting with the new German church council in Stuttgart, the ecumenical delegation indicated that a German confession of guilt was needed to restore ecumenical relations between the churches. Pinning the war on Germany, the ecumenical delegation urged a declaration from the German church as opposed to issuing a joint statement, which an ecumenical ethic might have genuinely inspired. The "Stuttgart Declaration of Guilt" that ensued aggravated the underlying tensions within the fragile German church. While reform-minded Protestants like Niemöller openly recognized Germany's guilt in the war, conservative leaders spoke of a collective guilt shared by all of humankind or of a personal guilt before God. Some even identified themselves as the true victims of the war and saw their present sufferings as enough atonement. Reflecting this debate over culpability, the "Stuttgart Declaration" vaguely spoke of the German people's "great solidarity of guilt" and acknowledged the "endless suffering" Germans had brought to "many peoples and countries." At the same time, it also spoke to the suffering of the German people themselves. When the declaration made its way to the German press, its release ignited a wildfire of controversy. Many lay German Protestants accused the council members of betraying their own people and nation. The response illustrated just how challenging it would be to replace nationalist sympathies with ecumenical perspectives among an occupied population.[33]

Moreover, the declaration's silence on the Jews indicated how difficult it would be for Protestants to broach the topic of Jewish-Christian relations. For his part, Herman saw the general language of the declaration as covering a litany of specific sins, from Protestant toleration of euthanasia campaigns to the military extermination units along the eastern front to the Nazi death camps. In contrast, American Lutheran pastor Sylvester Michelfelder wanted the Germans to speak "more clearly on matters like the persecution of the Jews." Niemöller proved one of the lonely souls in Germany who publicly acknowledged how his antisemitism had contributed to the Holocaust. He eventually argued that Germans needed to account for the fact that six million Jews had died under their watch. Here again, Herman read into Niemöller's repentance an act of atonement that seemingly applied to all of Germany. Yet in reality, Niemöller's ethic of responsibility failed to spread across the occupied land. Most Germans thought they carried no personal guilt for Nazi measures. Some simply wanted to forget the horrors of Dachau and Buchenwald and move on. Other Germans insisted that antisemitism was "not as deeply rooted" in Germany as these outsider ecumenists thought.

However, an ecumenist like Michelfelder was right to press the issue. After a tour of the British occupation zone, British ecumenists noted lingering signs of the same religious hatred of Jews and racial antisemitism that had enabled systematic genocide in the first place.[34]

In the United States, the Federal Council welcomed the Stuttgart Declaration while striking its own penitential tone. Cavert wrote that Americans were "deeply impressed" with the Germans' "frank avowal of moral responsibility." In return, he noted America's "own failure" to assume its "full share in the task of building an international order of justice." FCC leaders also used the moment to renew calls for reform at home and abroad. Here again, G. Bromley Oxnam noted that the American victory opened an opportunity for "enlightenment, the changing of hearts, and repentance" both in the United States and Germany. Americans could fully defeat Nazism in Germany through "educating" the Germans and keeping "the evangelism of the conquered nation" in focus. Meanwhile, Americans needed to defeat Jim Crow racism and promote a tolerant interfaith ethic in their own republic. In response to the Stuttgart Declaration, Cavert and Oxnam readily linked reforms abroad to changes at home. In this way, ecumenical engagement with Germany and the postwar occupation could work both ways. It could also prompt critical reflection on America's own flaws and inspire activism for racial justice at home.[35]

Despite this apparent ecumenical breakthrough, the struggle over guilt paralleled German opposition to other American-backed reforms. Such resistance signaled the development of a spiritual quagmire not only between the churches, but also between the occupiers and occupied. Church finances and financial independence from the state proved to be another hot-button issue that created gridlock and misunderstanding. American ecumenists and the AMG hoped the German Protestant churches would forgo receiving revenues from the state and instead rely on free-will offerings. Such a model, they believed, would inspire independence from the state and a more critical approach to public life. However, German Protestants pushed back and delivered an intense theological argument against free-will offerings. The destruction of the war, the growing refugee crisis, and the disappearance of the state placed the churches in dire financial straits, they argued. Conservative bishop Otto Dibelius now declared that depriving the churches "of its traditional fiscal benefits . . . would be disastrous" in such an unstable environment. He also maintained that "a connection to the state" was not "necessarily evil." Even a radical reformer like Niemöller eventually called for a "preliminary period of taxation while church and nation regain financial equilibrium." Preserving the taxation system, he believed, would provide a stable foundation for German churches. At the theological level, German Protestants also developed a strong rationale to reject American advances. They claimed that church taxes actually preserved the integrity of the Christian gospel. Through the tax support, German pastors were freed to truly preach the gospel and not turn their sermons into fundraising campaigns like the Americans did. Suggestions for reform could therefore also ignite opposition to American church practices within Germany.[36]

The resistance of conservative leaders also applied to Allied denazification efforts. Left to pursue its own denazification—a privilege given to no other national institution—the German Protestant church set up a test to identify pastors whose loyalty to National Socialism had compromised their ordination vows. While the policy removed some of the most egregious offenders, its ambiguity allowed the overwhelming majority of Nazi sympathizers to retain their pastoral posts. All told, Marshall Knappen estimated that only 321 out of 19,134 church workers in the American zone had been dismissed from office, while he projected that at least 4,000 had been actively involved in supporting Nazism. According to these numbers, ecclesial denazification proved exceedingly lax. Such an outcome led Knappen to write off the process as a farce and, more generally, to depict the occupation and postwar reconstruction as a failure. Nonetheless, ecumenical leaders desired to swiftly rehabilitate the image of German Protestantism and therefore praised Confessing Church leaders for "purifying" their churches. In defending such a mixed record, they arguably missed an opportunity to urge Germans to grapple seriously with their complicity with Nazism.[37]

More broadly, German Protestant leaders like Theophil Wurm contested the Allied denazification policy for all of Germany as a whole. Drawing lessons from their resistance to Hitler's interference in the churches, conservative Protestants challenged the occupiers as the new totalitarian powers that had now merely replaced the Nazis. While Wurm recognized the need to remove the vestiges of Nazism from German society, he disapproved of the Americans' indiscriminate policy that treated all Nazi party members the same. Such an approach failed, he argued, to determine each Nazi party member's degree of complicity and guilt. He also accused the denazification process of discrediting democratic liberties and rights, such as due process. For Wurm, American denazification policies felt like a new form of totalitarianism. He responded in an aggressive manner, even defending *Schutzstaffel* officers who had played a role in the murder of Jews and Eastern Europeans along the eastern front.[38]

In December 1945, Wurm voiced the widespread German frustration with the occupation by responding to the Anglican archbishop of Canterbury, Geoffrey Fisher, who had critiqued the Germans for exhibiting "self-righteousness" after the war. Fisher called for additional signs of genuine repentance from the Germans. In response, Wurm crafted a theological argument for the collective guilt of humanity in the war. He also challenged the Allies to acknowledge the unnecessary suffering caused by the occupation, including the forced expulsion of Germans from Eastern Europe and the dismantling of the German economy. Everyday German Protestants wrote in great support of Wurm and his theological rebuttal to the occupying powers. They felt they had found a national defender in the German bishop and the churches. In these ways, the occupation and its policies also ignited the fires of German religious nationalism.[39]

In response to the emerging spiritual quagmire, Herman feared that America's postwar opportunity was being lost. He began to defend Wurm and the German churches before the American state, arguing that the robust pursuit of denazification merely amounted to a "hard peace" that would alienate the Germans. He also feared the harsh occupation only discredited democracy and turned the Germans toward anarchy. Instead, Herman wanted to quickly rehabilitate the Germans as partners in his postwar cause. Moreover, the AMG's insistence, he wrote, on upholding "the strict American tradition of complete separation of church and state" in its religious policy was not getting the job done. In Herman's view, the AMG needed to devote more resources to the churches, starting by using military chaplains to promote spiritual reform in Germany. Herman had no qualms about using the power of the state to "Christianize" a country. A host of ecumenists concurred, including American realists like Reinhold Niebuhr and Henry Pitney van Dusen, as well as Swiss theologian Emil Brunner, who all critiqued AMG policies as being too restrictive and felt the AMG needed to pursue a more positive course of democratic and ecumenical reconstruction. The AMG was squandering a golden chance, the editors of *Christianity and Crisis* publicized, to build "a world of peace, reconciliation, democracy and practical Christianity."[40]

Herman also believed that the German people still had not gained the total "trust" of the Allies. In order to soothe these tensions, he proposed new programs of reconstruction and exchange between American and German

Protestants. In November 1945, Herman wrote to John Foster Dulles, who he hoped could get a word in with other ranking leaders in Washington. With Dulles, Herman shared his "feeling of disquietude" that the military had not yet implemented "a program of constructive support of the Christian church, the one element in Germany which offers some hope of moral reconstruction." He also warned that the churches were "scarcely in a better position than communism." Herman therefore asked for help in further impressing upon the military government and the White House the importance of the World Council's pursuit of Germany's "re-Christianization" and "democratization." He continued to argue that America's postwar cause was best advanced through a reconstructionist peace that quickly rehabilitated Germany into America's postwar democratic order. Through Dulles, he hoped he could turn the tides of the worsening occupation and make good on America's postwar opportunity to promote Christianity and democracy in the heart of Europe.[41]

Herman's mission on behalf of American ecumenists and diplomats marked the beginning of a longer American spiritual intervention in Germany. His proposals for reform were but the first in a series of American initiatives designed to remake the defeated nation along democratic and ecumenical lines. Herman and his ecumenical allies certainly professed belief in the "supranational" power of their faith and helped foster transnational reconciliation and new spiritual ties across the Atlantic. Yet their faith paradoxically proved just as captive to the reigning ideologies of their era, including American nationalism, world democratization, and anti-communism. While these ecumenists had clearly rejected "old-style imperialism" and had pushed their nation to forsake a vindictive peace, their postwar agenda turned the ecumenical movement into a vehicle of American expansionism. In that regard, ecumenists kept alive their own style of Christian nationalism in their efforts to remake Germany's spiritual and political culture.

Even as the occupation proved haphazard and German Protestants pushed back, American Protestants still drew confidence from their endeavors. Reviving the Protestant heartland seemingly confirmed their national purpose of bringing Christianity and democracy to the rest of the world. Reconstructing and rehabilitating Germany as a new Christian partner was but the first step in establishing a new Christian order across the Atlantic. Ecumenists soon launched an even wider program of continental spiritual recovery that sent aid, resources, and personnel abroad in order to revive Europe and strengthen the continent's defenses against secularism and communism. Already in 1945, some ecumenists were sounding the alarm about Soviet intentions in occupied Germany. Leaders within their ranks would soon rally the American people to oppose the "godless" communists in an emerging spiritual cold war. They likewise would energize ecumenical Protestants to oppose secularists, Catholics, and evangelicals in a new spiritual and cultural war for the West.

6

Battleground Europe

On March 6, 1946, President Harry Truman prepared with a troubled mind for his first ever speech before the Federal Council of Churches. A month earlier, Soviet premier Joseph Stalin had declared communism and capitalism to be inherent enemies. Now the Soviet premier refused to withdraw Soviet troops from oil-rich Iran. Meanwhile, on a state visit to the United States, British prime minister Winston Churchill had warned that an "iron curtain" of Soviet control had fallen across Eastern Europe from the Baltic to the Adriatic Sea. Truman grew alarmed as the Soviets' recalcitrance increased. One day after Churchill's stirring address, the American president addressed America's leading ecumenists and outlined what their nation stood for in the world. The Missourian Baptist affirmed that the United States had defended "religion and democracy" in the war against the "forces of evil." He now called on all God-fearing Americans to remain steadfast in their defense of these ideals. His speech was just one part of his emerging strategy to rally American religious groups to global vigilance against the Soviet threat.[1]

While the Federal Council assembly appreciated Truman's support of their spiritual diplomacy and humanitarian endeavors in Europe, the president actually proved too ecumenical for these Protestant ecumenists. While some Federal Council delegates were eager to "contain" communism, they were also growing increasingly concerned over the Vatican's "spiritual imperialism" and were wary of Truman's tri-faith idealism. They especially feared that Catholics were primed to retake the European continent and to undermine Protestants' privileged standing in Berlin and Washington. In response, American ecumenists aimed to forge a strong transatlantic Protestant coalition that would counteract "political and spiritual totalitarianism" in Europe.

Beyond the Vatican, ecumenists also noticed the new activism of American evangelicals both at home and abroad. Drawing energy from their mobilization for war, two rising evangelists—Torrey Johnson and Billy Graham—called for a "spiritual invasion" of "Battleground Europe." They pledged to transform Europe into a "continent for conquest" and called on American

God's Marshall Plan. James D. Strasburg, Oxford University Press (2021). © Oxford University Press.
DOI: 10.1093/oso/9780197516447.003.0007

Protestants to fight "for the hearts and minds" of the European people. Above all, they focused on gaining a foothold in occupied Germany, where they preached their conversionary gospel and commitments to freedom and free enterprise. Struggling to work with the "theologically liberal" military government, American evangelicals instead forged an enduring partnership with American military chaplains and fundamentalist officers that gave them access to a powerful American institution with an unprecedented global reach.[2]

Altogether, these competing postwar spiritual missions began to outline a religious rationale for a new Cold War against the Soviet Union. They also made Germany and the European continent into a "spiritual battleground" between ecumenists and evangelicals, Protestants and Catholics, and American democrats and Soviet communists. In this regard, postwar Protestant mission ultimately became about something much more than reviving Europe. It yielded a contest over the religious and political identity of the American nation itself. To many American Protestants, the souls of "Christian America" and the "Christian West" were now on the line in "Battleground Europe."[3]

As the bone-chilling European winter of 1945 began, American ecumenists warned of an impending humanitarian crisis in occupied Germany. In response, they outlined a program of humanitarian relief to war-torn Europe that would counteract communism and strengthen Protestant resolve. As food shortages mounted and material supplies grew scarce, World Council director Stewart Herman sounded the alarm that "millions of Germans" found themselves "on the verge of starvation." As German refugees flowed into the occupation zones, Federal Council leader Samuel McCrea Cavert likewise counseled that "weary cynicism" and psychological distress grew rapidly among the hungry and homeless Germans. The conditions were perfect, ecumenists warned, for societal collapse and perhaps even a desperate turn to communism. Seeing the threat, Herman and Cavert demanded a swift shift to reconstruction initiatives and pushed their government to start food shipments to Germany. The World Council had stored vast food supplies at the Swiss-German border and was merely waiting for American Military Government (AMG) approval. The AMG initially held off, hoping to strike a note of parity in rations between occupied Germany and the European neighbors it had attacked.[4]

Back home, Protestant leaders also went on the offensive, pressuring Truman to carry out the responsibilities of a "Christian nation" in a time of humanitarian crisis. The president of the Lutheran Church Missouri Synod, John Behnken, criticized America's occupation policies for being "unchristian" and "undemocratic." In order "to save Christian civilization in Europe," Behnken argued, Americans needed to provide aid and relief, not punishment. Behnken called on American Lutherans to undertake a coordinated campaign of advocacy. In a letter to Truman, he urged the president to "open channels for effective work of charity" and tied his request to America's newfound leadership of the free world: "upon America, touched least of all by the ravages of war, it will depend whether or not millions will die this winter." United Lutheran president Franklin Fry likewise met with Truman on January 16, 1946, and pressed the need to send material aid to Germany's churches, a move which he believed would not only reflect America's benevolent spirit but also aid Germany's democratization.[5]

Their labors translated into new foreign policy directives in an emerging Cold War. Yet in the hands of Truman, these initiatives reflected a trifaith sentiment. With Catholics and Jews also pressing the administration, Truman created in February 1946 the Council of Relief Agencies Licensed to Operate in Germany, a central committee which coordinated material relief from voluntary and religious relief agencies in the United States to Germany. In the summer of 1946, the AMG also approved the shipment of individual CARE (Cooperative for American Remittances to Europe) packages to Germany that everyday American citizens could ship to individual Germans. Millions of pounds of corporate and individual aid began to flow across the Atlantic in order to stave off a collapse of German society.[6]

For these ecumenists, however, their nation's moral responsibilities extended beyond just providing humanitarian relief. Protestant ecumenists also envisioned forging a powerful transatlantic Protestant coalition that would strengthen German Protestantism and halt the advance of totalitarian threats—both spiritual and political—in the beleaguered nation. After his initial tours of Germany, Herman in particular called on the American government to mobilize Protestant military chaplains in Germany's spiritual reconstruction and to send more Protestant ecumenical representatives to the country. In January 1946, American Methodist bishop G. Bromley Oxnam, fresh off his own ecumenical tour of occupied Germany, also recommended increasing the "informal" American Protestant presence in Germany. The two ecumenists desired to a send a bevy of Protestant advisors and relief workers to reconstruct the German Protestant churches on a democratic basis.[7]

The recommendations of Herman and Oxnam coincided with a growing suspicion in Washington about Soviet intentions. Already in February 1946, US Army intelligence reports began to depict Germany "as the scene of the decisive engagement between the forces of Western Christian civilization and those of the materialistic Marxist philosophy burgeoning in the East." In this harrowing landscape, the report continued, the German churches provided "the basis of a united front against 'the Bolshevist threat.'" Such military intelligence aligned with a dispatch from George Kennan, one of Herman's former colleagues in the US Embassy in Berlin, which provided a compelling explanation of Soviet behavior. Authored on February 22, 1946, from his diplomatic post in Moscow, Kennan's "Long Telegram" described the Russians as anxious, paranoid, ideologically driven, and eager to secure their standing through territorial expansion. The report would eventually lead Truman to adopt Kennan's recommendation to "contain" Soviet communism in Europe through economic and military aid to threatened regions. In March 1947, just one year after his Federal Council address, Truman took his first formal step against Soviet communism with the Truman Doctrine—a commitment of economic and military assistance to pro-democratic forces in Greece and Turkey.[8]

Yet before he authored the Truman Doctrine, the American president first sought to pursue a subtle program of spiritual diplomacy to the European continent. With the advent of atomic weapons, the stakes and costs of war had escalated beyond human imagination. In such a risky environment, building transatlantic, faith-based coalitions served as a discrete way to oppose the Soviets through fortifying Europe's democratic and spiritual resolve. In collaboration with the AMG, Truman authorized American Protestant, Catholic, and Jewish representatives to support German religious organizations and promote "democratic principles" in the occupation zones. Lucius Clay, the ranking deputy governor in the AMG, promised these religious ambassadors his "maximum aid" as they pursued the "spiritual reconstruction" of a "peaceful and democratic Germany."[9]

Washington's newfound spiritual diplomacy looked to these three monotheistic faiths to promote democratic commitments such as human dignity, ordered liberty, and religious toleration in the occupation zones. Meanwhile, Truman began penning letters to Pope Pius XII that called on "all who cherish Christian and democratic institutions" to "unite against the common enemy... the Soviet Union." He also re-dispatched Episcopalian industrialist Myron Taylor as a liaison to the pope and urged him to meet broadly with other spiritual leaders. In Germany, Taylor met with Konrad von Preysing and Otto Dibelius, the Catholic and Protestant bishops of Berlin. Their rejection of communism impressed Taylor, who ensured that both had the funds needed to counteract Soviet indoctrination in a city that was quickly becoming a hotspot in the emerging conflict. Deputy military governor Lucius Clay supported the two bishops as well, stating that stronger Christian relations would "help us in raising our resistance to communism to a high level." Germany's spiritual reconstruction thus led the American government to use religion as a new way to wage the Cold War.[10]

When Truman worked closely with the Vatican, Protestant ecumenists opposed such entreaties. During the war, some ecumenists like Herman had hoped the "common suffering" of Catholics and Protestants would foster "a greater measure of sympathy and understanding in the common task of rebuilding a postwar world." Yet despite these tokens of goodwill, ecumenists also renewed their historically deep hostility toward Catholicism. These ecumenists especially feared the Vatican's "imperial" designs for Europe. For them, Catholicism was a kind of spiritual totalitarianism, an "authoritarian" spiritual system that had historically partnered with monarchical, fascist, and tyrannical regimes. In contrast, they believed only ecumenical Protestantism could provide an authentic spiritual foundation for democracy. American ecumenists like G. Bromley Oxnam grew especially concerned that the Vatican was using communism as a rationale to reassert itself across Europe. For these reasons, he resisted collaborating with Catholics in Truman's emerging tri-faith coalition.[11]

Rankled by Truman's tri-faith activism, Oxnam sought to get a head start on the Catholics and dispatched Ewart Turner and Samuel McCrea Cavert in the winter and summer of 1946 to prepare the military government and churches in Germany for a wave of Protestant ambassadors to Germany. Turner reported that German Protestants still had much to do to overcome their "otherworldliness," or in other words, their lack of interest in temporal affairs and "international organization." He called on Americans to give Germans "a true vision of the democratic way." Meanwhile, Cavert counseled that the American Protestant presence would fill Germany's "spiritual vacuum" with a "positive faith" shaped by "the experience of the American churches." It also would secure "the fuller cooperation" of German Protestants in "developing" a "democratic Germany" and would "foster the emergence of a Christian world outlook." In the fall of 1946, Julius Bodensieck built upon these efforts as the first official Protestant ambassador to Germany. Bodensieck continued Herman's reform work through calling for a "decisive reversal" in how German Protestants treated the laity. As he saw it, only through activating the energies of the lay believers could the church counteract both political and spiritual totalitarianism.[12]

Yet Truman and the AMG held their ground. They soon dispatched Aloysius Muench, the Catholic bishop of Fargo, North Dakota, as their nation's Catholic envoy to Germany. A first-generation German-American, Muench viewed the German Catholic church as an anti-Nazi bastion that had "written a glorious chapter in the history of the Church" through its opposition to Hitler. The Catholic bishop wholly disassociated "Nazism and Christianity" from one another. They two were "as incompatible as fire and water," he wrote. Muench thus proved just as ready to promote a myth of Catholic resistance to Nazism. As a continuation of that heroic story, the American bishop now encouraged German Catholics to foster a "new spirit" and a "new state" in Germany. Like many American Catholics, Muench knew full well that Catholicism and democracy were not incompatible in the ways American Protestants claimed. Drawing on the democratic record of American Catholic luminaries such as John Carroll and Orestes Brownson, he urged American Catholics to now help their German partners in faith to embrace democracy. He encouraged "the spiritual and cultural rehabilitation of Germany ... based on the assumption of Western civilization (Europe and America)" and likewise worked closely with Christian Democratic Union politicians. During his multi-year tour of Germany, the American bishop also proved most active in dispatching American Catholic aid to German Catholic parishes. Such "magnificent charity" proved "unparalleled in the history of Christian civilization," he wrote.[13]

In contrast to the rather triumphant tone of American Protestants and Catholics, Rabbi Simon Kramer developed a posture of lament as he represented America's Jews in occupied Germany. Kramer first went to the occupation zones in 1948 and 1949 to encourage Jewish communities there. Hundreds of thousands of German Jews had been murdered in the Holocaust, leaving the German Jewish community devastated. More broadly, the Nazis had carried out a systematic genocide that had killed over six million of Europe's roughly nine million Jews.

In the shadow of the Shoah, Kramer mostly met with the thousands of European Jews who had fled to occupied Germany after the war in order to escape antisemitic persecutions that had broken out across Eastern Europe. As he praised these Jews for their "remarkable initiative" in restoring a semblance of Jewish religious life in Germany, he also notified the military authorities of lingering antisemitism in the German public. The "fundamental bias of the Germans" had not been removed, Kramer warned. He counseled that the military government would need to carefully observe "the processes of democratization." He found some solace, however, in the newly formed nation-state of Israel, which he and Harry Truman alike hoped would become a safe haven for Europe's Jews, even as Israel's creation unleashed a brutal war and refugee crisis that would decimate Palestinian communities.[14]

American ecumenists soon sought to gain the upper hand in occupied Germany through sending an additional ambassador from the World Council of Churches. The Soviets blocked the plan, alarming Americans, who had hoped the ecumenical representative would facilitate "direct contact with the thinking of democratic nations." While the British and French also supported the request, the Soviets argued that the German churches were not yet ready for such an international influence. Americans saw the Soviet response as indicative of the broader Marxist hostility toward religion. In response, the Western powers defiantly approved the liaison position within their zones. The Allied powers were beginning to split over religious policy, divisions that soon appeared in economic and political matters as well.[15]

As these confrontations with communism became more prevalent, the Federal Council called for cautious vigilance against the Soviets. In its 1946 statement on "Soviet-American relations," the Council struck a reserved yet firm tone about the emerging tensions between the United States and the Soviet Union. While it called for "tolerance" of political differences within a new international system, it also named Marxism a dangerous ideology that stood "clearly opposed to Christianity" and that rejected "the sacredness of personality." Far from proposing a direct confrontation, however, it advised its member churches to "retain antipathy to dictatorship" and to not retreat from shaping the postwar order. If Americans could make their democracy "vigorous and life-giving," they could ensure that their nation would "have a spiritual appeal to the masses of mankind." The Council thus called for the promotion of democratic and ecumenical values abroad, alongside a principled yet peaceful ideological opposition to communism, a stance that sought to not intensify the conflict but also not cede spiritual ground to Marxist irreligion. In outlining this view, the Council sought to mediate between the diverging interests of its pacifist wing, which called for accommodation and tolerance toward the Soviets, and its realist wing, which called for firm and steadfast opposition to communism. How to best respond to Soviet communism was thus proving to be a divisive issue within ecumenical ranks.[16]

Indeed, in contrast to the Federal Council's hesitant tone, other mainline Protestants called on American Protestants to "get tough" with the Russians. Protestant media mogul Henry Luce, who had already outlined the Protestant vision for a new "American Century," used his media empire to strengthen Protestant resolve against communism. In its March 1946 feature article, "Protestants Plan for Peace," *LIFE Magazine*, one of Luce's hallmark publications, reported on ecumenical meetings in Geneva, Switzerland, and Columbus, Ohio, where in addition to Truman's admonition to defend religion and freedom, John Foster Dulles urged American ecumenists to not "ignore the tensions" between "the Soviet Union and the Western democracies." Like the Federal Council, Dulles also drew a clear ideological distinction: Western Christians based their "view of life upon the belief in the dignity and worth of man as a child of God." The Soviets promoted a very different set of materialist and atheist ideals. Yet Dulles outlined an even more aggressive, Christian nationalist response. As he put it, Americans had always been called to spread their "gospel" of "human freedom" across the globe. "Christian America" now had a new "missionary opportunity," Dulles argued, in its global advocacy for these values. Dulles followed up his speech with two articles of his own in *LIFE* that portrayed the Soviet system as wholly incompatible with Christianity and Western democracy. In response, he outlined the need for firm resolve, ideological integrity, and military preparedness. He would eventually translate these Christian nationalist commitments into a new foreign policy that would not just "contain" communism but now more aggressively "roll back" the gains of Soviet communism in Eastern Europe.[17]

A Christian realist like Reinhold Niebuhr also supported Truman's harder line against communism. After a tour of Germany in the summer of 1946, Niebuhr outlined in *LIFE* how the Russians stood primed to assert their power throughout all of occupied Germany. While the Allies had allowed Eastern Europe to succumb to Soviet designs, Niebuhr counseled Americans to hold firm against the Russians in "the fight for Germany." Just months after Niebuhr's tour, Secretary of State James Byrnes gave a speech in Germany announcing a similar resolve to oppose Soviet intentions for the Western zones. Niebuhr supported the new direction. In response to the Truman Doctrine, he claimed that providing aid to Greece and Turkey would "do little good" if Americans simultaneously created "conditions" conducive "to the growth of communism" in Germany. Niebuhr thus called for a robust program of economic recovery. As such, realist commitments to democratization in Germany and assessments of structural sin proved easily adaptable to stances against communism. Niebuhr urged the United States to counteract all forms of political totalitarianism, whether fascist or communist.[18]

The American government concurred and sought to further expand its program of spiritual diplomacy. To further counter the Soviets and promote democracy in the occupation zones, Washington drafted new plans for religious exchanges between the United States and Germany. The exchanges reflected a novel occupation policy that engaged the German people in their own "reorientation" toward democracy and Christianity. American policymakers admitted that the shift modeled the "positive policy of cooperation with German churches" that American ecumenists had already been pursuing. The American government now sought to more fully engage the Germans as democratic partners and allies. To do so, it would look to forge faith-based partnerships between Protestants and Catholics on both sides of the Atlantic.[19]

To build a strong German-American Protestant coalition, Federal Council leaders were already planning trips for leading German Protestant clergy to come to the United States. Henry Smith Leiper especially desired more Americans to gain a stronger sense of the "brave minority" of Germans who had opposed Hitler. He hoped such exchanges could "break the conspiracy of silence" about the German resistance, as he put it. Leiper and the Federal Council thus first brought Martin Niemöller, the radical reformer who had also been billed by *TIME Magazine* as Hitler's personal prisoner, to the United States. Washington viewed Niemöller as a controversial choice, however. While Cavert had convinced General Dwight Eisenhower of Niemöller's appeal, Undersecretary of State Dean Acheson remained skeptical as he recalled Niemöller's anti-democratic remarks and record. Acheson wondered if the German pastor was the best German spokesperson for America's "occupation objectives." Disappointed with the choice, he refused to approve Niemöller's visa out of these exact concerns and only relented once Cavert, Herman, and Dulles persistently protested.[20]

With their visas approved, Martin and Else Niemöller arrived in the United States on December 4, 1946, as the first German citizens to visit America following the war. The stakes of his visit were exceedingly high. Leading ecumenists like Cavert hoped Niemöller would further influence the positive American view of Germany as a postwar Protestant partner, not a vanquished foe. In his estimation, Niemöller offered the American public a living example of Germany's "opposition to Hitler." Billing Niemöller as the "churchman who defied the Nazis," the Federal Council played up Niemöller's spiritual opposition to Hitler while silencing any discussion of his support of Hitler's political and racial aims. The decision revealed just how strong the desire to rehabilitate the Germans as transatlantic partners was in American ecumenical circles.[21]

Remembered by many Americans as a Nazi martyr, Niemöller received a barrage of requests for speaking engagements. After addressing the Federal Council annual assembly in Seattle, his barnstorming tour took him to over sixty cities, twenty-two states, forty pastoral conventions, and seventeen

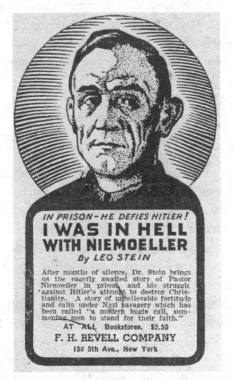

In honoring Martin Niemöller as a "living martyr" who suffered under the Nazis, both ecumenical and evangelical American Protestants sought to claim his fame and recruit him to their respective postwar causes. For his part, Niemöller began to forge his own "third way" in the Cold War.
Courtesy of Wichita State University Libraries, Special Collections and University Archives.

universities and theological seminaries in just over two months' time. In crowded churches, cozy fellowship halls, and seminary classrooms, he gave over two hundred public talks to an estimated 500,000 American Christians. If not for limits of time and stamina, Niemöller's tour would have multiplied those totals by five had he fulfilled all requests, so high was the demand.[22]

Niemöller's visit ultimately sought to foster sympathy for America's Protestant partners in embattled Germany. In his addresses, he thanked Americans for their generous aid and reflected poignantly on the need for stronger Christian fellowship between Americans and Germans. As he spoke on the deep Christian roots of the German people, he provided firsthand accounts of how Germany's Protestants had resisted Hitler. Additionally, he reported on the difficult material conditions Germans faced and called for continued assistance from American churches. His ecumenical hosts considered his trip a smashing success. In their view, the visit improved the ecumenical spirit tying the two nations together. As Cavert wrote to Evangelical Church in Germany (EKD) president Theophil Wurm, the visit had contributed to a "warmer feeling of fraternal fellowship" between the German and American peoples.[23]

Niemöller came to other conclusions. At the 1947 Treysa gathering, the German pastor shared with his German Protestant colleagues that they could learn from American Protestantism's remarkably strong congregations and robust public role. Yet he expressed his continued frustration with the American denazification policy. His portrayal of Germans as good Christians had little effect in getting the Americans to end their occupation or to unify his country. Moreover, Niemöller stated that Americans no longer feared the rise of German militarism but rather Soviet expansion. He worried that Germany had become a pawn in this broader international conflict. Niemöller stood out as one German Protestant who would ultimately resist enlistment into America's emerging Cold War Christian coalition.[24]

With time, the American government also looked to bring over Germans whose anti-communist commitments were stronger than Niemöller's. The National Catholic Welfare Conference (NCWC) readily worked with the government to host the Catholic bishop of Berlin, Konrad von Preysing, for a two-month tour of the United States that replicated Niemöller's in intensity and purpose. In his public addresses, von Preysing delivered a consistent message. He depicted the common German as immune to Nazism and claimed the war had discredited Nazism among the German public. The American press in turn depicted von Preysing as a staunch opponent to

Hitler and the Nazis. As news headlines praised the German cleric for taking a stand against dictatorship, American Catholics echoed the sentiment. The Holy Cross priests of the University of Notre Dame, for instance, honored von Preysing for his "staunch fight against Nazism."[25]

Von Preysing's tour also showcased the Catholic bishop's deep appreciation for Christian democratic values. With occupation tensions mounting in Berlin and the Soviet zone, von Preysing looked to connect with Americans through their shared commitment to religion. He especially praised the Americans as "a free people who freely acknowledge God's sovereignty." In his view, the United States stood as "a land where the sacred principles of humanity, based on belief in one God, are living and directing the life of a great nation." American Catholics in Buffalo, New York returned the praise by lauding von Preysing as a defender of "human rights, human dignity, and human freedom." At a special assembly in San Francisco, Earl Warren, the governor of California, likewise honored von Preysing as a Christian leader whose example emboldened "free men everywhere." Warren stated that von Preysing inspired Americans "to persevere in our devotion to the ideals of truth and justice and charity as expressed through the processes of democratic government." Americans identified in von Preysing the very ideals— human dignity, freedom, and democracy—that they believed their Christian nation protected in the world. Von Preysing's visit and the values it showcased, moreover, granted American Catholics an opportunity to dress themselves in the mantle of Cold War Americanism, thereby claiming a more prominent place in a society that had long been dominated by a Protestant establishment.[26]

Meanwhile, von Preysing stressed the great hope the devastated people of Germany placed in American material relief. He depicted the Americans as exceedingly generous and thanked them for their postwar aid. His visit also inspired new American Catholic relief initiatives, such as the announcement of a $5 million campaign to "help our afflicted brethren in Europe." In summoning America's humanitarian spirit, von Preysing charged the American people with an important role on the global stage: "since the war, America, more than ever before has become a land of promise and hope for the weary people of the Old World." In his opinion, the world needed less totalitarianism and more "Americanism." Von Preysing seemingly played upon the image of the United States as a benevolent Christian nation dedicated to humanitarian relief.[27]

Following von Preysing's tour, the Protestant bishop of Berlin, Otto Dibelius, especially highlighted German Protestantism's anti-communist commitments. In the winter of 1947–1948, Dibelius engaged in a similar national speaking tour of the United States and had a private meeting with President Truman in the Oval Office, who found the bishop quite impressive. One American church leader noted that Dibelius left "a profound impression" upon the American public and that his visit was of "great value to our churches." Herman lavished praise on Dibelius as a "fearless champion of the Christian cause" in response to dictators, both fascist and communist. For his part, Dibelius departed the country energized. In particular, the lay activism of American churches amazed him. He felt emboldened to infuse such activism into his leadership of German churches in response to the Soviet threat.[28]

Reflecting its tri-faith idealism, the Truman administration readily welcomed both von Preysing and Dibelius as Catholic and Protestant allies in the struggle against Soviet communism. Indeed, both Dibelius and von Preysing were beginning to resolutely oppose and condemn the Soviets. In pastoral letters, Dibelius described how Berlin had become a battleground between two competing ideologies, one rooted in freedom, the other in atheism and tyranny. State censorship of the press, the elimination of multi-party politics, and the organization of a national police force all pointed to the development of a totalitarian state in the Soviet zone. As the Soviets stifled freedom, Dibelius sought to ensure that a "red dictatorship" would not take the place "of a brown one." In response, he declared dictatorship to be "inconsistent with the will of God" and defended the church's autonomy. Moreover, the German bishop pushed for a Western orientation in Germany. He now dramatically shifted his view on democracy, stating that the Germans needed "a democratic state system for the sake of the Gospel." In effect, the Cold War had transformed even a conservative stalwart like Dibelius into a democratic partner. Von Preysing likewise highlighted Cold War tensions. He shared that the Soviets had begun to clamp down on the churches. He likewise affirmed that Germany needed to be "rebuilt on democratic and Christian foundations" and called on Americans to help realize that outcome. The commentary of the two bishops showed how commitments to Christianity and democracy glued Germans and Americans together after the war. While Protestant ecumenists opposed Catholicism's advance, the American government still believed that monotheistic religion, human dignity, and religious freedom could unite the United States and occupied Germany. As the

Cold War intensified, Truman's administration likewise secured partnerships with and supported Konrad Adenauer's pro-Western political party, the Christian Democratic Union. The "good Germans" were now those who could be faith-based, democratic allies in the struggle against Soviet communism.[29]

While Niemöller, von Preysing, and Dibelius generally received a warm public welcome, not all Americans approved of their visits. Eleanor Roosevelt critiqued the tours because they created "sympathy for Germany." She did not yet fully support the coalition building the American government had embraced as a foreign policy tool. Along with Roosevelt, other critical voices called into question the record of the three clergy in resisting Hitler. All three in fact had been fiercely loyal to the German nation in the war. Swiss theologian Karl Barth captured the difficulty of the situation when he stated that Niemöller was a "fervent German nationalist." He had been a "good—a too good—Lutheran" in his commitment to the nation. These churchmen also had done little to speak out against Nazi persecution of the Jews. Rabbi Stephen Wise wondered how Americans could openly welcome such anti-semitic Germans. Not all Americans could quickly gloss over these traces of their Nazi and antisemitic past. Finally, some pointed out that German Christianity's consistent anti-communism had actually led many Germans to welcome Hitler in the first place. This same loathing for communism, now broadly championed in the United States, in part had contributed to the unlawful imprisonment of numerous socialists and leftists in Hitler's Reich. Critics of the visits argued that the American way was in fact to grant freedom of political expression and to tolerate political difference.[30]

With communism threatening Europe, however, many Americans came to the defense of the three guests. In response to Roosevelt, one Protestant author heralded Niemöller as a pastor who stood "against tyranny" and fought "for freedom." Henry Smith Leiper also explained away Niemöller's offer to rejoin the German navy as a covert way "to continue opposing Hitler" outside of prison. Similarly, the national chairman of the Catholic War Veterans Americanism Committee defended von Preysing as someone who "fought for the same principles and for the same cause as we Americans fought." According to the chairman, the same could not be said about "godless visitors from Moscow" who stood "for the annihilation of religion and world revolution." American Protestants and Catholics thus easily discovered Cold War values such as freedom, opposition to tyranny, and support of human dignity in the work of their German co-religionists. Consequently, these Americans could sweep away their newfound partners' Nazi past as the confrontation with the Soviet Union grew. Their response also pointed to an emerging revival of American civil religion in the Cold War, wherein faith and anti-communism became near civic duties. While many ecumenists were not eager to see Catholics gain ground in Washington, the Cold War itself would also lead some American Protestants to see Catholics across the globe as their Cold War partners.[31]

Having identified religious alliances as new diplomatic tools in the emerging Cold War, American policymakers built on these high-level visits with grassroots, person-to-person exchanges. Immersions in American religious congregations, they suggested, could provide Germans with "practical experience in the democratic way of life" and facilitate the "political and moral reorientation" of the German people. Soon, hundreds of German pastors and religious educators crossed the Atlantic for religious "reorientation programs" sponsored by American religious groups and the American government. An AMG officer admitted that while the military could not "force a conquered people to accept new ideas and new ways of life," everyday American congregations could win over Germans to democratic principles. Protestant churches could provide a valuable service, she continued, to these "awakened" Germans, especially those in the Soviet sector where "cut and dried slogans" filled "Germany's intellectual and moral vacuum."[32]

Numerous Protestant congregations reached out directly to the AMG in response. For instance, the Congregational Church in Plymouth, Minnesota—"an active democratic fellowship of 1,800 members"—agreed to host a German Protestant for an exchange year and promised it would make the German partner "a part of our fellowship so that he might take home something from our ways." Through these everyday congregations, dozens of German religious leaders traveled to the United States for immersions in American religious life that ranged from placements in American youth ministries to studies of religious media to training in modern evangelistic methods. Additional exchange programs focused on American congregational life, interfaith relations, church-state relations, and community outreach. Upon return to Germany, one German participant noted the trip had significantly "enriched" his understanding of American religion's active role in society. Another felt emboldened to foster more "collaborative work" between clergy and laity in Germany. For American policymakers, such programs strengthened commitments to religion and democracy in Germany's parishes and pews. They expanded America's cultural and spiritual appeal and aimed to remake Germany's spiritual culture in America's trifaith and civil religious image. While high-ranking ecumenists proved wary of yielding ground to Catholics, everyday Americans in the pews proved ready and willing to join a transatlantic religious coalition against communism. For them, Europe had become the frontlines in a spiritual battle for both democracy and Christianity. From the pulpits to the pews, they widely promoted America's Christian identity against the Soviet threat.[33]

The American government likewise sent a wide range of American spiritual leaders to Germany to promote religious activism as an antidote to Soviet materialism. American Catholic priest George Higgins embarked on his own ninety-day tour of Germany to promote Christian democratic values among German Catholic workers and unions. Higgins sought to diminish communist sympathies among Catholic workers while advancing a democratic and economic agenda reminiscent of the New Deal. Meanwhile, the AMG also dispatched American Lutherans to steer conservative German Lutherans toward democracy. American Lutheran representatives at the 1948 Bad Boll Conference encouraged their German peers to embrace "the Christian democratic principles upon which the political, social, and economic structure of the United States are founded." Whether Catholic or Protestant, Truman welcomed the contributions of these various delegations to America's religious front against communism.[34]

Washington even looked to the eccentric evangelist Frank Buchman to promote moral renewal and reconciliation in Europe. After failing to convert Hitler, Buchman had made a name for himself in 1939 by founding "Moral Re-Armament" (MRA), which held massive rallies in Los Angeles and New York and called on Americans and Europeans to "morally rearm" themselves against totalitarianism through embracing the "four absolutes"— honesty, unselfishness, purity, and love. While Buchman faced increasing criticism for his earlier praise of Hitler, he now used anti-communism to clear his name. As the war ended, he went public with a secret Nazi document he claimed had been discovered during the German retreat from France. According to the confidential report, the Nazis had condemned the Oxford Group as a fierce foe and a defender of world democracy. Despite questions regarding its authenticity, Buchman used the document to rehabilitate his record and to portray himself as a perpetual opponent of totalitarian regimes. Reflecting his continued focus on moral holiness, Buchman hosted reconciliation conferences in Switzerland that encouraged French and German participants to repent with one another as a means to secure European peace. In Lucius Clay's view, the MRA gatherings fostered a new European politics rooted in reconciliation and anti-communism. The Truman administration thus forged even the most eclectic of partnerships as it activated the fires of American civil religion in response to the Soviet threat.[35]

While Truman often prioritized working with the ecumenical Federal Council, American evangelicals also stood ready to oppose the advance of communism in Europe. They too launched aggressive campaigns to promote their Christian and democratic ideals across the Atlantic. In contrast to the Federal Council, however, evangelicals spread in Germany commitments to evangelical conversion, free market economics, and militant anti-communism. The outbreak of the Cold War would only further galvanize evangelicals as America's fiercest spiritual warriors.

As the Second World War ended, American evangelicals immediately warned of the Soviets' insatiable desire for world domination. They likewise predicted that an impending third world war loomed on the horizon. As one fundamentalist put it, "RUSSIA IS TO DOMINATE THE EUROPEAN PICTURE as no country has ever dominated it in all of its history . . . Germany is to be her slave . . . Russian atheism and religious ungodliness are quite likely to spread themselves all over Europe as a result of Russian domination." Fundamentalist preacher Hyman Appelman concurred when he prophesied that "Europe is devastated . . . within the next ten years, twenty years at the most, communism will take over all of Europe." Appelman believed a third world war was imminent and therefore outlined a get-tough approach to the Soviet threat. As evidenced, American evangelicals did not shy away from an apocalyptic view of the globe that foretold cataclysmic conflict with the Soviets.[36]

Evangelical fears also spoke to the Soviet threat to German and European Christianity as a whole. Louis Patmont, a revivalist preacher who traveled widely across postwar Europe, especially sounded the alarm. Patmont warned that "Moscow" was out "to completely destroy the influence of German Churches" in the occupation zones. He reported that the Soviets were already pursuing "the complete liquidation of German Churches along with their industries." Across the continent, he added, Europe's Christians were "surpassing for privation and persecution the sorrows of the catacomb period in the ancient Roman Empire." In Patmont's estimation, Americans had never before encountered such a threat. They therefore needed to oppose it with all their might.[37]

The specter of Soviet communism strengthened evangelical calls for aggressive global intervention—both armed and spiritual. Following the war, many evangelicals firmly rejected isolationism. Hyman Appelman, for instance, called isolationist policies "a dead issue" for Americans. He heralded the United States as "the greatest nation in the world" whose "frontiers" had now expanded to "the ends of the earth." America's armed forces bestrode "fifty-nine countries" across the world, placing it in an advantageous position to check evil in its place and preach the life-giving gospel. Appelman's acclamations of military power especially focused on defending and resurrecting Europe as a new evangelical partner. Evangelicals warned that if their nation withdrew its military from the continent, there would be "a complete blackout of European civilization." The heartland of the faith would be thrown "back into the Dark Ages." They therefore demanded their government "open Germany to the Gospel and give missionary forces unhindered opportunity to minister in both spiritual and material ways." Only the evangelical tenets of "Christian America" could restore Europe, they affirmed. Their "Christian nation" was now providentially positioned to lead Europe back to Christ and defend it from the Soviets.[38]

Responding to such calls, Youth for Christ International (YFC) initially carried the evangelical torch to Europe. In the 1940s, YFC had emerged as one of America's leading neo-evangelical ministries under the leadership of aspiring dentist Torrey Johnson. Johnson had organized massive rallies of youth in order to call American youngsters to the highest ideals of Christ and country. In a time of growing concern over "juvenile delinquency," YFC's calls for Christian order and morality gained a wide public backing. Newspaper magnate William Randolph Hearst leant his support, while President Harry Truman's comment that YFC meetings "were just what America needed" showed his willingness to use all forms of faith to fortify American civil religion, even as evangelicals opposed his Fair Deal initiatives and national health insurance plan.[39]

As the nation worried how it would cope with totalitarianism abroad, YFC developed into a national ministry with international aspirations. Relying on the funding of evangelical business owners, it soon set its sights on taking its revivals to postwar Europe. In doing so, it transformed Europe into a battleground between the god-fearing and the godless. At YFC's first annual conference, Johnson announced, "I'm not interested in establishing YOUTH FOR CHRIST everywhere in America—I'M INTERESTED IN REACHING YOUNG PEOPLE FOR JESUS EVERYWHERE!" In 1946, the ministry soon

A Youth for Christ team, including Billy Graham, Torrey Johnson, Chuck
Templeton, and J. Stratton Shufelt, stopped to pray for a revival of European
souls before their first European tour in 1946.
Courtesy of Billy Graham Center Archives, Wheaton College.

sent a small evangelistic team, headlined by Johnson and Billy Graham, on a
first European tour to England and Scandinavia. As promotional materials
from this first tour made clear, the group's answer to the postwar threats of
secularism and communism lay in individual conversion to Christ. One promotional poster described Europe as "in the most desperate spiritual need
since the days of Wesley." In response, the ministry aimed to "win souls for
Christ" and asked for its backers to pray for "1,000 souls per month." In the
ruins of postwar Europe, it would focus on Europe's youth, who could lay the
foundation for a continental revival. Relying on the funding of evangelical
business owners, YFC developed into a national ministry with international
aspirations.[40]

In internationalizing its ministry, YFC drew upon the example of the
young Americans who had spread America's Christian civilization across
the globe at the turn of the twentieth century. In his speeches, Johnson

In the aftermath of a cataclysmic global war, Youth for Christ preachers Torrey Johnson, Billy Graham, and Chuck Templeton hoped to reach Germany, Europe, and the entire globe with their gospel message. With airplanes, radios, and corporate partners at their command, they felt confident they could evangelize the world "within their generation."
Courtesy of Billy Graham Center Archives, Wheaton College.

compared Youth for Christ to the Student Volunteer Movement, which had recruited thousands of American students to lead the American missionary endeavor in America's imperial age. In Johnson's view, both movements shared the same fundamentals in preaching a pure, evangelical gospel and affirming the infallible nature of Scripture. Yet YFC had some decisive advantages in its use of mass rallies and modern technologies like radio broadcasts. Along with new forms of transportation like airplanes, Johnson felt confident that "the evangelization of the world" would finally be accomplished.[41]

As YFC refined its European strategy, it narrowed in on Germany in particular as an evangelistic target. Just like fundamentalists in the era of World War I, Johnson attributed Germany's wayward path to its rejection of evangelical Protestantism and embrace of "heathendom." Echoing the fiery sermons of Billy Sunday, he thundered judgment upon the "disgraceful" nation that had "rejected the Word of God, turned its back upon Jesus Christ, and cast aside Martin Luther and the message of the Reformation." According to Johnson, the horrors of Dachau and Buchenwald had grown out of a theological modernism that had rejected the infallible Word of God. The solution was straightforward. Johnson envisioned igniting a European "great awakening" through his American-led ministry to German youth. Believing the "Christian West" stood at a "crossroads," he urged Americans to see that "this is the most critical hour in all history. This is America's hour of opportunity! This is Germany's hour of destiny!" Through launching new evangelical crusades, Americans could "stem the tide of Godlessness in Europe." With its youth rallies and ministry strategy, YFC planned to reach German youth and steer Germany back to authentic Christian foundations. As Johnson wrote, "the God of Martin Luther still lives and HE will yet give a great mass movement of spiritual revival to this land of the Reformation."[42]

In the context of the Cold War, Johnson readily emphasized the strategic spiritual importance of Germany. To make his case, he used American foreign policies as frameworks for corresponding spiritual strategies. As he warned in one postwar address, "as goes Germany, so goes Western Europe. If Germany goes communistic, then you can write France, Italy, Spain, and Portugal off in the same category." In these remarks, Johnson spiritualized America's "containment" strategy and the emerging Cold War "domino theory." He warned that Germany was the crucial spiritual and political edifice in Europe. If Americans failed to halt communism in that vital "spiritual center," the nations of the Western Europe would fall like cascading dominos one by one. Johnson thus urged the evangelical faithful "to get to Germany as soon as possible." As he made clear, "the destiny of Europe's civilization will be determined with what happens in Germany." Paralleling rhetoric ecumenical leader Stewart Herman had used just years before, the evangelist added, "If we fail . . . all of Europe will be overswept—yes, probably America very soon will be engulfed in the bitter hatred of Godlessness that is rising in the Old World." For Johnson and other evangelicals, reviving Germany therefore had tremendous spiritual implications for the "Christian West" and the United States. His use of foreign policy metaphors to make that case showed evangelicals' eagerness to integrate their movement into the mainstream currents of American life. It also revealed how American Protestants were not shy about weaponizing their faith in the Cold War. Evangelicals volunteered their theology as the surest way to contain and roll back communism in Europe.[43]

To shore up the West's spiritual defenses in Germany, Johnson reached out to the AMG to secure an entry permit and begin hosting revivals but received no response. As his petitions continued to go unheard, Johnson suspected a conspiracy was at work. The "very liberal" leaders of the Religious Affairs Branch must be opposing "bible-believing people," he surmised. Expressing the kind of fears that would soon ignite a domestic Red Scare, the American preacher stated that "communists and communistic fellow-travelers . . . of the American Military Government" were hindering his YFC teams from getting into Germany. These leaders instead gave "high priority" to the Protestant "liberalists" of the Federal and World Council of Churches.[44]

To counteract these liberal ecumenists, Johnson turned to personal contacts among American military chaplains, in particular Chaplain Paul Maddox, the chief chaplain of the US European Command, whom Johnson lauded as "a great man of God." Maddox was a textbook fundamentalist, affirming the authority of Scripture and the centrality of conversion. Johnson also nurtured connections to fundamentalist military officers, helping forge in the process an enduring postwar partnership between evangelical religion and America's armed forces. Praising American infantrymen and officers as an "army of occupation" bringing "the Gospel into Germany," Johnson called upon faithful American military members to form YFC clubs on military bases and local communities. Just as young American soldiers had stormed the beaches of Normandy to defeat the Nazis, so too would they now spiritually occupy Europe and foster its evangelical revival.[45]

Johnson's focus on working with the American armed forces also reflected the evangelical proclivity for a unilateral approach to foreign missions. Evangelicals initially believed they would find few German partners in evangelism. Germany was just too prone to theological modernism, they thought. As such, American evangelicals emphasized that Germany required "outside leadership" in order for it "to be revived." YFC thus first looked to American military chaplains to lead its affairs in Germany. In 1945, Johnson even reached out to Martin Niemöller to share with the German pastor that his youth organization was "prepared to send a battalion of young Americans to Germany . . . to show the young people the way back to God." Niemöller thanked him for his concern but stated that he and his peers would have to bear the responsibility of reviving their own country. Nonetheless, Johnson pressed onward undeterred, seeking to forge partnerships with American chaplains and military officers to carry out the task of evangelism. Evangelical soldiers in Heidelberg, Wiesbaden, and Nürnberg answered the call and organized hundreds of spontaneous rallies on American military bases. After the military lifted its restriction on "fraternization" between American soldiers and Germans, the Americans quickly moved to evangelize their local communities. American soldiers meeting at the Frankfurt YFC club, for instance, regularly distributed tracts at major pedestrian areas in Frankfurt. In one month alone, the soldiers handed out an estimated 230,000 tracts throughout the German city.[46]

In building these military partnerships, YFC readily used military terminology to describe its evangelical campaigns in Germany, Europe, and beyond. Postwar revivals were now "invasions," led by evangelical "battalions" that fought for "spiritual victories" across the continent. Their rhetoric mirrored the military-ministry partnership that grew as America's armed forces established an unprecedented global presence. Relying on the military's global reach, YFC's postwar operations indeed soon extended beyond just Germany into neighboring European nations and even stretched to China and Japan. In that corner of the globe, evangelical missionaries answered General Douglas MacArthur's call to Christianize and democratize occupied Japan in an offensive maneuver against "the crusade of Communism" in East Asia. President Truman praised the effort, noting that "democracy and progress" would only come to Japan through the spread of "fundamental Christian principles." America's military missionaries thus began to undertake a new evangelical and democratic "invasion" across the globe.[47]

With time, however, YFC's military strategy began to give way to more indigenous models of ministry. American soldiers began to invite German guests to attend their rallies, casting the seeds for a German-American evangelical alliance. Upon further reflection, Johnson began to recognize that these Germans indeed could be allies in evangelism and perhaps be even more effective evangelists due to their knowledge of German culture and fluency in the German language. Yet Johnson still noted they would need to be trained in American methods. He therefore began to draft plans for educating "one hundred German evangelists" in "American techniques" in order to spread the gospel message across the barren land. American military chaplains began to forge collaborative partnerships with German evangelicals, teaching them in the process American revival techniques. YFC clubs soon boasted a mixed German-American membership, such as the club in Wiesbaden, which relied on a core group of fifty Germans and twenty-five

Americans to organize its rallies. Johnson also looked to German-American businessmen and industrialists to strengthen his evangelistic network. John Bolten, a successful German businessman who had emigrated to the United States in the late 1920s, proved particularly helpful in connecting him to potential German Protestant allies. In these ways, YFC initially pursued an America-first approach to postwar evangelization that gradually gave way to new partnerships with German evangelicals. Eventually, these kinds of cross-cultural partnerships would foster among some American evangelicals a more critical perspective on just how intertwined American evangelicalism was with American militarism and other American Cold War values. Yet for the time being, most American evangelicals saw little dissonance between their faith and the American way.[48]

With Maddox's assistance, Johnson finally received approval to travel to Germany in the spring of 1947 in order to conduct religious rallies for German youth. Like a circuit preacher of old, he traveled a reported total of 4,000 miles across Germany, stopping in Frankfurt, Berlin, Wiesbaden, Stuttgart, Nürnberg, and Munich to meet with free church ministers, Baptists, Methodists, YMCA leaders, and army chaplains. He found willing partners in free church Germans who practiced their Christian faith independent of the EKD. In particular, Johnson connected with Baptist pastors Willi Sauer and Willy Diezel of the "Evangelical Alliance," who both agreed to take leadership roles in a newly constituted German chapter of the YFC. Increasingly, Johnson and other evangelicals would look to the "Alliance" as a faithful indigenous partner in the effort to reconvert Germany. He likewise wrote home of Germany's great spiritual and material need and called on American evangelicals to lead a robust material relief campaign that would complement their evangelization efforts.[49]

Johnson's interactions with the AMG during his tour pointed to broader theological and diplomatic rifts forming between Protestant ecumenists and evangelicals in the United States. Once on the ground in Germany, Johnson went toe to toe with what he described as a "liberal" Religious Affairs officer in the military government. As he recounted, this "young snipper" accused him of being a spiritual fascist akin to Hitler that believed in the truthfulness of a single book (the Bible) and a single person (Jesus). The encounter led Johnson to send off a series of accusatory letters to his congressional representatives and Lucius Clay. He accordingly warned Maddox of a "leadership coup" within the AMG. As he wrote, liberal elements were "laboring feverishly to unseat and undermine" Maddox's "authority." In response, Johnson

American military chaplain Paul Maddox (fourth from left), army servicemen, and German Youth for Christ members greet evangelical minister Torrey Johnson (fourth from right) upon his arrival in Frankfurt. The partnership of Maddox and Johnson signaled how postwar evangelicals would look to the American military to carry out a "spiritual occupation" of Germany.
Courtesy of Billy Graham Center Archives, Wheaton College.

praised the "scores of Godly chaplains" who served the cause of evangelical Christianity in occupied Germany. Johnson's letter drew clear spiritual battle lines that were quickly transcending occupied Germany and fostering a new anti-communist politics of Americanism at home.[50]

While Johnson dealt with liberal military officers and ecumenical representatives in Germany, he also faced headaches back home. Separatist fundamentalist Gerald L. K. Smith had sought to capitalize on YFC's growing fame through hosting "Christian Youth for America" rallies across the country. Johnson received a host of telegrams inquiring why his youth ministry had partnered with Smith. He went into damage control, clarifying to the American press that his organization had no official ties to Smith's movement, nor did it tolerate antisemitism or racism. Smith and his ally Gerald Winrod both bristled at Johnson disowning them in public. Fashioning themselves as "persecuted preachers" and "martyrs

Youth for Christ began to train German evangelistic teams, such as the one pictured here in Duisburg, in American revivalist techniques in order to inspire a postwar revival and strengthen democratic commitments across occupied Germany.
Courtesy of Billy Graham Center Archives, Wheaton College.

for true Christian Americanism," they affirmed God had chosen them "to help save America in this dark hour." They dedicated themselves to building a "great wall for God in America" through their extremist beliefs and continued to seek more recruits to their "Christian nationalist crusade." Battle lines thus also surfaced between old-school fundamentalists and the now more mainstream evangelicals. Even though a "new" evangelical like Johnson sought to distance himself from fundamentalists like Winrod and Carl McIntire, he in fact continued to share with them rather similar political and diplomatic convictions when it came to international organization, the threat of communism, and the apocalyptic potential of the Cold War.[51]

Postwar evangelicals were eager as well to use their crusades and connections to the military as means to advance these politically conservative commitments among the mainstream public on both sides of the Atlantic. Recognizing the rise of evangelicals as a new diplomatic force, the Department of State invited a National Association of Evangelicals (NAE) representative to join its religious affairs committee. Having gained the ear of America's foreign policymakers, NAE leader Harold Ockenga affirmed America's postwar role as "the guardian of the West" and expressed his concern over the spread of "communist propaganda" in postwar Europe. He also called on the government to enforce "democratization" in Germany, in particular to spread "the ideology of free enterprise, the infinite value of the individual, and the freedoms which we know in America." Ockenga's vision for foreign policy was confirmed at a 1950 NAE convention, which called for the promotion of "free enterprise," "private property," and "moral integrity" both at home and abroad.[52]

Here again, evangelicals differentiated themselves from their ecumenical counterparts. They helped ensure that Europe would be a battleground against not only communism but also New Deal liberalism and social democracy. So too did American evangelicals promote a unilateral, go-it-alone mentality in diplomacy that contrasted the multilateral approach of ecumenists. These competing postwar mobilizations stood as a reminder that ecumenism and evangelicalism were never about theology and doctrine alone. In particular, evangelical faith was interlaced with a set of political and diplomatic convictions, including commitments to limited government, individual freedom, free markets, rugged militarism, unilateralism, and Western civilization. To be sure, not all evangelicals shared these exact views or felt that such a political synthesis had much to do with the Jesus of the gospels. A spectrum of evangelicals existed in the United States, with some espousing a pacifist and prophetic ethic. Yet more often than not, the American evangelical gospel proved captive to the national, cultural, and political currents of Cold War America. On this point, American evangelicals were not alone. American ecumenists proved just as ready and willing to spread their understanding of the American way across the Atlantic.

These competing understandings of the "American Century" ultimately led American evangelicals and ecumenists to see one another as spiritual opponents in "Battleground Europe." In many ways, ecumenists and evangelicals shared the same concerns about Germany's spiritual rebirth and the growing tide of secularism and communism in Europe. Yet they ultimately preached competing interpretations of the American gospel. While ecumenists heralded a new ethic of civic activism, multilateral international order, and ideological opposition to communism, evangelicals promoted biblical fundamentals, economic and political liberty, and militant strength. All the while, both ecumenists and evangelicals felt uneasy about Truman's newfound alliance with the Vatican and Catholicism. "Battleground Europe" pit Protestants against Catholics, as well as God-fearing democrats against godless communists, in equal measure. To keep such spiritual opponents at bay, American ecumenists were beginning to plan a grand spiritual intervention in Europe of their own that they hoped would grant them a decisive advantage in the struggle for the continent's soul.

7

God's Marshall Plan

As Stewart Herman traveled across Europe in 1947 to coordinate the distribution of ecumenical aid, scenes of battle-scarred cities, long bread lines,
and homeless migrants seemed to meet him at every major turn. Europe's
spiritual landscape, he noted, was also in ruins. Countless churches had
been reduced to piles of rubble; scores of seminarians had been killed in the
war; Nazified youth lacked spiritual direction; and religious doubt grew in
the face of untold suffering. Protestant churches in Soviet-occupied lands
especially seemed to be faring poorly under the imposition of Stalinist
dictatorships. With the continued support of the American government,
Herman was among the first American Protestants to "slip behind the Iron
Curtain" and visit in person with Protestants now living underneath new
communist regimes. He reported back home on the "very precarious" situation of the churches there. In his words, these Protestants waged an "unequal
fight against the force applied against it by the Communist Party." Herman
warned that this "new system, the Communist East" saw Christianity as "a
superfluous, tolerated nuisance." It would perhaps not be long, he feared,
until the Soviets moved to eliminate the churches altogether. To give these
European Protestants a fighting chance and a "reason for hope in the future,"
he added, Americans would need to provide additional aid and support. As
hunger, despair, and disbelief stalked the continent, he and other Americans
indeed worried that Europe's Protestant institutions could soon fail, opening
the floodgates to a deluge of secularism, nihilism, and communism across
the continent.[1]

For all these reasons, ecumenists like Herman welcomed the European
Recovery Program (ERP) with high praise and hopeful optimism.
Announced that summer by US Secretary of State George Marshall, this bold
diplomatic initiative, known popularly as the Marshall Plan, pledged to stabilize Europe and to revive its economies through an infusion of $13 billion
in American economic aid. Herman saw in the plan a program "nearer to
being Christian" than any other postwar foreign policy to date. In peacefully
supporting Europe's reconstruction, he believed that "Christian America"

God's Marshall Plan. James D. Strasburg, Oxford University Press (2021). © Oxford University Press.
DOI: 10.1093/oso/9780197516447.003.0008

was making good on its spiritual commitments to creating a new Christian world order that kept spiritual disbelief and political disorder equally at bay.[2]

Yet the American ecumenist also thought dollar diplomacy alone would not restore Europe to full health. Only "spiritual reconstruction" could touch and restore the continent's soul. Herman therefore outlined a spiritual recovery program—"A Marshall Plan for the Churches," as he put it—that would activate the "spiritual forces" of "the brotherhood of man under the fatherhood of God." Such a program would foster "the religious renewal of the continent" and compliment the economic and political integration of Europe into the "West"—a new transatlantic postwar order predicated upon democracy, free markets, and belief in God. This spiritual Marshall Plan aimed to transform Europe's spiritual culture and thwart the spread of atheism and communism through reconstructing churches, providing material aid, and encouraging theological reform.[3]

It also made the World Council of Churches (WCC) into an agent of American foreign policy in Europe. In an era when American capital, consumer goods, popular culture, and military platoons poured into Europe and began to remake the continent's economics, society, and politics, this accompanying spiritual intervention sought to transform Europe's soul. At this crucial juncture in the Cold War, "God's Marshall Plan" provided critical spiritual support to the creation of a new Western order that was Christian, democratic, and capitalist. In response, however, a vocal number of European Protestants challenged this American spiritual crusade altogether. In particular, European theologians proposed a new "third way" theology that identified the world's Protestants as mediators between East and West in the emerging conflict. Far from remaking Europe or unifying the "Christian West," God's Marshall Plan instead splintered transatlantic Protestantism into spiritual factions.[4]

As the Cold War intensified in the summer of 1947, leading American and British voices echoed Herman's call for economic and spiritual aid as a means to counteract communism's advance. A host of prominent figures continued to describe Europe as a decisive spiritual battleground—one of the most crucial postwar landscapes where Protestants needed to vie for the primacy of Christ and democracy. Humanitarian administrator and former Republican president Herbert Hoover and Scottish ecumenist J. Hutchinson at least thought as much: both warned that the cradle of "Western civilization" was now in jeopardy. The usual suspects, such as Allen Dulles and John Foster Dulles, likewise called on American churches to complement American foreign policy with a "Marshall plan of the spirit for the people of Europe." Firm supporters of Herman's work, the Dulles brothers continued to look to the Protestant churches as a spiritual bulwark against communism across the continent. In Herman's spiritual recovery program, they saw another means to orient Europe westward. So too did Reinhold Niebuhr, who had grown increasingly concerned about Soviet expansionism. Niebuhr argued that the Marshall Plan was the ideal application of "American power" that promised to secure the "European destiny" and defend the continent from totalitarianism. Drawing from their realist ethic, Protestants like Niebuhr and diplomats like the Dulles brothers continued to pursue a hard line against Soviet communism through programs of spiritual and economic reconstruction.[5]

Having long supported European reconstruction, major mainline Protestant institutions likewise called for American spiritual and diplomatic activism in Europe. While less confrontational in its tone than Niebuhrian realists, *The Christian Century* urged increases in humanitarian aid in order to soothe material and psychological distress. It also voiced its support for new diplomatic maneuvers such as the 1947 merger of the American and British zones in occupied Germany. The leading mainline periodical especially hoped the creation of "Bizonia" would begin to end the occupied country's "economic strangulation" through promoting interzonal trade. Even more, the editors hoped, the merger could potentially lead to Germany's unification in the heart of a pacified Europe. The Federal Council also issued a statement celebrating the European Recovery Program as a "momentous affirmation" of "freedom" and "the creative capacity of free men." In particular, it defended a Western commitment to "inalienable rights . . . endowed by the Creator" and helped guarantee "a life of freedom and fellowship" for postwar Europe. The infusions of economic aid would moreover help secure the continent's "self-determination" in the face of Soviet expansionism. Yet on that note, the Federal Council also warned its government not to "remake Europe" in the "American political and economic image," just as the Soviets had done to Eastern European countries. The Council clearly condemned the Soviets' tactics as the maneuvers of an old-style empire. In contrast, it called on the United States to become a benevolent world power. Through its moral example, the United States could strengthen its global appeal and broadcast its values abroad.[6]

While President Harry Truman had declared that the United States sought "no territorial expansion of selfish advantage" through its postwar engagement, the Marshall Plan still revealed America's pursuit of a becoming a new globe-spanning hegemon. In particular, while policymakers presented it as a humanitarian endeavor, Marshall's program of reconstruction was also designed to economically integrate Western Europe into America's postwar sphere of influence. Such economic aid was just the beginning of America's dramatic expansion across the Atlantic. Beyond economic reconstruction, American policymakers also established their nation's postwar influence across the continent through trade networks, military alliances and bases, and cultural appeal. Such efforts effectively built up Western Europe as a key outpost of a new American order, one that was not defined by colonies, but rather by a shared market, a mutual security framework, and a federation of postwar democratic states. At the center of this European order stood the Western occupation zones in Germany and the Federal Republic of Germany that emerged out of them. With Marshall Plan funds strengthening its economy, American troops securing its borders, and a US-sponsored treaty guaranteeing its democratic form of government, some historians have argued that West Germany effectively became an unofficial "American state" in Europe in the early Cold War. In this regard, the Marshall Plan was but one part of a broader quest to establish a new American order across the Atlantic.[7]

To compliment these diplomatic efforts, American ecumenists outlined a campaign of spiritual reconstruction that identified Germany as the cornerstone of a new democratic and Christian order in the heart of Europe. They accordingly sought to work through the WCC and the American Military Government (AMG) to reconstruct German spiritual life along ecumenical lines. Exporting spiritual values such as congregationalism, lay voluntarism, and public activism, they hoped, would help create a spiritual foundation for a new democratic Germany. This vision of spiritual reconstruction drew upon a long tradition of theological reflection that had identified Germany's spiritual and political culture as authoritarian and in need of reform. In a telling phrase, one World Council field worker stated "the Führer principle" was "deeply rooted and not dead" in German churches. As a "top-down" hierarchy, the German Protestant church had historically failed to activate the energies of lay believers and local congregations. Instead, the church functioned as a cultural institution that existed to facilitate "the outstanding events of life: baptism, confirmation, marriage, and burial." In contrast to this stale system, ecumenists worked to make German Protestantism into a spiritual force that could "achieve a more Christian world." Herman especially urged on a new ethic of public engagement and activism, stating that "the post-war mood requires motion. Tabernacles, not temples! A static church attracts no interest." The American ecumenist added that the new German church would also need to forsake the long-standing Two Kingdoms teaching that bifurcated the world into two realms: "a spiritual one, embodied in the Church, and a worldly one, dominated by a complete secularization." Instead, American ecumenists hoped to help German Protestants secure Christ's "vast claim over the entire world."[8]

As ecumenists made clear, Germany's predicament was a continental one as well. Drawing from his travels for the World Council, Herman in particular argued that "millions of Europeans" were no longer authentic Christians, making the "cradle of Christian culture" itself a new and "major" Christian "mission field." Ecumenical reconstruction efforts in Germany would therefore serve as a blueprint for continent-wide operations. Herman accordingly called on "Christian America" to rally in response, starting with the "Christianization" of Germany and then proceeding to claim the entire continent for Christ.[9]

In coming to Germany and Europe's aid, mainline American Protestants also expressed an emerging postwar mentality that fused together an ethic of global responsibility with a long-standing notion of spiritual exceptionalism. For instance, one postwar American Protestant relief agency—the Emergency Committee for German Protestantism—noted that despite Germany's extensive contributions to "World Protestantism," the destruction of the war had left the country's spiritual reserves depleted. With much of the continent now under Soviet control, "World Protestantism" had "sustained . . . its greatest loss ever," the agency reported. In response, the relief committee called on American Protestants to "save German Protestantism!" While Germany had once been a citadel of the faith, it now fell upon American Protestants to assume the mantle of global leadership and breathe new life into Germany's churches. Such proclamations certainly reflected a newfound sense of global responsibility and growing commitment to ecumenical relief. Yet they also drew energy from the long-standing belief that American Protestants had a special mission to spiritually conquer the world and bring it underneath Christ's rule. Germany had quickly emerged as the major postwar stage upon which American Protestants would act out such convictions, often with conflicting results.[10]

Rebuilding the thousands of German churches destroyed in the war stood out as one of the most significant ways American ecumenists sought to reconstruct German Protestantism. The need was indeed tremendous and pressing. Herman's postwar reports had recounted scene after scene of bombed out and burned down churches in nearly every major German city he visited. With their churches in ruins, Herman wrote, German communities were hard pressed to organize worship services, youth education, and weekly prayer. An official 1948 World Council report confirmed Herman's reconnaissance. Nearly 7,500 churches had been "very severely" to "slightly damaged" in the war, rendering them either unusable or in need of repair. Valuable material resources, such as Bibles, hymnals, and theological literature, had also been damaged or completely destroyed in air raids. From a material standpoint, German Christianity faced an unprecedented crisis. As one World Council report put it, the German people had "lost their spiritual bearings" with the destruction of their "familiar spiritual landmarks." They were "wandering blindly in darkness and in the shadow of death." In response, the WCC began shipping makeshift Swiss military barracks into occupied Germany as temporary emergency churches, with additional barracks sent to Holland and France as well. Due to their wooden construction, the barracks could be dismantled, mass shipped, and then reassembled on site by teams of volunteers. After sending an initial shipment of forty-four barracks, the WCC launched a fundraising campaign for more purchases, with American churches providing the lion's share of funds.[11]

Beyond re-establishing spiritual landmarks across Germany, American ecumenists hoped these emergency structures would serve as a platform for democratic reforms within the German Protestant church as a whole. As Herman wrote, these humble barracks were meant in part to dismantle Germany's "expensive ecclesiastical machinery." Instead of towering Gothic cathedrals, these meek new structures, built in the midst of postwar ruins, would be the kind of living "tabernacles" that restored belief, revived hearts, and inspired activism across a secularized continent. In Germany's ruined cityscapes, their communal construction would also mark a grassroots initiative of lay activism and symbolize the "church in action." These lowly structures would begin to rebuild German Protestantism from the ground up, fostering a thriving congregational life and sense of spiritual responsibility that in turn would undergird a new democratic civic sphere. In this way, American ecumenists envisioned the barracks churches serving as the first spiritual schoolhouses of democracy for the new Germany. Such a renewal would in turn promote the spiritual culture that they believed was so central to a thriving democratic society.[12]

Ecumenical reports on the barracks suggested that the new structures promised to fulfill these purposes. After receiving a barracks church, for instance, the *Brüdergemeinde*, a Protestant parish in Berlin, immediately began to host three Sunday services, two weekly Bible studies, and its brass band and choir rehearsals within its wooden walls. The effects of such meeting spaces did not go unnoticed. The parish pastor noted the barracks "served as rallying points for Christian people" recovering from the trauma of war. Pursuing a weekly rhythm of prayer, worship, and fellowship provided a spiritual anchor for everyday Germans longing for direction. Beyond stabilizing communities, the barracks seemed to strengthen lay participation in the life of the church as well. The same pastor noted that his congregants poured "gifts of money and material and time" into clearing rubble and debris and constructing the makeshift structures. He added that his congregants "poured their love and labor into the construction of even a little barrack." The pastor likewise noted that the barracks had led to new ecumenical collaboration. His parish had invited a local Mennonite congregation to use their barracks structure, as well as the Young Men's Christian Association in Berlin. On this point, the barracks churches also symbolized the goodwill of Christians from the United States and thus were meant to further ecumenical fellowship between the two nations. All told, the *Brüdergemeinde* symbolized how the barracks churches were designed to empower the laity and foster spiritual renewal in a dire time.[13]

After the barracks project showed signs of success, World Council ecumenists began working closely with the German Protestant relief agency *Hilfswerk* to expand their reconstruction efforts. *Hilfswerk*'s director Eugen Gerstenmaier had tasked leading church architect Otto Bartning to design a church structure that could be built out of the rubble of destroyed churches and buildings. German congregations could gather these rubble materials, Gerstenmaier and Bartning suggested, while American churches could finance raw materials like wood, glass, and iron that were difficult to acquire in postwar Germany. American ecumenists lauded the idea. Just like the barracks project, the *Hilfswerk* design promised to cultivate lay activism, strengthen congregational identities, and nurture an ethic of responsibility. World Council leaders therefore began to raise the nearly half million US dollars it would take to construct forty-eight *Notkirchen* ("emergency churches") throughout all four occupation zones.[14]

The city of Pforzheim became the first test site for constructing Bartning's design. Nestled in the southwestern corner of the American occupation zone, the city had lost nearly all of its Protestant churches in a single bombing raid. With over 60,000 Protestant churchgoers, the lack of physical meeting space placed extraordinary burdens on the city's congregations. Brick by brick, stone by stone, Pforzheim congregants had begun gathering and salvaging building materials out of the ruin and rubble of their city. They cheered the arrival of World Council shipments that brought prefabricated items, including wooden support beams, windows, and doors, which they then paired with the rubble building materials. In just a year's time, their gritty hard work led to the completion of their emergency church.[15]

The dedication ceremony of the completed rubble church in Pforzheim sought to emphasize the city's spiritual renewal. As World Council officials and German congregants gathered together, church architect Otto Bartning compared Germany's postwar situation to Israel's Exodus journey through the wilderness. The "emergency church," Bartning explained, existed to guide Germans lost "in the desert of destructed cities." To congregations living in the rubble, he continued, the church offered orientation, hope, and renewal. The congregation affirmed Bartning's vision. Wanting to emphasize that their church's hour of spiritual renewal and rebirth had come, they intentionally changed the church's name from the "Church of St. John" to the "Church of the Resurrection." In his sermon that day, the church's pastor invoked the image of a mummified Lazarus coming forth from his tomb at the call of Jesus. He heralded the new church "as a symbol of life in a city... of death and destruction." In these ways, the dedication ceremony in Pforzheim spoke powerfully to the possibility of ecclesial renewal in the postwar hour.[16]

Ecumenists soon replicated the effort in over forty-seven additional locations. Just like the barracks, the construction of *Notkirchen* was meant to nurture spiritual and political transformation in occupied Germany. Above all, church reconstruction focused American and German efforts on forming new German citizens who would be active both spiritually and civically in postwar Germany. One *Hilfswerk* leader stated that the new housing structures being raised in destroyed cities through Marshall Plan funds would "remain dead shells" without a new kind of person to occupy them. These "new humans" were "the foundational element of our renewal," he declared. *Notkirchen* were designed to form these "new Germans" into vigorous citizens through inviting them to take an active role in the reconstruction of their churches. As German congregations salvaged hundreds of thousands of stones, bricks, and other raw materials from their ruined cities for church reconstruction, ecumenists hoped they were nurturing a stronger lay ethic and congregational spirit across Germany. These spiritual traits, they believed, not only formed the spiritual foundation of a democratic civic sphere, but also served as a bulwark against communism.[17]

Beyond the forty-eight "emergency churches," ecumenists also commissioned special reconstruction projects such as rebuilding the Reformed Church at Barmen. With Karl Barth helping raise funds abroad, the Barmen project aimed to reconstruct the church exactly as it looked in 1934 at the famous synod that authored the Barmen Declaration. Ecumenists hailed the declaration as "the most important occurrence" in the German Protestantism's modern history. It was the "Magna Carta" of their age and the foundation for an internal transformation within the church. They hoped the rebuilt church would provide an "enduring memorial" to future generations of the Germans who fought against the "false teachings and violent deeds" of the "national socialist worldview." In prioritizing the reconstruction of the Barmen church, the ecumenical council held up the Confessing Church as a model for the future of German Protestantism.[18]

As these new churches popped up across Germany, American ecumenists complemented their construction with infusions of spiritual aid. The American Bible Society, for instance, began to ship millions of Bibles, hymnals, catechisms, and devotional materials to fill the ecclesial spaces. A German pastor thanked the Americans for the gift, noting that "Germany has a hunger of the body, but also for the Gospel which has been almost crushed." Meanwhile, the WCC outfitted German pastors with bicycles, motorcycles, and automobiles to minister to congregants and supplied mass quantities of raw paper for the printing of spiritual literature. This spiritual aid, designed to accompany Marshall Plan dollars, sought to fill the defeated nation with a Christian spirit that Nazism and Soviet communism could not defeat.[19]

For more conservative Protestants, the construction of *Notkirchen* indeed was designed to "re-Christianize" the German nation and counteract "Bolshevism." Emergency church planners specifically earmarked funds for emergency church construction in major cities in the Soviet zone, such as Berlin, Dresden, Leipzig, and Weimar. While *Notkirchen* built in the eastern zone promoted solidarity between German churches across the Iron Curtain, they also served as a clear sign of the Protestant willingness to counteract "atheistic communism." This anti-communist resolve especially

American Lutherans and the Federal Council of Churches provided most of the funding for the construction of forty-eight "emergency churches" across occupied Germany. These rubble churches reflected the ecumenical focus on rebuilding German spiritual institutions on a democratic basis. The emergency churches likewise served as spiritual bulwarks against secularism and communism in the emerging Cold War.
Courtesy of World Council of Churches Archives.

appeared in the reconstruction of the small city of Anklam's church, which lay in the Soviet zone. A *Hilfswerk* report indicated how the damaged church had been left dormant, "dirty," and "full of refuse" after the war. It was "completely burnt out" from the war, with "enormous holes in the roof" and "windows destroyed." Even worse, "the Party" had begun to use the church "as a storehouse for arms." Neighbors had reported that the communists engaged in "wicked mischievousness" in the church's sacred halls. Yet the local congregants would have none of it. They pushed back against the local authorities, collected the necessary funds, and repaired the church. Meanwhile, Sunday School attendance skyrocketed, lay religion classes began, and "community life was revived." The WCC and *Hilfswerk* heralded this example under the bold headline: "This is Church Reconstruction." A 1948 promotional booklet on church reconstruction provided further visual evidence of the battle lines that had been drawn. Although the German Protestant church remained institutionally united across the four occupation zones, the booklet's map clearly demarcated the Soviet occupation zone from the Western zones. The map's boundaries illustrated how the imagination of ecumenical Protestants clearly conformed to Cold War geographies, even as they professed to transcend such boundaries.[20]

In addition to fostering anti-communism, church reconstruction also strengthened ties between God-fearing Germans and faith-filled Americans. Federal Council congregations and American Lutheran relief agencies led the global Protestant charge in raising funds for church reconstruction. In honor of these efforts, cornerstone ceremonies became occasions for Germans to celebrate the generous American aid that rebuilt their spiritual centers. At one dedication service, German clergymen expressed their gratitude "to our brothers in faith in America" who had bankrolled the construction of their emergency church. The church's pastor likewise heralded the Americans for their "spirit of reconciliation" and prayed that the "same spirit of peace and reconciliation would forever remain within the halls of the rubble-church." Individual church communities in the United States and Germany also found themselves bound together in new ways. Handwritten letters from German congregations thanked the Americans for their generosity and Christian charity. Such exchanges created tangible connections between Christians in the United States and Germany and vested churches on the opposite side of an ocean in each other's future.[21]

In these ways, church reconstruction aimed to promote American spiritual values abroad while also enhancing America's international appeal in the early Cold War. American ecumenists hoped that the reconstruction of churches—stone by stone, brick by brick—would ultimately transform German Protestantism into a democratic force in a spiritual battle against secularism and communism. Without question, church reconstruction aided congregations in need, promoted reconciliation, and provided spiritual orientation in a fragmented landscape. Yet for many American ecumenists, it was also about reforming Germany's soul and creating an American-led world order in the heart of Cold War Europe. Such efforts continued into the postwar era their long-standing mission of worldwide Christianization and democratization.

Beyond rebuilding destroyed churches, ecumenical reconstruction also distributed material relief across Germany and Europe in order to diminish the psychological distress of war, strengthen transatlantic bonds, and circumvent communist sympathies. Everyday Protestants from across the United States contributed weekly donations of money, food, and clothing to Germany in order to revive Europe's faith and counteract communism. In the "Christian Carloads" program, for instance, farmers from across the Great Plains filled their pickups and cars with surplus crops and donated the haul to Germany. *Hilfswerk* especially honored farmers from Oklahoma and Colorado who gave enough wheat to feed millions of Germans. Meanwhile, the women of Birmingham, Alabama, garnered German gratitude for their donation of syrup. As *Hilfswerk* put it, these gifts—both small and large—witnessed to Germans that "the spirit of Christianity is alive in America." Over time, these carloads of surplus crops and Sunday collections of canned goods, clothing, and offerings added up to hundreds of millions of pounds in material aid shipped from American Protestants to their anti-communist spiritual partners in Germany.[22]

This ecumenical material relief uplifted everyday Germans while also strengthening transatlantic ties. One widowed mother in postwar Germany found solace in providing her daughter with shoes and a used dress sent over from the United States. Her daughter wrote in gratitude, "the dress will keep me warm and last a long time. . . . I always think of the American girl who has worn it before and given it to me." Shipments of flour ensured the mother could provide daily bread to her family. Another widow noted the psychological impact American aid had upon her: the aid was "a spark of hope and of belief in mankind." Ecumenical Protestants affirmed such relief helped defeat the "weary cynicism" growing in Germany and promoted reconciliation between former enemies. More broadly, it illustrated that ecumenical ideas were not only promoted; they were actually felt, internalized, and acted on by everyday believers in the United States and Germany. Individual Protestants on both sides of the Atlantic forged new ties in their common faith and hope for postwar peace.[23]

Ecumenical material relief also focused on the severe refugee crisis developing in the Soviet occupation zone. Americans increasingly criticized Soviet occupation policies that promoted "rampant hunger" and "tremendous hardship" in the midst of the crisis. While the Soviet authorities curtailed the powers of the churches in education and politics, material relief proved to be one area where the churches had greater freedom. With most of the thirteen million German refugees pouring into the Soviet zone, the Soviet authorities needed religious relief agencies to quell a worsening humanitarian crisis, one that had the potential to dampen the appeal of Soviet communism across Europe. The Soviets therefore granted the churches this limited sphere of freedom with caution, fearing in particular external influences from the Vatican or American churches. To curtail such influence, the Soviet administrators ordered the churches to coordinate their relief underneath the Soviet's governmental relief agency. Many churches refused to cooperate and distributed aid independently, in the process opposing the "red dictatorship."[24]

To support the churches in this anti-communist cause, Americans pledged new aid for the construction of "diaspora and community centers" for German refugees who had fled the Soviet East. Billed as "fortresses of faith," the centers sought to spiritually and socially nourish refugee communities through combining a church and community center within one building. The worship space could be quickly repurposed as a social and community event center, in effect tying together spiritual and political causes into one civic mission. That civic mission accordingly was meant to halt the rise of secularism in postwar Germany and counteract the anti-religious policies of the Soviet Union.[25]

To further coordinate transatlantic Protestant aid, Eugen Gerstenmaier, the leader of *Hilfswerk*, toured the United States in the spring of 1948. News coverage of the journey portrayed Gerstenmaier as a stalwart anti-Nazi and partner in the postwar defense of democracy and freedom. As he discussed and coordinated humanitarian relief, he praised the Americans for their generous aid and democratic example, as well as their "true Christian spirit" that built bridges across the Atlantic. A supporter of Christian Democratic politics, Gerstenmaier also lauded freedom as "the ideal of Americans" and "the great hope of people throughout the world." In one interview, he reflected positively on the final scene of a film showing at the time, *The State of the*

Union, in which a lead character declared his intent to share "freedom" with the "cold, hungry, and scared" suffering under "communists and fascists." In addition to playing up his love of democracy, the German relief organizer praised American Protestants for being "more generous" than any other Christians in the world. They offered an example to all through their "extraordinarily active," "personal," and "lay influenced" churches. He found his spirit refreshed by this genuine "priesthood of all believers" and believed Germans could learn much "from the American way of Church life with its practical cooperation of clergy and laymen in the community." When asked by an American, "Do you like our country?," he responded enthusiastically: "I love it!"[26]

For their part, American Protestant ecumenists soaked up Gerstenmaier's praise, which spoke powerfully to their national self-understanding as a benevolent Christian nation. Yet Gerstenmaier's comments were also designed to win over the Americans to his own cause. The German relief leader was eager for the Americans to not just see Germany as spiritually bankrupt. Rather, he emphasized that the German people stood ready to become America's "full partners in the great work of moral and material reconstruction." He thus subtly challenged American ecumenists' sense of spiritual superiority and called for the mutual partnerships promised by a genuine Christian globalism. Nonetheless, many ecumenists continued to understand their ecumenical mission to be one of leading the spiritually weakened German churches into a democratic and ecumenical future. Yet in all of these initiatives, Germans proved vital partners, often molding and shaping American policy to their own ends. A growing contingent of reform-minded German Protestants was even beginning to challenge America's Cold War aims. The postwar religious exchange between the United States and Germany therefore was not just about collaboration against communism. It soon became a contest over America's spiritual crusade altogether.[27]

As aid flowed into Europe, America's "Marshall Plan for the Churches" also sought to change the actual theological substance of European Protestantism. American ecumenists cast these theological reform efforts as a "Second Reformation"—a transformative renewal of Protestant Christianity in its historic birthplace. As Herman put it, Europe had "an opportunity for reformation such as it has not possessed since the days of Martin Luther." With

Herman and other American ecumenists contributing to the mission, the WCC called for major programs in three key areas: lay discipleship, youth work, and theological education. Through these measures, ecumenists worked to promote a new theology of lay activism across the Atlantic, as well as to strengthen theological defenses against secularism, communism, and Catholicism in the West.[28]

Seeing Europe as spiritually barren and under threat from "hostile ideologies," American ecumenists sought to nurture a new theological focus on the laity across the continent. Drawing from the practical theology of Princeton theologian E. G. Homrighausen and Niebuhr's ethic of public responsibility, the ecumenical project promoted within European churches new theological ideas such as "lay stewardship" and the "responsible society." This theology sought to reform church hierarchies through looking to the lay congregation as the locus of Protestant activism. The congregation itself became the new ordering block of society and of a new civic sphere. The congregation, American ecumenists argued, was a form of voluntary association in which lay Protestants could learn and practice a new ethic of spiritual and civic responsibility. From the congregation up, ecumenists hoped, lay Protestants would begin to foster a "responsible society"—one that was critical in its public engagement and dedicated to the pursuit of justice. So too could lay believers evangelize a "de-Christanized Europe" and a "post-Christian world," albeit not through direct conversionary mission, but rather through their daily vocations. The churches would no longer need established missionaries as they would look to everyday parishioners to create a Christian society through their daily work in schools, political parties, media outlets, businesses, and hospitals. This new grassroots missiology became a crucial component of ecumenical Protestantism's Cold War mission. In particular, the WCC sought to promote this congregational lay theology through lay conferences and programming at new lay institutes, such as the Bossey Institute in Switzerland that John D. Rockefeller, Jr., had bankrolled.[29]

For their part, German and European Protestants also developed their own "evangelical academies" dedicated to the training of laity. After the war, these new lay academies popped up in Germany, France, Holland, and Finland. In 1949, German Protestant laity also pioneered the first ever *Kirchentag* ("Church Congress")—a gathering of lay Protestants designed to strengthen their engagement in the church, public politics, and ecumenical networks. The week-long event especially targeted lay Protestants who had been baptized but no longer actively participated in the life of the church. In these ways, the *Kirchentag* reflected the beginning of an indigenous trans-formation within German Protestantism that elevated the laity, prioritized a public presence for the churches, and sought the wholescale transformation of German society. Training the laity for spiritual and civic responsibility also received generous backing from the AMG, whose officials noted that the new academies and institutes "contributed vitally to a better understanding of the churches' responsibility in local community and national affairs" and promoted "a proper degree of separation of church and state." American ecumenists such as Reinhold Niebuhr and E. Theodore Bachmann likewise had high praise for how these developments promoted their ecumenical ethic of "personal religion" and "responsible Christian social action."[30]

Beyond these lay academies, the World Council also promoted a new dem-ocratic youth ministry throughout Europe. World Council reports warned that European youth, and German youngsters in particular, had experienced devastating disruptions in their moral formation. Behind the Iron Curtain, European youth especially faced "a completely secularized and politically one-sided world," one report cautioned. The Council fretted that "materialist philosophy" would reorient European youth away from Christian and demo-cratic values. American, British, and European ecumenists alike worried that this generation might be lost for good. In response, the Council sponsored the training of thousands of youth workers, catechists, and deacons to serve in youth ministry and summer youth camps. These educators and leaders were encouraged to integrate European youth into congregational life and grant them "important roles in church life and in the Church's relation to the community." The AMG likewise identified youth groups as laboratories for spiritual democracy. Church youth synods in Bavaria, for instance, were encouraged to "elect representatives from youth groups of the whole land" to discuss "in a democratic atmosphere" the "major problems" they faced. To further strengthen such trends, the Federal Council sent American youth leaders to work in the American occupation zone, where they had the oppor-tunity to share American youth ministry methods with their German peers. All told, youth ministry proved yet another part of an American-backed movement for democracy and faith in a hostile ideological environment.[31]

Building on this programming, Americans provided theological training to young German theologians and pastors as well. Drawing from his own studies, Herman argued that "fundamental changes" were needed within German theology faculties, which in his estimation focused far too much on doctrinal precision and not enough on ecumenical and civic engagement.

He therefore called on American seminaries to provide guidance to young German theologians in need of a new kind of theology. Reinhold Niebuhr made a similar case. At war's end, Niebuhr held up the transformation of Dietrich Bonhoeffer in the United States as a model for Germany's young theologians. Niebuhr claimed that Bonhoeffer's studies in the United States had led him to be "concerned about the inadequacies of Lutheran social ethics and particularly about the doctrine of the two realms." Bonhoeffer had accordingly emerged as a theologian committed to "actions which can be socially valued." Niebuhr thus argued that Bonhoeffer's example was a "source of grace for the new church in a new Germany" and provided hope "of a revitalized Protestant faith in Germany." Following Bonhoeffer's lead, Germans would learn "to overcome the one fateful error of German Protestantism, the complete dichotomy between faith and political life." Herman concurred. "We are accustomed to thinking of German theologians as musty scholars perpetually fighting paper wars about obscure and unimportant points of dogma," the American ecumenist wrote, adding that "Dietrich Bonhoeffer was a theologian, but not that kind. He not only believed that the Christian faith had to be related to life on earth, but he believed it was good theology to do so." Herman concluded, Bonhoeffer's "participation in the fight against Nazism was not a vacation from his vocation but an integral part of it." To train future Bonhoeffers, American ecumenists created a "Dietrich Bonhoeffer Fund" and petitioned the readership of *Christianity and Crisis* to provide scholarships to young and promising clergymen in the German Protestant church.[32]

In 1946, American Protestant seminaries such as Eden and Princeton had already begun to offer full-tuition scholarships to German theology students. They worked out arrangements with the Federal Council and the AMG, agreeing on a plan to require all exchange students to return to Germany immediately after their year abroad in order to share their experiences with German churches. With this process formalized by the summer of 1947, the Federal Council formally invited twenty-five German theology students through *Hilfswerk* to study at mainline seminaries. Over the following years, hundreds of German theology students studied for one year at an American Protestant seminary on scholarship. For their American hosts, the exchanges provided a chance to share American theology with this next generation of democratic and faith-based partners.[33]

While many of these young German students noted that American theology was less rigorous than German theology, they recognized that they could learn something from America's practical focus on service and ecumenism. One student at Eden Theological Seminary, for instance, compared the academic quality of distinguished American professors to that of a "gifted" and "diligent" German student. The young man wrote, "these men do not want to be scientists." At Union Theological Seminary, however, a young woman noted how the strength of American theology could be seen in its "orientation to practice in ecclesial and everyday life." To develop this practical orientation, almost every exchange student received a pastoral service placement. Reflecting on her time in one urban ministry, a student praised how American Protestants "took seriously their responsibility for their fellow man." Finally, a student reflected positively on the "international" and "ecumenical" focus of Hartford Theological Seminary, which sought to foster a "community where the borders of nation, of color, and of narrow confessionalism can be overcome."[34]

In addition to the practical focus of American Protestantism, these German students also reflected positively on the prominent role of the laity in American congregations. An exchange student at Princeton noted that American Protestants had a "much higher sense of responsibility and active participation" in congregational life than in Germany. If Germans could adopt this lay voluntarism, one reflected, Germany "would have the purest revolution in the church." Multiple students also stated their desire to spread the American Protestant concepts of "stewardship" and "responsibility" into German religious life. For these young Germans, stewardship constituted "the realization of belief in all areas of daily life." As one student reported, "the enormous activity of laymen in every church appears like a miracle to a European." He added, "there is no question that we are taught by the Americans a very necessary lesson in Stewardship." Immersion into American Protestantism provided these German students with new ideas and practices they hoped to spread in Germany. In particular, the exchanges motivated multiple students to seek to transform German Protestantism into a more practical and lay-oriented religion. One student ultimately wrote of her desire "to work with young people in the way in which I have seen it done in America." Her experience motivated her to "apply American experiences and aim at a more satisfactory congregational life" in Germany.[35]

While German students drew inspiration from American Protestantism, many expressed their concern that their hosts wanted to Americanize Germany. In response, one student remained adamant that the "American model" could not "be transplanted to Europe." He left the United States believing that Europeans should not "disregard" their "historical roots and foundations." Yet another student critiqued Americans for their careless consumerism and expansionist tendencies. He claimed the American "frontier existence" had infused into the American identity a relentless desire to consume and conquer. Others criticized the imperial impulse they saw at work in American Protestantism. For one young man, America's "conquering faith" showed itself in "the hope of many Americans . . . to Christianize the entire world and create a Christian society within a Christian world order." He was not fully convinced, however, that "democracy with a free market" was the "sole Christian state form." Another student added that Americans had forgotten "Christianity and Democracy are not the same." The Christian nationalism of America's mainline Protestants clearly showed in "the colourful harmony of State Flag and Church Flag in front of the pews." On this point, one young theologian concluded that America's Christian nationalism thwarted ecumenical fellowship in the world. He hoped Americans could still recognize and value the Christians behind the "Iron Curtain" and within "totalitarian regimes" in their rush to oppose the "godless" communists. Such efforts, he felt, often created greater division and tension than peace and understanding. For most students, then, their sojourns in America left them still desiring a broader ecumenical fellowship.[36]

These young German students also perceptively saw that "Christian America" was not free of nativism and racism. As they wrote back home, they reflected on the racial inequality and prejudice that permeated their host country. Like Bonhoeffer, they found their immersions in black Christianity to be among the most transformative experiences their time in America offered. One student reflected on the inspiration he discovered at a southside Chicago church. As he closed the service with the "Our Father" in German, the congregation's "amens," "hallelujahs," and "yessirs" stirred his soul. Yet given their nation's entrenched residential and ecclesial segregation, most white American Protestants had never come into such intimate spiritual fellowship with their black sisters and brothers in the faith. Since the 1920s, some American ecumenists had been drawing upon their faith's innate potential to overcome racial division through Christ, but racial progress often met stubborn and prejudiced opposition from many white Protestant congregations in the US.[37]

These reflections illustrated the conflicting insights these young students gained from their transatlantic exchanges. They indeed drew inspiration from American Protestantism's lay activism and congregationalism. They likewise expressed gratitude for the ecumenical relief that rebuilt German churches, fostered reconciliation, and supported the renewal of German Protestantism. Yet they also criticized how American Protestants and those very ecumenical initiatives heightened Cold War tensions and revived Christian nationalism. In their view, American ecumenists too readily coupled their spiritual mission to the advancement of the American system of faith, politics, and markets across the Atlantic. They feared that transatlantic ecumenism therefore dangerously risked becoming a vehicle of America's new Cold War activism in Europe. They saw clearly how American ecumenists had dangerously wed their faith to the prevailing national ideologies of their era.

American ecumenists indeed continued to hope that God's global kingdom could grow through their nation's global project. Their confidence that their churches and their nation possessed the spiritual resources needed to create a new Christian order led them to complement the American capital, consumer goods, and military troops that flowed across the Atlantic with spiritual aid. They accordingly celebrated their efforts to rebuild churches, provide material relief, and form new democratic citizens. As one ecumenist put it, the Germans had once "dismissed the social expressions of American Christianity as moralistic activism." But now, the author noted, "Continental church thought" was "moving much closer to the American idea." Even more, America's economic and spiritual aid had built a surefire Christian defense against the looming spiritual threats of the postwar era. American ecumenists were thus fulfilling their long-standing mission to make the continent more Christian and democratic, and in effect, to remake Europe in their spiritual image. For them, the missions of Christ and Wilson were seemingly one and the same.[38]

As indicated by these German students, German Protestants ultimately split in their response to America's conquering faith. While some welcomed American aid as generous and benevolent, others protested the Americanization of their church life. While some aligned themselves with the "Christian West," others feared a looming civil war that threatened to destroy their nation. When the Cold War intensified even further, reform-minded Protestants protested what they saw as a militant and ascendant United States in the world. They reminded their American peers that the Christ they followed had forsaken the ways of empire. They accordingly resisted conscription into America's Cold War coalition. As members of churches that transcended occupation zones, they feared the Cold War was tearing their nation irreparably apart and dividing the church for good. Having suffered alongside political leftists in Hitler's concentration camps, some radical clergy like Martin Niemöller had also begun to question their historic hostility to socialism and communism. With the publication of the "Word of Darmstadt" (*Darmstädter Wort*) in the summer of 1947, reform-minded Protestants like Niemöller, Hans Iwand, Hermann Diem, and Karl Barth followed up on the Stuttgart Declaration of Guilt in identifying key errors that German Protestants had made in their support of National Socialism. Not only did they forsake the nationalism and militarism of the German past, they also maintained that they had erred in totally condemning socialists. Moving forward, they called for fostering reconciliation among the peoples of the world. Their theological vision translated into political support of democratic socialism at home and peace, justice, and reconciliation abroad.

Developing these convictions further, German Protestants Hermann Diem and Friedrich Siegmund-Schultze began to call for a "third way" theology in the emerging Cold War. In their view, the German church was uniquely positioned "between Russia and America," "between East and West." As Siegmund-Schultze put it, only Christians could truly "love all human beings in East and West," including the "democrats" and "the communists and materialists." Siegmund-Schultze shuddered over the prospect of Germans from different occupation zones marching off to battle with each other in a proxy war between the Soviets and Americans. His "third way" theology championed the ethics of Christ above Cold War divisions and positioned Protestant ecumenism as a neutral, mediating force within the East-West conflict. In the emerging Cold War, it was therefore Europeans like Diem and Siegmund-Schultze who were beginning to lead the way in articulating a Christian globalist ethic, one that called on Christians to transcend nationality and ideology and profess their highest loyalties to the transnational body of Christ. In contrast to these "third way" currents, some American and German Protestants continued to draw a hard line against the Soviets. Above all, conservative Protestants in Germany like Otto Dibelius and Christian Realists in the United States like John Foster Dulles and Reinhold Niebuhr were wary of making such accommodations to the Soviet Union. The rise of "third way" theology thus began to drive a wedge within transatlantic Protestantism, as ecumenists began to assess the Soviet threat in diverging ways.[39]

These conflicting views came to a head in the late summer of 1948. Protestants on both sides of the Atlantic had been working for decades to formally create a global ecumenical church body. The first general assembly of the WCC, held in Amsterdam in 1948, therefore should have marked a moment of triumph. The ecumenical movement had survived the fiery trial of world war. Now many believed they were on the precipice of a just and durable world order. Inaugurating the WCC, they hoped, would only strengthen that effort. As Protestant ecumenists gathered in Amsterdam that August, however, they could not avoid the simmering tensions of the Cold War. That summer, the Soviets had blockaded all major transportation links into West Berlin. When Americans began the Berlin Airlift to keep the city tied to the West, any hope for a unified Germany had been buried under escalated Cold War hostilities. Protestant ecumenists had formed the Commission of the Churches on International Affairs to give the ecumenical churches a united voice on events such as these. Yet despite the Commission's intention to counteract the world's "power politics," the ideological conflict of the Cold War had fostered internal ecumenical division. Just like those young German theologians, not all Europeans were thrilled with "God's Marshall Plan," the American military presence in Europe, or the looming division of Germany. Some American ecumenists were also frustrated that the conference was not being held on American soil. They feared in particular that the soft stance on communism of some Europeans would dominate the agenda if the conference were held in Europe. The ecumenical gathering thus exposed these underlying tensions.[40]

Leading American ecumenists like Reinhold Niebuhr and John Foster Dulles had clear-cut contributions to share on the assembly's theme of "Man's Disorder and God's Design." Both voiced ecumenical commitments to the democratic West. Niebuhr continued his offensive against totalitarianism, arguing that both fascism and communism threatened to undermine world order. While he maintained a sober realism about America's own failures to promote peace and justice, he called on free countries "not under the dominion of communist totalitarianism" to foster a just world order. Dulles proved even more aggressive about America's role in the world. He resolutely believed in the power of Christian civilization. He depicted the world as split between "free societies" and totalitarian dictatorships and delivered a moral defense of laissez-faire capitalism. In contrast to communism, he argued, democracy rooted itself in moral law and human rights as the only legitimate source of human order. Both

Americans thus sought to rally Protestant ecumenism in defense of a democratic and Christian order in the world.[41]

In response, some European delegates protested. Karl Barth, for instance, criticized American ecumenists for advancing a "Christian Marshall Plan"—an improper blending of spiritual mission with political goals. He questioned the wisdom of American efforts to remake international politics and society. In Barth's view, the Americans had it all wrong. Christians should focus first and foremost on the otherworldly revelation to which the church alone could point. In a stinging critique of America's ecumenical mission, he declared that the church's responsibility was not to liberate the world. As the Swiss theologian put it, human efforts to "Christianize" all humanity or "to achieve a Christian world order" would only result in further disorder. The church therefore did not require "lawyers, engineers, managers, statisticians, and administrative directors" to transform the world. The church merely needed to point to Christ. More broadly, Barth's criticism aligned with his refusal to neither condemn communism nor support democracy.[42]

An even sharper critique came from Josef Hromádka, a Czech theologian who declared at Amsterdam that the West did not possess "the political skill, wisdom, and strength of conviction to rule our countries." Hromádka pushed back against the "Christian West" in condemning what he described as its reactionary, capitalist, and imperialist ways in the world. Instead, he defended socialism as representing "much of the social impetus of the living church." Hromádka thus forsook the cause of the democratic West and joined the socialist revolution in its quest for social justice and global fellowship. In reply, Niebuhr claimed Hromádka lacked a realistic understanding of "the horrible evils generated by the Communist alternative to our civilization." He also critiqued Barth for promoting political quietism and inaction in the world. In his view, human beings still possessed the capacity to act with a semblance of virtue. Democratic society was indeed flawed, but it was certainly superior to totalitarian dictatorship.[43]

Amsterdam thus left the ecumenical movement divided. The conference itself ultimately followed Barth's lead, declaring that the church should "reject the ideologies of both communism and laissez-faire capitalism." Visser 't Hooft made clear the intent: "the World Council refused . . . to let itself be used as an instrument in the Cold War." Ecumenical proponents of the "third way" cheered on the development. German Protestant Eduard Heimann encouraged ecumenists gathered together at the Bossey Institute to see Europe as a "THIRD FORCE in spirit and institutions." An "independent

Europe" could remain neutral in the Cold War, effectively mediating between the Soviet-dominated East and American-led West. In the aftermath of Amsterdam, so too did American ecumenist John Bennett praise the "third way" for envisioning how ecumenical Protestants could live "responsibly" within both capitalist and socialist systems. Yet with a permanently divided Germany in sight and Soviet control cemented over Eastern Europe, the "third way" still remained a tenuous idea within transatlantic ecumenical circles. Amsterdam left American and European ecumenists struggling to align their visions for international relations. While many could agree on commitments to multilateralism and European federation, they still disagreed sharply over the proper value to ascribe to democracy and communism. These competing Cold War convictions fostered division and disunity within the ecumenical movement.[44]

As Europeans protested America's "Christian Marshall Plan," American ecumenists also encountered opposition from fundamentalists and evangelicals back home. In particular, Presbyterian fundamentalist Carl McIntire, founder of the separatist American Council of Christian Churches, drew up plans for an international congress of fundamentalist Protestants in Amsterdam that was held just before the World Council assembly. McIntire's competing conference founded the International Council of Christian Churches to defend biblical fundamentals and counteract modernist ecumenism. The separatist fundamentalist claimed his council would "stand for the liberty and the faith once delivered unto the saints." He assured his peers that, unlike the World Council, neither "modernism" nor "socialism" would gain a hearing among attendees.[45]

In response, American ecumenists were more than a little annoyed. Through a series of memos, the editors of *The Christian Century* condemned McIntire's council for its "malevolent intentions" and aims to "wreck the World Council." "The devil" had "seduced" McIntire, they argued, who had been "blinded" by his "own vain imaginings." The editors likewise warned the American press not to give coverage to McIntire's "most extreme and sectarian" "splinter organization of American super-fundamentalists." In the same breath, they mocked the "rump council" by emphasizing that it only drew the paltry total of thirty attendees. They likewise condemned this "self-chosen clique" for their "schismatic, nationalistic, and reactionary" ways. Meanwhile, they attacked Pentecostal and holiness Christians who were newly active in Germany and were "speaking in tongues." These "sects" only alarmed the Germans, they claimed, and weakened the spread of the true ecumenical faith. Such commentary showed the rather aggressive ecumenical response to alternative forms of Protestantism. It likewise exposed how ecumenists viewed Europe as a spiritual battleground.[46]

Such critical opposition riled up Francis Schaeffer, the American missionary whom McIntire had dispatched to Europe in 1947. Schaeffer in particular had looked forward to the American Council gathering as an opportunity for fundamentalists to challenge their liberal-leaning counterparts. On the ecumenical smear campaign, Schaeffer wrote, "I am convinced that a clear-cut stand is necessary and that all of these things spring from the labor of the devil to try to get us to call off our international meeting." After the Amsterdam gathering, Schaeffer remained full-time in Europe, settling in the alpine foothills of Switzerland. From his new post, he opposed the World Council and derided Karl Barth's theology. In years to come, he would sharpen his critiques of Barth's "new modernism" and the trend of postwar secularization from L'Abri, the retreat center he founded in his Swiss chalet. L'Abri would attract thousands of young people from the United States and Europe eager to explore biblical fundamentalism in what they felt was an increasingly secularized world.[47]

Schaeffer was not the only fundamentalist concerned about ecumenical pressures. Other separatist fundamentalists accused the World Council of "using every possible means to silence our voice." McIntire in particular joined the chorus as he critiqued the World Council for its purportedly socialist leanings. In particular, the World Council promoted the "Social Gospel," which he slammed as "the principles of Karl Marx dressed up in Christian clothes." In his view, ecumenical Christianity and theological modernism led to a litany of evils—"socialistic principles, class strife, race bitterness, pacifism, atheism, and eternal destruction." In promoting such teachings, McIntire claimed that both the Federal Council and the World Council were promoting "world socialism," "collectivistic" economics, and "extreme materialistic modernism." He also warned that the ecumenists would ultimately use "the United Nations to influence the United States in the drive for world socialism."[48]

Some evangelicals, however, such as National Association of Evangelicals founder Harold Ockenga, took a more conciliatory approach to the World Council. Ockenga and his partners organized a "World Congress on Evangelism" that same fall in Beatenberg, Switzerland, an event that aimed not to undermine the WCC, but rather to issue a gentle yet principled correction to its missiology. Ockenga represented the commitment of the "neo-evangelicals" to engage mainstream Protestantism. Through principled dialogue, Ockenga hoped that liberal ecumenists could still be persuaded to head in a more evangelical direction. Under the auspices of Youth for Christ, Ockenga, Billy Graham, and Torrey Johnson called for the evangelization of Europe and the world "in this generation" and marveled at the modern technologies like planes and radios, not to mention corporate partners, that could make such a goal possible. The assembly brought together American, British, and European evangelicals to plan for the conversion of the European continent back to their old-time faith. They ended up founding their own evangelical Bible institute in Beatenberg, situated at the foot of the majestic Jungfrau mountain range. In the heart of Europe, evangelicals began to train a new crop of European evangelists to win back the continent for Christ.[49]

Beyond condemning ecumenists' liberalized mission, evangelicals also critiqued the US government for aid programs like the Marshall Plan. Evangelical leader Billy Graham especially criticized Marshall's "folly" as a "give-away program" of "deficit spending" that was "breaking our economic back." The rising evangelist claimed that such aid only alienated Europeans, who in his view resented handouts. In making this claim, Graham conveniently overlooked the formation of Western Europe's postwar welfare states rooted in Christian democratic thought. In contrast, he argued Americans could best help at the personal level through supporting evangelistic efforts or sending CARE relief packages to individual Germans. As Graham made clear in his condemnation of governmental programs, the "greatest need is not more money, food, or even medicine; it is Christ. . . . Give them the Gospel of love and grace first and they will clean themselves up, educate themselves, and better their economic conditions." On this point, separatist fundamentalist Carl McIntire concurred. He added the European Recovery Program had failed to stipulate what *kind* of economy Europeans should adopt. He rejected the initiative because it did not clearly defend laissez-faire principles.[50]

Graham's attacks on the Marshall Plan paralleled an emerging conservative movement against "collectivism," "big government," and Truman's Fair Deal in the United States. Aided by fundamentalists and evangelicals, political conservatives panned Truman's Fair Deal programs as creeping state socialism. They especially rejected his proposal for national health insurance as "socialized medicine" and a surefire path to "societal slavery." In contrast,

BRETHREN, PRAY FOR US! 1 Thess. 5:25.

STUDYING THE BIBLE. "The entrance of thy words giveth light." Ps. 119:130.

American evangelicals sought to challenge the World Council of Churches through holding the World Congress of Evangelism conference in Beatenberg, Switzerland. European youth soon flocked to their new Bible school, where they absorbed evangelical commitments to biblical inerrancy and conversionary mission.

Courtesy of Billy Graham Center Archives, Wheaton College.

an ecumenist like Herman saw such governmental measures as a necessary complement to the church's social mission. Moreover, some evangelicals and fundamentalists opposed Truman's civil rights initiatives as an abuse of federal power and called instead for the pure gospel to transform individual bigotry. Building off these critiques, the evangelical political alliance with a more conservative flank within the Republican Party was strengthening. For a growing number within their ranks, the only correct vote was now for the Republican ticket. As John R. Rice put it, a vote for the GOP would "put the New Deal radicals out of power and save the American way of life." The intensification of the Cold War further galvanized this new brand of anti-communist conservatism that would gradually claim the political center in Cold War America.[51]

A student at the world map ⟨presented by the American Airlines⟩ which greets every visitor in the hall of the Bible School.

Europe is calling - you!

The night cometh, when no man can work! God says "to-day" - so do not say "to-morrow"! To-morrow - it may be... too late!

For many American Protestants, Europe had become both a new mission field and a spiritual battleground for the soul of the North Atlantic world. Airplanes and corporate partners gave American evangelicals confidence they would triumph in the struggle.

Courtesy of Billy Graham Center Archives, Wheaton College.

Buoyed by the Cold War, evangelicals would soon seek to eclipse God's Marshall Plan with campaigns that promoted spiritual, political, and economic liberty alongside military strength against the Soviets. As Herman surveyed postwar Europe in the late 1940s, he saw these trends bursting out into the open. Not only did "international movements of all political complexions" compete for the European soul, he wrote, but so too had "aggressive American and British evangelistic movements . . . intensified their activity." Herman felt confident ecumenism's "community-wide generation" would prevail. Europeans, in his view, showed little interest in "individual salvation." American evangelicals thought otherwise. They would transform Germany into one of the most intense fronts in the struggle for the soul of the "Christian West."[52]

8

Spiritual Rearmament

Billy Graham sensed the significance of the moment. As a Youth for Christ evangelist, the young preacher had perfected his staccato-like delivery in crowded church halls across the United States and Europe. He had filled revival tents to the brim and had grown in renown since his successful 1949 evangelical crusade in Los Angeles. In 1954, he now set his sights on the renewal of a vital outpost of the "Christian West." He recognized that he had never before proclaimed the gospel in such a setting. As Graham stepped before thousands of Germans at the Nazi parade grounds in Nuremberg, "in Hitler's stadium" as he would later recall, he fell back on what he knew best. He took the podium at the "sacred shrine of the Nazis" and preached the old-time gospel of judgment and repentance. He sought to lead the German people back to Christ.[1]

Yet Graham's gospel did not just seek to save German souls; it also sought to win the Germans as spiritual allies in the fight against the Soviets. With the split of Germany into two separate nation-states in 1949, the European theater of the Cold War had changed dramatically. While Americans lamented that East Germany had been lost to the communists, they now looked all the more to West Germany as a citadel of Christianity and democracy in the heart of "Battleground Europe." Meanwhile, America's Cold War fears had led to robust expenditures on national defense, a foreign war in Korea, and a nuclear arms race. Cold War militarization had begun in earnest.

While some Protestant ecumenists proved hesitant to support these developments, evangelical Protestants in the US launched aggressive spiritual efforts to support American military strength in the Cold War. In particular, two conservative campaigns—the Wooden Church Crusade and the evangelical crusades of Billy Graham—sought to "spiritually rearm" West Germany as a complement to its literal rearmament in the Cold War. Led by a coalition of free-enterprise businessmen, Cold War hawks, and conservative clergy, these postwar crusades rallied God-fearing Americans to defend their values of faith, freedom, and free enterprise both at home and abroad against New Deal liberalism, Soviet communism, and postwar secularization.

God's Marshall Plan. James D. Strasburg, Oxford University Press (2021). © Oxford University Press.
DOI: 10.1093/oso/9780197516447.003.0009

Meanwhile, American evangelicals pursued Christian nationalist revivals that sought to make America and West Germany into nations "under God." In principle, these campaigns built upon the earlier opposition of Protestant ecumenists to secularism and communism. Yet as the Cold War became an increasingly militarized conflict, "spiritual rearmament" signaled the rising stature of American evangelicals in domestic and international politics.

In 1949, Protestant ecumenists and evangelicals alike observed the intensification of the Cold War with growing concern. That year, the Allied powers had divided the German occupation zones into two separate nation-states—the democratic Federal Republic of Germany (West Germany) and the communist German Democratic Republic (East Germany). Meanwhile, the Soviets had successfully detonated an atomic bomb, and China was "lost" to Mao Zedong's communists. These global developments confirmed what American Protestants had long feared: the Soviets were aggressively establishing their dominance across the globe. Seeing the Soviets as insatiable expansionists, evangelical Protestants especially supported a robust military-oriented foreign policy that aimed to "globally contain" communism through a "preponderance" of American power across the globe. The North Atlantic Treaty Organization (NATO) soon created a mutual defense arrangement between the United States and Western European nations, while National Security Council 68, a confidential foreign policy document, called for a drastic build-up in American military capabilities in order to counteract the Soviets' "fanatic faith." With these militaristic policies underway, American evangelicals felt confident their nation had taken a firm step against the Soviets. They now pledged to complement their nation's military maneuvers with spiritual support.[2]

American evangelicals especially looked to spiritually and militarily fortify West Germany. As the Korean War broke out in 1950, West German chancellor Konrad Adenauer, a German Catholic and leading politician of the Christian Democratic Union (CDU), felt the heat of the thirty-plus Soviet divisions sitting just east of the West German border. To protect West Germany against a potential Soviet invasion, Adenauer pushed forward a policy of integration with the West and asked the United States, Britain, and France to consider West Germany's inclusion in NATO. Although Britain and France expressed hesitation, the Korean War and the threat of Soviet expansionism demonstrated to the Americans that a strong West Germany would be needed to help defend the European continent. Linked by a common commitment to Christianity and democracy, Adenauer partnered with American president Dwight Eisenhower and his secretary of state, John Foster Dulles, to forge an alliance that made a remilitarized Federal Republic the bedrock of America's European security policy.[3]

Rearmament proved to be a lightning rod on both sides of the Atlantic that electrified and divided Protestants into competing Cold War factions. In August 1950, Adenauer's minister of the interior, Gustav Heinemann, resigned his post in protest of such policies and joined the opposition Social Democratic Party. Heinemann, who also was a noted leader in German Protestant circles, feared that any form of rearmament would further the divide between East and West Germany and cut off the possibility of cooperation between Protestant churches in each region. The German church was the one national German institution that still transcended the Iron Curtain. Heinemann believed the church needed to prevent a civil war that he feared would permanently destroy Germany. He therefore called on East and West German Protestants to foster spiritual unity amidst Cold War divisions.[4]

Drawing inspiration from the call for a "third way" in the Cold War, some German Protestants began to pursue dialogue with the Soviets. Protestant pastor Martin Niemöller came under particular scrutiny for his 1952 trip to Moscow and his robust opposition to West German rearmament. While many Americans had praised him in the 1940s, a growing number now criticized him as "Moscow's Red Dean" and condemned his "pro-Sovietism" and "anti-Americanism." Meanwhile, Niemöller criticized the CDU-led Federal Republic of Germany as "a child conceived in the Vatican and born in Washington." He especially believed the Christian Democratic Union was a front for an imperial Catholicism that aimed to destroy continental Protestantism. In a confession that shocked many in the West, he stated his preference for a united communist Germany over a divided one.[5]

German Protestant Friedrich Siegmund-Schultze also developed a strong position against the remilitarization of West Germany. In particular, Siegmund-Schultze criticized the US government for pushing rearmament on the West German people. In his view, rearming Germany tempted a civil war that could "destroy Germany" for good. As an alternative, the German ecumenist looked to Germany's identity as "a bridge between Eastern and Western Europe" and outlined a "spiritual mission" for the German people "inside the nations of Europe." Rejecting nuclear proliferation and remilitarization, Siegmund-Schultze furthered his "third way" theology through tying it to an ethic of pacifism and reconciliation in the Cold War.[6]

More conservative-leaning and nationalist leaders, however, such as Berlin's Otto Dibelius, avowed that churches needed to combat the spread of communism's atheist ideology. While Dibelius ultimately yielded the question of remilitarization to the state as a political matter, he still saw rearmament as an important hedge against Soviet expansionism and accepted that West Germany would need to be rearmed. Within German Catholicism, a clearer voice also emerged in favor of rearmament. Cardinal Josef Frings especially called on Catholics to be more vigilant in their defense of Christianity against communism. He cautioned against "sentimentality and false humanitarianism" in the Cold War. Pacifist ideals alone could not secure European security and peace, he reasoned. Influential Catholic periodicals likewise called for West Germans to accept greater responsibility for their security and to grow less dependent on the Western powers. Following the lead of Frings, Catholics launched a robust campaign of support for Adenauer's policies, which by 1955 had carried the day. That year, West Germany entered NATO under the careful watch of the United States. A key step had been taken in transatlantic relations: in addition to spiritual, political, and economic partnerships, West Germany was now a military ally of the Americans as well.[7]

In the United States, Protestants disagreed over how to best respond to these developments. While Christian realists continued their sober critique of communism and saw the need for German rearmament, many ecumenists grew concerned about the growing militarization and development of nuclear weapons. While they condemned Soviet policies in East Germany, the editors of *The Christian Century* especially warned that German rearmament would undermine the peace Americans had secured in Europe. In particular, it would alienate the French and British and create new hostilities within a recently pacified Europe. American ecumenical leader O. Frederick Nolde likewise criticized both the United States and the Soviet Union for creating a "new world catastrophe" in the Cold War. He stated that Americans should be willing to allow different political and economic systems to take hold elsewhere in the world. For a growing number of ecumenists, American foreign policy had taken the wrong track in its increasingly militarized approach to Soviet communism. While they had supported ideological, economic, and spiritual opposition, their nation's growing belief in military power concerned them.[8]

Stewart Herman's thinking on Cold War affairs also reflected this American ecumenical shift toward the European "third way" position. Drawing upon his pacifist streak, Herman stated that America's Cold War militarization was just as belligerent and disruptive to world order as Soviet expansionism. While he condemned Soviet totalitarianism, he also denounced America's new militaristic policies in equal measure. In his view, the emerging "rearmament race" and the militant "crusade against communism" subordinated "peaceful reconstruction to military defense." While Herman had once sanctioned the use of force to check evil, he now professed that faithful Christians in the Cold War could not support such military solutions to international disorder. Only "desperate anti-communists," he wrote, embraced America's new "war mentality." In contrast, Herman sought to rally Americans and European Protestants as an ecumenical force for peace in the world. He especially praised the "third force" Europeans who had adopted "a respectable middle position in the East-West conflict." He also looked to the World Council to transcend "narrower frontiers" and bridge "the rift between East and West through Jesus Christ." Cold War militarization had thus led Herman to begin to embrace Germany's "third way" theology that placed ecumenical loyalty to the ways of Christ over the ways of the nation.[9]

Yet even then, Herman's own reflections in the early Cold War showed the conflicted nature of the ecumenical mind, as well as the enduring ecumenical commitment to Christian nationalism. In particular, many American ecumenists continued to spiritually mobilize "Christian America" against totalitarian threats. For instance, even as Herman opposed Cold War militarization, he still urged American ecumenists to oppose the "menace of atheistic communism" through their own faith-based activism abroad. He also lamented that Europeans were overly enamored with "socialist solutions" to societal problems. There could be "no salvation through socialism," Herman wrote. Instead, the American ecumenist professed his confidence in American democracy as the highest form of Christian politics. In his view, Americans still had a special role to play in creating and preserving a Christian world order that circumvented communists, socialists, and secularists alike. The newly formed National Council of Churches also expressed these Christian and democratic convictions. In particular, the Council's 1950 inaugural assembly called on America to be a "nation under God" and affirmed that American democracy and culture could only rest upon the foundation of Protestant Christianity. National Council leaders urged "Christian and Protestant America" to oppose the "new and old paganisms that are contending for the mastery of the world." So too did they summon ecumenical Protestants to build a "Christian America in a Christian world." American ecumenists thus also contributed to the Cold War revival of Christian nationalism at home and continued to support a Wilsonian mission abroad.[10]

The ecumenists' opposition to socialism and communism paralleled their concerns regarding "political Catholicism" as well. Herman warned that the Vatican was "imperial" in its approach to political and spiritual affairs. The threat of its spiritual totalitarianism, he added, demanded that all faithful Americans "fight to keep Rome from occupying Washington." Ecumenists like Herman thus continued to call on a narrowly defined Protestant "Christian America" to defend democracy and faith from the Catholic threat. In expressing such views, they did not fully sense how their advocacy for ecumenical Protestantism had an imperial character of its own.[11]

Despite these professions of Christian nationalism, ecumenists still struck many fundamentalists as anti-American due to their "collectivistic" and "modernistic" tendencies. Protestant ecumenists soon became targets in a spiritual "Red Scare" that sought to purge religious institutions of communist sympathizers. As the National Council of Churches reaffirmed its stance against racial segregation in the United States, conservative reactionaries feared that ecumenism and civil rights could be part of a broader communist ploy to sow agitation and division within the nation. Carl McIntire, for instance, called National Council leader G. Bromley Oxnam "the prophet of Marx" and warned that "internal enemies" were threatening America. Gerald Winrod also condemned ecumenical leaders, civil rights activists, and communists alike as threats to America. He claimed that these "leftists" and "liberals" professed "hate for Christ" and were dead set on the downfall of "Western civilization." The absolutist politics and good-versus-evil worldview of McIntire and Winrod fit the emerging black-and-white Cold War conflict perfectly. Such views naturally drew fundamentalists to a new brand of politics that wove together commitments to Christian fundamentals, limited government, and anti-communism.[12]

Many neo-evangelicals also felt that ecumenists had grown too "soft" in their foreign policies toward Soviet communism. In particular, evangelical Protestants strongly supported John Foster Dulles's new foreign policy of "rollback," which sought to go beyond containing communism to liberating the world of Soviet control. Along with his brother Allen Dulles, who now led the CIA, the two brothers encouraged Eisenhower to enact coups and regime change in both Guatemala and Iran in order to counteract communism. In this regard, their ecumenical quest to defend Christian civilization easily transitioned into a fervent crusade against communism. Their support of global interventions also aligned with the go-it-alone unilateralism of evangelicals, who condemned the United Nations and multilateralism as potential tools of the Antichrist.[13]

As the Cold War intensified, evangelical Protestants continued to advance a rhetoric of "holy war" against communism that excited the American spiritual imagination. For these Protestants, "spiritual rearmament" appeared as a way they could actively complement their nation's armed forces in the standoff with the Soviets. Indeed, Protestant evangelicals identified religion as one of the most potent weapons in America's Cold War arsenal. In effect, they believed the Bible was just as powerful a defense against communism as an American B-52 bomber. Both of these spiritual and military weapons could be used to "roll back" communism. Their thinking aligned with their long-standing view that communism was not just a faulty political system. It was at its core a religious system that threatened the fundamental values of Western civilization altogether. They diagnosed communism as a disease of the soul that replaced God with man, faith with atheism, and freedom with tyranny. If communism was thus built on faulty spiritual foundations, it could easily be toppled through the power of faith.[14]

The call for "spiritual rearmament" resonated with an American public that itself was flocking to America's religious sanctuaries and embracing American civil religion in an age of nuclear anxiety. As church membership skyrocketed to all-time highs in the 1950s, nearly every American citizen identified with a religious tradition and began to see religious devotion itself as a civic duty. President Dwight Eisenhower led the way by becoming the first president to be baptized while in office. Meanwhile, he guided Congress to add "under God" to the Pledge of Allegiance and to make "In God We Trust" the national motto. As Eisenhower made clear shortly after his election, the American "form of government has no sense unless it is founded on a deeply felt religious faith." Eisenhower later added, "The churches of America are citadels of our faith in individual freedom and human dignity. This faith is the living source of all our spiritual strength. And this strength is our matchless armor in our world-wide struggle against the forces of godless tyranny and oppression." With monotheistic devotion and anti-communism functioning as near civic duties, American civil religion flourished. Even as the Judeo-Christian identity was more inclusive than evangelicals would have liked, many within their ranks still felt that a vote for Eisenhower would "help God save America" from "the quackery" of New Deal liberals. American evangelicals could therefore fully endorse Eisenhower's Cold War religious crusade, and indeed, even seize upon it as an opportunity to advance their standing in Washington's halls of power.[15]

In drawing on faith to oppose secularism and communism, ecumenists and evangelicals alike helped promote a Christian nationalist revival at home. Yet even as they desired to defend "Christian America" from such threats, the divisions between them grew, especially as they viewed the use of military force in the Cold War in opposing ways. While American ecumenists desired to Christianize and democratize the globe through non-military measures, many evangelicals leaned on their apocalypticism and fundamentalist roots to sketch out a more militant and muscular foreign policy that confronted Soviet communism with both the Bible and B-52 bombers. As such, it was ultimately in the hands of European Protestants—dealing with the Cold War division of their continent and the prospect of a third world war—to articulate a third way position— a Christian globalism that transcended Cold War hostilities and called on Protestants to declare higher loyalties to a peaceful transnational fellowship.

In the United States, such a pacifist ethic was seemingly out of step with the national mood. Domestic support of Cold War militarization exposed the fading power of the ecumenical establishment and the rising influence of evangelical conservatism in American public life. Under the strain of Cold War politics, a new constellation of alliances began to form within American Protestantism. Building on the crucial partnership that had formed between conservative religious leaders and capitalist corporations, some big business backers of the ecumenical establishment, including Henry Luce, the media magnate behind *TIME* and *LIFE*, and J. Howard Pew of Sun Oil Company, began to shift their support to Billy Graham's rising evangelicalism. Evangelicals in turn backed new crusades to "spiritually rearm" the United States and Europe. Through such efforts, they hoped to claim ecumenical Protestantism's prominence in Washington and to have an influential role in the West German–American relationship. The Cold War crusades that followed showcased not only their robust Christian nationalism, but also their rising prominence in American political, corporate, and diplomatic circles.

Drawing energy from this Cold War Christian nationalist revival, politically and religiously conservative Americans soon launched transatlantic campaigns to "spiritually rearm" West Germany. In the early 1950s, "The Wooden Church Crusade" stood out as one of the most prominent of these civil religious endeavors. Led by Baron Henning von Royk-Lewinski, a former Nazi naval captain, and Fulton Lewis, Jr., a conservative American radio host, the Wooden Church Crusade pledged to build houses of worship right alongside the Iron Curtain in West Germany as a "spiritual wall against communism." In 1950, Royk-Lewinski arrived in the United States to promote the idea, just as Adenauer began his push to rearm West Germany. In interviews and press releases, Royk-Lewinski portrayed himself to the American public as a faithful Protestant who had internally opposed the Nazis and all forms of totalitarianism. A nephew of Paul von Hindenburg, he claimed he belonged to the Prussian aristocratic military elite that loathed Hitler and found the excesses of Nazism distasteful. While Royk-Lewinski thus fulfilled his patriotic duty as a Nazi officer, he reported he slowly began to fear what would come of Hitler's aims to control all of Europe.[16]

As Royk-Lewinski would relay to his new audience, he only first witnessed the brutality of Hitler and the Nazis in Berlin in 1942. While on official business in the Reich's capital city, he came upon a burnt-down synagogue, destroyed in the vicious "Night of Broken Glass." As he put it, the charred remains of the structure haunted him. He entered the ruins, picked up a stone, and vowed that he would one day return to rebuild the house of worship. The naval officer kept the stone with him throughout the rest of the war, tucking it in his pocket as a reminder of the Nazi "hatred for man," even as he waged battles for that very regime. During the war's remaining years, Royk-Lewinski stated that he hoped for a quick end to the war and the destruction of Nazism. His story impressed many Americans. In the fervor of the Cold War, few Americans investigated Royk-Lewinski's complicated record. Many quickly welcomed the one-time Nazi as an anti-communist partner.[17]

After the war, Royk-Lewinski recounted how he felt the stone's weight as he surveyed the political changes sweeping over Germany. In his view, the Soviets were iron-willed occupiers, even more severe than the Nazis in their hatred of humankind. The growing German refugee crisis confirmed such suspicions. As Royk-Lewinski recalled, millions of Germans streamed into occupied Germany, driven from their homes in East Prussia in search of "the slightest vestige of shelter." While the Soviets had destroyed their lives,

Royk-Lewinski defiantly claimed they could not take away their religion. The refugees sought out churches, and where there were none, they prayed "in open meadows, groves, schools—even in beer halls." The religiosity of the refugees convinced Royk-Lewinski that "the outpouring of faith" constituted his "country's greatest hope for the future." As he asserted, the Soviets could "match our divisions, our planes and ships and weapons. But one weapon remained, one that Communism could never use: our religion, our belief in God." He thus vowed to rebuild "houses of God" throughout his homeland as an act of opposition to totalitarian regimes.[18]

With this insight, Royk-Lewinski believed the time had come to take that stone and use it as a foundation for a new Germany. Along with other conservative Protestants like Dibelius, Royk-Lewinski applauded the close alliance Adenauer had forged with the United States. While he commended Marshall's promise of economic aid, he claimed that "large-scale official economic aid" did not touch the soul. Echoing Herman's rhetoric just years before, he stated that West Germany most needed "a resurgence of religious values" if it were "to withstand the menace of atheistic doctrines." Beyond revived spirituality, he believed West Germany also required a spiritual relationship with the United States to survive on its side of the Iron Curtain. As Royk-Lewinski noted, "a strong bond of understanding between Americans and the free people of West Germany" could stabilize the new political and economic foundations of West Germany.[19]

Drawing these insights together, Royk-Lewinski developed a bold plan: to build American-financed houses of worship along the Iron Curtain in the eastern-most regions of West Germany. This "wall of faith" had a dual purpose. Not only would it provide a stalwart spiritual defense against a Soviet invasion, it also would promote Western values among forlorn refugees. Only the German churches, the baron believed, remained "steadfastly dedicated to Western civilized principles." Such houses of worship could especially "expand the number and influence of God-fearing citizens who believe in the dignity of man under divine guidance." America stood as the ideal partner in such a project. The two nations' "common devotion to spiritual traditions" would tie them together in a joint crusade against Soviet communism.[20]

While in Europe, the baron began to recruit West German governmental officials, American military authorities, Catholic and Protestant bishops, and as he told it, even Pope Pius XII in the Vatican. He then set his sights on securing more American allies in 1950. His persistent networking paid dividends in 1951 when a mutual acquaintance connected him to Fulton

Lewis, Jr., a conservative radio broadcaster who had risen to national prominence through his attacks on Franklin Delano Roosevelt and the New Deal. In 1951, Lewis had just returned from a four-week tour of West Germany. While the conservative broadcaster had seen firsthand the physical destruction of total war, he also wondered about the spiritual destruction wreaked by Nazism. In search of old-time religion that revived the soul, Lewis grew worried over "the lack of religious facilities and the disinterest of youth in their churches." Discrediting the World Council's theologically liberal programs, Lewis stated that "many thousands of German young and old are deprived with religious practice and training." Like ecumenists before him, he feared that communist propaganda would fill this spiritual vacuum.[21]

Meeting Royk-Lewinski could not have come at a more opportune moment. Lewis found a German partner to address Germany's glaring spiritual need. Inspired by Royk-Lewinski's idea, the American radio host agreed to publicize the church construction plan in his syndicated columns and radio program. He presented the idea to the American public as a "crusade" to build "wooden churches" along the Iron Curtain. He also linked the idea of "spiritual rearmament" to "military rearmament." While the two complemented one another, he argued that spiritually rearming the Germans should not be discounted. "Think of the influence one hundred of these wooden structures would exert on the youth of West Germany," Lewis stated, then adding, "What better weapons to fight Communism! A strong bulwark in Western Germany is the United States' best defense against Communism." The message hit home across an America increasingly concerned about the aggressive "reds." Richard Kinzer, a mill-owner and businessman out of Burlington, Wisconsin, reached out to Lewis after reading his column. After meeting personally with Royk-Lewinski, Kinzer volunteered to organize "The Wooden Church Crusade, Inc." A grassroots conservative organization had been born with aspirations to wage the Cold War through religion.[22]

Together, Lewis, Royk-Lewinski, and Kinzer laid a national foundation for the agency. While Royk-Lewinski embarked upon a countrywide speaking tour to Protestant and Catholic congregations, Kinzer worked his connections in the American business world. Meanwhile, Lewis began to close every radio broadcast with the exhortation: "Don't forget to send in your dollars for the Wooden Church Crusade." By the end of 1952, the Wooden Church Crusade had received half a million US dollars from individual donors across the country. For many Americans, supporting the

The Wooden Church Crusade sought to build a "spiritual wall against communism" along the Iron Curtain in West Germany.
Courtesy of Syracuse University Libraries, Special Collections Research Center, Fulton Lewis Jr. Papers.

Crusade was an ideal way they could be faithful citizens, simultaneously showcasing their anti-communist commitments and religious devotion.[23]

Despite the initial success, it was not until 1953 that the Wooden Church Crusade made more significant headway in fundraising. During that fateful summer, East German workers in East Berlin started an uprising that was violently suppressed by Soviet forces and the East German national police. With Soviet repression of freedom-loving East Germans in clear view, Fulton Lewis, Jr., threw his full weight behind the project. He took over as national chairman and embarked on another four-week tour of West Germany and

Berlin. While abroad, Lewis interviewed Protestant Bishop Otto Dibelius and Catholic Bishop Wilhelm Weskamm, both of whom oversaw church affairs in Berlin and Brandenburg. The American commentator then broadcast the dire need of Germany's churches. Forty-five percent of all churches had been destroyed in the war, Lewis claimed. He likewise reported on communist propaganda saturating East German society and undermining American credibility in the region. As he argued, rebuilding Germany's churches represented a way to counteract such propaganda, to prove the goodwill of Americans, and to send a firm message of resistance to the Soviets.[24]

While touring West Berlin, Lewis also identified a strategic site on the border with East Berlin. Along the East-West border, he envisioned building a "wooden church" with an impressive bell tower that would send a loud and clear message to those living behind the Iron Curtain. Richard Kinzer's daughter stated "the bell" of the church would be "heard all the way to Moscow . . . bearing witness to truth and freedom" in a land of "tyranny." In order to fill East Germany with that sweet sound of freedom, Lewis rallied everyday Americans to the cause. As he noted, "the defense of Western freedom relies heavily upon the strength of a new and very different Germany, bravely confronting Communist terror." He believed that American spiritual support could help form this "new Germany."[25]

Returning from Germany, Lewis developed an ambitious campaign featuring a national "one-state-to-one-church" fundraising strategy. He called for the construction of forty-nine "wooden" churches, one for each state in the continental United States and an additional church for the District of Columbia. In tri-faith fashion, the needs of the local population in Germany would determine whether a church would be Catholic or Protestant, or in rare instances, if a Jewish synagogue might be built. Regardless of confession, this "chain of simple churches facing the Iron Curtain" would form "God's Spiritual Beachhead" against the "communists" who sought "worldwide conquest." Meanwhile, Royk-Lewinski and Lewis sold the idea to the American public through consistently advertising that for the price of one American B-52 bomber, over forty-nine churches could be built in Germany. Billing church reconstruction as "cheaper than high taxes" and "easier than war," they employed libertarian rhetoric to rally the spiritual energies of everyday Americans into a "modern day Christian Crusade" against "atheistic communism."[26]

Lewis utilized his Washington contacts to gain sponsors from each state and raise the needed funds to construct a single church. He recruited a

The postwar crusade of Fulton Lewis, Jr., and Henning von Royk-Lewinski rallied together anti-communist Christians, foreign policy hawks, and conservative corporate titans to defend "faith, freedom, and free enterprise" both at home and abroad in the Cold War.
Courtesy of Syracuse University Libraries, Special Collections Research Center, Fulton Lewis Jr. Papers.

diverse array of state sponsors, in sum twenty-six state governors and fifty-one senators. Hawkish cold warriors and conservative politicians flocked to the cause. Republican Senator Barry Goldwater pledged to head up fund-raising in the state of Arizona to complement his anti-communist advocacy and states' rights politics. Democrats with strong anti-communist convictions also lent their support, with Senator J. W. Fulbright organizing efforts in Arkansas. Not only did the inclusion of American politicians bequeath the Crusade an air of national credibility, it also showed the willingness of American policymakers to use religion as a tool of diplomacy in the Cold War.

Beyond political support, the Crusade also gained the backing of some of America's leading religious figures who desired to advance conservative politics in a world under communist threat. Both James Fifield and Norman Vincent Peale especially jumped on the Crusade's bandwagon. In the 1930s, the two ministers had already fostered campaigns against the "pagan stateism" of the New Deal. By the 1950s, they were again joining forces against the collectivist trends of communism and Fair Deal liberalism. Fifield's Spiritual Mobilization campaign aggressively promoted free-market economics and limited government among Protestant clergy and in the public sphere. The pro-business, Christian ideals of the movement found fertile soil in Fifield's home base of Southern California, where postwar defense industries began to boom in an era of Cold War militarization. Meanwhile, grassroots anti-communist and evangelical groups across the region formed the basis of a new conservative coalition that would increasingly champion Fifield's ideals. Those values appeared in Spiritual Mobilization's 1951 "Freedom under God" ceremonies. On the occasion of the 175th anniversary of the signing of the Declaration of Independence, Spiritual Mobilization launched a series of national celebrations which sought to keep alive America's historic roots of limited and godly government. The Wooden Church Crusade proved a natural international extension of Spiritual Mobilization's focus on reviving conservative religion and politics as a means to preserve the West's true heritage. Peale also supported the Crusade given its libertarian leanings. He hoped his theory of positive thinking, outlined in his 1952 bestseller *The Power of Positive Thinking*, would have a twofold effect on the nation. Through making problems personal instead of societal, it could galvanize an individualist ethic of "self-help" and limit dependency on governmental programs. Moreover, through promoting the soothing psychological benefits of faith, it could ignite a national religious revival that would defend the nation against "atheistic communism."[27]

The Wooden Church Crusade also benefited from corporate titans like J. Howard Pew, J. C. Penney, and Conrad Hilton, who had been inspired to play a larger role in politics due to the rise of the New Deal state and the onset of the Cold War. These businessmen endeavored as well to promote "faith, freedom, and free-enterprise" at home and abroad. Through bankrolling national campaigns such as Spiritual Mobilization, the Freedom Foundation, and the National Prayer Breakfast, they worked to foster an image of "Christian America" defined by individual freedoms, small government, and a robust public faith. To extend these values internationally, partnering with Lewis and Royk-Lewinski proved a natural fit. Newspaper mogul William Randolph Hearst and Sunoco president J. Howard Pew both pledged funds to the Crusade and served on the organization's national board. The "American Business Consultants" likewise threw its weight behind the project, advertising a call for sponsors in their journal, *Counterattack: The Newsletter of Facts to Combat Communism*.[28]

Corporate supporter Baron Walter Langer von Langerdorff also organized the 1954 International Debutante Ball to raise funds for the Crusade and promote conservative values in Germany. Held at Conrad Hilton's Waldorf Astoria Hotel in New York City, the Ball presented eligible young ladies to international society. Along with department store magnate James C. Penney, von Langerdorff and Hilton put together a star-studded affair that celebrated German-American democratic and Christian friendship. The niece of Konrad Adenauer, Fräulein Gabriele Adenauer, especially stole the show and the tabloids. Beyond the glitz and glamor, the Ball celebrated the spread of individual freedoms around the globe through democratic governance. The festivities reached a high note with a special performance of the "Pathétique" theme from Tchaikovsky's Sixth Symphony. A performance titled "Darkness to Light" set to the musical piece depicted the spread of individual liberty and freedom through the Wooden Church Crusade.[29]

While these corporate titans padded the Crusade's coffers, Lewis especially worked to gain support from everyday Americans. His broadcasts called on every individual American to contribute. He emphasized "the place of solitary individual participation—the person-to-person aspect . . . in the world struggle against Godless totalitarian tyranny." He received a resounding reply from small-town clubs, local business societies, and city service organizations that sent in small dollar donations. To Lewis, each individual sponsor and agency affirmed that the American people stood behind West Germany. The Crusade illustrated to the Germans and Soviets, Lewis claimed, that "this is not just money from the Government. It is from the people." With a personal touch, officials at the Wooden Church Crusade sent handwritten notes of gratitude to each individual contributor. American donors also were promised to have their name enshrined in a "Golden Book" to be placed in each "wooden" church.[30]

Beyond small donors, the Crusade also drew the support of heavy-hitting national organizations and clubs that advanced anti-communism across Cold War America. In addition to support from the Sons and Daughters of the American Revolution, the American Legion Auxiliary named the Crusade as its 1954 "National President's Project." The organization's periodical affirmed that "the wooden churches" provided "concrete evidence that Americans understand and have feeling for the spiritual, as well as the material needs, of the individual Germans." The Auxiliary's support aligned with the all-male Legion's "Back to God" campaign, which encouraged Christians across the nation to propagate their faith in their homes, schools, and sites of worship. One Auxiliary author also included a passionate plea that exhibited the tri-faith idealism of the project. After invoking the Golden Rule present in the world's major religions, the author wrote, "Communism, a godless tyranny, has no such words. It is vulnerable because it denies God." She continued to reflect on how communism would ultimately fail as a polit-ical and societal system due to its rejection of religion. Through supporting the Crusade, concerned Americans could "help strengthen the influence of religion in a region where freedom stands face to face with Communism." The article concluded by invoking God's blessing upon donors. Channeling the positive thinking of Peale, it declared that fighting communism abroad would lead to personal fulfillment and happiness at home.[31]

The Wooden Church Crusade illustrated how the American public, from governors and senators down to everyday citizens and parishioners, rallied behind the cause of spiritual rearmament. In doing so, they helped put into motion the grassroots origins of a postwar conservatism that was anti-communist in its politics and tri-faith in its religion. In this regard, the Cold War and the Wooden Church Crusade actually created space for new interfaith partnerships under the banner of "Judeo-Christian" America, as conservative Catholics and Jews joined conservative Protestants in a spir-itual offensive against communism and secularism. Even some Protestant evangelicals suspended their strong anti-Catholicism in order to support the crusade's spiritual cause. These Americans acted on their conviction that the Cold War required a spiritual and religious response that complemented ec-onomic and military partnerships. In this way, the Wooden Church Crusade continued to advance America's sacred cause of defending democracy and faith in the world. While European ecumenists had begun to call for a "third way," conservative crusaders like Lewis and Royk-Lewinski continued to weaponize American religion in order to defeat the "godless communists" both at home and abroad.

With such broad national support, the Crusade finally broke ground in 1954 on its first church outside of Hamburg, six kilometers from the East-West German border. By the end of the year, sixteen churches had been constructed, with eight more in the works for the following year. By the end of 1956, a total of twenty-eight houses of worship had been built, including several synagogues. Along the Iron Curtain, individual congregations in need gratefully accepted the aid and celebrated the German-American partnership in the Cold War. German Protestants in Wildenheid-Meilschnitz, for instance, proved receptive to Royk-Lewinski's mission to "build a spiritual wall against communism." The small village lay not far from the Fulda Gap, one of the Cold War's hottest spots in Europe given its suitability for a Soviet tank invasion of West Germany. At the dedication of their "Wooden Church" on October 16, 1955, expressions of German-American friendship abounded. As an American flag flew in the German breeze, the church reinforced American-German friendship through its display of a Golden Book, in which "the names of their American friends under the same God" stood enshrined for ages to come. The congregants also celebrated the church as a symbol of defiance to communism and solidarity with the oppressed peoples of East Germany. Reports on the affair stated that the "sound of bells" rang out as a "sign of freedom and unity" to the occupied peoples of East Germany.[32]

Although the Crusade received support from individual congregations, church leaders in Germany split over the cause. Conservative-leaning bishops like Otto Dibelius went on record for Lewis, noting the "essential necessity" of church reconstruction. Dibelius was more than willing to work with both liberal ecumenists and conservative evangelicals in his quest to hold off secularism and communism. Berlin's Catholic Bishop Wilhelm Weskamm, the successor to Konrad von Preysing, also welcomed the construction of new Catholic parishes in West Berlin and supported West Germany's entry into NATO. In Bavaria, Cardinal Michael von Faulhaber coordinated with Royk-Lewinski to construct multiple Catholic parishes. The Crusade also found a willing institutional partner in the Gustav-Adolf-Werk, a church agency which existed to strengthen the spiritual life of refugee communities. The organization's leaders claimed to overlook the "political" nature of the work and focused instead on providing church buildings to refugees in need.[33]

In contrast, officials in *Hilfswerk* expressed their concern over the "quasi-political program." Initially, *Hilfswerk* workers scrambled for information about the Crusade as they had difficulty determining its origin. Their correspondence suggested that Dibelius had gone rogue in his cooperation with Royk-Lewinski. One worker in the central *Hilfswerk* bureau feared the Crusade would only lead to East German authorities taking a harsher stance on the churches there, perhaps even forcing them to sever ties with churches in West Germany. These German Protestants noted the need for careful and open diplomacy with East Germany. In one editorial, Protestant pastors accused the Crusade of "carrying the character of a political action" that cast all of East German as "pagan." They pointed out there were "Christian and living congregations" behind the Iron Curtain that needed ecumenical support.[34]

Although Protestant ecumenists in the United States had argued for religion's importance in the Cold War, they proved lukewarm about backing this tri-faith, conservative campaign that supported West German rearmament. Federal Council leader Samuel McCrea Cavert and ranking American Lutheran Franklin C. Fry both refused Lewis's call for sponsorship. Church World Service, the relief agency of the National Council, also declined to back the Crusade. These ecumenists ultimately expressed concern over the "quasi-political nature of the crusade" and felt skittish about "rearming" Germans militarily. They ultimately criticized the Crusade for turning religion into a utilitarian weapon that complemented military strength and worsened Cold War tensions. Their lack of support revealed how they had begun to track out of orbit of the new mainstream commitments of Americans in the Cold War.[35]

As conservative and liberal Christians split on both sides of the Atlantic, the Wooden Church Crusade never reached its goal of building forty-nine houses of worship. Ultimately, fundraising began to stall in light of the *Wirtschaftswunder*, West Germany's miraculous economic recovery. As fundraising dried up, Royk-Lewinski came under increasing scrutiny. In particular, suspicions lingered regarding his wartime service on behalf of the Nazi regime. As immigration officials first suspected in 1950, he certainly knew of Hitler's horrors long before 1942. He in fact represented one of many Germans eager to erase their complicity with Nazism through anti-communism. Questions also arose over how Royk-Lewinski used the Crusade's funds. While the Crusade had succeeded remarkably in garnering publicity and donations, accountability and oversight of those funds proved another story. Royk-Lewinski's annual salary and his frequent stays at the posh Hotel Continental in Munich on Crusade business seemingly drained the organization's bank accounts. All the while, at least one case emerged in which a German congregation received a pledge of a donation from the Crusade that never arrived. After Royk-Lewinski personally promised the funds would materialize, the West German Protestant congregation began construction on its new "wooden church" building. When the Crusade failed to deliver, however, it was forced to take out a loan and found itself shortly thereafter in default. In response to their repeated inquiries, Royk-Lewinski finally wrote back that the actual funds from the United States had never arrived. Americans had taken stock of Germany's economic recovery, he claimed, and were no longer donating. In the end, Royk-Lewinski could only send a fraction of the promised funds to the congregation, leaving it with a large debt. Meanwhile, Royk-Lewinski pressed on undeterred. In the fervor of the Crusade, the US Congress had granted him permanent residency. Using that to good measure, he went on to pursue a business career in Hawaii.[36]

Although the Crusade never reached its full goal, Crusade backers nonetheless celebrated what they had accomplished. In their view, the Wooden Church Crusade had united a diverse array of conservative Americans, from the halls of power in Washington to everyday Protestant and Catholic parishes, to form a spiritual offensive against Soviet communism. As West Germany joined NATO in 1955, the Crusade's leaders celebrated how they had already provided spiritual support for this Western outpost along the Iron Curtain. They had marshalled the energies of a Christian national revival that called on the United States and West Germany to be nations "under God" and to oppose "godless" communists both at home and abroad.

As the Wooden Church Crusade reached its peak in 1954, evangelical Protestants also looked to Billy Graham to advance their particular evangelical cause in West Germany. West German rearmament—both militarily and spiritually—found a major promoter in the rising evangelist. As he put it in one sermon, communism was a dangerous movement that had "decided against God, against Christ, against the Bible, and against all religion. Communism is not only an economic interpretation of life—communism is a religion that is inspired, directed, and motivated by the Devil himself who has declared war against Almighty God." Graham's black-and-white, apocalyptic worldview motivated him to take his crusades directly to West Germany to defend the faith before the Iron Curtain.[37]

In 1954, Graham made "spiritual rearmament" a guiding motif for his first West German crusade, which included mass rallies in Frankfurt, Düsseldorf, and Berlin. After landing in West Germany, the globetrotting evangelist made a splash when he called West Germans his "brothers in arms" and declared his support for West Germany's remilitarization. The German press took notice and soon began calling Graham "God's Machine Gun" due to his militant stance against communism and his staccato-like preaching style.

Building upon his 1954 success, Graham returned again to West Germany in 1955, stopping in Mannheim, Stuttgart, Nuremberg, Dortmund, Frankfurt, and at select American military bases. He would return three more times, in 1960, 1963, and 1966, for bigger and longer tours in Germany and Europe, including stops in London, Paris, Amsterdam, Copenhagen, Stockholm, Helsinki, and Zürich. In his crusades, Graham revived the image of Europe as a "spiritual battleground" of "conquest" between God-fearing Americans and godless Soviets.[38]

Many German Protestants welcomed Graham's crusades as a means to counteract secularization and communism. In particular, some Germans lauded Graham's modern methods that seemed to connect with the postwar West German public. His crusades used popular media to create a publicity buzz, featured modern music styles, and had high production value. For instance, the 80,000 Germans gathered at Berlin's Olympic Stadium in the summer of 1954 were treated to a choir of 2,000 West Germans, an ensemble of 400 trombonists, and the American gospel singer Beverly Shea. Graham offered a distinctly American religious experience to this West German audience that was also beginning to consume Coca-Cola and listen to American rock 'n' roll.[39]

Leading German Protestants such as Otto Dibelius and Hanns Lilje emerged as two of Graham's strongest supporters. They saw Graham as a useful ally in their postwar campaign to "re-Christianize" their nation and stave off secularization and materialism. Dibelius recognized that if he could not evangelize Germans, perhaps an outsider could. As he put it, "If I do not succeed, then there is nothing else to do but to say, 'Billy Graham, come again.'" Lilje also affirmed that Graham had a "mission in today's Christianity." Even as ecumenical and evangelical American Protestants disagreed in theology and politics, Dibelius and Lilje used both groups to "re-Christianize" their country.[40]

Yet not all West Germans were sold. While Graham's personable demeanor disarmed some, others saw his methods and persona as superficial. The German press, for instance, described him as a shallow "actor" and "Hollywood prodigy." News headlines pointed out that his crusades cost millions of dollars and ran like Hollywood mass productions. West Germans also criticized Graham for simplifying the gospel and turning it into an item of mass consumption. According to one Düsseldorf newspaper, Graham was an "adman" who "advertised the Bible like toothpaste and chewing gum." The popular periodical Der Spiegel also disparaged the American evangelist

American evangelist Billy Graham often filled his revival tents to the brim during his postwar West German crusades. Graham aimed to preach the old-time gospel in modern ways. In this 1960 West Berlin revival, he spoke underneath a large banner declaring in German that Jesus was "the way, the truth, and the life."
Courtesy of Billy Graham Evangelical Association.

for "preaching the ABCs of Christianity, religious commodities, designed for mass consumption." In the estimation of these Germans, Graham "sold the gospel like soap" and amounted to nothing more than a "Protestant Goebbels." Others wondered if Graham's method and technique were the only way forward for the German churches. They emphasized that Germans had led the Protestant world "for centuries" and questioned whether there could be German alternatives to Graham's mass meetings.[41]

Some West Germans also opposed the massive size of Graham's gatherings, seeing in them events too reminiscent of Germany's own fascist past. One Protestant leader compared Graham's mass rallies to "mass intoxication." Drawing a parallel to Hitler's misleading ways, he warned, "a people so wounded as the Germans must not be subjected to the temptation of intoxication and must find time to let its wounds heal." Graham and his allies, however, actively drew upon the Nazi past as a rationale for their crusades.

"Battleground Europe," a 1955 promotional video produced by Graham's production company, emphasized how Germans naturally responded to a "forceful voice" at "great outdoor gatherings." The narrator contrasted Graham's sermon at the Nuremberg parade grounds by affirming that "the swastika was replaced by the cross, the hate by the love of God." The narrator continued: "sixty-five thousand persons, the largest crowd in the stadium since Hitler's day, stood in the stadium to listen. No plan for a race of supermen here. Rather, the solemn declaration that all have sinned and come short of the glory of God." While Germans had erred grievously, the promotional film claimed Graham's salvific message provided them with a means to atone for the Nazi past—and seemingly to defend themselves against a Soviet future as well.[42]

While American ecumenists had used rather similar language to describe their mission in postwar Germany, they split over Graham's style and methods. Reinhold Niebuhr emerged as one of Graham's harshest domestic critics. When Graham came to New York in 1957 for a month-long crusade, Niebuhr spared no ink. He described Graham's religion as "obscurantist" and "oversimplified." For Niebuhr, conversion was not just signing a decision card for Christ; nor was it drawing sinners to the cross through the glitz and glamor of Madison Avenue. The Christian faith entailed a "painful religious experience" that demanded responsible action in the public sphere. In contrast, Protestant ecumenist Henry van Dusen defended Graham. In his own student days, van Dusen's soul had been stirred by preachers similar to Graham. In his view, a decision for Christ could begin a process that led the individual into a deeper and more complex practice of Christianity.[43]

Ecumenical Protestants also worried, however, that Graham's evangelical crusades would splinter German Protestantism. At a 1960 rally, one of Graham's German translators contributed to that effect through a subtle yet intentional translation decision. When Graham invited his audience to come to the altar and join an "evangelical church," the young translator decided not to use the traditional German word for evangelical—*evangelisch*—because he feared German attendees might mistake Graham to mean attending a traditional Protestant church. Instead, he riffed and used the new adjective *evangelikal*. Through his translation, he hoped to differentiate "evangelical free churches" from the liberal Protestant state churches. The spontaneous use of the adjective further galvanized *evangelikal* Protestants in Germany. Free church believers reported that they were prepared to open up a "battlefront" against the state churches' "counterfeit Gospel" and "modernist theology." These Germans thus found in Graham an ally against the theological modernism and liberalism that had long defined German Protestantism.[44]

Beyond strengthening evangelical identity abroad, Graham's crusades also hardened the political battle lines of the Cold War. Graham's Cold War messaging led many German journalists to interpret his stardom entirely within the political context of the East-West conflict. The editors of *Der Spiegel*, one of West Germany's leading news journals, pointed out Graham's 1949 breakout as an evangelist could only be understood in light of the dramatic events of that year, including the "loss of China" to communism, the Berlin Blockade, and the news of the Soviet Union's first successful atomic bomb. "Before then," the editors wrote, Graham "was an unknown Baptist pastor." The magazine argued that "anti-communism"—not authentic faith—was the strongest impulse in Graham's crusade. Other media outlets pondered the connection between Graham's revivals and the new American militarism of the Cold War. One Munich newspaper portrayed Graham preaching his message from the top of an American tank. In the cartoonist's view, Graham emboldened recently pacified West Germans to now take up arms against the existential foe of communism.[45]

The East German press was even more critical: it argued that Graham was a covert agent of American empire. In a 1960 political cartoon, East German satirists depicted Graham flying over Berlin on wings made out of American flags. "God's Machine Gun" carried a Bible emblazoned with a dollar sign on its cover. In the eyes of these East Germans, Graham proclaimed a gospel message of capitalist wealth and militarism reminiscent of the Nazi past. Another East German paper characterized Graham's crusades as a tool of "American propaganda in the psychological Cold War." Other outlets claimed that the CIA, American industrialists, and the "warmongers" in Washington and Bonn funded his crusades in order to foster the "stultification" of the working classes. Such viewpoints captured the intense political ramifications of Graham's crusades in the Cold War. His crusades inspired polemical opposition on both sides of the Iron Curtain to American religion and American foreign policy.[46]

Although Graham insisted on the apolitical nature of his crusades, he also readily drew upon the Cold War itself as a framework for his revivals. Even as he claimed he came only to preach the Gospel, he still carried out significant political work. In particular, he often depicted his transatlantic preaching tours as linking together the crucial centers of the "free world," from New York to Amsterdam and London to West Berlin. His crusades in these cities sought to foster an imagined community of faithful Christians, united in their commitments to spiritual, economic, and political liberty. Graham's rallies in Berlin especially highlighted such efforts. The American preacher gave the beleaguered city a privileged standing in the North Atlantic world. As he announced to Germans gathered in Berlin's Olympic Stadium in 1954, "millions of Christians in the entire world know about the particular situation of Berlin. Berlin is prayed for in the world more than any other city. The citizens of Berlin are not forgotten." For many Americans, West Berlin had become a defiant outpost of liberty in a sea of communist red. Graham's crusades sought to strengthen the spiritual defenses of this crucial Western garrison. As he made his way across "Battleground Europe" in the mid-1950s and early 1960s, he brought this same message to other crucial strongholds. In sermon after sermon, he gave his European attendees a central place in the transatlantic "Christian West." They were the spiritual foot soldiers in the front lines of an unfolding drama against the globe's godless forces. Moreover, his efforts strove to foster religious and political solidarity across the North Atlantic world. With each crusade, he worked to forge a new conservative, anti-communist coalition committed to freedom, democracy, and capitalism.[47]

Berlin's status as a central European outpost of the "free world" especially came to light during Graham's 1960 crusade there. In the 1950s, millions of East Germans had used West Berlin to escape from East Germany. The city therefore had simultaneously become a symbol of the free world and a source of Soviet embarrassment. Graham's 1960 Berlin crusade took place against this tense backdrop. When the crusade organizers constructed a large tent right in front of the German *Bundestag* and close to the East-West border crossing at the Brandenburg Gate, the city government of East Berlin sharply criticized the provocative location and demanded that West Berlin's city government remove it. The mayor of West Berlin, Willy Brandt, replied, "Billy Graham can preach in West Berlin where he wants and as long as he wants, your protests notwithstanding." In response, East Berlin leaders threatened to arrest Graham if he crossed over into their city. They also called on Protestant theologian Emil Fuchs, East Germany's "best-known theologian," to challenge Graham in a public debate. When the crusade began, East Berliners found their normal routes into West Berlin blocked by border guards. Soviet tanks also lined Berlin's main boulevard in order to discourage East Berliners from attending. Six months later, East German and Soviet officials would follow up on the presence of soldiers and tanks with the construction of the Berlin Wall that made such crossings permanently impossible.[48]

Graham's crusades certainly did not cause East German authorities to build the Berlin Wall. But they did worsen Cold War tensions between East and West Germans, as well as the Soviet Union and the United States. Moreover, they indicated how evangelical Protestants welded their spiritual and political convictions together as they campaigned for the rearmament of the "Christian West." In the 1950s, evangelical Protestants were therefore at the helm of reviving a new kind of Christian nationalism, one that called for a defense of biblical fundamentals, democratic liberty, and free markets both at home and abroad. They also called on Americans to build up the kind of military power needed not only to check Soviet communism in its place, but to actually "roll it back." As the Cold War intensified in the 1950s, these evangelical commitments began to more fully shape their nation's global engagement. The quest to spiritually rearm Germany gave American evangelicals newfound confidence to pursue spiritual interventions abroad and political campaigns at home. To be sure, not all evangelicals stood for this kind of militant God-and-country-faith. In fact, the international engagement of American evangelicals would soon begin to inspire a global turn within some of their churches. Yet on the whole, "God's Machine Gun" and the politics of West Germany's spiritual rearmament quickened the rise of a muscular conservative evangelicalism, a style of faith that would soon remake American political and religious life.

Epilogue

In March 1963, Stewart Herman took the podium at the Seabury House in Greenwich, Connecticut, to address a gathering of American and Soviet pastors. The National Council of Churches was hosting sixteen Russian Orthodox priests and Protestant pastors in an effort to build international goodwill and Christian unity between the United States and the Soviet Union. In his address, Herman declared that "the Christian church" was "supra-national" and that ecumenical Christianity was focused solely on "universal interests." He added, "If nations of the world are ever to enjoy orderly procedures and peaceful change, surely it is incumbent upon the Christian churches to furnish practical examples in the conduct of their own national and international affairs."[1]

The American Protestant journey to this kind of Christian globalist ethic had been complex. American ecumenists had often expressed the central tenets of Christian globalism in their mission to Europe, including opposition to nationalism, racism, and imperialism, as well as a focus on mutual partnerships within global organizations. In response to the international challenges and disorder of their day, they sought to infuse diplomacy and international relations with a Christian character and worked to create a just and peaceful international order out of the world's chaos.

Yet their ministry in practice had also illustrated that they were just as quick to serve their nation's interests and advance its global project. Ironically, their quest to build a most just, tolerant, and peaceful world order also yielded a mission to spread the American way of democracy, capitalism, and Christianity across the Atlantic. Their long-standing commitment to "Christianizing and democratizing" the globe, as well as their concerns about fascism, communism, secularism, and Catholicism, led them to seek to rebuild Germany as the European cornerstone of an American-led Christian world order. They accordingly transformed the ecumenical movement into a vehicle of America's global democratic mission and provided vital energy

God's Marshall Plan. James D. Strasburg, Oxford University Press (2021). © Oxford University Press.
DOI: 10.1093/oso/9780197516447.003.0010

and spiritual support to their nation's international expansion. All the while, they sought to preserve the power of ecumenical Protestantism at home and abroad and struggled to forge a hospitable posture toward Jews and Catholics. In this regard, Protestant ecumenists played an underacknowledged yet significant role in keeping alive the flames of American Christian nationalism in the twentieth century.

In more ways than perhaps recognized, then, the boundary between Christian globalism and Christian nationalism proved blurry within American ecumenical circles. Although ecumenists tended to tell their movement's story in heroic and transcendent terms, the historical truth actually lay somewhere more in the complex middle. Indeed, the ecumenical response to Hitler and Nazi fascism did not just entail righteous resistance and transnational solidarity. It also involved degrees of accommodation, resignation, inaction, and even admiration. The ecumenical vision for Germany's reformation also did not just call for peaceful reconstruction and collaborative partnership. It was also about fulfilling a Wilsonian mission of spiritual conquest and opposing the perceived spiritual foes of communism and Catholicism.

Yet these Protestant ecumenists were also not singular or unique in their struggle with the theology of Christian nationalism. Indeed, the challenge for many Protestant Christians in the twentieth century involved untangling their faith from the creeds of nation, race, and empire. That struggle continues to this day. In today's context, the history of twentieth-century Protestantism ideally can clarify the ramifications of Protestant Christianity's ideological captivity. That history demonstrates how Christian nationalism led Protestants to go to war against one another and to narrowly pursue their nation's interests. Christian nationalism likewise corrupted the core tenets of the Christian faith—namely the command to love one's neighbor—in favor of exclusionary politics that compelled Christians to see fellow human beings as outsiders and enemies. Christian nationalists more often than not deployed their faith as a weapon in cultural and spiritual wars at home and abroad and as a tool of power and control. In these regards, Christian nationalism clearly distorted the Christian faith.

Over the course of that same century, however, some American Protestants learned through their struggle for the soul of Europe, as well as their engagement with other parts of the globe, that Christian nationalism tainted their theology and witness. It became clearer to them that the tenets of Christian nationalism had little to do with the Jesus of the gospels. For the American Protestants who sought to remake Europe, this shift especially came about through the German and European Protestants who challenged them to become a mediating and reconciling force in the Cold War.[2]

For their part, Germany's Protestants had walked a fine line between collaboration and contestation in response to America's spiritual crusade to their continent. Through the Great War and interwar years, they had long maintained their suspicions of America's spiritual empire. The postwar peace and the Allied occupation of Germany activated these concerns yet again. In response, some German Protestant leaders certainly rose up as defenders of their nation during the postwar military occupation. At the same time, some also began to come to terms with their own commitments to Christian nationalism. These radical reformers began the slow work of building an entirely different kind of German Protestant church out of the ashes of war. Critical reflection on the Nazi past, new ecumenical networks, and Cold War divisions inspired reform. These German reformers took spiritual values like ecumenism, civic activism, and public responsibility into their own hands and increasingly used them to challenge American and West German policies in the Cold War itself. They combined their critiques of Cold War militarization with a vision for social democracy, international solidarity, and global peace. This wave of radical reformers in Germany indeed became some of the world's strongest proponents of Europe's "third way" theology.

The stories of Karl Barth and Martin Niemöller especially showcased these developments. In the 1960s, both emerged as leading spiritual ambassadors of Europe's "third way" approach. In the spring of 1962, Barth made his first transatlantic journey to the United States. Fresh off his retirement from the University of Basel, the Swiss theologian accepted an invitation to lecture at American Protestant seminaries, such as Princeton Theological Seminary and the Divinity School at the University of Chicago. Despite his graying hair, the Swiss theologian undertook a grand tour of the United States, which included stops in New York City, San Francisco, the Grand Canyon, and Gettysburg, where Barth stopped to fire a nineteenth-century musket. The American press honored him with a front cover on *TIME Magazine* and headlines that praised him as "the most creative Protestant theologian since John Calvin" and a "fearless fighter" against "Hitler and the Nazis."[3]

In response, the Swiss theologian proceeded to deliver a fiery critique of the capitalist and democratic "Christian West." As one *New York Times* profile put it, Barth warned that "the 'fleshpots' and 'complacency'" of "the American way of life" were "a greater danger to the Christian soul than

communism." In a harsh rebuke of his hosts, he added, "I regard anticommunism as a matter of principle an evil even greater than communism in itself."
In his view, Cold War hostilities had resulted primarily from American aggression. Diplomatic maneuvers such as the creation of the Federal Republic
of Germany, as well as the stockpiling of nuclear weapons, had only alienated
the Soviet Union. The Cold War "madness" of American Protestants likewise
undermined the true mission of the church, namely being a "superior witness to the peace and hope of the kingdom of God."[4]

Barth also delivered a blistering condemnation of American inequality as
he visited three prisons across the nation and met with civil rights activists
and socialist groups. Americans had grown so enamored with "moon shots,"
he stated, that they had neglected to care for "the least of these." He especially
condemned the American prison and criminal justice system as "Dante's
hell." While staying in Chicago, he also expressed his deep concern over "the
plight of Negroes in nearby slums." If he were an American theologian, he
counseled, he would work on a "theology of freedom," but not freedom as
Americans understood it. It would not be the freedom of unbridled choice,
consumption, and individualism, nor the kind of freedom that appeared, as
he saw it, in the myth of American exceptionalism. That American theology
needed to be "demythologized," he stated. Rather, an authentic "theology
of freedom" would make clear that true freedom came from Christ alone.
Such freedom was available to all, regardless of nationality, ideology, race, or
class. And it always entailed responsibility for one's neighbor and "the least
of these."[5]

Niemöller also joined Barth in offering a prophetic critique of American
militarism and Cold War hostilities. The German pastor's postwar ethic of
pacifist protest only grew with time. The repentant nationalist soon found
himself at the helm of the World Council of Churches, serving as president
and advocating pacifism among the world's Protestants. In 1967, Niemöller
even visited Ho Chi Minh on a mission of peace and solidarity in the thick of
the Vietnam War. The apostle of détente called for an end to all Cold War hostilities and carried his mission of penance and reform onward until his death
in 1984. Niemöller had indeed helped transform German Protestantism into
an emerging beacon of Christian globalism.[6]

Both Barth and Niemöller helped further the "third way" shift within
American and European ecumenical circles. As American Protestants spent
more time listening to European partners during the German occupation
and the Cold War, their views indeed began to change. They had pressed

abroad to remake Europe, but in the end, Europe ultimately remade them. In particular, the "third way" theology and newfound Christian globalism of Germany's radical reformers in the Cold War spoke back to American Protestants in powerful ways. For those who had ears to hear, the prophetic witness of these European Protestants in the Cold War challenged Americans to rethink their commitments. This European example ultimately proved an important factor in leading American ecumenists to strengthen their dedication to a global fellowship of believers that placed the ethics of Christ above the nation.

In response, some American ecumenists began to more fully embrace a Christian globalist ethic that called for reconciliation, mediation, and toleration of ideological difference in the Cold War. They argued the bipolar conflict had created artificial boundaries that could be overcome through Christian fellowship. They returned back to theologies of protest and pacifism in order to challenge America's militant Cold War policies both at home and abroad. As the United States imposed its will through coups, established alliances with dictators, carried out wars in Vietnam and across Latin America, and struggled to uphold liberty and justice for all at home, they also began to see their country less as a "city on the hill" and more as one of the "principalities" and "powers" that the Apostle Paul had warned of in his letter to the Ephesians. In response, they took up a prophetic role, speaking truth to power and seeking to aid the victims of such power. They practiced a healthy and critical love of country as a civic good, but one that was always tempered by a higher allegiance to the love of neighbor both near and afar. As they stretched their global imagination, they reconsidered whether God's global kingdom could be advanced through their nation's global strength. They questioned more thoroughly whether the cause of Christ and country could be truly one and the same. To a growing number in their ranks, what mattered the most now was empowering Protestants to be witnesses to a Christian ethic in whatever sociopolitical, national, or economic context they found themselves. As such, ecumenists began to see themselves not as citizens of Christian America, but rather as citizens of a global kingdom that knew no borders. Such citizenship did not entail a quest for dominion, the imposition of ideologies, or the spiritual conquest of the globe. Rather, it encouraged solidarity, mutual partnership, and humble service. For these Protestants, Christian mission accordingly no longer meant advancing their understanding of America's global project. It ultimately became about joining God and others in creating a more loving world for all creaturely life.

Such developments especially appeared in the work of Stewart Herman. Herman's own sojourn in Europe, along with his postwar experiences across Latin America, led him in particular to develop a more inclusive view of other faiths and a stronger ethic of responsibility for his neighbor. Encountering the horrors of the Holocaust firsthand and the repentance of reformers like Niemöller led him to increasingly believe that Protestants had "entirely failed" the Jews. He now urged his fellow Christians to take "quick public action" in response to signs of antisemitism and racism. After working for the World Council, he also began to serve the Lutheran World Federation and helped relocate German refugees to Latin America. That ministry opened him to the currents of Latin American liberation theology and Vatican II. Increasingly, he welcomed Catholics as newfound partners in the global pursuit of peace and justice. While at one time he had deemed Judaism and Catholicism the spiritual inferiors of Protestantism, Herman's experiences abroad expanded his ecumenism to now include other faiths outside of a narrow Protestant confessionalism. Herman sought to make good on his transformation at home, forging new interfaith partnerships in response to the world's challenges.[7]

Herman's critical reflections on his own religious and racial prejudice—in particular, his failure to oppose such currents in Hitler's Berlin—also fostered within him a stronger willingness to act in response to these currents at home. In March 1965, Herman sat down on a Sunday evening for a televised showing of *Judgment at Nuremburg*, only to have a breaking news report interrupt his viewing. That same day, Alabama state troopers in Selma had used vicious force to beat back peaceful civil rights activists who had sought to cross the Edmund Pettus Bridge. The scene shocked him. He had not seen such brutality since his years in Hitler's Berlin. While he had largely remained on the sidelines in Germany at that time, he resolved now to "stand up and be counted." He left the next evening for Selma with a group of Chicago-based clergy. Two days later, he marched hand in hand with other civil rights activists. Herman's longer journey to the commitments of Christian globalism stood as a reminder of how American Protestants who pressed abroad to change the world often could find themselves just as much changed in return.[8]

For a time, it appeared as if this globalist ethic would take hold of American Protestantism and the United States. Civil rights legislation in 1964 and 1965 ended years of state-sponsored racism and political inequality, and a new immigration policy in 1965 opened the United States to immigrants from across the decolonizing world. The quagmire of the Vietnam War gave way to a new spirit of openness and cooperation with the Soviet Union. More tolerant views developed toward non-Christian religions in the United States. Reflecting critically upon the connection between imperialism and conversion, ecumenical Protestants focused more on humanitarian work than missionary boards. In some corners of America, it appeared as if this cosmopolitan ethic was carrying the day.[9]

Yet the spiritual reconstruction of Europe had also exposed deep fractures within American Protestantism. Not all American Protestants welcomed the third way critique of Barth and Niemöller. Transatlantic events continued to create divisions within American and German Protestantism as wide as the Grand Canyon that left Barth breathless. For instance, in a four-page profile of Barth, *TIME* wrote that theologically conservative Americans "variously damned" the aging emeritus professor "as a heretic, a narrow-minded Biblicist, and an atheist in disguise." Anti-communist hardliners also described Barth's views on communism as "naïve." His neutral politics riled up American fundamentalists like Carl McIntire, who cabled to Konrad Adenauer that "Barth's attitude" on Soviet communism failed to "represent the position of orthodox Christianity." Under McIntire's machinations, Barth endured attacks reminiscent of McCarthy's Red Scare in the 1950s.[10]

The spiritual battles of the early to mid-twentieth century had thus equally strengthened Christian nationalism across the United States. In particular, the twentieth century's three major wars spurred on the rise of evangelical Protestants as the proponents of a more militant and muscular form of Christian nationalism. Galvanized by the threat of theological modernism and German *Kultur* in the First World War, fundamentalist Protestants began their decades-long struggle against domestic and foreign threats. The liberalization of Protestant mission and fears of the impending apocalypse likewise committed them to "occupying" their world and pursuing conversionary mission. Seeing Nazi fascism and communism as intertwined and related evils, Protestant evangelicals mobilized for holy wars and fought for the soul of their nation and the "Christian West." As the Cold War began, they fashioned themselves as patriotic defenders of "Christian America" and proudly enlisted as their nation's spiritual cold warriors. In that role, they strove to establish a different kind of spiritual order of evangelical Christianity, anti-communism, and free markets across the North Atlantic West. Meanwhile, they tended to support interventionist and militant foreign policies and proved slower to support the movement for civil rights within their nation.

Billy Graham's ministry especially featured the prevalence of Christian nationalism among mainstream American evangelicals as they became major players in transatlantic affairs. In the same year that Herman spoke with Soviet pastors, Graham sat down to coffee with West German chancellor Konrad Adenauer. As the German chancellor prepared to step down from his post, he and Graham connected over their faith and opposition to communism. As Graham met with Adenauer, the evangelical standard *Christianity Today* ran a favorable piece on Otto Dibelius. The periodical lauded Dibelius as the bold bishop who stood with "Christ against the tyrants." Henry Luce in particular praised Dibelius for "keeping the flame of Christian hope alive for his people under two tyrannies, Nazism and Communism." The article described Berlin as the site of not only a "struggle between world powers" but also a struggle for the entire "spiritual fate of humanity in our times." Graham and his evangelical allies saw the Cold War as a decisive spiritual battle to be waged, and they refused to back down.[11]

Graham's 1963 meeting with Adenauer likewise highlighted his strategy of connecting with powerful politicians and cultural figures in order to bolster evangelicalism's standing in the United States and Europe. He especially relished his role as a trusted political advisor to Republican presidents Dwight Eisenhower and Richard Nixon. His meeting with the German chancellor also showed how evangelicals would carry forward America's sacred cause into a new Cold War era. Graham tied his coffee hour with Adenauer to evangelical crusades across West Germany and the United States, and he soon reached out even farther, taking his revivals to a global audience in Australia, across the African continent, and in East Asia. Along the way, he preached a gospel of individual conversion and proclaimed commitments to freedom and capitalism. Meanwhile, he voiced his support for the Vietnam War and proved slow to counteract the racial legacy of Jim Crow. While he racially integrated his crusades, he cautioned against swift change and ultimately argued that Christians ought to focus their energies on changing hearts instead of transforming society. In these ways, Graham illustrated how evangelical Protestantism remained largely captive to Christian nationalism in the Cold War.[12]

Yet Graham's story also revealed the growing global evangelical challenge to American Protestantism. In particular, his international travels opened his eyes to the rapid growth of indigenous Christianity across the decolonizing world. For some American evangelicals, these global "kingdom partners" worked a change in them. The 1966 World Congress on Evangelism in West Berlin showcased these developments in particular detail. On the one hand, the Congress clearly reflected the triumphant spirit of American evangelicalism. Entrepreneurial American speakers dominated the Congress's public talks and shared their energetic mission to win the world to Christ. An all-American planning committee also intentionally chose West Berlin as the host city due to its Cold War symbolism. The Berlin Wall served as the perfect backdrop for marketing the American evangelical mission that defended Christianity, free markets, and democracy. The Congress likewise featured vocal, anti-communist evangelicals from across the decolonizing world. In these ways, the Congress clearly reflected American evangelical commitments to an entrepreneurial, anti-communist, and pro-business gospel. Yet the American organizers had also capped American participation at 100 delegates, allowing a significant contingent of non-Western Protestants to attend. In discussion groups and prayer sessions, African, Asian, and Latin American delegates began to challenge America's spiritual dominance. They openly pointed out their Western counterparts' complicity with racism and colonialism. They critiqued the American gospel of free markets, and they challenged fellow delegates to focus on the evils of sinful human structures. These Congress delegates therefore issued a rebuke of American Christian nationalism. In response, they summoned American evangelicals to join a genuinely transnational movement.[13]

The 1966 World Congress in Berlin foreshadowed the 1974 Lausanne Congress on World Evangelization, an evangelical gathering which drew 2,700 evangelical delegates from 150 countries. Evangelicals from Latin America and across the "Global South" continued to invite their American peers to see social concern and social transformation as important components of gospel-inspired evangelism. Increasingly, some American evangelicals looked to their counterparts in Africa, Asia, and Latin America to lead and revive their global faith. Lausanne also highlighted the efforts of a more liberal group of American evangelicals both at home and abroad who had been working to tie the evangelical focus on conversion to a concern for social justice, humanitarianism, refugees, and human rights. With these shifts, evangelicals worked to disentangle their faith from Christian nationalism. American evangelicals attentive to the currents of Lausanne recognized that American foreign policy, despite the good it could work in the world, could also do tremendous harm. As Graham confessed at Lausanne, he had readily advanced the cause of "Christian America" in the world. He

American evangelicals joined evangelical delegates from across the globe at the 1966 World Congress of Evangelism in Berlin. In events such as the "March on Christian Witness," pictured here before the Kaiser Wilhelm Memorial Church in West Berlin, evangelicals from Latin America, Africa, and East Asia increasingly called on American Protestants to re-examine their Christian nationalist commitments.

Courtesy of Billy Graham Evangelical Association.

repented, stating that "to tie the Gospel to any political system, secular program, or society is dangerous." He added, "When I go to preach the Gospel, I go as an ambassador of the kingdom of God—not America." Beyond Graham's encounter with global evangelicals, Nixon's criminal activity in the

Watergate Scandal also shocked him. Graham more fully began to question pairing his faith with American politics. In response, the American evangelist sought to renew his focus on the conversionary gospel. While he pledged to simply preach a pure and simple gospel message, it still took time to separate his faith from his cultural and national commitments. In some respects, Graham never fully stopped being a spiritual warrior for God.[14]

Despite such acts of repentance, the political and spiritual battle lines of Christian nationalists endured. Seeing the early Cold War as an initial proving ground, conservative Christians in the United States launched an even larger struggle to reclaim the soul of their nation and the transatlantic West. Francis Schaeffer in particular galvanized conservative Christians into becoming a powerful political coalition set on reclaiming "Christian America" and planting the seeds of an evangelical revolution across a secularizing Europe. With the rise of the Moral Majority just five years after Lausanne, conservative evangelicals signaled their intent to defend "Christian America" against the evils they associated with secular humanism, liberal government, and ecumenical modernism. In the culture wars that ensued, they yoked their moral vision to a political agenda of limited government and interventionist foreign policy against the "evil empire" of the Soviet Union. They defended their nation's Christian identity and its providential, messianic role in the world. In the 1980 election, Moral Majority evangelicals played a crucial role in securing a presidential victory for Ronald Reagan. Under Reagan's watch, the United States underwent a neoliberal revolution of deregulation, free markets, and limited government—policies American evangelicals had called for since the early twentieth century. Reagan also proved a strident cold warrior, and in 1987, stood defiantly before the Berlin Wall and demanded of Soviet premier Mikhail Gorbachev: "Mr. Gorbachev, tear down this wall!"[15]

While the diplomacy of Gorbachev and Reagan certainly helped bring the Cold War to a close, the work of everyday citizens behind the Iron Curtain, and in the particular cases of East Germany and Poland, the activism of Protestants and Catholics against communist regimes, arguably played the more crucial and underacknowledged role. The story of Protestant Christianity on the other side of the Iron Curtain highlighted the human hunger for faith and justice, as well as the power of grassroots faith-based activism. Such activism began in part in 1966, when East German Protestants experienced a landmark transition of their own. That year, Otto Dibelius resigned from his post as bishop of Berlin and Brandenburg. The conservative nationalist leader had proven one of America's most faithful Cold War allies. With his departure, the East German church lost one of its most vocal and confrontational critics of the communist state. In addition to Dibelius's absence, the construction of the Berlin Wall led a growing number of East Germans to give up hopes of German unification. Some Protestant leaders began to accept the East German state as a fixed reality. In response, they pushed forward the theology of accommodation that Dibelius had opposed. Their theology of cooperation with socialism, which in 1967 they termed *Kirche im Sozialismus* ("The Church in Socialism"), called on Protestants to work within the socialist system and to pursue social equality.[16]

Such accommodation with a communist regime had its consequences. In 1968, East German churches cut formal ties with the West Protestant churches in order to placate the East German state. Numerous agents of the East German secret police also infiltrated the church from the highest ranks of leadership to everyday parishes. Yet a new grassroots ethic of faith-based activism was also beginning to surface within those same parishes. A fresh wave of East and West German students began to reject the conservative legacy of a prior generation. They opposed the militarism of the Cold War and reflected on potential connections between Christianity and socialism. Rudi Dutschke, one young West German activist, described Jesus as the "greatest revolutionary" who had secured the most "decisive revolution of world history . . . the revolution of the world through all-transcendent love." A new student-led movement of pacifism, protest, and social reform was thus gaining prominence on both sides of the Atlantic in the turbulent 1960s. The same grassroots activism that had come alive in West Germany also found expression across the border. In the 1970s and 1980s, low-ranking East German clergy and lay Christians carved out spaces in their local parishes for dissension and protest against the totalitarian state. Using the small sliver of independence hard earned by Dibelius and his supporters, they pushed for a new order in East Germany. As they called for a *Kirche von Unten* ("church from below"), they opened their doors to an expanding constellation of "basis groups" and civic dissidents who were protesting economic, social, political, and environmental injustice in German Democratic Republic. Churches such as the *Nicholaikirche* in Leipzig and the *Zionskirche* in Berlin played a crucial role in transforming prayer services into public demonstrations that preceded the fall of the Berlin Wall in November 1989. Through grassroots activism and organizing, the churches strengthened the

East German dissident movement that toppled the East German state and helped bring the Cold War to a close.[17]

As the Cold War ended, Christians in the United States and Europe alike cheered the conclusion of an era of totalitarian politics. While many Germans celebrated the end of their national division and pushed for the unification of Europe, President George H. W. Bush called for a "new world order" rooted in the West's democratic norms. Reflecting the euphoria of the moment, political scientist Francis Fukuyama declared "the end of history" and proclaimed that democratic liberalism had won the ideological battle of the twentieth century. It seemed to some as if a global system of American and democratic principles was finally within reach. In response, Americans began speaking about their country as the "indispensable nation" and proclaimed a new "Pax Americana" in which American values would flourish across the globe. A fresh wave of evangelical missionaries spread out across once-communist countries in Eastern Europe and the Soviet Union, eager to bring their gospel message, as well as democracy and free markets, to those who had lived behind the Iron Curtain. Meanwhile, the swift US victory in the Persian Gulf War helped exorcise the ghost of Vietnam and renewed American confidence in military power as a means to shaping the world. In the aftermath of the conflict, one prominent conservative commentator spoke of America's "unipolar moment." The United States was now a solitary world power that could create a "new American century."[18]

Yet such exuberance did not last long. America's overwhelming preponderance of power could not halt ethnic genocide in Rwanda, sectarian conflict in Bosnia, or warlords in Mogadishu. American commentators also identified new challenges looming on the horizon, such as the threats of rogue weapons states "armed with weapons of mass destruction." Others spoke of a potential "clash of civilizations" between Islamic fundamentalism and the "Christian, democratic West." Terrorism began to rattle America's sense of national security and global strength. In response to the September 11, 2001, terrorist attacks, the administration of George W. Bush made the case for a new global war on terror, as well as an offensive against a new "Axis of evil" that threatened the globe. Against this backdrop, American Protestants drew on theological commitments that stretched back to the early twentieth century. Christian nationalists were among the most vocal supporters of the new foreign wars in Afghanistan and Iraq, approving of both the "shock and awe" tactics and the use of torture to defeat terrorism. Beyond renewing American militarism, these wars also revived Wilson's spirit in their promotion of liberal democracy and pursuit of the Middle East's regional transformation. Meanwhile, Christian nationalists also maintained that "Christian America" was under attack from enemies both internal and external. The spiritual warriors of the twenty-first century pledged to defend America's "Christian heritage" against religious pluralism, global migration, and secularization. Christian nationalism resurfaced on the other side of the Atlantic as well, with calls emanating from Hungary, Germany, and France to protect "Christian Europe" against a wave of refugees from Syria, who were fleeing a civil war in Syria that had been worsened by America's invasion and occupation of Iraq. Fierce debates also broke out over Europe's religious and cultural identity. Nationalists across the European Union argued that the "European character" was being diluted under a wave of "Islamization."[19]

Yet in response to these events, some Protestants also rallied around a globalist ethic that championed interfaith dialogue, human rights, and global peacemaking. They expressed considerable caution about America's new wars abroad and warned against overconfidence in American military power. The tenets of Christian globalism also led them to refuse to cast the world in a bipolar struggle between competing civilizations. At home, they defended the American constitutional tradition of religious freedom and celebrated America's "multi-religious" identity. Meanwhile, in Germany, numerous Protestant churches opened their doors to Syrian, Afghan, and Iraqi refugees in a spirit of hospitality and care. Christian Democratic Union leaders such as Angela Merkel also sought to strengthen Germany's commitments to a multicultural society.[20]

The 2016 presidential candidacy of Donald Trump proved another source of division between Protestants on both sides of the Atlantic, as well as an indicator of a popular resurgence of Christian nationalism. Exit polls from the 2016 election revealed that 81% of white evangelicals and a sizable number of mainline Protestants had cast their vote for the New York real estate mogul and reality television celebrity. While these Protestants undoubtedly had diverse and varying rationales for their votes, the Christian nationalist character of Trump's candidacy certainly resonated with some. On the campaign trail, Trump had promised to "make America great again" and outlined an "America First" foreign policy. He targeted "illegal aliens" as threats to the American people, proposed to build a border wall, and outlined an immigration ban on Muslims. He likewise espoused an anti-internationalism that opposed the United Nations and other multilateral bodies. As he put it, "I'm a nationalist, okay? I'm a nationalist. Nationalist! Use that word! Use that word!" The underlying principles of such views in fact had deeper roots in twentieth-century Christian nationalism. In response, Christian globalists protested how the Trump presidency closed the United States to refugees and asylum seekers, inflamed racial tensions, and damaged long-standing diplomatic and multilateral relationships. The struggle for the soul of the nation continued. Meanwhile, many Germans grew perplexed at the new direction of the United States and puzzled over American Protestant support for the Trump administration. Major German periodicals described the state of America's politics as a catastrophe. Germans who had once looked to the United States as a partner and ally grew increasingly dismayed.[21]

As the twenty-first century matured, it became clear that American Protestantism's past theologies of global engagement continued to have staying power. The roots of these contemporary theological expressions in part appeared in the American Protestant responses to Germany and Europe in the early to mid-twentieth century. American activism in the Great War, the Second World War, and the Cold War had led American Protestants to reimagine and redefine their place and role in the world in lasting and fractious ways. Their transatlantic activism also had shaped competing blueprints for global engagement that endured well after the Berlin Wall and the Fulda Gap lost their geopolitical significance. As a new set of global trials arose, Christian nationalism continued to challenge Christian globalism as American Protestantism's definitive mode of global engagement. Ideally, careful study of these past episodes might play a part in helping American Protestants foster and practice theologies and a style of politics that more fully reflect the ways of a border-defying faith.

Notes

Introduction

1. Stewart Winfield Herman, Jr., *American Church in Berlin: A History* (n.p.: Self-published, 2001), 87–91. Stewart Winfield Herman, Jr., *It's Your Souls We Want* (New York: Harper and Brothers, 1943), 296.
2. Reinhold Niebuhr, "The German Problem," *Christianity and Crisis (CAC)*, January 10, 1944, 2. Herman, *It's Your Souls We Want*, 296. For a comparative look at how leading intellectuals of Herman's time assessed the "crisis" of their era, see: Alan Jacobs, *The Year of Our Lord 1943: Christian Humanism in an Age of Crisis* (New York: Oxford University Press, 2018).
3. In using "ecumenical" to describe these "mainline" and "liberal" Protestants, I follow the lead of historian David Hollinger. In general, these "ecumenical" Protestants stemmed from the mainline American Protestant denominations and affirmed the theological tenets of Protestant modernism. See: David Hollinger, *After Cloven Tongues of Fire: Protestant Liberalism in Modern American History* (Princeton, NJ: Princeton University Press, 2013), 18–55.

    For examples of the use of "World Christianity" in Protestant thought of this era, see: Henry Smith Leiper, *World Chaos or World Christianity: A Popular Interpretation of Edinburgh and Oxford, 1937* (New York: Willet, Clark, 1937). Henry van Dusen, *World Christianity: Yesterday, Today, and Tomorrow* (New York: Abingdon & Cokesbury, 1947). On the history of "imagined communities," see: Benedict Anderson, *Imagined Communities: Reflections on the Origin and Spread of Nationalism* (New York: Verso, 2006).
4. On postwar American evangelicalism and its fundamentalist roots, see: George Marsden, *Fundamentalism and American Culture: The Shaping of Twentieth-Century Evangelicalism, 1870–1925* (New York: Oxford University Press, 1980). Joel Carpenter, *Revive Us Again: The Reawakening of American Fundamentalism* (New York: Oxford University Press, 1997). Matthew Avery Sutton, *American Apocalypse: A History of Modern Evangelicalism* (Cambridge, MA: Harvard University Press, 2014). Molly Worthen, *Apostles of Reason: The Crisis of Authority in American Evangelicalism* (New York: Oxford University Press, 2016). On the Vatican's postwar operations, see: Giuliana Chamedes, *A Twentieth-Century Crusade: The Vatican's Battle to Remake Christian Europe* (Cambridge, MA: Harvard University Press, 2019).
5. The history of Christian nationalism has been a theme of growing interest to historians of American religion. Recent works discussing and defining Christian nationalism include: John Fea, *Was America Founded as a Christian Nation? A Historical Introduction* (Louisville, KY: Westminster John Knox, 2016). Matthew McCullough,

The Cross of War: Christian Nationalism and U.S. Expansion in the Spanish-American War (Madison: University of Wisconsin Press, 2014). Mark Edwards, ed., *Christian Nationalism in the United States* (Basel, Switzerland: MDPI, 2018). Samuel Perry and Andrew Whitehead, *Taking America Back for God: Christian Nationalism in the United States* (New York: Oxford University Press, 2020), ix–22. On the theme of American exceptionalism, see: Abram C. Van Engen, *City on a Hill: A History of American Exceptionalism* (New Haven, CT: Yale University Press, 2020). On American Protestantism's "conquering faith," see: Matthew Avery Sutton, *Double Crossed: The Missionaries Who Spied for the United States during the Second World War* (New York: Basic Books, 2019), 63–66. On the "American Century," see: Henry Luce, "The American Century," *LIFE*, February 17, 1941, 61–65.

6. On Protestant "internationalism" and Protestant "cosmopolitanism," see: Michael Thompson, *For God and Globe: Christian Internationalism in the United States between the Great War and the Cold War* (Ithaca, NY: Cornell University Press, 2015). David Hollinger, *Protestants Abroad: How Missionaries Tried to Change the World but Changed America* (Princeton, NJ: Princeton University Press, 2017).

7. On the broader history of German-American relations, with limited reference to its religious components, see: Frank Trommler and Eliot Shore, eds., *The German-American Encounter: Conflict and Cooperation between Two Cultures, 1800–2000* (New York: Berghahn Books, 2001). Manfred Berg and Philipp Gassert, eds., *Deutschland und die USA in der internationalen Geschichte des 20. Jahrhunderts.* (Stuttgart: Steiner, 2004).

   On German-American Protestant connections that this work builds upon, see: Uta Balbier, "Billy Graham in West Germany: German Protestantism between Americanization and Rechristianization, 1954–1970," *Zeithistorichse Forschungen / Studies in Contemporary History* 7 (2010). Mark Ruff, "The German Churches and the Specter of Americanization," in *The United States and German in the Era of the Cold War, 1945–1990*, Volume 1: *1945–1968* (New York: Cambridge University Press, 2004). James Enns, *Saving Germany: North American Protestants and Christian Mission to West Germany, 1945–1974* (Montreal: McGill-Queen's University, 2017).

8. On these episodes in American history, see: Greg Grandin, *The End of the Myth: From the Frontier to the Border Wall in the Mind of America* (New York: Metropolitan Books, 2019), 113–147. Matthew Frye Jacobson, *Barbarian Virtues: The United States Encounters Foreign Peoples at Home and Abroad* (New York: Hill and Wang, 2000), 3–58, 139–178. On the rise of the German empire, see: James Retallak, ed., *Imperial Germany: 1871–1918* (New York: Oxford University Press, 2008); Mark Correll, *Shepherds of Empire: Germany's Conservative Leadership, 1888–1919* (Minneapolis: Fortress Press, 2014). For a comparative account on the rise of Germany and the United States as naval empires, see: Dirk Bonker, *Militarism in a Global Age: Naval Ambitions in Germany and the United States before World War I* (Ithaca, NY: Cornell University Press, 2012).

9. On transatlantic revivals, see: Jan Stievermann, "American Evangelicalism and the Prussian *Erweckungsbewegung*, 1815–1850," Paper presented at *Religious Revivals and Their Effects: Perceptions, Media, and Networks in the Modern World,*

Amsterdam Centre for Religious History, Amsterdam, 2018. Andrew Z. Hansen, "Nineteenth-Century Transatlantic Protestantism: Charles Hodge and the Prussian *Erweckungsbewegung*," *Pietismus und Neuzeit* 37 (2011): 191–210. On social reform and liberal theology, see: Christopher Evans, *The Social Gospel in American Religion* (New York: New York University Press, 2017), 58–65. Carl Diehl, *Americans and German Scholarship, 1770–1870* (New Haven, CT: Yale University Press, 1978).

For an example of one American assessment of Germany's spiritual and political culture, see: Niebuhr, "The German Problem." For an example of one German assessment of American spiritual imperialism, see: Henrich Frick, *Die Evangelische Mission* (Bonn: Schroeder, 1922), 375, 392, 395–396.

10. These American Protestants were a significant part of the United States' overarching twentieth-century project of global democracy promotion. On US efforts to promote democracy abroad, see: Emily Rosenberg, *Spreading the American Dream: American Economic and Cultural Expansion, 1890–1945* (New York: Hill and Wang, 1982). Reinhold Wagnleitner, *Coca-Colonization and the Cold War: The Cultural Mission of the US in Austria after the Second World War* (Chapel Hill: University of North Carolina, Press, 1994). Tony Smith, *America's Mission: The United States and the Worldwide Struggle for Democracy in the Twentieth Century* (Princeton, NJ: Princeton University Press, 1994). Stephen Porter, *Benevolent Empire: U.S. Power, Humanitarianism, and the World's Dispossessed* (Philadelphia: University of Pennsylvania Press, 2017).

For specific attention to Protestant contributions to such efforts, see: Richard Gamble, *The War for Righteousness: Progressive Christianity, the Great War, and the Rise of the Messianic Nation* (Wilmington, DE: Intercollegiate Studies Institute, 2003). Andrew Preston, *Sword of the Spirit, Shield of Faith: Religion in American War and Diplomacy* (New York: Knopf, 2012). Ian Tyrrell, *Reforming the World: The Creation of America's Moral Empire* (Princeton, NJ: Princeton University Press, 2013). Cara Lee Burnidge, *A Peaceful Conquest: Woodrow Wilson, Religion, and the New World Order* (Chicago: University of Chicago Press, 2016).

11. For primers on the Fundamentalist-Modernist Controversy, see: Marsden, *Fundamentalism and American Culture*; Martin Marty, *Modern American Religion*, Volume 2: *The Noise of Conflict, 1919–1941* (Chicago: University of Chicago Press, 1984), 155–214.

12. For the definitive histories on liberal Protestant modernism, see: William Hutchinson, ed., *Between the Times: The Travail of the Protestant Establishment in America, 1900–1960* (Cambridge, MA: Harvard University Press, 1989). William Hutchinson, *The Modernist Impulse in American Protestantism* (Durham, NC: Duke University Press, 1992). Hollinger, *After Cloven Tongues of Fire*. On the transatlantic rise Protestant liberal theology, see: Gary Dorrien, *The Making of American Liberal Theology: Idealism, Realism, and Modernity 1900–1950* (Louisville, KY: Westminster John Knox Press, 2003).

The primary Protestant mainline denominations included the Episcopalian Church, the Presbyterian Church (USA), United Methodist Church, northern Baptist churches, Congregationalists, Disciples of Christ, and United Lutherans.

Together, these denominations formed the core of the Federal Council of Churches and represented the chief players in the ecumenical movement. See: Elesha Coffman, *The Christian Century and the Rise of the Protestant Mainline* (New York: Oxford University Press, 2013).

13. On the history of American Protestant mission, see: William Hutchinson, *Errand to the World: American Protestant Thought and Foreign Mission* (Chicago: University of Chicago Press, 1993). Xi Lian, *The Conversion of Missionaries: Liberalism in American Protestant Missions in China, 1907–1932* (University Park: Pennsylvania State Press, 1997). Hollinger, *Protestants Abroad.* Emily Conroy-Krutz, *Christian Imperialism: Converting the World in the Early American Republic* (Ithaca, NY: Cornell University Press, 2015). On the Social Gospel, see: Evans, *The Social Gospel in American Religion: A History*, 21–46, 77–134.

    On American Protestants and Wilson's foreign policies, see: Burnidge, *A Peaceful Conquest.* Gamble, *The War for Righteousness.* For the definitive historical survey of American religion and diplomacy, see: Preston, *Sword of the Spirit, Shield of Faith.* Preston's portrayal of Wilsonianism (pp. 233–252), "spiritual diplomacy (pp. 342–364), and the "apostles of progress" and "apostles of liberty" (pp. 465–496) have especially informed this study.

14. On interwar and postwar Protestant ecumenism, see: Elisabeth Engel, James Kennedy, and Justin Reynolds, "The Theory and Practice of Ecumenism: Christian Global Governance and the Search for World Order, 1900–1980," *Journal of Global History* 13 (2018): 157–164. Gene Zubovich, "The Global Gospel: Protestant Internationalism and American Liberalism, 1940–1960" (PhD diss., University of California–Berkeley, 2015). Justin Reynolds, "Against the World: International Protestantism and the Ecumenical Movement between Secularization and Politics, 1900–1952" (PhD diss., Columbia University, 2016). Mark Edwards, *The Right of the Protestant Left: God's Totalitarianism* (New York: Palgrave Macmillan, 2012). Lucian Leustean, *The Ecumenical Movement and the Making of the European Community* (New York: Oxford University Press, 2014).

    Most of the history of Protestant ecumenism has been written by its first-hand practitioners, often in triumphal ways. For a selection of these histories, see: Samuel McCrea Cavert, *The American Churches in the Ecumenical Movement* (New York: Association Press, 1968). Stephen Neill and Ruth Rouse, *A History of the Ecumenical Movement, 1517–1948* (Philadelphia: Westminster Press, 1968). William Adolph Visser 't Hooft, *The Genesis and Formation of the World Council of Churches* (Geneva: World Council of Churches, 1982).

15. On American fundamentalism and evangelicalism, see: Marsden, *Fundamentalism and American Culture.* Carpenter, *Revive Us Again.* Sutton, *American Apocalypse.* Worthen, *Apostles of Reason.*

16. I draw here on Matthew Avery Sutton's description of premillennialist fundamentalists as "radical evangelicals." See: Sutton, *American Apocalypse*, 1–8, 113. For a discussion of premillennial dispensationalism, see: Sutton, *American Apocalypse.* Ernest Sandeen, *The Roots of Fundamentalism: British and American Millenarianism, 1800–1930* (Chicago: University of Chicago Press, 1970).

17. Sutton, *American Apocalypse*, 1–8, 113. On the history of Christian libertarianism and "faith, freedom, and free enterprise," see: Kevin Kruse, *One Nation, Under God: How Corporate America Invented Christian America* (New York: Basic Books, 2015). On evangelical anti-internationalism, see: Mark Ruotsila, *The Origins of Christian Anti-Internationalism: Conservative Evangelicals and the League of Nations* (Washington, DC: Georgetown University Press, 2007). On these major schools of thought in American foreign policy, including the Wilsonian and Jacksonian schools, see: Walter Russel Mead, *Special Providence: American Foreign Policy and How It Changed the World* (New York: Routledge, 2002).

18. Carpenter, *Revive Us Again*, 141–160. Sutton, *American Apocalypse*, 263–292. Worthen, *Apostles of Reason*, 45–46.

19. On the history of twentieth-century Christianity and nationalism, see: Brian Stanley, *Christianity in the Twentieth Century: A World History* (Princeton, NJ: Princeton University Press, 2018), 1–11, 36–56, 150–171, 357–366. As a historical phenomenon, nationalism originated in Enlightenment-era efforts to tie and bind a people together through a shared history, often mythical in nature, as well as a common language, culture, and faith. Yet nations also contained within their borders tremendous historical, linguistic, cultural, and religious diversity. In this sense, nationalism was also about who belonged and who did not, who was in and who was out. Perhaps even more so, it existed in order to oppose those who posed threats to the nation itself. Such opposition to perceived enemies was the fuel of nationalism itself. For an exploration of these themes in the context of the Great War, with special focus on how religion shaped this conflict, see: Philip Jenkins, *The Great and Holy War: How World War I Became a Religious Crusade* (New York: Harper One, 2015).

20. For a poignant and practical examination of these ideologies in the context of 1930s America, see: Ira Katznelson, *Fear Itself: The New Deal and the Origins of Our Time* (New York: Liveright, 2013). For "love of neighbor," see: Matthew 22:36–40 (ESV); Mark 12:31 (ESV); Luke 6:27 (ESV). For the "peace and welfare of the city," see Jeremiah 29:7 (ESV). On a higher citizenship, see: Philippians 3:20 (ESV). For the "kingdom of God has no borders," see: Melani McAlister, *The Kingdom of God Has No Borders: A Global History of American Evangelicals* (New York: Oxford University Press, 2018).

21. On the construction of national identities, see: Anderson, *Imagined Communities*. Jill Lepore, *This America: The Case for the Nation* (New York: Liveright, 2019). On the growth of Christianity across the "Global South," see: Andrew Walls, *The Missionary Movement in Christian History: Studies in the Transmission of Faith* (Maryknoll, NY: Orbis Books, 1996). Lamin Sanneh, *Disciples of All Nations: Pillars of World Christianity* (New York: Oxford University Press, 2007). Dana Robert, *Christian Mission: How Christianity Became a World Religion* (Malden, MA: Wiley-Blackwell, 2009). Mark Noll, *The New Shape of World Christianity: How American Experience Reflects Global Faith* (Downers Grove, IL: Intervarsity Press, 2009). Philip Jenkins, *The Next Christendom: The Coming of Global Christianity* (New York: Oxford University Press, 2011).

22. On the nineteenth-century roots of Christian nationalism, see: Sam Hasselby, *The Origins of American Religious Nationalism* (New York: Oxford University Press, 2015). Fea, *Was America Founded as a Christian Nation?*, 1–56. McCullough, *The Cross of War*, 3–11. Edwards, ed., *Christian Nationalism in the United States*. On "Christian imperialism," see: Conroy-Krutz, *Christian Imperialism*, 1–19.

    Christian nationalism was at times closely tied to American civil religion. Whereas civil religion emanated primarily from the state officials of Washington, this study is more focused on the thought of American Protestant ecumenists and evangelicals, although it indeed considers the often seamless overlap of the interests of Protestant leaders and state figures. In a nutshell, the American civil religious tradition argued that a providential being had singled out the United States to be a beacon of republican liberty in the world. In contrast, Christian nationalism made specific claims about the Protestant nature of the American nation and its particular Christian mission in the world. For a recent history of American civil religion in its historical iterations, see: Philip Gorski, *American Covenant: A History of Civil Religion from the Puritans to the Present* (Princeton, NJ: Princeton University Press, 2019).

23. On this history of American nativism and exclusion, see: Linda Gordon, *The Second Coming of the KKK: The Ku Klux Klan of the 1920s and the American Political Tradition* (New York: Liveright, 2017). Erika Lee, *America for the Americans: A History of Xenophobia in the United States* (New York: Basic Books, 2019).

24. On this kind of "cautious patriotism," see: David Sittser, *A Cautious Patriotism: The American Churches and the Second World War* (Chapel Hill: University of North Carolina Press, 1997). On the difference between civic patriotism and illiberal nationalism, see: Lepore, *This America*. On the "beloved community," see: Martin Luther King, Jr., "Letter from Birmingham Jail," April 16, 1963, King Papers, Martin Luther King, Jr., Research and Education Center, Stanford University.

25. For academic studies of Christian nationalism among fundamentalists and evangelicals, see: Matthew Avery Sutton, *Aimee Simple McPherson and the Resurrection of Christian America* (Cambridge, MA: Harvard University Press, 2007), 212–266. Sutton, *American Apocalypse*, 47–78. Ruotsila, *The Origins of Christian Anti-Internationalism*. Kruse, *One Nation, Under God*, 3–164.

26. Thompson, *For God and Globe*, 4, 14. Although Thompson uses the term "Christian internationalism" in his work to describe this countermovement, I have opted to use "Christian globalism" to describe the thought of these Protestant missionaries, in part because of the connections American Protestants drew between "Christian internationalism" and the Wilsonian quest to remake the globe in America's image. As the first chapter of this book argues, "Christian internationalism" as a term concealed an underlying notion of moral and spiritual exceptionalism within ecumenical circles. In using this term, ecumenists of that era expressed their hope that "Christian America" could spiritually support Wilson's foreign policies, enter the League of Nations, and elevate the international relations of all nations. In this regard, "Christian internationalism" was not fully shorn of the imperial and racial undertones of the Wilsonian project. In contrast, I find "Christian globalism" to speak more fully to the *global* identity and fellowship that these ecumenists sought within the Christian church, one

that transcended the nation-state itself, as well as the antiracist, anti-imperial, and anti-nationalist convictions they held. "Christian globalism" likewise speaks to the ways in which ecumenists began to prioritize the church over the nation-state as an agent of global order.

27. Hollinger, *Protestants Abroad*, 1–3, 288–299. On human rights and Christian globalism, see: Sam Moyn, *Christian Human Rights* (Philadelphia: University of Pennsylvania Press, 2015). Gene Zubovich, "For Human Rights Abroad, against Jim Crow at Home: The Political Mobilization of American Ecumenical Protestants in the World War II Era," *The Journal of American History* 105, no. 2 (September 2018): 267–290. Bastiaan Bouwman, "From Religious Freedom to Social Justice: The Human Rights Engagement of the Ecumenical Movement from the 1940s to the 1970s," *Journal of Global History* 13 (2018): 252–273.

28. On American Protestantism's "cautious" approach to the Second World War, see: Sittser, *A Cautious Patriotism*. For histories exploring these nationalist currents within mainline, liberal Protestantism, see: Gamble, *The War for Righteousness*. Edwards, *The Right of the Protestant Left*. Sutton, *Double Crossed*, 59–74. Mark Edwards, "From a Christian World Community to a Christian America: Ecumenical Protestant Internationalism as a Source of Christian Nationalist Renewal," *Genealogy* 3, no. 30 (2019). On Christian imperialism, see: Conroy-Krutz, *Christian Imperialism*, 1–19. On the ecumenists' "conquering faith," see: Francis B. Sayre to William Eddy, December 14, 1938, and February 8, 1939, Princeton University Library, Department of Special Collections, Mudd Manuscript Library, William Eddy Papers, Box 8, Folder 5. Sutton, *Double Crossed*, 63–66. On the "American Century," see: Henry Luce, "The American Century."

29. On Christian realism, see: Warren, *Theologians of a New World Order*, 19–93. Edwards, *The Right of the Protestant Left*, 17–120.

30. On this wartime mobilization, see: Sittser, *A Cautious Patriotism*. Warren, *Theologians of a New World Order*, 94–128. On Protestantism's "conquering faith" and ecumenists' work as spies, see: Sutton, *Double Crossed*, 1–12, 59–74.

31. This book benefits from a host of studies on the Allied occupation of Germany, including: James Tent, *Mission on the Rhine: Reeducation and Denazification in American Occupied Germany* (Chicago: University of Chicago Press, 1985). Thomas Schwartz, *America's Germany: John McCloy and the Federal Republic of Germany* (Cambridge, MA: Harvard University Press, 1991). Carolyn Eisenberg, *Drawing the Line: The American Decision to Divide Germany* (New York: Cambridge University Press, 1996). Marc Trachtenberg, *A Constructed Peace: The Making of the European Settlement, 1945-1963* (Princeton, NJ: Princeton University Press, 1999). Petra Goede, *GIs and Germans: Culture, Gender, and Foreign Relations, 1945-1949* (New Haven, CT: Yale University Press, 2003). Susan Carruthers, *The Good Occupation: American Soldiers and the Hazards of the Peace* (Cambridge, MA: Harvard University Press, 2016).

For greater focus on the military government's use of religion in the occupation, see: Heike Springhart, *Aufbrüche zu neuen Ufern: Der Beitrag von Religion und Kirche für Demokratisierung und Reeducation im Western Deutschlands nach 1945* (Leipzig: Evangelische Verlagsanstalt, 2008). Steven Schroeder, *To Forget It All and*

Begin Again: Reconciliation in Occupied Germany, 1944–1954 (Toronto: University of Toronto Press, 2013).

For a comparative study of democratization efforts in occupied Japan, see: Jennifer Miller, *Cold War Democracy: The United States and Japan* (Cambridge, MA: Harvard University Press, 2019).

32. On American empire in the twentieth century, see: Geir Lundestad, "Empire by Invitation: The United States and Western Europe, 1945–1952," *Journal of Peace Research* 23 no. 3 (1986): 263–277. Daniel Immerwahr, *How to Hide an Empire: A History of the Greater United States* (New York: Farrar, Straus, and Giroux, 2019). On the Marshall Plan, see: Benn Steil, *The Marshall Plan: Dawn of the Cold War* (New York: Simon and Schuster, 2018).

On America's postwar empire, see: Walter McDougall, *Promised Land, Crusader State: The American Encounter with the World since 1776* (New York: Houghton Mifflin, 1997), 101–198. Victoria de Grazia, *Irresistible Empire: America's Advance through Twentieth-Century Europe* (Cambridge, MA: Harvard University Press, 2005). Paul Kramer, "Power and Connection: Imperial Histories of the United States in the World," *American Historical Review* 116, no. 5 (2011): 1348–1391. On the Protestant effort to "Americanize" Christian internationalism, see: Thompson, *For God and Globe*, 167–189.

33. For specific reference to American religion and foreign policy in the Cold War, see: T. Jeremy Gunn, *Spiritual Weapons: The Cold War and the Forging of an American National Religion* (Westport, CT: Praeger, 2009). William Inboden, *Religion and American Foreign Policy, 1945–1960: The Soul of Containment* (New York: Cambridge University Press, 2008). Jonathan Herzog, *The Spiritual-Industrial Complex: America's Religious Battle against Communism in the Early Cold War* (New York: Oxford University Press, 2011). Preston, *Sword of Spirit, Shield of Faith*, 411–496.

34. On this cosmopolitan turn, see: Hollinger, *Protestants Abroad*, 1–23.

35. Otto Dibelius, *The Strange Case of Bishop Dibelius: A Selection of Documents* (Berlin: Rütten & Loening, 1962), 47. See also: Günther van Norden, *Der deutsche Protestantismus im Jahr der nationalsozialistische Machterfreigung* (Gütersloh: Verlaghaus Mohn, 1979), 54. The historiography on German Protestantism is expansive and too exhaustive to list in full here. Particular studies that have proven especially helpful include: Mark R. Correll, *Shepherds of the Empire: Germany's Conservative Protestant Leadership, 1888–1919* (Minneapolis: Fortress Press, 2014); Matthew Hockenos, *A Church Divided: German Protestants Confront the Nazi Past* (Bloomington: Indiana University Press, 2004). Matthew Hockenos, *Then They Came for Me: Martin Niemöller, the Pastor Who Defied the Nazis* (New York: Basic Books, 2018). Benjamin Ziemann, *Martin Niemöller: Ein Leben in Opposition* (Munich: Deutsche Verlags-Anstalt, 2019). Martin Greschat, *Protestanten in der Zeit: Kirche und Gesellschaft vom Kaiserreich bis zur Gegenwart* (Stuttgart: Kohlhammer Verlag, 1994). Martin Greschat, *Die evangelische Christenheit und die deutshe Geschichte nach 1945. Weichenstellungen in der Nachkriegszeit* (Stuttgart: Kohlhammer Verlag, 2002). Martin Greschat, *Protestantismus im Kalten Krieg: Kirche, Politik und Gesellschaft im geteilten Deutschland, 1945–1963* (Paderborn: Ferdinand Schöningh Verlag,

2010). Martin Greschat, *Der Protestantismus in der Bundesrepublik (1945–2005)* (Leipzig: Evangelische Verlagsanstalt, 2010). Claudia Lepp and Kurt Nowack, *Evangelische Kirche im geteilten Deutschland (1949–1989)* (Göttingen: Vandenhoeck & Ruprecht, 2001). Claudia Lepp, *Tabu der Einheit? Die Ost-West-Gemeinschaft der evangelischen Christen und die deutsche Teilung, 1945–1969* (Göttingen: Vandenhoeck & Ruprecht, 2005).

On German-American Protestant connections, see: Balbier, "Billy Graham in West Germany." Ruff, "The German Churches and the Specter of Americanization." Enns, *Saving Germany.*

Although this book primarily focuses on Protestant history, for comparative treatments of German Catholicism, see: Mark Ruff, *Wayward Flock: Catholic Youth in Postwar Germany, 1945–1965* (Chapel Hill: University of North Carolina Press, 2005). Maria Mitchell, *The Origins of Christian Democracy: Politics and Confession in Modern Germany* (Ann Arbor: University of Michigan Press, 2012). Lauren Faulkner-Rossi, *Wehrmacht Priests: Catholicism and the Nazi War of Annihilation* (Cambridge, MA: Harvard University Press, 2015). Mark Ruff, *The Battle for the Catholic Past in Germany, 1945–1980* (New York: Cambridge University Press, 2017).

On Catholic internationalism, see: James Chappel, *Catholic Modern: The Challenge of Totalitarianism and the Remaking of the Church* (Cambridge, MA: Harvard University Press, 2018). Chamedes, *A Twentieth-Century Crusade.*

On postwar German democratization, see: Heinrich August Winkler, *Der lange Weg nach Westem* (Bonn: C. H. Beck Verlag, 2002). Konrad Jarausch, *After Hitler: Recivilizing Germans, 1945–1995* (New York: Oxford University Press, 2008). Jan-Werner Müller, *Contesting Democracy: Political Ideas in Twentieth Century Europe* (New Haven, CT: Yale University Press, 2011). Heinrich August Winkler, *Geschichte des Westens: Vom Krieg zum Mauerfall* (Munich: Beck Verlag, 2015).

36. On the origins of evangelical internationalism, see: David Swartz, *Moral Minority: The Evangelical Left in an Age of Conservativism* (Philadelphia: University of Pennsylvania Press, 2012). McAlister, *The Kingdom of God Has No Borders.* David King, *God's Internationalists: World Vision and the Age of Evangelical Humanitarianism* (Philadelphia: University of Pennsylvania Press, 2019). David Swartz, *Facing West: American Evangelicals in an Age of World Christianity* (New York: Oxford University Press, 2020).

37. For this particular iteration of "Christian libertarian" politics, see: Kruse, *One Nation, Under God.* On evangelical politics, with special reference to the role of religion in the rise of Cold War conservatism, see: Darren Dochuk, *From Bible Belt to Sunbelt: Plain-folk Religion, Grassroots Politics, and the Rise of Evangelical Conservatism* (W. W. Norton, 2010). Daniel Williams, *God's Own Party: The Making of the Christian Right* (New York: Oxford University Press, 2010). Lisa McGirr, *Suburban Warriors: The Origins of the New American Right* (Princeton, NJ: Princeton University Press, 2015). Sutton, *American Apocalypse,* 293–325. Kristin Kobes du Mez, *Jesus and John Wayne: How White Evangelicals Corrupted a Faith and Fractured a Nation* (New York: Liveright, 2020).

Chapter 1

1. Leiper to Parents, January 19, 1918, in *The Collected Letters of Henry Smith Leiper*, Volume 1, Presbyterian Historical Society (PHS), Pearl Digital Collections, 10. Leiper to Parents, November 16, 1919, *Collected Letters*, PHS, 232. For an overview of Leiper's life, see: William J. Schmidt and Edward Ouellette, *What Kind of a Man? The Life of Henry Smith Leiper* (New York: Friendship Press, 1988). On ecumenical Protestants in World War I, see Burnidge, *A Peaceful Conquest*. Gamble, *War for Righteousness*.

2. For an overview of Riley's life and times, see: William Trollinger, *God's Empire: William Bell Riley and Midwestern Fundamentalism* (Madison: University of Wisconsin Press, 1991). On fundamentalism and World War I, see: Sutton, *American Apocalypse*, 47–78.

3. Frederick Jackson Turner, "The Significance of the Frontier in American History," American Historical Association Meeting, Chicago, Illinois, July 12, 1893. Josiah Strong, *Our Country: Its Possible Future and Its Current Crisis* (New York: Baker and Taylor, 1885), 14, 161, 165.

4. "The Ecumenical Conference on Foreign Missions," *The Spirit of Missions* 65 (1900): 358–359. "Missions and Modern History," *The Congregationalist and Christian World* 90 (1905): 50. On Protestant mission in the early twentieth century, see: Conroy-Krutz, *Christian Imperialism*. Heather Curtis, *Holy Humanitarians: American Evangelicals and Global Aid* (Cambridge, MA: Harvard University Press, 2018), 1–15. McCullough, *The Cross of War*. Tyrrell, *Reforming the World*. On the racial and imperial framework behind such mission, see: Matthew Frye Jacobson, *Barbarian Virtues: The United States Encounters Foreign Peoples at Home and Abroad, 1876–1917* (New York: Hill and Wang, 2000).

    A fierce debate indeed raged at this time over how to best conduct Protestant foreign mission. While some American Protestants viewed Protestant mission as primarily a spiritual task that involved preaching the gospel and then leaving, others argued that mission also required "civilizing" the world with all the blessings of American civilization. In 1900, for instance, missionary organizer Robert Speer had cast Protestant mission as "implanting the life of Christ in the hearts of men" as opposed to completely reorganizing a people's "whole social fabric." He added he would rather plant the "seed" of the gospel in a "heathen" society than cover that society with the "veneer" of "Western civilization." In doing so, Speer echoed the voice of American missionary Rufus Anderson, who in the mid-nineteenth century had advocated for the indigenous model of "self-supporting, self-propagating, and self-governing" foreign churches. In contrast, John R. Mott desired to spread American religion and civilization in tandem, but he wanted to "neutralize and supplant" the more sinister aspects of American civilization that went along with America's expanding global reach. Mott thus believed both religion and empire could serve the same cause, but only if faithful Protestants reformed American imperialism to be more authentically Christian. See: Robert E. Speer, *Missionary Principles and Practices* (New York: Fleming H. Revell Co., 1902), 34–37. John R. Mott, *The Evangelization of the World in This Generation* (New York: Student Volunteer Movement for Foreign Missions, 1901), 28.

5. Samuel McCrea Cavert, *The American Churches in the Ecumenical Movement* (New York: Association Press, 1968), 52–71.

6. Arthur S. Link, ed., *The Papers of Woodrow Wilson* (Princeton, NJ: Princeton University Press, 1994), 227–228. "Must Oppose Graft, Says Church Delegates," *New York Times* (*NYT*), November 22, 1905. "Roosevelt Encourages Christianizing Japan," *NYT*, November 16, 1905.

7. Mott, *The Evangelization of the World in This Generation*. Robert Handy, *A History of Union Theological Seminary in New York* (New York: Columbia University Press, 1987), 135.

8. On this transatlantic flow of theology, see Evans, *The Social Gospel in American Religion*, 58–65. Andrew Z. Hansen, "Nineteenth-Century Transatlantic Protestantism: Charles Hodge and the Prussian *Erweckungsbewegung*," *Pietismus und Neuzeit* 37 (2011): 191–210. Carl Diehl, *Americans and German Scholarship, 1770–1870* (New Haven, CT: Yale University Press, 1978).

9. On the social gospel, see: Evans, *The Social Gospel in American Religion*, 21–46, 77–134. Gary Dorrien, *The Making of American Liberal Theology: Idealism, Realism, and Modernity, 1900–1950* (Louisville, KY: Westminster John Knox Press, 2003). On the working-class origins of the social gospel, see: Heath Carter, *Union Made: Working People and the Rise of Social Christianity in Chicago* (New York: Oxford University Press, 2015).

   German theological developments strongly shaped Rauschenbusch, the son of a German Baptist immigrant. In 1883, Rauschenbusch complimented his American theological training with a sabbatical at the University of Berlin. In 1891, he returned to Berlin yet again to study the New Testament and ponder a response to America's urban-industrial capitalism. Reflecting on his theological formation, Rauschenbusch wrote, "the intellectual life of America and Germany cross in my thinking like warp and woof."

10. Hockenos, *Then They Came for Me*, 7–28. Ziemann, *Martin Niemöller*, 19–58. See also: Martin Niemöller, *Vom U-Boot zur Kanzel* (Berlin: Martin Warneck Verlag, 1934).

11. John Conway, "The Political Role of German Protestantism, 1870–1990," *Journal of Church and State* 34, no. 4 (Autumn 1992): 819–842. Correll, *Shepherds of the Empire*.

12. Strong, *Our Country*, 159–160. Many American Protestants indeed recognized the German Pietists as a notable exception. Both groups shared a commitment to social mission and activism. Both also tended to identify the congregation as the heart of the church. In response to rigid orthodoxy and confessionalism within German Protestantism, Pietists sought a religion of the heart and individual conversion. Whereas Germans often viewed the church as an institution, Pietist ecclesiology portrayed the church as a movement on a mission. Nonetheless, key differences remained that showed the limits of American-backed reform. Above all, even Pietists supported Germany's conservative monarchism, which championed autocratic rule and offered formalized support for Pietist mission in return. See: Stievermann, "American Evangelicalism and the Prussian Erweckungsbewegung, 1815–1850."

13. Strong, *Our Country*, 159–160. This American synthesis of democracy and Protestantism often found its diplomatic expression in support of Protestant liberty abroad. On "Christian republicanism," see: Preston, *Sword of the Spirit*, 92–101. Anna Su, *Exporting Freedom: Religious Liberty and American Power* (Cambridge, MA: Harvard University Press, 2016). For an exploration of the antebellum origins of this synthesis, see: Nathan Hatch, *The Democratization of American Christianity* (New Haven, CT: Yale University Press, 1989). On America's "informal" Christendom, see Mark Noll, *In the Beginning was the Word: The Bible in American Public Life, 1492– 1783* (New York: Oxford University Press, 2016), 3–8.

14. Strong, *Our Country*, 45, 172. On "racial providentialism," see: McCullough, *The Cross of War*, 83–97.

15. "Appeals for Union in Mission: Gospel Commission at World Conference Wants to Make Christianity Supreme," *NYT*, June 16, 1910, 5. "Roosevelt Praises Missions: Writes to World Conference Regretting His Inability to Attend It," *NYT*, June 17, 1910, 2. "Americans Were Brief," *NYT*, July 15, 1910, 6. World Missionary Conference, quoted in David Bosch, *Witness to the World: The Christian Mission in Theological Perspective* (London: Marshall, Morgan, and Scott, 1980), 160. While roughly 170 delegates came from continental Europe, only seventeen non-Westerners were seated at Edinburgh. Hutchinson, *Errand*, 93, 135; Brian Stanley, *The World Missionary Conference, Edinburgh 1910* (Grand Rapids, MI: William B. Eerdmans, 2009), 246, 273.

16. "The Story of the Conquest Flag," *Peloubet's Select Notes on the International Lessons for 1911* 37 (First Quarter), 52. H. Augustine Smith, *A Pageant of the Stars and Stripes* (Boston: American Institute of Religious Education, 1918), 4. Carleton Case, *Church Socials and Entertainment* (Chicago: Shrewesbury, 1916), 52. Dennis Stovall, "Christian Crusade for Rally Day," *The Church School Journal* 47 (1915): 668.

17. Gustav Warneck, "Thoughts on the Missionary Century," *Missionary Review of the World* 23, no. 6 (1900): 415–516. Henrich Frick, *Die Evangelische Mission* (Bonn: Schroeder, 1922), 375, 392, 395–396.

18. Heinrich Frick, *Nationalität und Internationalität der christlichen Mission* (Gütersloh: C. Bertelsmann, 1917), 73–79, 149–150. For a discussion of German *Volksmission*, see: Brian Stanley, *Christianity in the Twentieth Century: A World History* (Princeton, NJ: Princeton University Press, 2019), 197. Werner Ustorf, *Sailing on the Next Tide: Missions, Missiology, and the Third Reich* (Frankfurt am Main: Peter Lang, 2000).

19. Cavert, *The American Churches*, 85. Warren, *Theologians of a New World Order*, 16. As Brian Stanley puts it, "The planting of churches and educational institutions closely patterned on Western models, funded by Western money, and controlled by Western personnel . . . was all-pervasive throughout the missionary movement in the first half of the twentieth century" (Stanley, *Christianity in the Twentieth Century*, 196).

20. Quoted in Hartmut Lehmann, "'Es ist eine tiefernste, aber eine herrliche Zeit': Adolf von Harnack und die Kaiser-Wilhelm-Gesellschaft im Ersten Weltkrieg," in *Adolf von Harnack: Christentum, Wissenschaft, und Gesellschaft*, ed. Kurt Nowack (Göttingen: Vandenhoeck & Ruprecht, 2003), 189–206. On European religious

nationalism and the Great War, see: Philip Jenkins, *The Great and Holy War: How World War I Became a Religious Crusade* (New York: Harper Collins, 2014).

21. Friedrich Siegmund-Schultze, "Ein praktischer Versuch zur Lösung des sozialen Problems," *Die Innere Mission im Evangelischen Deutschland* 7 (1912): 97–104. John Conway, "Friedrich Siegmund-Schultze (1885–1996), *Evangelische Theologie* 43 (1983): 221–250. Heinz-Elmar Tenorth, Rolf Lindner, Frank Fehner, and Jens Wietschorke, *Friedrich Siegmund-Schultze 1885–1969: Ein Leben für Kirche, Wissenschaft und soziale Arbeit* (Stuttgart: Kohlhammer, 2007). Friedrich Siegmund-Schultze an Gräfin Schwerin-Loewitz, May 29, 1915, EZA 51/6262/I/6,3.

22. Woodrow Wilson, *The Papers of Woodrow Wilson*, Volume 35, 329–334. Burnidge, *A Peaceful Conquest*, 1–4.

23. Andrew Bacevich, *The New American Militarism: How Americans are Seduced by War* (New York: Oxford University Press, 2013), 10–11. See also: Gamble, *The War for Righteousness*.

24. Thomas Sugrue and Glenda Gilmore, *These United States: A Nation in the Making 1890 to the Present* (New York: W.W. Norton, 2015), 109. Bacevich, *The New American Militarism*, 10. On the Wilsonian and religious roots of this order, see: Burnidge, *A Peaceful Conquest*. On the history of "imagined communities," see: Anderson, *Imagined Communities*. On the course's origins, see: Columbia College, "The New Freshman Course in Columbia College," *Columbia University Quarterly*, July 1919, 247–250. On the American invention of the "West," see: Patrick Jackson, *Civilizing the Enemy: German Reconstruction and the Invention of the West* (Ann Arbor: University of Michigan Press, 2006).

25. Leiper to Parents, January 19, 1918, *Collected Letters*, PHS, Pearl Digital Collections. Leiper to Parents, November 16, 1919, *Collected Letters*, PHS, Pearl Digital Collections, 232. Henry Churchill King, quoted in Gamble, *The War for Righteousness*, 7. James Donahue, "In Search of a Global, Godly Order: The Ecumenical Movement and the Origins of the League of Nations, 1908–1918" (PhD diss., University of Notre Dame, 2015).

26. William Pierson Merrill, *Christian Internationalism* (New York: Macmillan, 1919), 49, 78–79, 132, 140.

27. Frank Lowden, "Shall the German God Prevail?," *Christian Century* (*CC*), March 7, 1918, 8–10. John Chadwick, "Are We Worthy of This Opportunity?," *Christian Advocate*, May 20, 1921, 617.

28. Charles MacFarland, ed., *Library of Christian Cooperation*, Volume III: *The Church and International Relations* (New York: Missionary Education Movement, 1917), 173, 189. "Program of the World Alliance for International Friendship," *The Christian Student* 18, no. 2 (August 1917): 80–81. Lyman Abbott, "Triumphing Christianity," *The Outlook*, May 1, 1918, 26–27.

29. Reinhold Niebuhr, "The Failure of German-Americanism," *Atlantic Monthly*, July 1916, 13–18. "Letter to Samuel Press," August 14, 1915, Library of Congress, Reinhold Niebuhr Papers, June Bingham Collection, Box 27. Richard Fox, *Reinhold Niebuhr: A Biography* (New York: Pantheon Books, 1985), 42. Mary Todd, *Authority Vested: A Story of Identity and Change in the Lutheran Church-Missouri Synod* (Grand Rapids,

MI: William B. Eerdmans, 2000), 105. In the Evangelical Lutheran Synod of Missouri, Ohio, and Other States, for instance, parishes holding liturgies in English went from one-sixth of all congregations to three-fourths between 1917 and 1920.

30. Sutton, *American Apocalypse*, 1–45.

31. Leonard Newby, "Light on the Present Crisis," *The Christian Workers' Magazine*, December 1916, 277–278. "Has Christianity Failed, or Has Civilization Failed, or Has Man Failed?," *The King's Business (KB)*, November 1914, 595. "What Are We Fighting For?," *KB*, October 1917, 867–868. Sutton, *American Apocalypse*, 52–59.

32. Shirely Jackson Case, "The Premillennial Menace," *Biblical World*, July 1918, 20. "Calls Pacifist Judas," *Washington Post*, February 19, 1938, 3. "German War Methods Diabolical," *Greater Iowa* 9, no. 6 (July 1917): 2. "40,000 Cheer for War and Religion Mixed by Sunday," *NYT*, April 9, 1917.

33. "German War Methods Diabolical." "Sunday Roasts and Damns Kaiser," *The Sun*, March 5, 1918, 16. "Good for You, Billy," *The Sun*, March 15, 1918, 8. Billy Sunday, "Curses, Not Loud, But Deep," *Cartoons Magazine* 13, no. 3 (March 1918), 388.

34. William Bell Riley, *The Antievolutionary Pamphlets of William Bell Riley* (New York: Garland, 1995), 175, 207. William Bell Riley, *Inspiration or Evolution* (Cleveland: Union Gospel, 1923), 16, 36, 46, 251.

35. French Oliver, "Signs of the Times," *KB*, September 1915, 770. R. A. Torrey, "The Second Coming of Christ," *KB*, September 1918, 746. David Kennedy, *The Presbyterian* 90 (January 8, 1920): 3.

36. A. C. Dixon, quoted in Marsden, *Fundamentalism and American Culture*, 161. Kennedy, *The Presbyterian* 90, 3.

37. *KB*, May 1918, 365–66. The original quote comes from Henry Watterson in the *Louisville Courier-Journal* (Henry Watterson, "The World's Hope," *The Christian Worker's Magazine*, March 1918, 547–548). Cortland Myers, "War on German Theology," in *Light on Prophecy: A Coordinated Constructive Teaching, Being the Proceedings and Addresses at the Philadelphia Prophetic Conference* (New York: The Christian Herald, 1918), 176. Sutton, *American Apocalypse*, 1–8, 112–113.

38. Charles MacFarland, ed., *Library of Christian Cooperation*, Volume III: *The Church and International Relations* (New York: Missionary Education Movement, 1917), 173, 189. "Program of the World Alliance for International Friendship," *The Christian Student* 18, no. 2 (August 1917): 80–81. Rob Guild, ed., *Community Programs for Cooperating Churches: A Manual of Principles and Methods* (New York: Association Press, 1920). Sidney Gulick, *The Christian Crusade for a Warless World* (New York: Macmillan, 1922). National Conference on the Christian Way of Life, *International Problems and the Christian Way of Life: A Syllabus of Questions for Use by Forums and Discussion Classes* (New York: Association Press, 1923).

39. "The World Is My Parish," *Fort Worth Star-Telegram*, May 15, 1919. George Henry Hubbard, *Spiritual Messages of the Miracle Stories* (Boston: Jordan & More Press, 1922), 43–44. John Chadwick, "Are We Worthy of This Opportunity?," *Christian Advocate*, May 20, 1921, 617. Robert Wells Veach, *The Meaning of the War for Religious Education* (New York: Fleming Revell, 1920), 211.

40. Merrill, *Christian Internationalism*, 3–5, 13, 50, 56, 61, 73–78, 83–85.

41. "Introduction," *God Hath Spoken: Twenty-Five Addresses Delivered at the World Conference of Christian Fundamentals* (Philadelphia: Bible Conference Committee, 1919), 7–8. William Bell Riley, "The Present Crisis in the Professing Church!," in *Inspiration or Evolution* (Cleveland, OH: Union Gospel, 1923), 180.

42. Sutton, *American Apocalypse*, 75–77. Ruotsila, *The Origins of Christian Anti-Internationalism*.

43. Henry Cabot Lodge, "Opposing the League of Nations," in *Ideas and American Foreign Policy: A Reader*, ed. Andrew Bacevich (New York: Oxford University Press, 2018), 180. Ruotsila, *The Origins of Christian Anti-Internationalism*.

44. John McDowell, "Our National Inheritance and Our National Responsibility," *Record of Christian Work* 40 (1921): 748–750. Billy Sunday, quoted in "Remarkable Remarks, *The Independent*, February 7, 1920, 193. Arno Gaebelein, quoted in Marsden, *Fundamentalism and American Culture*, 156. On the revival of Protestant nativism in the 1920s, see: Gordon, *The Second Coming of the KKK*.

45. On the rise of the tri-faith movement, see: Schultz, *Tri-Faith America*. Gaston, *Imagining Judeo-Christian America*, 46–71. On Christian internationalism, see: Thompson, *For God and Globe*, 1–21. On this postwar disillusionment, see: Erez Manela, *The Wilsonian Moment: Self-Determination and the International Origins of Anticolonialism* (New York: Oxford University Press, 2009).

46. Daniel Fleming, *Marks of a World Christian* (New York: Association Press, 1919), 47, 134, 165. On the liberalization of Protestant mission, see: Stanley, *The World Missionary Conference*, 205–247. Xi Lian, *The Conversion of Missionaries*. Grant Wacker, "Pearl S. Buck and the Waning of the Missionary Impulse," *Church History* 72, no. 4 (2013): 852–874. Hollinger, *Protestants Abroad*.

47. Harry Emerson Fosdick, "Shall the Fundamentalists Win?," May 21, 1922. *CC*, quoted in Riley, *The Antievolution Pamphlets*, 27. "Women's Aid to World Christianity Stressed. Objectors to Foreign Missions Assailed at Presbyterian General Assembly. Evangelism is Sought," *Washington Post*, June 1, 1927, 5. On the rise of apocalyptic fundamentalism, see: Sutton, *American Apocalypse*, 79–206.

48. Henry Smith Leiper, "The Vindication and Challenge of a World's Revised Estimate of Mission," Leiper Family Papers, Presbyterian Historical Society, RG 490, Box 3, Folder 23. Leiper to Parents, November 16, 1919, *Collected Letters*, PHS, 232.

49. Julius Richter, "Germany's Struggle for Life—II," *CC*, September 11, 1924, 1170–1173. Stanley, *Christianity in the Twentieth Century*, 4, 35.

50. "Committee for Christian Relief in France and Belgium," *Annual Reports of the Federal Council of the Churches of Christ in America* (New York: Missionary Education Movement, 1918), 137. *American Relief Administration, European Children's Fund, Germany: Reports*, Volume 1 (Hamburg: Ackermann & Wulff, 1921). On American humanitarian relief to postwar Europe, see: Guy Aiken, "Feeding Germany: American Quakers in the Weimar Republic, *Diplomatic History* 43, no. 4 (2019): 597–617. See also: Julia Irwin, *Making the World Safe: The American Red Cross and a Nation's Humanitarian Awakening* (New York: Oxford University Press, 2013), esp. 141–184.

51. Reinhold Niebuhr, "The Despair of Europe," in William Chrystal, ed., *Young Reinhold Niebuhr: The Early Writings: 1911–1931* (New York: Pilgrim Press, 1977), 135. Calvin Coolidge, "Address Delivered at the Dedication of a Monument to Lafayette," September 6, 1924, in Calvin Coolidge, *Foundations of the Republic: Speeches and Addresses* (New York: Charles Scribner and Sons, 1926), 97–100.

52. "New York Pastor Tells League Audience World Christianity Must Prevail," *NYT*, September 14, 1925.

53. *The Relation between the Younger and Older Churches: Volume 3 of Report of the Jerusalem Meeting of the International Missionary Council* (Oxford: Oxford University Press, 1928). Robert E. Speer, *The Finality of Jesus Christ* (New York, 1933), 372. See also: Edwards, *The Right of the Protestant Left*, 72–73.

Chapter 2

1. Henry Smith Leiper, *World Chaos or World Christianity* (Chicago: Willett and Clark, 1937). On Protestant ecumenism as "God's totalitarianism," see: Edwards, *The Right of the Protestant Left*, 3, 53–106.

2. On the commitments of transatlantic ecumenists, see: Thompson, *For God and Globe*, 120–144. Edwards, *The Right of the Protestant Left*, 3, 53–106.

3. Victoria Barnett, *For the Soul of the People: Protestant Protest against Hitler* (New York: Oxford University Press, 1992), 9–29.

4. On interwar German Protestant mission, see: Hartmut Lehman, "Missionaries without Empire: German Protestant Missionary Efforts in the Interwar Period (1919–1933), in Brian Stanley, ed., *Missions, Nationalism, and the End of Empire* (Grand Rapids, MI: William B. Eerdmans, 2003): 34–53. On the divine orders, see: Robert P. Ericksen, *Theologians under Hitler* (New Haven, CT: Yale University Press, 1985), 98–104. On the meaning of the German *Volkskirche*, see: Kurt Meier, *Volkskirche 1918–1948: Ekklesiologie and Zeitgeschichte* (München: Kaiser Verlag, 1982), 7–46.

5. Frick, *Mission*, 352, 392. Althaus, quoted in Rasmussen, "Editor's Introduction to the English Edition," *Dietrich Bonhoeffer Works (DBW)*, Volume 12: *Berlin, 1932–1933*, 20, note 69.

6. Hockenos, *Then They Came for Me*, 7–69. Ziemann, *Martin Niemöller*, 89–144.

7. Karl Barth, *Der Römerbrief* (Zürich: Theologischer Verlag Zürich, 1922). For a discussion of Barth's life and times, see: Eberhard Busch, *The Great Passion: An Introduction to Karl Barth's Theology* (Grand Rapids, MI: William B. Eerdmans, 2010), 3–30.

8. Barnett, *For the Soul of the People*, 30–46. Hockenos, *Then They Came for Me*, 71–94.

9. On the German Christians and their theology, see: Doris Bergen, *Twisted Cross: The German Christian Movement in the Third Reich* (Chapel Hill: University of North Carolina Press, 1996). Susannah Heschel, *The Aryan Jesus: Christian Theologians and the Bible in Nazi Germany* (Princeton, NJ: Princeton University Press, 2008).

10. On the Nazis and "positive Christianity," see: Richard Steigmann-Gall, *The Holy Reich: Nazi Conceptions of Christianity, 1919–1945* (New York: Cambridge University Press, 2004), 13–50.

11. Otto Dibelius, *The Strange Case of Bishop Dibelius: A Selection of Documents* (Berlin: Rütten & Loening, 1962), 47. See also: Günther van Norden, *Der deutsche Protestantismus im Jahr der nationalsozialistische Machterfreifung* (Gütersloh: Verlaghaus Mohn, 1979), 54. Barnett, *For the Soul of the People*, 30–46. Hockenos, *A Church Divided*, 17–18. Hockenos, *Then They Came for Me*, 71–94.

12. Barnett, *For the Soul of the People*, 30–103. Hockenos, *A Church Divided*, 15–41.

13. Henry Smith Leiper to Samuel McCrea Cavert, September 2, 1933, Union Theological Seminary (UTS) Burke Library, Henry Smith Leiper Papers (Leiper Papers), Series 1, Box 1, Folder 7. Henry Smith Leiper, *The Church-State Struggle in Germany* (London: Friends of Europe, 1935), 8. See also: Victoria Barnett, "Christian and Jewish Interfaith Efforts during the Holocaust: The Ecumenical Context," in Maria Mazzenga, ed., *American Religious Responses to Kristallnacht* (Palgrave MacMillan, 2009), 13–29.

14. Hockenos, *Then They Came for Me*, 71–122. Ziemann, *Martin Niemöller*, 169–224.

15. Barnett, *For the Soul of the People*, 30–73. Hockenos, *A Church Divided*, 15–41.

16. For Homrighausen's commentary, see: "Hitler and German Religion," *CC*, March 29, 1933, 418–420. "Barth Resists Hitler," *CC*, July 26, 1933, 954–955. "The Ethical Dilemma of German Christians," *CC*, August 30, 1933, 1085–1087. "What of Germany Now?," *CC*, August 29, 1934, 1090–1092. "The Nub of the German Church Crisis," *CC*, February 6, 1935, 174–176. Samuel McCrea Cavert, "Hitler and the German Churches," *CC*, May 24, 1933, 683–685. Reinhold Niebuhr, "Religion and the New Germany," *CC*, June 28, 1933, 843–845.

17. Warren, *Theologians of a New World*, 56–76. Edwards, *The Right of the Protestant Left*, 1–106. For Niebuhr's breakout book, see: Reinhold Niebuhr, *Moral Man and Immoral Society* (New York: Scribner and Sons, 1932).

18. On Niebuhr's critique of Barth, see: Reinhold Niebuhr, "Barth—Apostle of the Absolute," *CC*, December 13, 1928, 1523–1524. Niebuhr to Bennett, June 10 and 20, 1930, in Richard Fox, *Reinhold Niebuhr: A Biography* (Ithaca, NY: Cornell University Press, 1996), 123. Karl Barth, *Church and State* (London: Student Church Movement, 1939), 24–25, 69, 77–78.

19. Reinhold Niebuhr, "The Death of a Martyr," *CAC*, June 25, 1945, 6–7. For an exhaustive biography of Bonhoeffer, see: Eberhard Bethge, *Dietrich Bonhoeffer: A Biography* (Minneapolis: Fortress Press, 2000).

20. "An den akademischen Austauschdienst," January 9, 1930, UTS, Burke Library, Dietrich Bonhoeffer Papers, Series 1, Box 2, Folder 4. *DBW*, Volume 10: *Barcelona, Berlin, New York, 1929–1931* (Minneapolis: Fortress Press, 2008), 265, 307. For the definitive study of Bonhoeffer in America, see: Charles Marsh, *Strange Glory: A Life of Dietrich Bonhoeffer* (New York: Alfred Knopf, 2014).

21. *DBW 10*, 261, 266, 313, 320.

22. *DBW 10*, 318, 320, 602. Harry Ward's "Ethical Interpretations" seminar also guided Bonhoeffer into new theological waters. Ward, a Methodist minister and activist, was one of Union's most radical Christian Socialists. In the course, Bonhoeffer read newspaper articles, political journals, and government reports, and analyzed them within a Christian socialist framework.

23. *DBW 10*, 305, 451, 602. *DBW*, Volume 8: *Letters and Papers from Prison* (Minneapolis: Fortress Press, 2010), 24.

24. "Basic Questions of a Christian Ethic," *DBW 10*, 359–379. Bethge, *Bonhoeffer*, 151. *DBW 10*, 222. Bonhoeffer, quoted in Mary Bosanquet, *The Life and Death of Dietrich Bonhoeffer* (New York: Harper & Row, 1968), 98. On Bonhoeffer's lifelong relationship to ecumenism, see: Keith Clements, *Bonhoeffer's Ecumenical Quest* (Geneva: World Council of Churches, 2015).

25. *DBW 10*, 315. For a definitive overview of how Harlem shaped Bonhoeffer's theology, see: Reggie Williams, *Bonhoeffer's Black Jesus: Harlem Renaissance Theology and an Ethic of Resistance* (Waco, TX: Baylor University Press, 2014).

26. *DBW 10*, 257–258, 321.

27. *DBW*, Volume 15: *Theological Education Underground, 1937–1940* (Minneapolis: Fortress Press, 2011), 457–458. James Whitman, *Hitler's American Model: The United States and the Making of Nazi Racial Law* (Princeton, NJ: Princeton University Press, 2017).

28. *DBW*, Volume 12: *Berlin, 1932–1933* (Minneapolis: Fortress Press, 2009), 279–280.

29. Dietrich Bonhoeffer, "The Church and the Jewish Question," in *No Rusty Swords: Letters, Lectures and Notes 1928–1936*, ed. Edwin H. Robertson (New York: Harper and Row, 1965), 226.

30. Hockenos, *A Church Divided*, 22–28. Hockenos, *Then They Came for Me*, 71–122. Ziemann, *Martin Niemöller*, 169–224.

31. Henry Smith Leiper, *The Church-State Struggle in Germany* (New York: Universal Christian Council for Life and Work, 1934), 18.

32. Samuel McCrea Cavert, "Points of Tension between Church and State in America Today," in Henry van Dusen ed., *Church and State in the Modern World* (New York: Harper & Brothers, 1937), 187–188. "Brethren in Christ," February 11, 1938, UTS, Leiper Papers, Series 1, Box 3, Folder 6. "Text of the proposed letter to the churches of the world," 1938, UTS, Leiper Papers, Series 1, Box 1, Folder 7.

33. "Statement by Dr. Henry Smith Leiper," Evangelisches Zentralarchiv Berlin (EZA) 5/195. "Significant developments in American Church relations to the German Churches," UTS, Leiper Papers, Series 1, Box 1, Folder 7. "Nazi Church Defies All World Critics," *NYT*, August 28, 1934, 6.

34. "Baptist World Congress in Berlin Condemns Racial Animosity," *The Jewish Exponent*, August 17, 1934, 8.

35. Leiper, *The Church-State Struggle*, 31. Henry Smith Leiper, *The Ghost of Caesar Walks: The Conflict of Nationalism and World Christianity* (New York: Friendship Press, 1935). Leiper, *World Chaos or World Christianity*.

36. Leiper to Homelanders, August 30, 1935, PHS, Pearl Digital Collections. Henry Smith Leiper, "A Protestant Protests," *Opinion: A Journal of Jewish Life and Letters*, December 1938, 9. Henry Smith Leiper, "The Olympic Games in Berlin: A Question of Fair Play," November 12, 1935, PHS, Pearl Digital Collections. "Statement by Dr. Henry Smith Leiper," Evangelisches Zentralarchiv Berlin (EZA) 5/195.

37. Leiper, "A Protestant Protests."

38. "To the Jew Pastor Leiper," undated, PHS, Leiper Family Papers, RG 490, Box 9, Folder 9. On the rise of tri-faith idealism, see: Schultz, *Tri-Faith America*, 15–67. Gaston, *Imagining Judeo-Christian America*, 42–44, 46–96.

39. William Ernest Hocking, *Rethinking Missions: A Laymen's Inquiry after One Hundred Years* (New York: Harper and Brothers, 1932), 326–327. On the history of Rockefeller's oil-fueled philanthropy and interreligious ecumenism, see: Darren Dochuk, *Anointed with Oil: How Christianity and Crude Made Modern America* (New York: Basic Books, 2019).

40. Leiper, "A Protestant Protests."

41. "Labor Sunday Message, 1933," *Federal Council Bulletin*, September 1933, 12. On mainline Protestants and the New Deal, see: Vanessa Cook, *Spiritual Socialists: American Religion and the Left* (Philadelphia: University of Pennsylvania Press, 2019), 20–95. Allison Collis Greene, *No Depression in Heaven: The Great Depression, the New Deal, and the Transformation of Religion in the Delta* (New York: Oxford University Press, 2015), 101–129.

42. Reinhold Niebuhr, quoted in Charles Samuel Braden, *Modern Tendencies in World Religion* (New York: Macmillan, 1933), 260. G. Bromley Oxnam, *Russian Impressions* (Los Angeles: Self-published, 1927). Gene Zubovich, "The Protestant Search for 'the Universal Christian Community' between Colonization and Communism," in Mark Edwards, ed., *Christian Nationalism in the United States* (Basel, Switzerland: MDPI, 2018).

43. Sutton, *American Apocalypse*, 1–8, 112–113.

44. Ibid., 207–262.

45. Gerald Winrod, *Hitler in Prophecy* (Wichita, KS: Defenders of the Faith, 1933), 13–14, Michigan State University Special Collections (MSU), Radicalism Collection (RC). On Winrod's place within fundamentalism, see: Leo Paul Ribuffo, *The Old Christian Right: The Protestant Far Right from the Great Depression to the Cold War* (Philadelphia: Temple University Press, 1983), 80–127.

46. Gerald Winrod, *The NRA in Prophecy and a Discussion of Beast Worship* (Wichita, KS: Defender, 1933), 41–42, MSU RC. Gerald Winrod, *World Trends Toward Antichrist* (Wichita, KS: Defender, 1934), 22–23, MSU RC. See as well: Calvin B. Waller, "The Mark of the Beast," *Arkansas Baptist*, September 28, 1933, 1–7. For varying religious responses to the early New Deal, see: Greene, *No Depression in Heaven*, 101–129. For an excellent discussion of fundamentalism and the New Deal, see: Matthew Avery Sutton, "Was FDR the Antichrist? The Birth of Fundamentalist Antiliberalism in a Global Age," *Journal of American History* 98, no. 4 (March 2012): 1052–1074.

47. J. Frank Norris, quoted in Maynard Shipley, *The War on Modern Science: A Short History of the Fundamentalist Attacks on Evolution and Modernism* (New York: Alfred A. Knopf, 1927), 171–172. J. Frank Norris, "Secretary of Agriculture Advocates 'Totalitarian' or Communistic State," *Fundamentalist* (*TF*), July 31, 1936), 1–3. J. Frank Norris, "Shall America Remain Under Present Dictatorship?," *TF*, April 8, 1938. J. Frank Norris, "The Second American Revolution," *TF*, November 6, 1936.

On Norris, see: Barry Hankins, *God's Rascal: J. Frank Norris and the Beginnings of Southern Fundamentalism* (Lexington: University of Kentucky Press, 1996).

48. Gerald Winrod, "Christian Americanism," *Defender Magazine (DM)*, July 1935, 3, 16–17. Dan Gilbert, "Biblical Basis of the Constitution," *DM*, May 1937, 29.

49. Gilbert, "Biblical Basis of the Constitution." Louis Patmont, "The Assault on Americanism," *DM*, May 1937, 23–24. Gerald Winrod, *The U.S. at the Crossroads* (Wichita, KS: Defender, 1934), MSU RC. Curiously, Winrod warmed to Catholics in the 1930s due to their anti-communism. He sought to forge a Christian alliance with notable antisemites like Father Charles Coughlin. See: Gaston, *Imagining Judeo-Christian America*, 62–63.

50. Gerald Winrod, "Unmasking the Hidden Hand—A World Conspiracy," *DM*, March 1933, 3, 5. Gerald Winrod, *Communism and The Roosevelt Brain Trust* (Wichtia, KS: Defender, 1933), MSU RC. Gerald Winrod, *The Jewish Assault on Christianity* (Wichtia, KS: Defender, 1935), MSU RC. Gerald Winrod, *The German Church Situation* (Wichtia, KS: Defender, 1936), MSU RC. William Bell Riley, "Facts for Fundamentalists," *The Pilot*, July 1933, 298–299. William Bell Riley, "Why Recognize Russia and Rag Germany?" *The Pilot*, January 1934, 126;

51. Gerald Winrod, "The German Church Situation," *DM*, October 1937, 5–7. For an overview of Melle's foreign engagements, see: Roland Blaich, "A Tale of Two Leaders: German Methodists and the Nazi State," *Church History* 70, no. 2 (June 2001): 199–225.

52. Winrod, "The German Church Situation." John Lewis Spivak, *Secret Armies: The New Technique of Nazi Warfare* (New York: Starling Press, 1939). George Britt, *The Fifth Column Is Here* (New York: Funk, 1940), 108–112. Ralph Lord, *Apostles of Discord: A Study of Organized Bigotry and Disruption on the Fringes of Protestantism* (Boston: Beacon Press, 1953), 27–33. As a comparison, Elesha Coffman notes *The Christian Century* only carried a circulation of 40,000 in the same decade.

53. "22,000 Hold Rally in Garden," *NYT*, February 21, 1939. For documentary footage of the rally, see: Marshall Curry, *A Night at the Garden* (New York: Field of Vision, 2017). On pro-Nazi Americans, see: Bradley Hart, *Hitler's American Friends: The Third Reich's Supporters in the United States* (New York: St. Martin's Press, 2018).

54. Oswald Smith, "My Visit to Germany," *DM*, September 1936, 15–18.

55. J. Frank Norris, "Interesting Discussion in Oxford Group on Board the Queen Mary," *TF*, July 30, 1937. J. Frank Norris, "Happy Service in Bethel Church Sunday," *TF* (August 6, 1937). J. Frank Norris, "Seventeen Years Ago in Germany and Now," *TF*, August 6, 1937. "Germany in the Religious World Situation," *TF*, August 20, 1937.

56. John R. Rice, "Persecution of Jews and Bible Prophecies," *Sword of the Lord (SL)*, December 2, 1938).

57. "Rally on Belle Isle," *TF*, June 10, 1938. "Teacher Burns Nazi, Soviet Flags on Isle," *TF*, June 10, 1938. "Hitler Is Demon-Possessed," *TF*, August 22, 1941. J. Frank Norris, "The Protocols of the Wise Men of Zion: A Spurious and Fradulent Document," *TF*, October 22, 1937. "Hitler Is Demon-Possessed," *TF*, August 22, 1941.

Chapter 3

1. Stewart Herman, "The American Church in Berlin," A. R. Wentz Library and Seminary Archives, United Lutheran Seminary Gettysburg, Stewart Winfield Herman Papers (Herman Papers), Box 3. Very few scholars have made use of Herman's papers. For accounts of Herman's time in Berlin, see: Stephen Herr, "An American in Nazi Berlin: A Look at Stewart W. Herman, Jr. in 1936," *Lutheran Theological Seminary Bulletin* 76, no. 4 (1996): 43–56. Ronald Webster, "Stewart W. Herman, Pastor of the American Church in Berlin, 1935–42, and Hitler's Persecution of the Jews," in John Roth, Elisabeth Maxwell, Margot Levy, Wendy Whitworth, eds., *Remembering for the Future: The Holocaust in an Age of Genocide* (London: Palgrave MacMillan, 2001), 635–644. Sutton, *Double Crossed*, 31–57.

2. For a sense of Herman's intellectual and ecumenical formation, see: Stewart Herman, "Muhlenberg's Type of Lutheranism," Herman Papers, Box 1. Stewart Herman, "Life and Work vs. Faith and Order," Herman Papers, Box 1. Stewart Herman, "Modern Missions," Herman Papers, Box 1. Stewart Herman, "Ecumenics: The World Mission of the Church," Herman Papers, Box 22. Herman was ordained into the United Lutheran Church, which stemmed from an ecumenical and evangelical strain of Lutheranism developed by Henry Melchoir Muhlenberg and Samuel Schmucker. On the history of American Lutheranism, see: Mark Granquist, *Lutherans in America: A New History* (Minneapolis: Fortress Press, 2015).

3. Herman to parents, September 19, 1934, Herman Papers, Box 16.

4. Herman to parents, September 19, 1934, Herman Papers, Box 16. Herman to parents, January 16, 1935, Herman Papers, Box 16. Herman to parents, March 16, 1935, Herman Papers, Box 16. Herman to parents, January 22, 1936, Herman Papers, Box 16.

5. Herman to parents, October 22, 1935, Herman Papers, Box 17. Herman to parents, October 29, 1935, Herman Papers, Box 17.

6. Herman to parents, October 30, 1935, Herman Papers, Box 17. On the mixed Protestant reception of Hitler and Nazi antisemitism, see: Robert W. Ross, *So It Was True: The American Protestant Press and the Nazi Persecution of the Jews* (Eugene, OR: Wipf and Stock, 1980). Kenneth Barnes, "The Missouri Synod and Hitler's Germany," *Yearbook of German-American Studies* 24 (1989): 131–148. Caitlin Carenen, *The Fervent Embrace: Liberal Protestants, Evangelicals, and Israel* (New York: New York University Press, 2012), 1–48.

7. Herman to parents, November 5, 1935, Herman Papers, Box 17. Herman to parents, January 22, 1936, Herman Papers, Box 18. Herman to parents, October 1, 1936, Herman Papers, Box 17.

8. Herman to parents, November 24, 1935, Seminary Archives, Herman Papers, Box 17. Herman to parents, December 10, 1935, Herman Papers, Box 17. Herman to parents, May 6, 1936, Herman Papers, Box 17. Herman to parents, January 22, 1936, Herman Papers, Box 17.

9. Herman to parents, February 17, 1935, Herman Papers, Box 16.

10. Herman to Parents, March 25, 1935, Herman Parents, Box 16.

11. Herman to parents, November 4, 1935, Herman Papers, Box 17. Herman to parents, January 15, 1936, Herman Papers, Box 17.

12. Herman to parents, February 23, 1936, Herman Papers, Box 17.

13. Herman to parents, January 26, 1936, Herman Papers, Box 17. Herman to parents, January 23, 1936, Herman Papers, Box 17. Herman, *American Church*, 69. Herman to parents, February 23, 1936. Herman was not the only American to develop firsthand observations of Hitler's Berlin. For comparative treatments of major American figures in Berlin and their mixed assessments of Nazism, see: Erik Larson, *In the Garden of Beasts: Love, Terror, and an American Family in Hitler's Berlin* (New York: Crown, 2011). Andrew Nagorski, *Hitlerland: American Eyewitnesses to the Nazi Rise to Power* (New York: Simon & Schuster, 2013).

14. "American Church Pastor Attacked by Nazi," March 28, 1936, Herman Papers, Box 21. "Rev. Herman Gets Shove by Nazi," March 27, 1936, Herman Papers, Box 21. Sutton, *Double Crossed*, 44–45.

15. Herman, *It's Your Souls We Want*, x. Stewart Herman, "Annual Report, 1937–1938," Herman Papers, Box 14. Stewart Herman, "Speech of Acceptance at American Church," February 23, 1936, Herman Papers, Box 20. Stewart Herman, "The American Church in Berlin," Herman Papers, Box 3. Herman to parents, November 30, 1936, Herman Papers, Box 17.

16. Herman to parents, July 5, 1936, Herman Papers, Box 17.

17. Herman to parents, July 5, 1936, Herman Papers, Box 17.

18. Herman to Congregation, May 1, 1938, Herman Papers, Box 18. Herman to parents, March 2, 1938, Herman Papers, Box 18.

19. Herman to parents, February 10, 1936, Herman Papers, Box 17. Herman to parents, March 18, 1936, Herman Papers, Box 17. Herman to parents, November 30, 1936, Herman Papers, Box 17.

20. Herman to parents, July 29, 1936, Herman Papers, Box 17. Herman to parents, June 28, 1938, Herman Papers, Box 18. Despite Herman's critique, these internationalist seminars in fact gave many American Protestants a deep understanding of European affairs; see: Thompson, *For God and Globe*, 1–8.

21. On Buchman, see: Philip Boobyers, *The Spiritual Vision of Frank Buchman* (University Park: Pennsylvania State University Press, 2013). Garth Lean, *Frank Buchman: A Life* (London: Constable, 1985). Garth Lean, *On the Tail of a Comet: The Life of Frank Buchman* (Colorado Springs: Helmers and Howard, 1985). For a comparative Quaker "mission" to the Nazis, see: Guy Aiken, "The American Friends Service Committee's Mission to the Gestapo," *Peace & Change* 42, no. 2 (April 2017): 209–231.

22. Buchman, quoted in Tom Driberg, *The Mystery of Moral Re-Armament* (New York: Alfred A. Knopf, 1965), 69. "God-Controlled Dictatorship," *TIME*, September 7, 1936.

23. "The Oxford Groups Reach Out," *NYT*, July 19, 1936.

24. Reinhold Niebuhr, *Christianity and Power Politics* (New York: Charles Scribner's Sons, 1940), 160–161. *DBW Volume 13: London, 1933–1935* (Minneapolis: Fortress Press, 2007), 205.

25. Herman to parents, August 19, 1936, Herman Papers, Box 17. Herman to parents, February 17, 1936, Herman Papers, Box 17. Quoted in Sutton, *Double Crossed*, 41–42. Herman, *American Church*, 72. For an alternative and more critical contemporary view, see: A. S. Esker, "Nazi Propaganda Rules Olympics," *CC*, March 11, 1936, 412–413.

26. Herman to parents, November 10, 1935, Herman Papers, Box 20. Herman to parents, August 19, 1936, Herman Papers, Box 17.

27. Herman to parents, August 19, 1936, Herman Papers, Box 17; Herman to parents, November 10, 1935, Herman Papers, Box 17; Herman to parents, March 3, 1936, Herman Papers, Box 17. Herman to parents, April 20, 1936, Herman Papers, Box 17. Herman to parents, August 15, 1940, Herman Papers, Box 18.

28. Herman to parents, May 4, 1937, Herman Papers, Box 17.

29. Ewart Edmund Turner, "The Prisoner of Sachsenhausen," *CC*, June 28, 1939, 818–819. Ewart Edmund Turner, "Remember Martin Niemöller!," *CC*, January 11, 1939, 53–56. Harold Fey, "The German Church Says No!," *CC*, September 1, 1937, 1067–1069. See also Hockenos, *Then They Came for Me*, 142. Had American ecumenists listened more resolutely to more critical German voices, however, they might have seen more clearly that German Protestants were too loyal to Hitler. See for instance: Wilhelm Sollmann, "Have the German Churches Broken with Hitler?," *CC*, March 29, 1939, 414–417.

30. On the Oxford conference, see: Thompson, *For God and Globe*, 120–144. On this Protestant "counter-totalitarian" order, see: Edwards, *The Right of the Protestant Left*, 3, 9–10, 53–120. For an overview of Dulles's role in shaping Federal Council policies in the pre-1945 era, see: Martin Erdmann, *Building the Kingdom of God on Earth: The Churches' Contribution to Marshal Public Support for World Order and Peace, 1919–1945* (Eugene, OR: Wipf and Stock, 2005).

31. "Absage der deutschen Teilnahme an Oxford 1937," June 16, 1937, EZA 5/23. Herman to parents, June 21, 1937, Herman Papers, Box 17. Herman to parents, June 28, 1937, Herman Papers, Box 17; Herman, "What Has Oxford to Say?," July 25, 1937, Herman Papers, Box 3.

32. Herman to parents, February 17, 1936, Herman Papers, Box 17. Herman to parents, March 16, 1938, Herman Papers, Box 18. Reinhold Niebuhr, "Must Democracy Use Force, II: Peace and the Liberal Illusion," *The Nation*, January 8, 1939, 117–119.

33. Herman to parents, March 3, 1936, Herman Papers, Box 17. Herman to parents, November 4, 1935, Herman Papers, Box 16. Herman to parents, September 24, 1936, Herman Papers, Box 18. On Christian antisemitism, see: Leonard Dinnerstein, *Antisemitism in America* (New York: Oxford University Press, 1994), 58–149. John Connelly, *From Enemy to Brother: The Catholic Teaching on the Jews, 1933–1965* (Cambridge, MA: Harvard University Press, 2012), 1–93. Robert Ericksen, *Complicity in the Holocaust: Churches and Universities in Nazi Germany* (New York: Cambridge University Press, 2012), 24–60, 94–138. Herman's views in part grew out of his Lutheran faith. Following the Reformation, Luther hoped the Protestant gospel would lead to Jewish conversions. His views hardened with time. Eventually, he suggested Christian rulers could force conversions if necessary. If the Jews resisted, the Reformer called on Germans to burn Jewish

synagogues and homes, confiscate their prayer books, and show them no mercy. On his own Luther tour of Germany, Herman expressed his deep admiration for the reformer. Seeing Luther sites in Erfurt, Eisenach, and Wittenberg stirred "deep thoughts" within him and "constrained" him to "silence rather than words." On Luther's writings, see: Martin Luther, "On the Jews and Their Lies (1543)," in *The Essential Luther*, trans. Tryntje Helfferich (Indianapolis, IN: Hackett, 2018), 284–303. Christopher Probst, *Demonizing the Jews: Luther and the Protestant Church in Nazi Germany* (Bloomington: Indiana University Press, 2012), 1–58. Thomas Kaufmann, *Luther's Jews: A Journey into Antisemitism* (New York: Oxford University Press, 2017), 125–152.

34. Herman to parents, December 9, 1936, Herman Papers, Box 17. Herman to parents, March 23, 1938, Herman Papers, Box 18. Herman to parents, July 26, 1938, Herman Papers, Box 18.

35. Herman to parents, September 24, 1936, Herman Papers, Box 17.

36. Herman to parents, June 21, 1938, Herman Papers, Box 18. Herman to parents, June 28, 1938, Herman Papers, Box 18. Herman to parents, July 26, 1938, Herman Papers, Box 18. Sutton, *Double Crossed*, 47.

37. Herman to parents, June 28, 1938, Herman Papers, Box 18. Herman to parents, November 9, 1938, Herman Papers, Box 18.

38. Herman to parents, June 28, 1938, Herman Papers, Box 18. Herman to parents, July 19, 1938, Herman Papers, Box 18. Herman to parents, July 26, 1938, Herman Papers, Box 18. Herman to parents, November 25, 1938, Herman Papers, Box 18. Herman to parents, March 15, 1939, Herman Papers, Box 18. On the prevalence of Christian antisemitism in the United States, see: Dinnerstein, *Antisemitism in America*.

39. Herman to parents, January 22, 1936, Herman Papers, Box 17. Herman to parents, June 10, 1936, Herman Papers, Box 17. "Yom Kippur Is Observed in Synagogs [sic] of City," *Harrisburg Telegraph*, September 15, 1937.

40. Herman to parents, January 22, 1936, Herman Papers, Box 17. Herman to parents, November 11, 1937, Herman Papers, Box 17. Quoted in Webster, "Stewart W. Herman," 638. On Nazi admiration for American eugenics and Jim Crow laws, see: James Q. Whitman, *Hitler's American Model: The United States and the Making of Nazi Race Law* (Princeton, NJ: Princeton University Press, 2017).

41. Herman to parents, November 14, 1938, Herman Papers, Box 18.

42. Herman to parents, November 14, 1938, Herman Papers, Box 18. On the Federal Council response, see: Kyle Jantzen, "The Fatherhood of God and the Brotherhood of Man: Mainline American Protestants and the Kristallnacht Pogrom," in Maria Mazzenga, ed., *American Religious Responses to Kristallnacht* (New York: Palgrave Macmillan, 2009), 31–55. On American perceptions of Germans in the 1930s, see: Michaela Hoenicke Moore, *Know Your Enemy: The American Debate on Nazism, 1933–1945* (Cambridge: Cambridge University Press, 2009).

43. Herman, *American Church*, 78. Herman to parents, December 1, 1938, Herman Papers, Box 18.

44. Herman to parents, November 25, 1938, Herman Papers, Box 18. Herman to parents, December 1, 1938, Herman Papers, Box 18. Herman, *American Church*, 78.

45. Herman to parents, November 14, 1938, Herman Papers, Box 18. Herman to parents, November 25, 1938, Herman Papers, Box 18.

46. Herman to parents, November 14, 1938, Herman Papers, Box 18. Herman to parents, December 8, 1938, Herman Papers, Box 18. Herman to parents, January 2, 1939, Herman Papers, Box 18.

47. Herman to parents, February 22, 1939, Herman Papers, Box 18.

48. Reinhold Niebuhr to Henry Smith Leiper, May 1, 1939, UTS, Bonhoeffer Papers, Series 1, Box 2, Folder 2. Leiper to Bonhoeffer, May 11, 1939, UTS, Bonhoeffer Papers, Series 1, Box 2, Folder 2.

49. Niebuhr to Lehmann, July 8, 1939, Burke Library Archive, UTS, Bonhoeffer Papers, Series 3, Box 1, Folder 15. Reinhold Niebuhr, "The Death of a Martyr," *CAC, June* 25, 1945, 6–7. *DBW 8,* 52.

50. Herman to parents, August 25, 1939, Herman Papers, Box 20. Sutton, *Double Crossed,* 53–55.

51. Sutton, *Double Crossed,* 53–55.

52. Herman to parents, October 3, 1940, Herman Papers, Box 20. Herman to parents, November 3, 1941, Herman Papers, Box 18.

53. Herman to parents, October 6, 1941, Herman Papers, Box 18.

54. Herman to parents, October 17, 1941, Herman Papers, Box 18. On Roosevelt's response, see: Richard Breitman and Allan J. Lichtman, *FDR and the Jews* (Cambridge, MA: Harvard University Press, 2013).

55. Herman to parents, October 17, 1941, Herman Papers, Box 18. Herman to parents, October 24, 1941, Herman Papers, Box 18. Herman to parents, November 17, 1941, Herman Papers, Box 18.

56. Herman to parents, December 6, 1941, Herman Papers, Box 18.

57. Stewart Herman, "End of Year 1941," Herman Personal Diary.

Chapter 4

1. On the Christian realists in wartime, see: Warren, *Theologians of a New World Order,* 94–115; Edwards, *The Right of the Protestant Left,* 71–120; Preston, *Sword of the Spirit,* 297–314. On Protestant evangelicals during the war, see: Sutton, *American Apocalypse,* 263–292.

2. On this "cautious patriotism," see: Sittser, *A Cautious Patriotism,* 1–76.

3. Herman to parents, August 15, 1940, Herman Papers, Box 18. On this pacifist approach to the war, see: Sittser, *A Cautious Patriotism,* 1–76. Preston, *Sword of the Spirit,* 297–314, 365–383.

4. Herman to parents, September 6, 1940, Herman Papers, Box 18.

5. "Reinhold Niebuhr, "The Christian Faith and the World Crisis," *CAC,* February 10, 1941, 4. Reinhold Niebuhr, "The Crisis," *CAC,* February 10, 1941, 1.

6. Niebuhr, "The Crisis," 1. Fox, *Reinhold Niebuhr,* 199.

7. Francis B. Sayre to William Eddy, December 14, 1938, and February 8, 1939, Eddy Papers, Box 8, Folder 5. "President Roosevelt's Navy Day Address on World

Affairs," *NYT*, October 28, 1941. On the ecumenists' "conquering faith," see: Sutton, *Double Crossed*, 63–66. On Roosevelt's foreign policy, see: Robert Dallek, *Franklin D. Roosevelt and American Foreign Policy, 1933-1945* (New York: Oxford University Press, 2005); Warren Kimball, *The Juggler: Franklin Roosevelt as Wartime Statesman* (Princeton, NJ: Princeton University Press, 1991). For special reference to Roosevelt and religion, see: Preston, *Sword of the Spirit*, 315–326.

8. Herman to parents, December 22, 1941, Herman Papers, Box 18. Herman, "Ecumenics: The World Mission of the Church," Herman Papers, Box 22.

9. Everton to Herman, November 20, 1942, Herman Papers, Box 14. "An American Visitor," *The Manchester Guardian*, March 20, 1943. "Says Bombs Fail to Subdue Nazis: Rev. Herman, American Ex-Pastor in Berlin, Asserts Only Invasion Will Succeed," *NYT*, May 1, 1943. "Ex-Captive of Nazis Will Speak Sunday from Local Pulpit," Herman Papers, Box 22. "English BCC Trip," Herman Papers, Box 22.

10. Flack to Herman, July 23, 1943, Herman Papers, Box 14. Herman, "Ecumenics: The World Mission of the Church," Herman Papers, Box 22.

11. Herman to Lovell, July 7, 1943, Herman Papers, Box 14.

12. Herman to Dulles, "Personnel Survey of Possible Candidates for Staff of Austrian Operatives," October 13, 1944, NA RG 260, Box 333, Folder 66, Entry 190. Donovan to Flack, August 23, 1943, Herman Papers, Box 14. For Herman's OSS file, see: NA RG 226, Entry 125, Box 8, Folder 133. Figures like Herman made excellent spies due to their language skills and evangelistic training. For more on Herman's work in the OSS, see Sutton, *Double Crossed*, 144–156, 199–218.

13. Henry Luce, "The American Century," *LIFE*, February 17, 1941. Reinhold Niebuhr, "American Power and World Responsibility," *CAC*, April 5, 1943. Herman to parents, August 15, 1940, Herman Papers, Box 20. "Concerning Flags in the Sanctuary," *Federal Council Bulletin* 25, no. 3 (March 1942): 11.

14. Stewart Herman, *It's Your Souls We Want* (New York: Harper Brothers, 1943). *The New Republic*, March 22, 1943, 389. Leiper to Oxman, February 24, 1943, Herman Papers, Box 11. Van Dusen to Herman, June 16, 1943, Herman Papers, Box 11.

15. Herman, *It's Your Souls We Want*, 178, 234. Douglas Miller, "The Nazis Versus God," *NYT*, March 14, 1943. On the rise of this postwar myth, see: Barnett, *For the Soul of the People*, 197–208, 280–282. Hockenos, *A Church Divided*, 42–61.

16. Herman, *It's Your Souls We Want*, 178, 234. Miller, "The Nazis Versus God." On the rise of this postwar myth, see: Barnett, *For the Soul of the People*, 197–208, 280–282. Hockenos, *A Church Divided*, 42–61.

17. Herman, *It's Your Souls*, 104–107. In developing these interpretations, Herman contributed to an emerging historiography known as the *Sonderweg*, which claimed that Germany had taken a "special path" that deviated from the "normal" pattern of democratic developments of other Western nations. While widely accepted in the mid-twentieth century, the *Sonderweg* thesis has been since largely discredited by historians, who have criticized the school of thought for making it seem that Nazism was the only possible historical outcome for Germany and have convincingly argued that Germany's imperial development paralleled that of other Western nations.

18. Herman to parents, July 25, 1944, Herman Papers, Box 20. Herman, *It's Your Souls*, 296.

19. Arnold Jahr, "A Chance to Pay our Debt," *Lutheran Standard*, June 26, 1943, 2. Reinhold Niebuhr, "American Power and World Responsibility."

20. Reinhold Niebuhr, "The German Problem," *CAC*, January 10, 1944, 2. Reinhold Niebuhr, "The Peace Settlement with Special Reference to Germany," *CAC*, June 26, 1944, 6.

21. Walter W. Van Kirk, "Christian Mission Prepares Ground for Church Action," *Post War World*, December 15, 1943, 1. "Drive for World Order of Nations Opened by Christian Church Group," *NYT*, October 29, 1943. Niebuhr, "The Christian Faith and the World Crisis," 6. See also: G. Bromley Oxnam, "The Crusade for a New World Order," *CAC*, July 26, 1943, 12–14. Preston, *Sword of the Spirit*, 384–409.

22. Bishop G. Bromley Oxnam, "The Nazis Aren't Licked Yet," October 1945, UTS, Leiper Papers, Series 1, Box 4, Folder 4.

23. James Thompson, "Should I Sacrifice to Live Half-America? Double Victory against Axis Forces and Ugly Prejudices on the Home Front," *Pittsburgh Courier*, January 31, 1942. Horace Cayton, "Hitlerism: Real Fight for Democracy Has Only Begun; Hitler's Race Theory Still Lives," *Pittsburgh Courier*, May 19, 1945. See also: Sittser, *Cautious Patriotism*, 168–192.

24. Willem A. Visser 't Hooft, "Germany and the West," March 1940, World Council of Churches Archive (WCCA), 301.9.1.

25. Visser 't Hooft to A. Dulles, "The Situation of the Protestant Church in Germany," National Archives (NA) RG 226, Entry 190, Box 27, Folder 99. *DBW*, Volume 16: *Conspiracy and Imprisonment, 1940-1945* (Minneapolis: Fortress Press, 2006), 2/12, 536–539. Willem A. Visser 't Hooft, "Germany and the West," March 1940, WCCA, 301.9.1. W. A. Viser 't Hooft, "The Place of the German Church in Post-War Reconstruction," *CAC*, June 11, 1945, 4–7.

26. W. A. Visser 't Hooft, *Memoirs* (Amsterdam: SCM Press, 1971), 177–181. Samuel McCrea Cavert, "The American Churches and the Churches of Europe," *Federal Council of Churches Biennial Report* (1942): 27. Lucian Leustean, *The Ecumenical Movement and the Making of the European Community* (New York: Oxford University Press, 2014), 1–51.

27. A. Dulles to Washington, "Opposition of the German Churches," November 23, 1943, NA RG 226, Entry 134, Box 341, Folder 1821. Emmy Rado, "History and Significance of the Confessional Church in Germany," November 1944, NA RG 226, Entry 92, Box 588, Folder 6. Herman to J. F. Dulles, November 10, 1945, Herman Papers, Box 20.

28. Reinhold Niebuhr, "The German Problem," 2. Reinhold Niebuhr, "The Peace Settlement with special reference to Germany," 6. "Too Harsh a Peace Opposed for Reich," *NYT*, June 1, 1944. Reinhold Niebuhr, "Airplanes Are Not Enough," *CAC*, February 7, 1944, 1–2. Reinhold Niebuhr, "The Vengeance of Victors," *CAC*, November 26, 1945, 1–2. On the Morgenthau plan, see: Hans Morgenthau, *Germany Is Our Problem* (New York: Harper and Brothers, 1945). Warren Kimball, *Swords or Ploughshares: The Morgenthau Plan for Defeated Nazi Germany, 1943-1946* (Philadelphia: Lippincott, 1976). For the internal debates within Washington over

postwar Germany, see: Carolyn Eisenberg, *Drawing the Line: The American Decision to Divide Germany, 1944–1949* (New York: Cambridge University Press, 1996), 14–70; Jackson, *Civilizing the Enemy*, 112–149.

29. Reinhold Niebuhr, "The Fight for Germany," *LIFE*, October 21, 1946. Martin Hall, "The Kind of Germans We Need," *CC*, April 18, 1945, 488–489. "Are Germans Incurable," *CC*, October 6, 1943, 1128–1129. "Germany's Regeneration," *CC*, June 13, 1945, 702–703. Niebuhr was joined in these organizations by a host of intellectuals, including German émigré Paul Tillich. See: "A Program for a Democratic Germany," *CAC*, May 15, 1944, 3–5. Herman to family, July 25, 1944, Herman Papers, Box 19.

30. Herman to A. Dulles, October 17, 1944, Herman Papers, Box 14. Herman to parents, August 19, 1944, Herman Papers, Box 20.

31. Herman to parents, June 7, 1944, Herman Papers, Box 20. Herman to parents, July 13, 1945, Herman Papers, Box 20. Herman to Leiper, September 7, 1944, Herman Papers, Box 14.

32. Herman to Leiper, October 13, 1944, Herman Papers, Box 14.

33. Stewart Herman, "End of Year 1942," and "End of Year 1944," Herman Personal Diary.

34. Visser 't Hooft, quoted in William Schmidt, *Architect of Unity: A Biography of Samuel McCrea Cavert* (New York: Friendship Press, 1978), 134. "Million Dollar Gift," *The Living Church*, December 16, 1945, 11. Visser 't Hooft, *Memoirs*, 187–188.

35. Gerald Winrod, "Europe's Crisis in Prophecy," *DM*, October 1939. Oliver E. Williams, *The Changing World Order in the Light of the Prophetic Word* (Wichita, KS: Defender, 1941), MSU RC.

36. Gerald Winrod, *Radio Speeches on War and Peace* (Wichtia, KS: Defender, 1939), MSU RC. Gerald Winrod, "American Foreign Policy," *DM*, April 1938. Gerald Winrod, *A Prayer to Almighty God in Time of War* (Wichita, KS: Defender, 1941), MSU RC. For a time, globetrotting pilot Charles Lindbergh emerged as a prominent America First leader. Like Winrod, Lindbergh had visited Nazi Germany in the 1930s and left with high praise, especially for the Nazi *Luftwaffe*. The American aviator argued that the war only aimed to suppress Germany's rising stature and threatened to "reduce the strength and destroy the treasures of the White race." See: Charles Lindbergh, "Aviation, Geography, Race," *Reader's Digest*, November 1939, 64–67.

37. John R. Rice, "War: Human Wickedness and the Certain End of Civilization," *SL*, June 21, 1940. J. Frank Norris, "War Conditions Changed Our Route," *TF*, July 21, 1939. J. Frank Norris, "Hitler Will Be Cast Alive into a Lake of Fire," *TF*, December 20, 1940. John R. Rice, "War: Human Wickedness and the Certain End of Civilization," *SL*, June 21, 1940. John R. Rice, "Four Reasons Why Christians Should Fight," *SL*, June 19, 1942. John R. Rice, "Duties of Christians Concerning Hitler and World War," *SL*, August 22, 1941. John R. Rice, "Can America Keep Out of War?," *SL*, March 31, 1939, 1.

38. J. Frank Norris, "Is Hitler the Anti-Christ?," *TF*, May 17, 1940. J. Frank Norris, "Norris to Osborn," *TF*, November 15, 1940. J. Frank Norris, "Hitler's Fifty Million Dollar Bismarck Sent to the Bottom," *TF*, May 27, 1941.

39. John R. Rice, "Duties of Christians Concerning Hitler and World War," *SL*, August 22, 1941. Hyman Appelman, "How God Is Using Hitler (And How the Democracies Must Win)," *KB*, June 1942, 212. *DM*, January 1942.

40. Gerald Winrod, *The Prophetic Destiny of the United States* (Wichita, KS: Defender, 1941), MSU RC. Harold John Ockenga, *God Save America* (Boston: Park Street Church, 1939).

41. Harold John Ockenga, "Letter to the Times," *NYT*, March 9, 1944, 16. Elwin Wright, "The Federal Council and National Defence," *SL*, December 1, 1944. William Blackney, "A Tribute to the Flag," *DM*, June 1943. William Stidger, "Gernal Marshall's Religious Beliefs," *DM*, October 1943. On the evangelical partnership to the US military, see: Anne Loveland, *American Evangelicals and the U.S. Military, 1942–1993* (Baton Rouge: Louisiana State University Press, 1996).

42. "Fundamentalists: Dr. Rood Declares War Can Be Won by Prayer Bands," *Daily Boston Globe*, May 11, 1942, 16.

43. For a helpful introduction to Youth for Christ, see: Joel Carpenter, ed., *The Youth for Christ Movement and Its Pioneers* (New York: Garland, 1988).

44. John R. Rice, "Pray for Invasion Armies," *SL*, June 16, 1944. "McIntire Revival Starting Monday," *Nashville Tennessean*, May 5, 1943, 9. John R. Rice, "Can America Keep Out of War?," *SL*, March 31, 1939, 1.

45. Carl McIntire, *What Is the Difference between the American Council of Christian Churches and the National Council of Churches of Christ in the U.S.A.?* (Collingswood, NJ: Twentieth Century Reformation Hour, 1950). Carl McIntire, "The Modernist-Communist Threat to American Liberties," *SL*, September 14, 1945. Carl McIntire, "Private Enterprise in the Scriptures," *SL*, September 21, 1945.

46. John R. Rice, "Duties of Christians Concerning Hitler and World War," *SL*, August 22, 1941. "Rally on Belle Isle," *TF*, June 10, 1938. "Teacher Burns Nazi, Soviet Flags on Isle," *TF*, June 10, 1938. "Hitler Is Demon-Possessed," *TF*, August 22, 1941. Gerald Winrod, "Niemöller, A Symbol of Christian Heroism," *DM*, June 1942. Gerald Winrod, "Martin Niemöller—Persecuted for Christ," *DM*, January 1944.

47. "Gerald L. K. Smith Dead; Anti-Communist Crusader," *NYT*, April 16, 1976. Gerald L. K. Smith, "This Is Christian Nationalism," Phonograph Record, Gerald L. K. Smith Papers, Bentley Historical Library, University of Michigan. On Smith's life, see: Glean Jeansonne, *Gerald L. K. Smith: Minister of Hate* (Baton Rouge: Louisiana State University Press, 1997).

48. Carpenter, *Revive Us Again*, 141–160. Sutton, *American Apocalypse*, 285–290.

49. "National Association of Evangelicals (NAE)," Wheaton College, NAE Archival Collections. Harold Ockenga, "Christ for America," *United Evangelical Action*, May 4, 1943, 1.

50. "The San Francisco Charter," *United Evangelical Action*, August 1, 1945, 13. "Showers of Blessing: A Weekly Paper in Loyalty to Christ," February 12, 1943, PHS, Federal Council of Churches Records, RG 18, Box 8, Folder 24.

51. J. Frank Norris, "Hitler's Funeral," *TF*, May 25, 1945.

52. Adolf Keller, *Christian Europe Today* (New York: Harper, 1942), 225–226, 228.

Chapter 5

1. Herman to J. F. Dulles, November 10, 1945, Herman Papers, Box 20. Stewart Herman, *The Rebirth of the German Church* (New York: Harper Brothers, 1946), xiv. Stewart Winfield Herman, "Letter to the German Churches," July 29, 1945, in *The Rebirth of the German Church*, 187–188.

   Few scholars have made use of Herman's postwar reports and papers. For compendiums of these sources, see: Clemens Vollnhals, ed., *Die evangelische Kirche nach dem Zusammenbruch: Berichte ausländischer Beobachter aus dem Jahre 1945* (Göttingen: Vandenhoeck und Ruprecht, 1988). Gerhard Beiser, "Ökumenische Mission in Nachkriegsdeutschland: Die Berichte von Stewart W. Herman über die Verhältnisse in der evangelischen Kirche 1945–46. Drei Teile," *Kirchliche Zeitgeschichte* 1, no. 1 (May 1988): 151–187; 1, no. 2 (October 1988), 316–352; 2, no. 1 (May 1989): 294–358.

2. Ruff, "The German Churches and the Specter of Americanization."

3. Herman to J. F. Dulles, November 10, 1945, Herman Papers, Box 20. "Memorandum and Request re: Liaison between American Military Government, Protestant Churches of Germany, World Council of Churches," WCCA, 301.10.10. Sylvester Michelfelder, "Report of Dr. Sylvester C. Michelfelder on his visit to Germany and Alsace, October 15th–25th, 1945," NA, RG 260, 5/344-2/6. Among his State Department contacts, Herman counted Secretary of State James F. Byrnes, Ambassador Robert D. Murphy, and Foreign Service advisor Donald Heath.

4. "Potsdam Condemned," *CC*, December 12, 1945, 1377–1378. Herman, *Rebirth*, xix, 236. On the postwar refugee crisis, see: R. M. Douglas, *Orderly and Humane: The Expulsion of the Germans after the Second World War* (New Haven, CT: Yale University Press, 2012).

5. Beryl McClaskey, *The History of US Policy and Program in the Field of Religious Affairs under the Office of the US High Commissioner for Germany, Research Project No. 104*, Historical Division, Office of the Executive Secretary, 17, 77. "In Memoriam," *The American Political Science Review* 60, no. 2 (June 1966): 486–488. Marshall Knappen, "Report on Munich-Stuttgart Mission (May 18–21, 1945)," NA, RG 84, 842/37. For a discussion of the AMG's broader aims, see: Tent, *Mission on the Rhine*. Carruthers, *The Good Occupation*, 15–49.

6. "Education and Religious Affairs Branch," National Archives 260/390/46/15/5 Box 158. Chaplain William S. Purrier, "Impressions of Germany," *CAC*, June 25, 1945, 3–6. "Reports on Non-Fraternization," quoted in Faulkner-Rossi, *Wehrmacht Priests*, 198.

7. "For What I Am," *TIME Magazine*, June 18, 1945. Stewart Herman, "Memorandum on Conversation with Pastor Niemöller in Frankfurt on July 31, 1945," UTS, Leiper Papers, Series 1, Box 4, Folder 7. See also: G. Bromley Oxnam, "The Attack on Niemöller," *CC*, August 19, 1945, 977–979. Chaplain Ben Lacy Rose, "An Interview with Pastor Martin Niemöller," *CAC*, December 10, 1945, 4–6.

8. Karl Barth, *The Church and the War* (New York: Macmillan, 1944), 39.

9. *DBW 16*, 1/92a, 1/116a, 1/126a.

10. Hockenos, *A Church Divided*, 15–41.

11. "Reporting Two Hour Interview with Dr. Martin Niemoeller," WCCA 301.43.26/6. "Report on Conferences with Bishop Wurm's Party," June 25, 1945, NA 260/390/46/ 15/5, Box 199. For an excellent survey of Niemöller's postwar activities, see: Hockenos, *Then They Came for Me*, 157–186. Ziemann, *Martin Niemöller*, 357–496. The AMG likewise helped Catholic bishops organize a similar gathering of Catholic leaders in the fall of 1945 at Fulda.

12. Marshall Knappen, "Informal Conference on Distinction between Religious Freedom and Political Activity of Churchmen, 6 August, 1945," NA RG 84, 737/ 1. Marshall Knappen, *And Call It Peace* (Chicago: University of Chicago Press, 1947), 100. Brennan, *The Politics of Religion*, xii. For a broader survey of Soviet policy, see: Naimark, *The Russians in Germany: A History of the Soviet Occupation Zone, 1945–1949* (Cambridge, MA: Harvard University Press, 1995), 1–8, 141–204, 353–464.

13. Herman, *Rebirth*, 119. Knappen, *And Call It Peace*, 118.

14. Herman, *Rebirth*, 107. Herman to J. F. Dulles, November 10, 1945, Herman Papers, Box 20.

15. Herman, *Rebirth*, xiv, 18, 154–189, 270. Stewart Herman, "Memorandum of Conversation with Professor Iwand at Lünen on September 11, 1945," in Vollnhalls, *Die evangelische Kirche*, 141–143. Stewart Winfield Herman, "Berlin," August 9, 1945, WCCA 301.43.14/9. Herman to J. F. Dulles, November 10, 1945, Herman Papers, Box 20.

16. Herman, "Letter to the German Churches," July 29, 1945, in *Rebirth*, 187–188. Stewart Winfield Herman, "The World Council of Churches (August 13, 1945)," in *Die evangelische Kirche*, 106–109. Stewart Winfield Herman, "Memorandum on Conversation with Pastor Niemöller in Frankfurt on July 31, 1945," UTS, Leiper Papers, Series 1, Box 4, Folder 7. Sylvester Michelfelder, "Botschaft an die Kirchen in Deutschland, (27. Juli 1945)," Archiv für Diakonie und Entwicklung (ADE), ZB 7.

17. Stewart Herman, "General Panorama (Beginning August 1945)," in *Die evangelische Kirche*, 79–84. Stewart Winfield Herman, "Memorandum of Conversation with Pastor Fricke on July 31, 1945 at his parsonage in Frankfurt, Franz Rücker Allee 10," UTS, Leiper Papers, Series 1, Box 4, Folder 7. Herman, *Rebirth*, 12–14.

18. Herman, "Memorandum of Conversation with Pastor Fricke." Stewart Herman, "Baden (July 30 and August 5, 1945)," in *Die evangelische Kirche*, 64–69; Stewart Winfield Herman, "Report on German Reaction to the Stuttgart Declaration (December 14, 1945)," WCCA 301.43.13/2. Stewart Herman, "Treysa," Herman Papers, Box 3. Stewart Herman, "General German Church Situation (September 1945)," UTS, World Council of Churches Papers, Box 71, Folder 6.

19. Herman, "General German Church Situation." Herman, "Memorandum of Conversation with Pastor Fricke." Herman, *Rebirth*, 16, 29, 70, 160–163, 168. Martin Niemöller to Wilhelm Niemöller, November 10, 1945, in *Die deutsche Schuld, Not und Hoffnung*, Martin Niemöller (Zürich: Evangelischer Verlag, 1946), 21, 28. Herman, "Treysa." Herman, "The World Council of Churches."

20. Cecil Northcott, "The Treatment of Germany," *CC*, *February* 14, 1945, 205. A. L. Warnshuis, "Help for European Churches," *CAC*, May 28, 1945, 2–3. "Germany's Regeneration," *CC*, July 13, 1945, 703.

21. Herman, *Rebirth,* 10, 61. Herman, "Berlin." For more on this deeply divided postwar landscape, see: Hockenos, *A Church Divided,* 42–62. Annemarie Smith Von Osteen, *Von Treysa 1945 bis Eisenach 1948: zur Geschichte der Grundordnung der Evangelischen Kirche in Deutschland* (Göttingen: Vandenhoeck und Ruprecht, 1980). Thomas Martin Schneider, *Gegen den Zeitgeist: Der Weg zur VELKD als lutherischer Bekenntniskirche* (Göttingen: Vandenhoeck & Ruprecht, 2008).

22. Herman, "Berlin." Herman, "General Panorama." Herman, *It's Your Souls,* 104–107. Herman, *The Rebirth of the German Church,* 2, 10. Stewart Herman, "Memorandum on Conversation with Bishop Wurm in Stuttgart on August 6, 1945," UTS, Leiper Papers, Series 1, Box 4, Folder 7. On Dibelius, see: Robert Stupperich, *Otto Dibelius: ein evangelischer Bischof im Umbruch der Zeiten* (Göttingen: Vandenhoeck & Ruprecht, 1989). Hartmut Fritz, *Otto Dibelius: ein Kirchenmann in der Zeit zwischen Monarchie und Diktatur* (Göttingen: Vandenhoeck und Ruprecht, 1998).

23. Herman, "Berlin." Herman, *Rebirth,* 27. Stewart Winfield Herman, "Memo: Contacts in Berlin, August 7–15, 1945," UTS, Leiper Papers, Series 1, Box 4, Folder 7.

24. Theodore Lapp, "Treysa Conference of Evangelical Church Leaders, held at Hephata Institution, August 27–September 1, 1945," NA 260/390/46/15/5, Box 179. For a primary source comparison of the competing Protestant views, see the "Message to the Congregations," *Ecumenical Press Service* 32 (September 1945): 155–156, and "Message to the Pastors," *Ecumenical Press Service* 35 (September 1945): 173–174.

25. Herman, *Rebirth,* 160–162. "Wort zur Verantwortung der Kirche für das öffentliche Leben," EZA 2/39.

26. Herman, *Rebirth,* 166–168. "Drei Jahre Hilfswerk: was das Hilfswerk ist, was das Hilfswerk bekam, was das Hilfswerk tat," 1948, WCCA 301.43.14/7. "Addendum to German Agenda," September 1947, WCCA 425.3.62. "Mitteilungen aus dem Hilfswerk der evangelischen Kirchen in Deutschland," Nummer 1, April 1947, Zentralbüro Stuttgart, WCCA 452.3.58. E. Theodore Bachmann, "Self-Help in German Churches," *CC,* December 31, 1947, 1609–1610. The call for self-help bubbled forth from indigenous springs of practical and lay-oriented theology in German Protestantism, which originated in the *Innere Mission* theology of Johann Hinrich Wichern, the German Protestant pastor who in the nineteenth century had called German Protestants to practice "home missions."

27. Stewart Herman, "World Council of Churches: Department of Reconstruction and Inter-Church Aid: General German Church Situation," September 1945, WCCA 425/3/8/15. Herman, *Rebirth,* 185–189, 206–207. On Soviet religious policies, see: Brennan, *The Politics of Religion in Soviet-Occupied Germany.*

28. Herman, *Rebirth,* 206–207, 257–258.

29. Herman, *Rebirth,* 152, 175–177. See also: Stewart Herman, *Report from Christian Europe* (New York: Friendship Press, 1953), 133.

30. Stewart Herman, "Treysa," Herman Papers, Box 3. Herman, *Rebirth.,* xvi, 1–9, 13, 21, 59, 70, 152.

31. On postwar Protestantism and the Jewish question, see: Matthew D. Hockenos, "The German Protestant Church and its *Judenmission,* 1945–1950," in Kevin P. Spicer,

ed., *Antisemitism, Christian Ambivalence, and the Holocaust* (Bloomington: Indiana University Press, 2007), 173–200. Hockenos, *A Church Divided*, 135–170.

32. Earl Crumm, "Observations on the Conference of the German Evangelical Church Held at Treysa, 27–31 August 1945," NA 260/390/46/15/5, Box 179. Robert Murphy, "Conference of the German Evangelical Church, held at Treysa, August 27–September 1, 1945," NA 260/390/46/15/5 Box 179. Theodore Lapp, "Treysa Conference of Evangelical Church Leaders, held at Hephata Institution, August 27–September 1, 1945," NA 260/390/46/15/5 Box 179.

33. "Not Strangers but Brethren! Report on the Visit of the World Council Delegation to Germany, October 1945," UTS, Leiper Papers, Series 1, Box 4, Folder 4. "Stuttgarter Schuldbekenntnis," October 18–19, 1945, UTS, Leiper Papers, Series 1, Box 4, Folder 4. Samuel McCrea Cavert, "The New Birth of the German Church," CC, December 12, 1945, 1380–1381. Martin Niemöller, "Niemöller about the Question of Guilt," CAC, July 8, 1946, 5–6. On the backlash that Council members received, see: EZA 2/34. Hockenos, *A Church Divided*, 84–90. Armen Boyens, "Das Stuttgarter Schuldbekenntnis vom 19 Oktober 1945. Entstehung und Bedeutung," *Vierteljahrhefte für Zeitgeschichte* 29 (1971): 374–397.

34. Sylvester Michelfelder, quoted in *Die evangelische Kirche*, xxxix. Herman, *The Rebirth of the German Church*, 145–146. Arthur Cotter, "Report on the Visit of the Delegation of the British Council of Churches, November 27–December 14, 1945," in *Die evangelische Kirche*, 271. Hockenos, *A Church Divided*, 98.

35. Samuel McCrea Cavert, "Response to the Declaration of the Council of the German Church," WCCA 301.10.3. Bishop G. Bromley Oxnam, "The Nazis Aren't Licked Yet," October 1945, UTS, Leiper Papers, Series 1, Box 4, Folder 4.

36. Herman, *Rebirth*, 156–158. "Reconstruction of Church Organisation," NA 260/390/46/16/5–6, Box 206. "Kirchliches Finanzwesen," August 20, 1945, EZA 2/735. "An die Herren Superintendenten, betrifft: Neuordnung im Kirchensteuerwesen," January 15, 1946, EZA 2/735. "An die Dekanatämter, betr.: Kirchensteuer und freiwilliger Kirchenbeitrag," August 13, 1946, EZA 2/735.

37. "The Council of the Evangelical Church in Germany: Directives for the Restoration of a Professional Clergy Bound by Confessional Tenets," NA 260/390/46/15/5, Box 177. Knappen, *And Call It Peace*, 49, 135–136. "Confessionals Seek to Continue German Church Purification," CC, May 22, 1946, 644–645. "German Churches to Direct Own Denazification," CC, June 19, 1946, 771–772.

38. "To the United States Military Government in Germany Re: Act for the Liberation from National-Socialism and Militarism," April 26, 1946, NA 260/390/46/15/5, Box 199. On the German churches and denazification, see: Clemens Vollnhals, *Evangelische Kirche und Entnazifizoerung, 1945–1949: die Last der nationalsozialistischen Vergangenheit* (Munich: R. Oldenbourg, 1989). Clemens Vollnhals, *Entnazifizierung und Selbstreinigung im Urteil der evangelischen Kirche. Dokumente und Reflexionen 1945–1949* (Munich: Kaiser Verlag, 1989). Clemens Vollnhals, *Entnazifizierung. Politische Säuberung und Rehabilitierung in den veir Besatzungszonen 1945–1949* (Munich: Deutsche Taschenbuch Verlag, 1991). On the broader Protestant attempt to

whitewash the Nazis, see: Ernst Klee, *Persilscheine und falsche Pässe: wie die Kirchen den Nazis halfen* (Frankfurt am Main: Fischer Taschenbuch, 2011).

39. For Wurm's letter and Fisher's address, see Herman, *The Rebirth of the German Church*, 273–279.

40. Herman, *Rebirth*, 107, 120–122. "Army Rule for the German Church," *CC*, April 24, 1946, 518. Henry Pitney van Dusen, "American Rule—In Germany and in Japan," *CAC, February* 4, 1945, 1–2. Reinhold Niebuhr, "A Report on Germany," *CAC*, October 14, 1946, 6–7. Stewart W. Herman, "Kirche und Entnazifizierung im Urteil eines Amerikaners," *Neubau: Blätter für neues Leben aus Wort und Geist* Jahrgang 7, no. 8 (August 1952). For European critiques publicized by American ecumenists, see: Johannes Schattenmann, "Memorandum from Germany," *CAC*, June 23, 1947, 5–7; Emil Brunner, "Germany's Distress," *CAC*, August 4, 1947, 3–5.

41. Herman, *Rebirth*, 100, 257–258, 271. Herman to J. F. Dulles, November 10, 1945, Herman Papers, Box 20.

Chapter 6

1. "Address in Columbus at a Conference of the Federal Council of Churches," March 6, 1946, Harry S. Truman Public Papers, Harry S. Truman Presidential Library. On Truman's theology and spiritual diplomacy, see: Preston, *Sword of the Spirit*, 417–439. Inboden, *Religion and American Foreign Policy*, 105–156.

2. "Battleground Europe," Billy Graham Center Achive, Collection 113, Film 37. On postwar evangelicalism, see: Sutton, *American Apocalypse*, 293–325.

3. On the role of American religion in the outbreak of the Cold War, see: Gunn, *Spiritual Weapons*. Inboden, *Religion and American Foreign Policy*, 29–156. Preston, *Sword of the Spirit*, 411–417. Jonathan Herzog, *The Spiritual-Industrial Complex*.

4. Stewart Herman, "World Council of Churches: Department of Reconstruction and Inter-Church Aid: General German Church Situation," September 1945, WCCA 425/3/8/15. Samuel McCrea Cavert, "Report of a Mission to Germany," September 26, 1945, NA 260/390/46/16/5–6, Box 170. "Aktennotiz über die Besprechung mit Pastor Michelfelder und weitern amerikanischen Vertretern am 3. Dezember 1945," ADE ZB 619. Sylvester Michelfelder, "Report of Dr. SC Michelfelder on his visit to Germany and Alsace, October 15th–25th, 1945," November 7, 1945, WCCA 425/3/335.

5. "To Save Christian Civilization in Europe," *Lutheran Witness*, December 18, 1945, 414. "Appeal to the President," *Lutheran Witness*, January 1, 1946, 6. "Ask Lifting Ban on Clothes to Germans," *CC*, January 28, 1946, 3.

6. On CRALOG and CARE, see: Rachel McCleary, *Global Compassion: Private Voluntary Organizations and U.S. Foreign Policy since 1939* (New York: Oxford University Press, 2009), 53–70. Karl-Ludwig Sommer, *Humanitäre Auslandshilfe als Brücke zu atlantischer Partnerschaft: CARE, CRALOG und die Entwicklung der deutsch-amerikanischen Beziehungen nach Ende des Zweiten Weltkriegs* (Bremen: Selbstverlag des Staatarchives Bremen, 1999).

7. Herman, *Rebirth*, 104, 110.

8. "The German Church View," February 28, 1946, NA 260/390/46/15/5, Box 186. George Kennan, "The Sources of Soviet Conduct," *Foreign Affairs*, July 1947, 566–582. On Kennan's "containment" doctrine, see: Wilson Miscamble, *George F. Kennan and the Making of American Foreign Policy, 1947-1950* (Princeton, NJ: Princeton University Press, 1992). John Lewis Gaddis, *Strategies of Containment: A Critical Appraisal of Postwar American National Security Policy* (New York: Oxford University Press, 1982), 24–52.

9. "Clay to Archer Lerch," September 21, 1945, NA 260/390/46/15/5, Box 179. Clay to Cavert, August 1946, NA 260/390/46/15/5, Box 166. "Draft: For Release to the Religious Press of the United States," NA 260/390/46/15/5, Box 180. Lucius Clay, *Decision in Germany* (New York: Doubleday, 1950), 305. "Liaison Representatives from U.S. Churches," NA 260/390/46/15/5, Box 166. Truman to Cavert, June 28, 1946, NA 260/390/46/15/5, Box 180.

10. Truman to Pius XII, August 11, 1948, Harry S. Truman Presidential Library, Myron Taylor Papers, Box 1. Clay to Taylor, September 15, 1947, Harry S. Truman Presidential Library, Myron Taylor Papers, Box 1.

11. Herman, *It's Your Souls We Want*, 206. G. Bromley Oxnam, *On This Rock: An Appeal for Christian Unity* (New York: Harper and Brothers, 1951), 77. "Is the Cold War a Holy War?," *CC*, January 11, 1950, 39–41. See also: Preston, *Sword of the Spirit*, 413–414. John McGreevy, *Catholicism and American Freedom* (New York: W. W. Norton, 2003).

12. Ewart Turner, "German Churches in the Crucible," *CC*, February 6, 1946, 173–174. Samuel McCrea Cavert, "What Hope for Germany," *CC*, October 23, 1946, 1274–1276. "Laien schaffen Gemeinde," *Mitteilungen aus dem Hilfswerk*, Nummer 18, September 1948.

13. Aloysius Muench, "National Catholic Welfare Conference: A Brief Survey, The Church in Germany," 1947, Catholic University of America Archives (CUAA), Aloysius Muench Papers, Box 49, Folder 4. Aloysius Muench, "Begrüßungsansprache Bischofzkonferenz Fulda, Aug. 19, 1947," CUAA, Muench Papers, Box 42, Folder 16. Boarman to Muench, October 1, 1951, CUAA, Office of the General Secretary Papers, Box 38, Folder 17. Aloysius Muench, "Problems Old and New in Germany: A Brief Report, Fall 1950," CUAA, Muench Papers, Box 49, Folder 7. Aloysius Muench, "For Christ's Sake: A New Social Order" (Lent 1948), University of Notre Dame Archives, Drop File Collection, 2/14. On American Catholicism and democracy, see: John McGreevy, *Catholicism and American Freedom* (New York: W.W. Norton, 2003). For a broader discussion of postwar German Catholicism, see: Ruff, *Wayward Flock*. Ruff, *The Battle for the Catholic Past*.

14. "Religious Affairs," *Monthly Report of the Military Governor* 44 (1949): 47. "Anti-Semitism on Rise in Germany," *The Jewish Exponent*, May 20, 1949, 22. "Begegnung mit Leo Baeck," *Aufbau*, July 13, 1945, 1. Charlotte Weber, "Jews in Germany," *Jewish Advocate*, March 31, 1949, 6.

15. "Liaison Representative Between the World Council of Churches, Geneva, and the Protestant and Non-Roman Catholic Churches of the U.S. Zone," NA 260/390/46/46/15/5, Box 166. "Minutes–September 1946," NA RG 260, Allied Religious Affairs

Committee, 46/11. Frank Keating to Willem Visser 't Hooft, April 2, 1947, NA 260/390/46/15/5, Box 166. Keating to Cavert, May 22, 1947, NA 260/390/46/15/5, Box 166.

16. The Federal Council of Churches, *A Statement on Soviet-American Relations* (Samford, CT: Overbrook Press, 1946). On the ecumenical struggle to forge a foreign policy consensus, see: Inboden, *Religion and American Foreign Policy*, 29–62.

17. "Protestants Plan for Peace," *LIFE*, March 18, 1946, 31–36. John Foster Dulles, "Thoughts on Soviet Foreign Policy and What to Do about It," *LIFE*, June 3, 1946, 112–126; June 10, 1946, 118–130. John Foster Dulles, "A Policy of Boldness," *LIFE*, May 19, 1952, 146–157. On Dulles and rollback, see: Preston, *Sword of the Spirit*, 440–464. Inboden, *Religion and American Foreign Policy*, 226–256.

18. Niebuhr, "The Fight for Germany," *LIFE*, October 21, 1946. "U.S. Is Seen Losing Contest in Germany; Truman Urged to Allow Production There," *NYT*, June 16, 1947, A2.

19. Telegram Cable to Sec. State Washington, NA 260/390/46/15/5, Box 180. "Cultural Objectives of U.S. Military Government," NA 260/390/36/15/5, Box 167. On this transition in occupation policy, see: Tent, *Mission on the Rhine*, 254–311. Thaddeus, *Civilizing the Enemy*, 149–195.

20. Henry Smith Leiper, "Is There a Conspiracy of Silence on German Anti-Nazi Resistance?," *CAC*, March 4, 1946, 1–2. Hockenos, *Then They Came for Me*, 189–190.

21. "A Prophetic Voice Hitler Tried to Silence Speaks after 8 Years in Prison," WCCA 301/43/26/2. Matthew Hockenos, "Martin Niemöller, the Cold War, and His Embrace of Pacifism, 1945-1955," *Kirchliche Zeitgeschichte* (October 2014): 87–101. Hockenos, *Then They Came for Me*, 187–210.

22. "Pastor Niemöller at Seattle," *CC*, December 18, 1946, 1524. "Treysa 1947: Kirchenversammlung der Evangelischen Kirche in Deutschland am 5/6.6.1947," EZA 2/42.

23. "Bericht über meine Reise nach den Vereinigten Staaten von Pastor D. Martin Niemöller," June 5, 1947, EZA 2/42. Hockenos, *Then They Came for Me*, 206.

24. "Bericht über meine Reise nach den Vereinigten Staaten von Pastor D. Martin Niemöller," June 5, 1947, EZA 2/42. "Treysa 1947: Kirchenversammlung der Evangelischen Kirche in Deutschland am 5/6.6.1947," EZA 2/42.

25. "Feted in 15 Cities, Berlin Prelate met 3 US Cardinals, 11 Archbishops, 40 Bishops," March 24, 1947, NCWC News Service, Diözesanarchiv Berlin (DAB) V/16-10. "Von Preysing talks on Nazis; Stresses Suffering and Want in Germany," *New York Sun*, February 14, 1947, DAB V/16-9. "Von Preysing Here to Visit US: Anti-Nazi Bishop of Berlin Brings Thanks for Americans for Relief Aid," New York City Sun, February 13, 1947, DAB V/16-9. "Introduction of His Eminence Konrad Cardinal von Preysing," University of Notre Dame Archives, Department of Information Services, 115/65.

26. "Von Preysing Goes Home," *NYT*, March 26, 1947, DAB V/16-9. "Cardinal Flays Dictatorship," *San Francisco Call-Bulletin*, February 27, 1947, DAB V/16-9. "German Cardinal Visiting Buffalo, Lauds Good Deeds," DAB V/16-9. "Gov. Warren Greets German Cardinal," DAB V/16-9.

27. "Von Preysing talks on Nazis; Stresses Suffering and Want in Germany," *New York Sun*, February 14, 1947, DAB V/16–9. "Berlin Cardinal to End Visit Here Tomorrow," *Washington DC Star*, March 16, 1947, DAB V/16–9. "Compassion Beseeched for European Peoples: Berlin Cardinal Asks Charity and Assails Totalitarianism," *Dubuque Iowa Telegraph Herald*, March 5, 1947, DAB V/16–9. "Text of Cardinal von Preysing's Address at Welcome in Dubuque," DAB V/16–9.

28. L. W. Goebel to Martin Niemöller, March 8, 1948, EZA 6/7027. Herman, *Report from Christian Europe*, 163. Otto Dibelius, "Wir warten auf Euch!," Evangelisches Landeskirchliches Archiv Berlin (ELAB) 603/A7.1.I.

29. ELAB 603/A7–1.1. Brennan, *The Politics of Religion*, 12. Otto Dibelius, *Der Tagesspiegel*, May 1946. "Germans Need Foreign Aid, Cardinal Holds," March 16, 1947, DAB V/16–9; "Preysing Asserts Family Life Big Need for Europe," *Muncie Press*, February 26, 1947, DAB V/16–9. "Bishop Dibelius Asks Germans to Fight Tyranny," *CAC*, June 7, 1948, 78.

For a broader overview of German Protestantism's relationship to democracy, see: Kurt Nowak, "Protestantismus und Demokratie in Deutschland: Aspekte der politischen Moderne," in Martin Greschat and Jochen-Christoph Kaiser, eds., *Christentum und Demokratie im 20. Jahrhundert* (Stuttgart: W. Kohlhammer, 1992). Maria Mitchell, *The Origins of Christian Democracy: Politics and Confession in Modern Germany* (Ann Arbor: University of Michigan Press, 2006), 33–55.

30. Eleanor Roosevelt, "My Day: Mrs. Roosevelt on Clergymen from Germany; Wonders Why Religious Groups Must Bring Such Visitors," February 21, 1947, *St. Louis Post-Dispatch*, DAB V/16–9. "Cardinal Preysing's Visit to America," *New York PM*, March 12, 1947, DAB V/16–9. Karl Barth, "Niemöller's Offer to Fight," *The Watchman-Examiner*, February 22, 1948, WCCA 301/43/26/4.

31. "Play Fair with Niemoeller!," WCCA 301/43/26/2. Henry Smith Leiper, "This Man Niemoeller," WCCA, 30/43/26/2. "Mrs. Roosevelt Inflammatory Says Catholic Leader," March 6, 1947, *Armonk Sun*, DAB V/16–9.

32. "Long-Range Policy Statement for German Re-Education: U.S. Policy on German Activities," NA 260/390/46/15/5, Box 199. "Introducing You to the GYA Program," NA 260/390/46/15/5, Box 199. Bachmann to Empie, December 8, 1948, NA 260/390/46/15/5, Box 178. Elizabeth Lam, "German Youth to America," *CC*, December 22, 1948, 1396–1398.

33. Conn to Lam, January 29, 1949, NA 290/360/46/15/5, Box 199. "Harpprecht," January 5, 1949, NA 260/390/36/15/5, Box 178. "An die amerikanische Militärregierung," October 20, 1949, NA 260/390/36/15/5, Box 200. Alfons Fleischmann, "Bericht über die Studienreise," September 1949, NA 260/390/36/15/5, Box 200.

34. On Higgins NCWC work, see: "The Catholic Social Movement in Europe," July 25, 1944, CUAA, United States Conference of the Catholic Bishops Social Action Department (USCCB SAD), Box 13, Folder 10. George Higgins, "Address at Katholikentag," August 31, 1949, CUAA, USCCB SAD, Box 48, Folder 23. George Higgins, "Reports and Recommendations," August 23, 1949, CUAA, USCCB, Office of General Secretary Papers, Box 39, Folder 2.

On the Lutheran mission, see: Olson to Behnken, July 22, 1948, NA 260/390/46/15/5, Box 182. "Meeting of American and German Lutheran Theologians at Bad Boll, Wuerttemberg, June 23 to July 25, 1948," NA 260/390/46/15/5, Box 182. "Concerning Request of Lutheran Church, Missouri Synod to Send Fifty Educational Workers to Germany," February 6, 1948, NA 260/390/46/15/5, Box 182. Lawrence Meyer, "Our Share in the Rebuilding of Europe," *Lutheran Witness*, May 8, 1945, 51.

For studies on how the world wars shaped American Lutheranism, see: Clifford Nelson, *Lutherans in North America* (Minneapolis: Fortress Press, 1980). Mark Granquist, *Lutherans in America* (Minneapolis: Augsburg Fortress, 2015). James Strasburg, "Reviving the Heartland: American Lutherans, Postwar Internationalism, and the Crisis of German Protestantism, 1940-1949," *Journal of the Lutheran Historical Conference* 5 (2015): 62–84.

35. "12,000 at Garden in Buchman Rally," *NYT*, May 15, 1939, 1. "M.R.A. Bowl Rally Draws Thousands," *Los Angeles Times*, July 20, 1939, 1. "Moral Rearmament Backed by Governors of 29 States," *Los Angeles Times*, July 17, 1939, 1. DeWitt MacKenzie, "End of Christianity was Hitlerian Goal," December 10, 1945, Syracuse University Library and Archive (SULA), DeWitt McKenzie Papers. Steven Schroeder, *To Forget It All and Begin Again: Reconciliation in Occupied Germany, 1944–1954* (Toronto: University of Toronto Press, 2013), 112–119.

36. William Ward Ayer, "Will Atheism Conquer Europe," *DM*, June 1946. Hyman Appelman, "The Third World War: Will Russia Fight?," *SL*, September 27, 1946.

37. Louis Patmont, "Europe Faces Darkest Christmas," *DM*, December 1946; "Dr. Patmont Report," *DM*, January 1947.

38. Hyman Appelman, "American Issues," *SL*, June 13, 1946. Patmont, "Europe Faces Darkest Christmas." "Dr. Patmont Report."

39. Carpenter, *Revive Us Again*, 168–169. For a helpful introduction to Youth for Christ, see: Joel Carpenter, ed., *The Youth for Christ Movement and Its Pioneers* (New York: Garland, 1988).

40. Torrey Johnson, "Accepting the Challenge," July 28, 1945, First Annual Conference of Youth for Christ, Billy Graham Center Archives (BGCA), CN 285, Box 28, Folder 5 (emphasis original). "Youth for Christ International Going to Europe . . . With the Gospel!," 1946, BGCA.

41. Johnson, "Accepting the Challenge."

42. Torrey Johnson, "The Challenge of the Future for Youth for Christ," June 16, 1945, BGCA, CN 285, Box 28, Folder 5. Oswald Smith, "The Miracle of Youth for Christ in Europe," *The People's Magazine* (First Quarter, 1949), BGCA, CN 48, Box 16, Folder 21. Torrey Johnson, "Why Is Youth for Christ Going into Germany?," April 1947, BGCA, CN 285, Box 28, File 5.

43. Johnson, "Accepting the Challenge." Johnson, "Why Is Youth for Christ Going into Germany."

44. Johnson to Maddox, May 1, 1947, BGCA, CN 285, Box 27, Folder 13. Torrey Johnson, "Progress Report on Youth for Christ Movement in Germany," BGCA, CN 285, Box 28, Folder 5.

45. "YFCI Representatives News Letter #3," May 2, 1947, BGCA, CN 285, Box 28, Folder 5. Torrey Johnson, "Message Delivered by Dr. Torrey Johnson, Sunday Morning, July 29, 1945 in the Billy Sunday Tabernacle, Winona Lake, Indiana"—"God is in it!" BGCA, CN 48, Box 9, Folder 4.

On the role of the American military chaplaincy during this era, see: Stahl, *Enlisting Faith*, 134–164. Loveland, *America Evangelicals and the U.S. Military*.

46. "Youth for Christ World Congress on Evangelism," BGCA, CN 285, Box 24, Folder 10. Johnson to Niemöller, May 23, 1945, BGCA, CN 285, Box 26, Folder 5. Niemöller to Johnson, September 9, 1945, BGCA, CN 285, Box 26, Folder 5. Torrey Johnson, "Progress Report on Youth for Christ Movement in Germany," BGCA, CN 285, Box 28, Folder 5. Gray to Johnson, September 17, 1946, BGCA, CN 285, Box 25, Folder 6. Duffett to Youth for Christ, April 22, 1947, BGCA, April 22, 1947, CN 285, Box 25, Folder 6. Fisher to Johnson, February 21, 1947, BGCA, CN 285, Box 26, Folder 6. Bill Zulker, "Frankfurt Germany Youth for Christ," BGCA, Accession 10–86. *Frankfurt Youth for Christ News*, 2, no. 1, May 1947, BGCA, CN 285, Box 45, File 5. Hanisch to Johnson, undated, BGCA, CN 285, Box 26, Folder 5. Diezel to Johnson, January 23, 1947, BGCA, CN 285, Box 26, Folder 5.

47. Rockford, IL YFC Telegram, March 19, 1946, BGCA, CN 285, Box 45, Folder 4. Owosso, MI YFC Telegram, March 15, 1946, BGCA, CN 285, Box 45, Folder 4. Johnson to Niemöller, May 23, 1945, BGCA, CN 285, Box 26, Folder 5. Preston, *Sword of the Spirit*, 435.

48. Torrey Johnson, "Progress Report on Youth for Christ Movement in Germany," BGCA, CN 285, Box 28, Folder 5. Duffett to Youth for Christ, April 22, 1947, BGCA, April 22, 1947, CN 285, Box 25, Folder 6. Hanisch to Johnson, undated, BGCA, CN 285, Box 26, Folder 5. Diezel to Johnson, January 23, 1947, BGCA, CN 285, Box 26, Folder 5.

49. "Johnson to Commanding General of EUCOM," May 20, 1947, NA 260/390/46/15/ 5, Box 199. "Hilfswerk Circular Letter Concerning Youth for Christ," May 30, 1947, BGCA, CN 285, Box 26, File 5. Torrey Johnson, "Will the German Nation Be Lost for God?," BGCA, CN 285, Box 25.

50. Torrey Johnson, "Sermon at Calvary Baptist Church," May 25, 1947, BGCA, CN 285, Box 26, Folder 7. Johnson to Commanding General, May 20, 1947, BGCA, CN 285, Box 27, Folder 13. Johnson to Maddox, May 1, 1947, BGCA, CN 285, Box 27, Folder 13.

51. Torrey Johnson, "Youth for Christ Head Repudiates Bias Charge," BGCA, CN 285, Box 25, Folder 12. Gerald L. K. Smith, "America First Party Letter," April 17, 1946, BGCA, CN 285, Box 25, Folder 12. Larry Asman, "Christian Youth for America," April 22, 1946, BGCA, CN 285, Box 25, Folder 12. *Persecuted Preachers* (1946), MSU RC.

52. "Flash Sheet Newsletter," March 4, 1948, BGCA, Collection 165, Box 1, Folder 49. Harold Ockenga, "This Is Our Problem," *Moody Monthly*, November 1947. "Resolutions Adopted by the 8th Annual NAE Convention," April 21, 1950, BGCA, Collection 20, Box 67, Folder 9.

Chapter 7

1. "Foreign Aid Urged on Spiritual Basis," *NYT*, November 19, 1947. "The Churches and the European Recovery Program," UTS, Commission on a Just and Durable Peace, Box 2, Folder 2. Stewart Herman, "A Marshall Plan for the Churches," *Golden Rule Fellowship*, Winter 1947, 10–11. Herman, *Report from Christian Europe*, 12–13.

2. "Foreign Aid Urged on Spiritual Basis," *NYT*, November 19, 1947. "The Churches and the European Recovery Program," UTS, Commission on a Just and Durable Peace, Box 2, Folder 2. On the Marshall Plan and its place in the early Cold War, see: Benn Steil, *The Marshall Plan: Dawn of the Cold War* (New York: Simon and Schuster, 2018). James Patterson, *Grand Expectations: The United States, 1945–1974* (New York: Oxford University Press, 1996), 127–133. Geir Lundestad, "Empire by Invitation: The United States and Western Europe, 1945–1952," *Journal of Peace Research* 23, no. 3 (1986): 263–277.

3. Herman, "A Marshall Plan for the Churches."

4. On the cultural and imperial history of the Marshall Plan, see: Odd Arne Westad, *The Cold War: A World History* (New York: Basic Books, 2017), 209–211. Victoria De Grazia, *Irresistible Empire: America's Advance through Twentieth-Century Europe* (Cambridge, MA: Harvard University Press, 2005). Lundestad, "Empire by Invitation." Reinhold Wagnleitner, *Coca-Colonization and the Cold War: The Cultural Mission of the US in Austria after the Second World War* (Chapel Hill: University of North Carolina Press, 1994).

5. "Hoover Says German Civilization Dying," *CC*, March 12, 1947, 324. J. Hutchinson Cockburn, "The Renewal of Church Life in Europe—The Next Four Years," Report of the Director on the First Meeting of the Executive Committee, Department of Reconstruction and Inter-Church Aid, December 18–19, 1947, ADE, ZB 335. "Foreign Aid Urged on Spiritual Basis," *NYT*, November 19, 1947. Reinhold Niebuhr, "American Power and European Health," *CAC*, June 9, 1947, 1.

6. "Zone Merger is a Hopeful Sign," *CC*, January 8, 1947, 52. "The Churches and the European Recovery Program," UTS, Commission on a Just and Durable Peace, Box 2, Folder 2.

7. Harry Truman, "Address on Foreign Policy at the Navy Day Celebration," October 27, 1845, in *Public Papers of the Presidents of the United States: Harry S. Truman, April 12 to December 31, 1945* (Washington, DC: United States Government Printing Office, 1961), 433. For this interpretation of West Germany's status, see: Thomas Schwartz, *America's Germany: John McCloy and the Federal Republic of Germany* (Cambridge, MA: Harvard University Press, 1991).

8. Niebuhr, "The German Problem." Stewart Herman, "The Mission Field in Europe," WCCA, 425/3/29. Herman, *Rebirth*, 155. "Projects VI: Lay Leadership," WCCA, 425/1/66. "Report of Ecumenical Youth Workers in Germany," WCCA, 301/23/22/4.

9. Stewart Herman, "The Mission Field in Europe," WCCA, 425/3/29.

10. "Emergency Committee for German Protestantism: Save German Protestantism!," ADE, ZB 387.

11. Herman, "Report on Baden, July 30–August 5, 1945," WCCA 425.3.2. "A Staggering Legacy," April 20, 1948, WCCA 425.3.57. "Notkirchen," January 1948, WCCA, 452.3.062. "Wooden Churches," WCCA 425.3.001. "An das Reconstruction Department im Weltrat der Kirchen," February 18, 1946, WCCA 425.3.57. "Rebuilding," 1948, WCCA 425.1.66.

12. Herman, "A Marshall Plan for the Churches." Stewart Herman, "An American's View of the European Churches," February 7 and 8, 1947, Bossey Switzerland, Herman Papers, Box 20. Stewart Herman, "Chapter 1: The Mission Field in Europe," WCCA, 425.3.029.

13. "Die Kirchenbaracke der evang. Brüdergemeinde in Berlin," April 27, 1948, WCCA 425.3.57.

14. "Die 48 Notkirchen," 1949, WCCA 425.3.57. "Mitteilungen aus dem Hilfswerk der evangelischen Kirchen in Deutschland," Nummer 1, April 1947, Zentralbüro Stuttgart, WCCA, 452.3.058.

15. "Notkirchen," January 1948, WCC Archive, 452.3.62. "Drei Jahre Hilfswerk," WCCA 301.43.14/7.

16. "Dedication of the Rubble Church at Pforzheim," WCC Archive 425.3.62. "Lazarus, Come Forth," 1949, WCCA 425.3.6. "Dedication of the Rubble Church at Pforzheim," 1948, WCCA 425.3.62.

17. "Die 48 Notkirchen," WCCA 425.3.57. "Mitteilungen aus dem Hilfswerk," Nummer 8, November 1947, WCCA 452.3.058. "Report on Condition of Emergency Church, Ludwigshafen," June 15, 1948, WCCA 425.3.62. "Report from Heinrich Schmitz," May 5, 1949, WCCA 425.3.62.

18. "The Reconstruction of the Reformed Church at Barmen, Germany," March 22, 1946, WCCA 425.3.57. "Denkschrift des Presbyteriums der evang.-reformierten Gemeinde Barmen," February 8, 1946, WCCA 425.3.57.

19. "Bibles for Germany: A Report of Achievements," ADE, ZB 387. In total, the Society sent to Germany alone one million New Testaments, 368,000 full Bibles, and 775,000 gospels during the occupation.

20. "This Is Church Reconstruction," July 1947, WCCA 425.3.57. "Die 48 Notkirchen," WCCA 425.3.57.

21. "Notkirchen," January 1948, WCCA 452.3.62. "Report on Mannheim-Waldhof Church Dedication," May 1949, WCCA 425.3.62. "Report to the Reconstruction Department of the WCC on the Laying of the Cornerstone of the Evangelical Church at the Gartenstadt Mannheim-Waldhof," September 19, 1948, WCCA 425.3.062.

22. "Mitteilungen aus dem Hilfswerk," Nummer 8, November 1947, WCCA 452.3.58. *Jahresbericht des Hilfswerks der EKD* (Stuttgart: Evangelisches Verlagswerk, 1951).

23. Eugen Gerstenmaier, "Church in Action: Protestant Relief Work in Germany," 1947, ADE, ZB 11. Samuel McCrea Cavert, "Report of a Mission to Germany," September 26, 1946, NA 260/390/46/16/5–6, Box 170.

24. "Bericht über die 31 Notkirchen aus der Spende der Amerikanischen Sektion des Lutherischen Weltbundes," March 1, 1949, WCCA 425.3.57. On material relief in the Soviet zone, see: Brennan, *The Politics of Religion*, 135–164.

25. "Bericht über die 31 Notkirchen aus der Spende der Amerikanischen Sektion des Lutherischen Weltbundes," March 1, 1949, WCCA 425.3.57. "Fortresses of Faith," Hilfswerk Bulletin, 1949 no. 20, WCCA 452.3.58; "Gemeindezentren 1949/50," WCCA 452.3.58; "Request No. 223: Spiritual Reconstruction in Germany: Congregational Centers for the Lutheran Diaspora," WCCA 452.3.58. On material relief in the Soviet zone, see: Brennan, *The Politics of Religion*, 135–164.

26. *New York Staats-Zeitung und Herold*, April 11, 1948, ADE, ZB 387. "Hilfswerk Director Here to Thank America," *The St. Louis Lutheran*, April 3, 1948, 9, ADE, ZB 387. "Aus Amerika zurück," "Mitteilungen aus dem Hilfswerk," Nummer 15 Juni 1948, WCCA 452/3/48. "Hilfswerk Leader Thanks America," April 13, 1938, NA 260/390/46/15/5, Box 177. Eugen Gerstenmaier, "Kirche in Aktion," 1947, ADE, ZB 11.

27. "Hilfswerk Leader Thanks America," April 13, 1938, NA 260/390/46/15/5, Box 177.

28. Herman, *Rebirth*, 155. J. Hutchinson Cockburn, "The Renewal of Church Life in Europe—The Next Four Years," Report of the Director on the First Meeting of the Executive Committee, Department of Reconstruction and Inter-Church Aid, December 18–19, 1947, ADE, ZB 335.

29. "Projects VI: Lay Leadership," WCCA 425.1.66. *Evangelism: A Survey and Study of Modern Methods of Presenting the Gospel*, May 1947, No. 5, Spiritual Status of the Church in the Post-War World (WCC Commission), ADE, ZB 334. Stewart Herman, "The Mission Field in Europe," WCCA 425.3.29. See also: J. H. Oldham, "A Responsible Society," in *The Church and the Disorder of Society: The Amsterdam Assembly Series* (New York: Harper and Brothers, 1948).

30. Herman to Olsen, July 11, 1946, NA 260/390/46/15/5, Box 199. Herman, *Report from Christian Europe*, 23–27. Reinold von Thadden-Trieglaff, "Deutsche Evangelische Woche 1949 in Hannover," June 22, 1949, EZA 71/86/1. NA RG 260, Box 881, Folder 209.3. E. Theodore Bachmann, "Laymen Rouse German Church," *The Christian Century*, July 11, 1951, 818–820. Niebuhr, quoted in Eberhard Müller, *Widerstand und Verständigung: Fünfzig Jahre Erfahrungen Kirche und Gesellschaft, 1933–1983* (Stuttgart: Calwer Verlag, 1987), 91. On the academies and Kirchentag, see: Rulf Jürgen Treidel, *Evangelische Akademien im Nachkriegsdeutschland: Gesellschaftspoliti sches Engagement in kirchlicher Öffentlichkeitsverantwortung* (Stuttgart: Kohlhammer Verlag, 2001). Springhart, *Aufbrüche zu neuen Ufern*, 175–192. Benjamin Carl Pearson, "Faith and Democracy: Political Transformations at the German Protestant Kirchentag, 1949–1969" (PhD diss., University of North Carolina, 2007).

31. "Training Centers for Youth Leaders in the Eastern Zone of Germany," August 10, 1953, WCCA 425.3.57. "Youth," WCCA, 425.3.57. "Training Centers for Youth Leaders in the Eastern Zone of Germany," WCCA 425.3.57. Project 7: Youth Work," WCCA, 425.1.66. "Report of Ecumenical Youth Workers in Germany," WCCA 301.43.22. "Report by Roswell P. Barnes to the Committee on Cooperation with the Churches in Europe, 15 June 1949," PHS, National Council of Churches RG 8, Series VII: Church World Service, Box 82. See also: Martin Hall, "German Youth—A Lost Generation?," CC, September 27, 1944, 1098–1100. Iain Wilson, "German Churches Fail Youth," CC, March 30, 1949, 397–398.

32. Herman, *Rebirth*, 179–180. Niebuhr, "The Death of a Martyr," 6–7. "Bonhoeffer—Book of Martyrs," Seminary Archives, Herman Papers, Box 11.

33. Herbert Krimm, "Aufzeichnung," November 8, 1946, ADE, ZB 1334; Bush to Krimm, December 19, 1946, ADE, ZB 1334. Herman to Krimm, June 21, 1947, ADE ZB 1334.

34. Brose to Hahn, January 6, 1952, ADE, ZB 1575. Ganz to Hahn, September 30, 1955, ADE, ZB 1576. Ganz to Schmidt-Lauber, September 30, 1955, ADE, ZB 1576. Werner Otto Köstlin, "Bericht über meinen Aufenthalt in den USA," November 1949, ADE, ZB 1575.

35. Hans-Wilhelm Kirchofer, "Bericht über das Leben in den amerikanischen Gemeinden und über den Studienverlauf an den theologischen Seminaren," March 1952, ADE, ZB 1575. Eva Ganz, "Letter to the Department of Inter-Church Aid and Service to Refugees," September 28, 1955, ADE, ZB 1576. Jasper to Hahn, February 11, 1952, ADE, ZB 1575. "Bericht über meine Erfahrungen während des Studiums in den USA," February 1955, ADE, ZB 1576. Peter Stolt, "Bericht über Erfahrungen eines Jahres als Stipendiat des Weltkirchenrates in Des Moines, IA," ADE, ZB 1576. Eva Ganz, "Letter to the Department of Inter-Church Aid and Service to Refugees," September 28, 1955, ADE, ZB 1576.

36. Hans-Dietrich Caspary, "Bericht," April 7, 1953, ADE, ZB 1576. Brose to Hahn, January 6, 1952, ADE, ZB 1575. Horst Haefelin, "Bericht an das Zentralbüro der EKiD," ADE, ZB 1576. Erich Rudolph, "Abschrift eines englischen Berichtes an den Weltkirchenrat über ein Studienjahr in den Vereinigten Staaten von Amerika," October 1955, ADE, ZB 1576. Karl-Theodor Grashof, "Erster Erfahrungsbericht," February 1954, ADE, ZB 1576.

37. Karl-Theodor Grashof, "Zweiter Erfahrungsbericht," October 1954, ADE, ZB 1576.

38. Herman, *Report from Christian Europe*, 2. "German Christianity Is Changing," *CC*, January 28, 1948, 101.

39. Friedrich Siegmund-Schultze, "Der Christ zwischen Ost und West," EZA 51/QII/L4. Hermann Diem, "Die Kirche zwischen Rußland und Amerika," *Theologische Existenz Heute*, Nummer 10, September 1947, Evangelisches Zentralarchiv Bibliothek, Signatur 4459. Friedrich Siegmund-Schultze, "Der Christ zwischen Ost und West," EZA 51/QII/L4. See also: Heinz-Horst Schrey, "The German Church between Russia and America," *CAC, August* 2, 1948, 107–108.

40. "U.S. Churchmen Urge Agency on World Affairs," *New York Herald Tribune*, August 6, 1946, 19A. "Dulles Discounts Paris Peace Conference," *NYT*, July 30, 1946, 5. O. Frederick Nolde, "The European Christian Mind on World Affairs," January 30, 1948, UTS, Henry van Dusen Papers, Box AA.

41. Reinhold Niebuhr, "God's Order and the Present Disorder of Civilization," October 1947, Yale Divinity School Archives, World Council of Churches Papers, RG 162, Box 3, Folder 15. John Foster Dulles, "Concerning Christian Responsibility in a Changing World," October 1947, Yale Divinity School Archives, WCC Papers, RG 162, Box 3, Folder 17.

42. Karl Barth, "No Christian Marshall Plan," *CC*, December 8, 1948, 1330–1333.

43. "World Council: Communism and Capitalism Both Found Inadequate," *The Living Church* 117 (September 12, 1948): 5–7.

44. *The First Assembly of the World Council of Churches*, 80. Visser 't Hooft, *Memoirs*, 213. Eduard Heimann, "Factors in International Tension," WCCA 24.076/2, 9. John Bennett, "Introductory Statement on 'Toward a Third Way,'" June 1949, WCCA 24.152/I/6, 1. On ecumenical support of the Schuman Plan and French-German integration, as well as the Ecumenical Commission on European Cooperation, see: Lucian Leustean, *The Ecumenical Movement and the Making of the European Community* (New York: Oxford University Press, 2014), 1–51.

45. Carl McIntire, "The Drive for World Socialism through the World Council of Churches," *SL*, February 18, 1949.

46. "Still trying to wreck the Ecumenical Movement," *CC*, November 5, 1947, 1324. "Memo to the American Press," *CC*, August 4, 1948, 774–775. Harold Edward Fey, "Rump Council Meets," *CC*, September, 1, 1948, 895. "Press Misrepresents Fundamentalists," *CC*, November 17, 1948, 1229–1230. "Growth of Sects Alarms Germans," *CC*, July 23, 1948, 760.

47. Schaeffer to Youngs, March 17, 1948, BGCA, CN 285, Box 27, Folder 13. Francis Schaeffer, "An Exmination of the New Modernism," *That Baptist Bulletin*, January 1951, February 1951. On Schaeffer, see: Worthen, *Apostles of Reason*, 209–219.

48. ACCC to Youngs, March 11, 1948, BGCA, CN 285, Box 27, Folder 13. Carl McIntire, "The Drive for World Socialism through the World Council of Churches," *SL*, *February* 18, 1949.

49. Ockenga, "This Is Our Problem," *Moody Monthly*, November 1947. "Bible School Beatenberg Switzerland Bible Home," BGCA, CN 285, Box 25.

50. Billy Graham, quoted in William McLoughlin, *Billy Graham: Revivalist in a Secular Age* (New York: Ronald Press, 1960), 108–109. Carl McIntire, "The Drive for World Socialism through the World Council of Churches," *SL*, February 18, 1949.

51. Carl McIntire, "Bishop Oxnam, Prophet of Marx," *SL*, *May* 29, 1953. Stewart Herman, *The Church in the World Today*, 38. John R. Rice, "Who for President," *SL*, September 24, 1948.

52. Stewart Herman, "The Mission Field in Europe," 1953, WCCA 425/3/029. Herman, *Report from Christian Europe*, 32.

Chapter 8

1. "Battleground Europe," BGCA, Collection 113, Film 37. John Pollock, *The Billy Graham Story: The Authorized Biography* (Grand Rapids, MI: Zondervan, 2003), 77.

   For an overview of Graham's life and times, see: Grant Wacker, *America's Pastor: Billy Graham and the Shaping of a Nation* (New York: Cambridge University Press, 2014). Andrew Finstuen, *Original Sin and Everyday Protestants: The Theology of Reinhold Niebuhr, Billy Graham, and Paul Tillich in an Age of Anxiety* (Chapel Hill: University of North Carolina Press, 2009), 123–154.

2. "A Report to the National Security Council—NSC 68," April 12, 1950, Harry S. Truman Papers, Harry S. Truman Presidential Library, President's Secretary Files. Gaddis, *Strategies of Containment*, 87–124. Melvyn Leffler, *A Preponderance of*

Power: National Security, the Truman Administration, and the Cold War (Stanford, CA: Stanford University Press, 1992).

3. On this transatlantic partnership, see: Stephen Brady, *Eisenhower and Adenauer: Alliance Maintenance under Pressure, 1953-1960* (Lanham, MD: Lexington Books, 2010).

4. For more on these political and ecclesial developments, see David Clay Large, *Germans to the Front: West German Rearmament in the Adenauer Era* (Chapel Hill: University of North Carolina Press, 1996). Claudia Lepp, *Tabu der Einheit? Die Ost-West-Gemeinschaft der evangelischen Christen und die deutsche Teilung, 1945-1969* (Göttingen: Vandenhoeck & Ruprecht, 2005). Claudia Lepp, *Wege in die DDR. West-Ost-Übersiedlungen im kirchlichen Bereich vor dem Mauerbau* (Göttingen: Wallstein, 2015).

5. Eugen Tillinger, "Niemoeller: Germany's Red Dean," *The New Leader*, March 10, 1952, 12-14. American Jewish Committee, *Commentary* 15 (1953): 128. Herman, *Report from Christian Europe*, 172. Martin Niemöller, "No German Rearmament Now," *CC*, March 21, 1951, 367-368. "German Churchmen Push for Unification of Germany," *CC*, November 14, 1951, 1299-1300.

6. Friedrich Siegmund-Schultze, "Against the Remilitarization of Germany," EZA 51/ KII/b2.

7. David Clay Large, *Germans to the Front*, 78-79. For a broader discussion of postwar Catholicism, see: Ruff, *Wayward Flock*; Ruff, *The Battle for the Catholic Past*.

8. "Russia Establishes an East German State," *CC*, October 19, 1949, 1220-1221. "Push West German Rearmament," *CC*, December 21, 1949, 1508. "German Rearmament: Another Intelligence Failure," *CC*, September 27, 1950, 1123. Ewart E. Turner, "East German Church under Pressure," *CC*, September 13, 1950, 1074-1075. Ewart E. Turner, "The Stature of Bishop Dibelius," *CC*, October 11, 1950, 1199-1201. Iain Wilson, "German Churchmen and Rearmament," *CC*, January 10, 1951, 43-44. Douglas Steere, "As Germans See Us," *CC*, May 16, 1951, 610-611. "U.S., Soviets Blamed for World's Tensions," *NYT*, August 3, 1952, 19.

9. Herman, *Report from Christian Europe*, 43, 45, 51, 144, 195-196.

10. Herman, *Report from Christian Europe*, 50-51, 68, 114, 197. On this transition in American ecumenical thought from Christian globalism to Christian nationalism, see also: Edwards, "From a Christian World Community to a Christian America." "This Nation Under God," in *Christian Faith in Action: The Founding of the National Council of Churches in Christ in the United States of America*, ed. Robbins Barstow (New York: National Council of Churches in Christ, 1951). Henry Knox Sherrill, "The Presidential Message," in *Christian Faith in Action*, 143. Hermann Morse, "The Church in the Nation," in *Christian Faith in Action*, 94-95.

11. Herman, *Report from Christian Europe*, 107-121. Stewart Herman, "1951," Herman Personal Diary. See also: "Is the Cold War a Holy War?," *CC*, January 11, 1950, 39-41.

12. Carl McIntire, "Bishop Oxnam, Prophet of Marx," *SL*, May 29, 1953. Carl McIntire, "How Communism is Using the Churches," *SL*, January 8, 1954. Gerald Winrod, *God's Judgments on Russia* (Wichtia, KS: Defender, 1947), MSU RC. Gerald Winrod, *Communism and Corruption at Washington* (Wichita, KS: Defender, 1952). On

the evangelical role in the rise of the "New Right," see: Darren Dochuk, *From Bible Belt to Sunbelt: Plain-folk Religion, Grassroots Politics, and the Rise of Evangelical Conservatism* (New York: W. W. Norton, 2010). Lisa McGirr, *Suburban Warriors: The Origins of the New American Right* (Princeton, NJ: Princeton University Press, 2015).

13. Preston, *Sword of the Spirit*, 450–458.

14. Carl McIntire, "How Communism is Using the Churches," *SL*, January 8, 1954. Gerald Winrod, *The United Nations and the Tower of Babel* (1953), MSU RC. Preston, *Sword of the Spirit*, 465–467.

15. Eisenhower, quoted in *NYT*, December 23, 1952, 16. Dwight Eisenhower, "Message to the National Co-Chairmen," Commission on Religious Organizations, National Conference of Christians and Jews, July 9, 1953. John R. Rice, "Christians Ought to Vote!," *SL*, October 31, 1952. By 1957, 96% of the nation's population identified with a religious tradition; and by 1960, up to 70% of the population claimed membership in a religious congregation. For more on these postwar religious developments, see: Finstuen, *Original Sin and Everyday Protestants*, 1–46. Kruse, *One Nation under God*, 35–66.

16. *Newsweek* 43 (April 5, 1954): 54. "Wooden Churches to Be Built by US Near Iron Curtain," *Daily Boston Globe*, May 31, 1954, 65.

17. "Baron Tells How Americans Helped German Church Rebirth," *Washington Post and Times Herald*, August 10, 1957, B4.

18. "Curtain of Wooden Churches: H. von Royk-Lewinski, as told to Curtis Mitchell," *Washington Post and Times*, April 18, 1954, AW2.

19. "Wooden Churches to Be Built by US Near Iron Curtain," *Daily Boston Globe*, May 31, 1954, 65. John Manners, "One Man Radio Crusade," *Philanthropy* (1952): 43–44.

20. "Wooden Churches to Be Built," 65.

21. "Curtain of Wooden Churches, H. von Royk-Lewinski, as told to Curtis Mitchell," *Washington Post and Times*, April 18, 1954, AW2. Gordon Caroll and Booton Herndon, *Praised and Damned: The Story of Fulton Lewis, Jr.* (Washington, DC: Human Events, 1954). "The Wooden Church Crusade, Inc.," *Daughters of the American Revolution (DAR)*, 88 (1954): 236.

22. "The Wooden Church Crusade, Inc.," *DAR*. Dorothy Parnell, "International Deb Ball Nov. 23," *The Milwaukee Sentinel*, October 2, 1954.

23. Manners, "One Man Radio Crusade."

24. "Wooden Churches to Be Built," 65.

25. Caroline Lawrence Kinzer, *Men, Music, and Mirth* (Pittsburgh, PA: Lauriat Press, 2010), 115. "Wooden Churches to Be Built."

26. "Wooden Church Advertisements," Syracuse University Library University Archives (SUUA), Fulton Lewis Papers, Box 96. "Curtain of Wooden Churches," *Washington Post and Times*, April 18, 1954, AW2.

27. On Fifield and Spiritual Mobilization, see: Kruse, *One Nation*, 12, 27–34. On Peale's life, see: Christopher Lane, *Surge of Piety: Norman Vincent Peale and the Remaking of American Religious Life* (New Haven, CT: Yale University Press, 2016). Carol V. R. George, *God's Salesman: Norman Vincent Peale and the Power of Positive Thinking* (New York: Oxford University Press, 2019).

28. Kruse, *One Nation*, 7–8. American Business Consultants, *Counterattack: The Newsletter of Facts to Combat Communism* (1952), 6–7.

29. Parnell, "International Deb Ball Nov. 23." "Debutante Ball Assists Crusade: First International Fete, at Plaza, Is Benefit for the Wooden Church Drive," *NYT*, November 24, 1954, p. 20.

30. Manners, "One Man Radio Crusade." "Service Club Aids Wooden Church Crusade," *Atlantic Coast News Line* 35, no. 1 (1954). Women's Overseas Service League, *Carry On*, 32–34 (1953): 52–58. "Baron Tells How Americans Helped German Church Rebirth," *Washington Post and Times Herald*, August 10, 1957, B4. The Dartnell Corporation, *Sales Management* 71 (1953): 198. *Newsweek* 43 (April 5, 1954): 54.

31. "Moose Will Aid in Wooden Church Crusade," *The Fraternal Monitor* 63/64 (1952): 17. *Sons of the American Revolution* 48 (1953): 32. "The Wooden Church Crusade, Inc.," *DAR*. American Legion Auxiliary, "Wooden Church Crusade," *National News* 27 (1953): 9; *National News* 28 (1954): 15. Kruse, *One Nation*, 73.

32. "A Word from the President," February 21, 1955, SU Fulton Lewis Jr. Papers, Box 96. "Letter to the Editor from Fulton Lewis Jr.," October 31, 1956, SU Fulton Lewis Jr. Papers, Box 96. *Newsweek* 43 (April 5 1954): 54.

33. "Besuch von Baron von Royk-Lewinski am 25. März, 1955," EZA 200/5/98. "Brief an D.E. Wagner," May 14, 1954, EZA 200/5/98. "Brief an Baron Henning von Royk-Lewinski," July 26, 1954, EZA 200/5/98.

34. "Ihr Schreiben vom 12.9.1955, Holzkirchenkreuzzug," September 16, 1955, ADE, ZB 1379. "Abschrift an Herrn Pastor Trede," September 24, 1955; "Bau einer Kirche in Hengersberg," October 11, 1955. "Ihr Schreiben vom 1.9.1955," October 14, 1955; ADE, ZB 1379. "Noch einmal: Kirchenbau entlang der Zonegrenze?" *Kirche in der Zeit*, Heft 8, August 1954, ADE, ZB 1379.

35. "Letter from Wynn Fairfield," October 12, 1953, WCCA 425.3.57.

36. "An Baron Henning von Royk-Lewinski," July 30, 1956, EZA 200/5/98. "Brief an D. Wagner," June 22, 1955, EZA 200/5/98. "An Gustav Adolf-Werk, betr.: Kirchenbau in Eiterfeld," February 5, 1957. "An E. Wagner," February 11, 1957, EZA 200/5/98.

37. Billy Graham, "We Need Revival," in *Revival in Our Time* (Wheaton, IL: Van Kampen Press, 1950), 72–73.

38. "Billy Graham predigt Waffenbrüderschaft," *Bild Zeitung*, June 24, 1954, BGCA, CN 360, SB 52. On Graham's crusades in Germany, see: Uta Balbier, "Billy Graham in West Germany: German Protestantism between Americanization and Rechristianization, 1954–1970," *Zeithistorische Forschungen/Studies in Contemporary History* 7 (2010): 343–363.

39. "400 Posaunen bei Billy," *Essener Allgemeine Zeitung*, BGCA, CN 360, SB 61.

40. Otto Dibelius, December 1966, BGCA, Collection 506, Box 2, Folder 9. "Billy Graham: Zwölf Ernten im Jahr," *Der Spiegel*, June 23, 1954, ELAB 55/1/190.

41. "Nennt mich nur Billy," *Frankfurt Nachtausgabe*, June 24, 1954, BGCA, CN 360, Scrapbook 52. "Billy Graham ein Schausteller?," *Nacht-Depesche Berlin*; "Heilendes Wunderkind aus Hollywood," *Kasseler Zeitung*, May 25, 1956, BGCA, CN 360, SB 52. "Billy will Europa bekehren: der Kreuzzug William Franklin Grahams kostet Millionen," BGCA, CN 360, Volume 52. "Ein Werbefachmann Gottes," *Düsseldorfer*

Nachrichten; "Er preist die Bible an wie Leute Zahnpasta und Kaugummi," BGCA, CN 360, SB 52. "Billy Graham: Zwölf Ernten im Jahr," *Der Spiegel*, June 23, 1954, Evangelisches Landeskirchliches Archiv in Berlin 55/1/190. "Graham 'verkauft das Evangelium wie Seife': 'Ein Protestantischer Goebbels,'" *Märkische Union*, Potsdam, October 1, 1960, BGCA CN 360, SB 291. "Managertum auf religiösem Gebiet," *Neue Zeitung*, June 29, 1954, ELAB 55/1/190.

42. "Umstrittener Graham: Pfarrer diskutieren seine Methoden," *Frankfurter Allgemeine Zeitung*, July 2, 1955, ELAB 55/1/190. "Das ist kein Gottesdienst mehr, sondern Volksbelustigung," BGCA, CN 360, SB 61. "Battleground Europe."

43. Reinhold Niebuhr, quoted in Mark Silk, "The Rise of the New Evangelicalism," in *Between the Times*, 286. Reinhold Niebuhr, "Differing Views on Billy Graham," *Life*, July 1, 1957, 92. Henry Pitney van Dusen, "Billy Graham," *CC*, April 2, 1956, 40.

44. Gisa Bauer, *Evangelikale Bewegung und evangelische Kirche in der Bundesrepublik Deutschland* (Göttingen: Vandenhoeck & Ruprecht, 2012), 29–30.

45. Billy Graham: Zwölf Ernten im Jahr," *Der Spiegel*, June 23, 1954, ELAB 55/1/190. BGCA, Micro Reel, Volumes 52–58.

46. "Billy schießt unterm Zirkuszelt," BGCA, CN 360, SB 291. *Neue Zeit Sonnabend,* August 7, 1954, ELAB 55/1/190.

47. "Graham für moderne Werbung," *Der Tag*, ELAB 55/1/190. See also: Balbier, "Billy Graham in West Germany," 343–363.

48. "Billy Graham in Berlin: The Tent on the Frontier," *The Presbyterian Outlook* 142, no. 38 (1960): 7. *The Christian* 98, no. 52 (1960): 1165. "Billy Graham Chided: East German Theologian Said to Decry U.S. Evangelist," *NYT*, October 2, 1960, 30.

Epilogue

1. Stewart Herman, "Christian Responsibility and International Affairs," March 9, 1963, PHS, NCC Records, RG 17, Box 5, Folder 8.

2. Brian Stanley, *Christianity in the Twentieth Century: A World History*, 366.

3. "Witness to an Ancient Truth," *TIME* April 20, 1962. "Barth is Honored by U. of Chicago," *NYT*, April 28, 1962, 26.

4. Sydney Gruson, "Swiss Theologian Assails the West," *NYT*, January 19, 1959. Karl Barth, "Recapitulation Number Three," *The CC*, January 1, 1960, 72–76.

5. "Our Prisons Shock Dr. Karl Barth," *The Hartford Courant*, May 8, 1962. George Dugan, "Barth is Shocked by U.S. Prisons," *NYT*, May 2, 1962, 39. "Barth in America," *Newsweek*, April 23, 1962, 64–65. Barth, quoted in Eberhard Busch, *Karl Barth: His Life from Letters and Autobiographical Texts* (Eugene, OR: Wipf and Stock, 2005), 459. On Barth's US tour, see also: Jessica DeCou, "The First Community: Barth's American Prison Tours," in Clifford Anderson and Bruce McCormack, eds., *Karl Barth and the Making of Evangelical Theology: A Fifty Year Perspective* (Grand Rapids, MI: William B. Eerdmans, 2015), 67–90.

6. Hockenos, *Then They Came for Me*, 235–262.

7. Stewart Herman, *The Church in the World Today* (Philadelphia: Muhlenberg Press, 1950), 56–58, 73. Herman, *Report from Christian Europe*, 160. On these shifts in Jewish-Christian relations, see: Carenen, *The Fervent Embrace*, 1–92. On Herman's work with refugees and resettlement, in particular in Latin America, see: Stewart Herman, "Lutheran Service to Refugees," *Lutheran Quarterly*; Reuben Baetz, *Five Year Report of LWF Service to Refugees* (Geneva: Lutheran World Federation, 1952). Stewart Herman, "Latin America: Get In or Get Out?," in Jacob Meyers, ed., *Theological and Missionary Studies in Memory of John Aberly* (Gettysburg, PA: Times and News Publishing Company, 1965).

8. Herman, quoted in Sutton, *Double Crossed*, 335. On the "boomerang" effect, see: Hollinger, *Protestants Abroad*, 1–23.

9. Wade Coggins, "What's Behind the Idea of a Missionary Moratorium," *Christianity Today* (*CT*), November 22, 1974, 8.

10. "Witness to an Ancient Truth," *TIME*. McIntire, quoted in *Karl Barth and the Making of Evangelical Theology*, 3.

11. Graham, *Just As I Am*, 696–697. "Otto Dibelius: Christ against the Tyrants," *CT*, July 5, 1963.

12. On Graham's national and global legacy, see: Grant Wacker, *America's Pastor: Billy Graham and the Shaping of a Nation* (Cambridge, MA: Belknap Press of Harvard University, 2014).

13. Carl Henry and W. Stanley Mooneyham, *One Race, One Gospel, One Task: World Congress on Evangelism, Berlin 1966, Official Reference Volumes: Papers and Reports* (Minneapolis: World Wide Publications, 1967). William Martin, *A Prophet with Honor: The Billy Graham Story* (New York: W. W. Morrow, 1991), 325–337. Uta Balbier, "The World Congress on Evangelism 1966 in Berlin: US Evangelicalism, Cultural Dominance, and Global Challenges," *Journal of American Studies* 51, no. 4 (2017): 1171–1196.

14. Billy Graham, "Why Lausanne?," in J. D. Douglas, ed., *Let the Earth Hear His Voice: Official Reference Volume, Papers, and Responses; International Congress on World Evangelization, Lausanne, Switzerland* (Minneapolis: World Wide Publications, 1975).

On Lausanne, see: McAlister, *The Kingdom*, 85–102; Darren Dochuk, "Lausanne '74 and American Evangelicalism's Latin Turn," in Heath Carter and Laura Rominger Porter, eds., *Turning Points in the History of American Evangelicalism* (Grand Rapids, MI: William B. Eerdmans, 2017), 247–281.

On the rise of evangelical internationalism, see: McAlister, *The Kingdom of God Has No Borders*. Swartz, *Facing West*. David Kirkpatrick, *A Global Gospel of the Poor: Global Social Christianity and the Latin American Evangelical Left* (Philadelphia: University of Pennsylvania Press, 2019).

15. Worthen, *Apostles of Reason*, 209–219. On the rise of the Christian Right, see: Daniel K. Williams, *God's Own Party: The Making of the Christian Right* (New York: Oxford University Press, 2012).

16. On the history of Protestantism in the German Democratic Republic, see: Sean Brennan, *The Politics of Religion*, 165–194. John Conway, "The Stasi and the

Churches: Between Coercion and Comprise in East German Protestantism, 1949–89," *Journal of Church and State* 36, no. 4 (1994): 738. Gerhard Besier, *Der SED-Staat und die Kirche. Der Weg in die Anpassung* (Munich: W. Bertellsmann Verlag, 1993). Peter Maser, *Die Kirchen in der DDR* (Bonn: Bundeszentrale für politische Bildung, 2000).

17. Rudi Dutschke, *Jeder hat sein Leben ganz zu leben. Die Tagebücher 1963–1979* (Cologne: Kiepenheuer & Witsch Verlag, 2003), 17. On the Protestant opposition to the German Democratic Republic, see: Hermann Geyer, *Montags um Fünf. Die politischen Gottesdienste der Wendezeit in Leipzig* (Darmstadt: WBG Academic, 2007). John Burgess, *The East German Church and the End of Communism* (New York: Oxford University Press, 1997). Stephen Cotkin, *Uncivil Society: 1989 and the Implosion of the Communist Establishment* (New York: Random House, 2009).

18. George H. W. Bush, "Toward a New World Order," September 11, 1990, University of Minnesota Government Publications Library. Francis Fukuyama, "The End of History," *The National Interest* 16 (1989): 3–18. "Document 14.9: The Indispensable Nation," in Andrew Preston, Jeffrey Engel, Mark Atwood Lawrence, eds., *America in the World: A History of Documents from the War on Spain to the War on Terror* (Princeton, NJ: Princeton University Press, 2014), 346. Charles Krauthammer, "The Unipolar Moment," *Foreign Affairs* 70, no. 1 (1990–1991): 23–33.

19. Krauthammer, "The Unipolar Moment." Samuel Huntington, "The Clash of Civilizations," *Foreign Affairs* 72, no. 3 (1993): 22–49. George W. Bush, "State of the Union Address," January 29, 2002, in *America in the World*, 361. On American evangelicals and the Iraq War, see: McAlister, *The Kingdom of God Has No Borders*, 213–230. On European Protestants and Muslim migration, see: Matthew Kaemingk, *Christian Hospitality and Muslim Immigration in an Age of Fear* (Grand Rapids, MI: William B. Eerdmans, 2018).

20. On American Protestant engagement with Islam and the Middle East, see: Thomas Kidd, *American Christians and Islam: Evangelical Culture and Muslims from the Colonial Period to the Age of Terrorism* (Princeton, NJ: Princeton University Press, 2009). Melani McAlister, *Epic Encounters: Culture, Media, and U.S. Interests in the Middle East since 1945* (Berkeley: University of California Press, 2005). On "multi-religious" America, see: Gaston, *Imagining Judeo-Christian America*, 230–256.

21. "How the Faithful Voted: A Preliminary Analysis," Pew Research Center, November 9, 2016. On the Trump presidency and Christian nationalism, see: Fea, *Believe Me*. Perry and Whitehead, *Taking America Back for God*.

Index

For the benefit of digital users, indexed terms that span two pages (e.g., 52–53) may, on occasion, appear on only one of those pages.